THE COMPLETE
HISTORY
OF
GUITAR WORLD

CONTENTS

30 YEARS

GUITAR WORLD

MAGAZINE

1980-2010

YEARS

INTRODUCTION

HELLO, AND WELCOME to an incredible milestone. What you hold in your hands is a complete record of *Guitar World*'s 30 years in publication. To put it in context, we're 30 in human years, which means we can legally buy beer and that we are probably older than half of you. At a time when magazines are collapsing at an alarming rate, our longevity and stamina are something of a modern publishing miracle.

If that fails to impress, consider all of the guitar magazines over the years that *have* fallen by the wayside: *Guitar Shop*, *Guitar for the Practicing Musician*, *Maximum Guitar*, *Guitar One* and *Country Guitar* are just some of the six-string publications that are no longer with us. We're happy to report that, despite the high mortality among guitar rags, we are not only surviving but also bigger and healthier than at any point in our history.

While thinking about the reasons for our success, I stumbled upon the first editorial I composed as editor-in-chief of *Guitar World*, which appeared in the May 1991 issue.

"At its best, guitar playing is *liberation*," I explained. "It is a forum that enables you to vent frustrations with your school, your job or foreign governments. To create or destroy anything your heart desires. And all this, amazingly, can be expressed with one well-placed, cleanly executed vibrato.

"The catch is, you gotta pay your dues. The more you play, the better you get. The better you get, the more forceful your declaration. And if your statement rings loud, clear and true, you may actually earn the privilege of expressing yourself for all to hear."

I would like to think those ideals apply to *Guitar World*. For more than 325 issues over 30 years, we've been playing hard, paying our dues and kicking guitar butt. Because we've been putting in the time, *GW* has gotten better with each passing issue, and it is our hope that our editorial continues to ring loud, clear and true. It's been our privilege to serve you for the past three decades, and it's one that we will continue to work hard to earn.

We hope you enjoy this wild ride down memory lane and that the content in this book is as much fun for you to read as it has been for us to create. Here's to 30 more!

—**Brad Tolinski**
editor-in-chief, *Guitar World*

HISTORY

A TRUE ANECDOTE: It is December 1992, and a shroud of snow and mourning blankets all of Prague, Czechoslovakia. The citizens are weeping for the recently deceased Alexander Dubcek, the man who had led his nation's unsuccessful revolt against the Soviet Union in 1968. When the Soviets finally quit the country in late 1989, Dubcek, after years of internal exile, returned to his city to a hero's welcome. Now he is dead.

The funereal quiet permeating the beautiful center of Prague's Old Town is abruptly shattered by a shriek of joy: "Yes!" An American tourist hurries toward the source of the exclamation to see what could have caused such unbounded happiness in such a somber place. "It's this," says a greasy, bearded man, triumphantly waving a magazine he has just purchased from a street vendor. "I've been here for two years and haven't been able to get it. Cost me 10 bucks, but it was worth it."

It is the January 1992 issue of *Guitar World* magazine, featuring Steve Vai on its cover.

"Well, no wonder," says the tourist.

What manner of magazine would inspire a seedy expatriate to shatter the calm of a bereaved eastern European capital? What is its history? To put it more succinctly: Daddy, when was *Guitar World* born, and what made it so cool?

The answer, or answers, lie buried in the mists of time, in the events of a year so remote that most current *Guitar World* readers were not even a lascivious glint in their father's eyes when they transpired. Sometime in 1980—the same year that witnessed the U.S. Olympic hockey team's victory over the Soviet Union, the assassination of John Lennon and the introduction of the Post-it note—Stanley Harris, a New York publisher who specialized in magazines about hair care and guns, and circle-the-word puzzle books, decided to launch a guitar publication. Yes, there already existed such an entity, a California-based journal that reported with dull but authoritative regularity on developments in blues, jazz, country, surf and, after a fashion, rock guitar. The fact that this magazine sounded and often looked like a church bulletin was entirely appropriate for a publication that was perceived by itself and its aging readership as "The Guitar Bible."

So enter Harris, an amiable capitalist blessed with an extraordinary eye for recognizing a situation ripe for a little competition. It's as if a little light bulb switched on in his head: "Look, that other magazine is ignoring the needs of a gigantic segment of the guitar marketplace—rock guys who dress in tight black jeans and leather jackets and who care about what's happening in their world. These people want a magazine they can call their own."

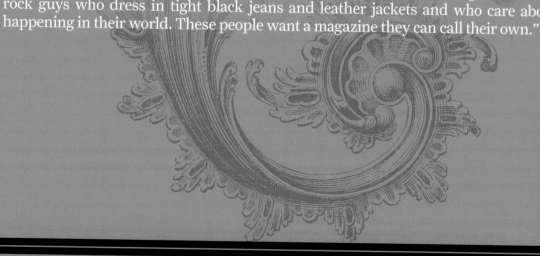

And so, in July 1980, with little public fanfare, Harris launched *Guitar World* magazine. The cover story of that maiden effort was an interview with blues-rock legend Johnny Winter, then in the prime of his career. Also featured in the issue were interviews with Allman Brothers Band second guitarist Dan Toler and retro rocker George Thorogood, who'd made it big with revved-up covers of classic tunes like Bo Diddley's "Who Do You Love" and Hank Williams' "Move It On Over."

While this was clearly a magazine a self-respecting rocker could dig his decaying teeth into, there were also indications that *Guitar World* had yet to truly set itself apart from that older guitar magazine. For along with the Winter, Toler and Thorogood pieces were articles on the "Revolution in Jazz Fingerstyle," "Pedal Steel Guitar" and a feature piece on the great country guitarist Merle Travis—all interesting but hardly rockin'.

"Although that first issue sold well from the get-go, I knew what we really needed was a hipper rock alternative to what was already out there," recalls Dennis Page, an advertising rep Harris enlisted to handle the business end of his new guitar magazine. "While *Guitar World*'s original editor, Art Maher, was a good guy, he was obviously into musty country stuff, which wasn't really the direction we needed to go."

When *Guitar World*, which began its life as a bimonthly, followed up its debut with issues featuring jazzman Pat Metheny and fusion star Al Di Meola, respectively, Page says he told himself, "I need to get involved with this freakin' book." And so he did, hooking up with Harris full time to become publisher of *Guitar World*, a position he would hold until 2003, when the magazine was sold to Future US. Page shook things up by hiring a new editor-in-chief, Noë Goldwasser, whose qualifications apparently extended beyond the fact that he spelled his name with an umlaut.

"He was a hippie quasi-rock writer dude," says Page, "who brought with him a lot of good editorial talent, like [*Rolling Stone*] writer John Swenson." Under Goldwasser, the magazine's appearance began to improve as well, losing some of the offhand scruffiness that characterized its earliest issues. Nevertheless, it took several years—and the 1985 arrival of a new advertising director, Greg Di Benedetto—for *Guitar World* to show real hints of the powerhouse publication it would become.

"The thing about Greg is that, unlike myself, he was a player, a guy who loved and knew all about the guitar," says Page. "Advertisers liked and trusted him instinctively." Di Benedetto, a talented rock guitarist who was not entirely satisfied with his day job—selling classified ads to doctors for a telephone directory—says he'd always viewed working at *Guitar World* "as a dream gig, where I could work with guitars in advertising." When a position in retail sales opened up at the magazine, he jumped, and within a short time he took charge of the entire department.

"I walked the walk and talked the talk," he says of the bond he shared with the guitar and guitar-related gear manufacturers who comprised his clientele. "They were part of the same rock guitar culture that I belonged to."

What ultimately rocketed *Guitar World* into the stratosphere was the infusion of "rock guitar culture" in the magazine's editorial content, and the arrival of Brad Tolinski as editor-in-chief. In 1988, Goldwasser began having the proverbial "creative differences" with publisher Dennis Page. "There were several problems there," recalls Page, "but the most important one was that we were being seriously challenged by the arrival on the scene of *Guitar for the Practicing Musician*, which cut into our readership because they had song transcriptions in their magazine. I thought that we ought to follow suit, but Noë resisted."

Ultimately, Goldwasser and *Guitar World* parted company, and despite successfully introducing transcriptions into its pages, the magazine, as Page recalls, "lost its way" for a time. "We started including a lot of jazz, which our readers didn't care about. I knew that the key was for us to get younger, not older."

The fountain of *Guitar World*'s youth movement was Tolinski, who prior to assuming the magazine's editorial helm had worked for Page as editor of the brilliant but ill-fated *Modern Keyboard*.

"I knew *Guitar World* was in trouble when its editors came to me and asked if I thought it made sense for them to run a cover story on Slash and Izzy Stradlin of Guns N' Roses," recalls Tolinski. "*Appetite for Destruction* was then a gigantic success, and I thought it odd that anyone would hesitate to go with the most important rock guitar band in the world."

Slash and Izzy did appear on the cover of *Guitar World*, and the issue was enormously popular. Tolinski officially joined the staff as associate editor, and in relatively short order became editor-in-chief, a position he holds to this day. "Brad was a dream-come-true editor," says Dennis Page. "With him, for the first time we not only had a player, a guy who understood guitar *and* rock music, but also someone who understood the magazine business and magazine design and had a personal vision for what *Guitar World* should be. Brad understood that we had to be young, young, young, yet without abandoning our older readers. He was the missing piece, and along with Greg Di Benedetto, he took the magazine to the Promised Land."

In other words, absolute ascendancy among guitar magazines. In his first year as editor, Tolinski scored time and again with exciting, vibrantly designed issues that struck a careful balance in focus between rising young stars (Zakk Wylde, Nuno Bettencourt), classic rockers (Aerosmith, Eric Clapton) pure players (Steve Vai, Joe Satriani, Stevie Ray Vaughan) and, of course, *Guitar World*'s mainstay, Eddie Van Halen. If one had to single out one aspect of his skill that accounted, and continues to account, for the magazine's success, it's his ability to put himself in the shoes of the reader. This hearkens back to Di Benedetto's concept of "rock guitar culture." A lifelong guitarist, Tolinski not only belonged to and understood that culture but also was able to translate his understanding into every aspect of his success as an editor.

What ultimately rocketed *Guitar World* into the stratosphere was the infusion of "rock guitar culture" in the magazine's editorial content.

"I wanted the magazine to convey to readers that we understood what it means to play guitar and be in a band," says Tolinski, "and that, above all else, it is *fun*. Taking a dry, technical approach to things has its place, and we certainly are committed to teaching the guitar, but *Guitar World* wouldn't be as popular as it is if that's all there were to it. Our readers relate to us—so much so that when they complain about something in a letter or an email, it's with the kind of vehemence you usually reserve for a relative. That's a good sign."

That *Guitar World* is serious about the technical and educational side of the magazine equation is clear by the quality of the song transcriptions and

lessons. "Jimmy Brown, our music editor, does a great job with our transcribers, some of whom—like Andy Aledort—have an enormous following among guitarists," says Tolinski. "We never stop trying to devise the best possible tablature system, which readers know has improved incredibly over the years. We also feature lessons and columns by the best guitarists out there—players like Kirk Hammett and Steve Vai have been part of the magazine for years, and we've had landmark contributions by people like Eddie Van Halen and Jimmy Page."

Guitar World has come a long way since Stanley Harris decided to compete with *Guitar Player* back in 1980. Tolinski attributes much of the magazine's staying power and consistent quality to his staff, many of whom—like him and Greg Di Benedetto—are active musicians. "We work together like a band—everyone feels like they play important roles in a creative collective, not like some industrial cog. There's lots of pressure at times, but it's also fun—and I believe our readers are intuitively hip to that, because it shows up in our writing, design, headlines and photographs."

Perhaps the ultimate barometer of *Guitar World*'s success is that so many players featured in the magazine today fondly remember growing up with the magazine. That also applies to the staff. Senior editor Richard Bienstock says he began reading the magazine as a 12-year-old metalhead in 1989. "I took lessons," he says, "but I learned much more about the guitar—the players, songs, techniques—by reading the magazine." Bienstock, who like so many *GW* staffers began his career as an intern, says he'll never forget his first day on the job. "I knew so many of the editors just from being a reader. I'd never seen Jimmy Brown before, but I recognized him immediately from having seen his photo next to his column for so many years. It occurred to me then that I was probably more familiar with his face—and hair—than I was my own father's."

Now that's a fan. ✳

THE COMPLETE

HISTORY

OF

GUITAR WORLD

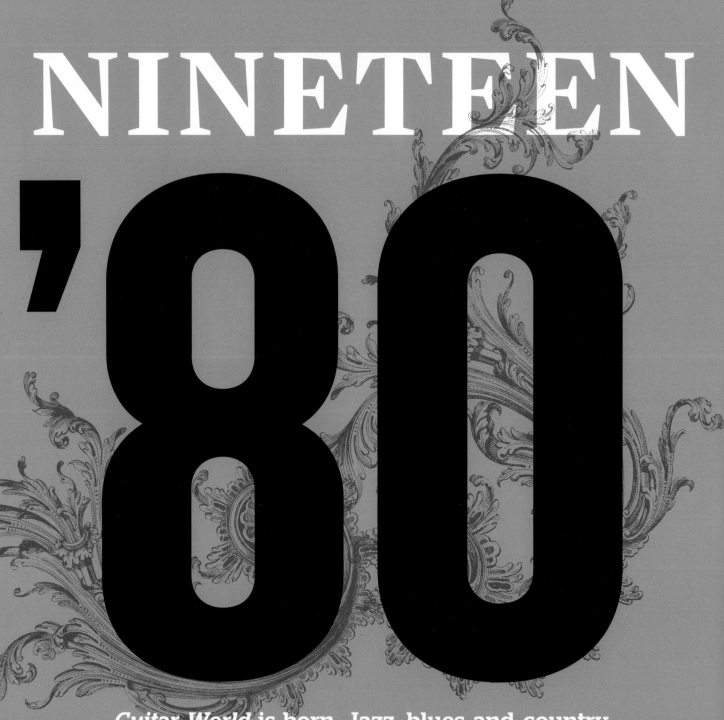

NINETEEN '80

Guitar World is born. Jazz, blues and country reign supreme across the first three issues.

Dear *Guitar World*,

Just wanted to take the time to write a note complimenting you on your new magazine. As a George Thorogood fan and a Johnny Winter nut, I was ecstatic to see well-written articles on these two great guitarists. If your forthcoming issues are anywhere near as good as this first one, your popularity should soar!

—Rob Shapiro

Guitar World

02135 $1.50   JULY 1980

JOHNNY WINTER
Rockin' Better Than Ever !

50 Best Guitar Records Ever Made

Revolution In Jazz Fingerstyle

PEDAL STEEL
The Bars That Made Nashville Famous

GEORGE THOROGOOD
Underdog Makes It Big

THE TRAVIS MAGIC

A Living Legend

JULY

Issue Number One features interviews with Johnny Winter, George Thorogood and Merle Travis, as well as the magazine's first official list: The 50 Best Guitar Records Ever Made. "Knowledge and excitement can help you improve your skills and heighten the pleasure you receive from playing," wrote original editor-in-chief Arthur J. Maher, "and that is our primary goal."

COVER STORY BY JOEL SIEGEL; PHOTO BY JOHN STIX

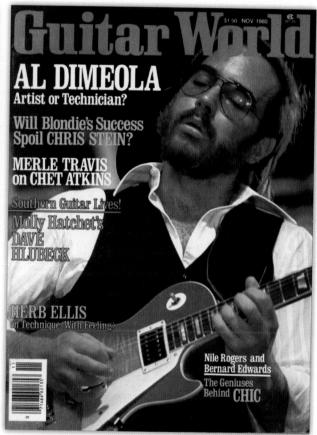

SEPTEMBER 26-year-old jazz star Pat Metheny gives a detailed interview on a range of topics, including the crucial elements of his distinctive guitar tone, his development as a musician and his disdain for the word "fusion." "I hate that word. It makes no sense and whenever I hear it applied to my music, I want to kill."

COVER STORY BY JOEL SIEGEL; PHOTO BY ROB VAN PETTEN

NOVEMBER *GW* continues its jazz coverage with this profile of legend-in-the-making Al Di Meola. In it, Di Meola opens up about his perfectionist nature when it comes to writing and recording. "There's a certain sound I want to create. My band is here to recreate what I have in mind. It's not loose."

COVER STORY BY JOHN STIX; PHOTO BY RICHARD AARONS

JOHNNY WINTER

Still Rockin' with the Blues

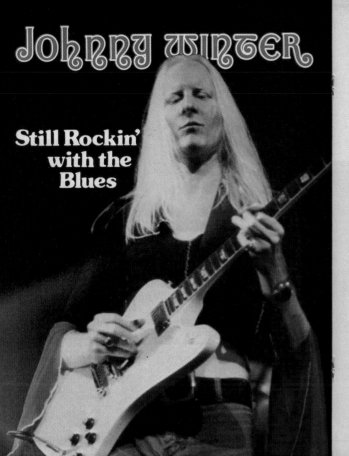

by Joel Siegel

Way back in the late 60's a slew of English guitarists emerged on the popular music scene whose blues-based rock captured the imagination of many young musicians. Names like Eric Clapton, Jimmy Page, Jeff Beck, and Peter Green were new then. Their exciting music, along with the already established influence of the Rolling Stones, sent many guitarists in America on a blues search pondering names like Chester Burnett (Howlin' Wolf) and McKinley Morganfield (Muddy Waters) that appeared in rock record song credits.

That same period produced an American guitarist whose association with the blues was perhaps more intimate than that of the English players. In 1969, when he came out of a Texas town just west of the Louisiana border, Johnny Winter was hot property. Word spread out from the Southwest about a lanky, long-haired, albino guitarist who could play like a monster.

During the next three years, Johnny Winter continuously toured North America, astounding audiences and building an enormous following. In that short period of time, he was transformed into a rock star, filling arenas, selling hundreds of thousands of records, and influencing a generation of musicians who were in awe of his lightning fast, blues-based rock style. With the exception of a one-year hiatus, Johnny Winter has been going strong ever since.

And he has been going it alone. While Eric Clapton, Jimmy Page, Jeff Beck and most other guitarists of the periods have all abandoned blues as the major thrust of their work, Johnny Winter has maintained his love for this great American heritage. His commitment goes be-

Photographer: Fin Costello/Retna

"I used to wonder if you had to be suffering all the time to play the blues. It wouldn't be worth it. When you're really down, it is pretty hard to be creative. When you are looking back at the time you were down, then you can write songs."

Photo © London Features International, Ltd./Retna

Photographer: Russell Walczak/Globe Photo

JULY 1980

VOL. 1 / NO. 7

Johnny Winter

In *Guitar World*'s debut issue, Johnny Winter describes his love for the blues as well as the career problems and drug addiction that led to his downward spiral in the Seventies and, ultimately, his salvation.

Johnny recalls the late Sixties, when rock and roll fans "discovered" the blues. "Things were better in terms of blues appreciation," says the guitarist. "The Rolling Stones and some of the other English groups were starting to do blues. People came on to the blues through those guys, but most of those English guys didn't stick with it.

"Before that time, things were really rough for real blues musicians. Even black people didn't want to have anything to do with the blues for a long time. They thought the blues was not an educated music, and it brought back to many people the memories of the bad times. There is still an appalling lack of appreciation in this country for blues. To me, it is the finest music."

And what does it take to play this fine music?

"I used to wonder if you had to be suffering all the time to play the blues. It wouldn't be worth it. Everyone has pain in their lives. Everyone has problems, some more than others. When you're really down, it is hard to be creative. When you are looking back at the time you were down, hindsight, then you can write songs. When you're going through the process, through some really horrible life or death situation, it's hard to even care about music."

Johnny experienced some of those real bad times while trying to cope with the rigors of his three years of constant touring. "It would take me a long time to go into the whole thing, but the one thing to keep in mind is that there was always something in me saying 'stay alive.' I felt for quite a while like killing myself. I couldn't stand the life I was leading. I was real down, and death seemed like an easy way out. If you want to make up your mind that you're not going to die, then you have got to figure out a way to make yourself happy. You have to figure out what is making your life so miserable and set out to change it.

"To me, it was everybody wanting to get on the Johnny Winter bandwagon, everybody wanting a little piece of the action—give me a loan, give me some of your hair, have sex with me, show me how to play guitar, how did you make it? There was no time for sleep, or for friends, or for doing normal things like watching television and eating. It didn't look like things were going to change. I could picture it being like that forever and ever—everybody taking their 10 or 20 percent out of my money and leaving me with nothing.

"It was a real lonely time. The people I'd meet were all after something. It was mentally and physically draining. After three years of that I knew that if I didn't get away from it, the business, the people, the drugs, the whole bit—at least for a while—I wouldn't have been able to live with myself. I didn't know if I was ever going to play again. The main thing, for me, was to figure out what went wrong.

"I locked myself up. I checked myself into a hospital where I was getting constant psychotherapy. I couldn't get any letters. The first three months were real painful, coming off the drugs and just being in one place, not having a job to go to. At the time, it was real horrible, but I wouldn't take it back. I am real glad I went through it. After I decided that there was a chance for me to be happy, I began to learn a lot. I can look back at that time with enjoyment, now, as I have gone through it on to better times." ✳

SEPT. '80

GEORGE THOROGOOD

The blues-rock warrior is mystified about being featured in *Guitar World*'s premiere issue.

WRITER JOEL SIEGEL conducted *Guitar World*'s first interview with rising star George Thorogood—who was just 24 at the time—at the Deer Park Inn, the "most hopping bar" in Thorogood's home town of Newark, Delaware. Thorogood was already known for such bluesy anthems as "Move It On Over," "It Wasn't Me" and "Who Do You Love," but couldn't quite understand why this new magazine called *Guitar World* wanted to talk to him.

"I can't see why anyone would be interested in me at all," said Thorogood. "I don't know that much about guitar. I don't know how to play it all that well. I just enjoy doing it for others that enjoy it as much as I do, but who can't play or they would be doing it themselves. Some of them are scared like I used to be. If I can get them off their asses then I won't have to play as much and they can get interviewed.

"I don't think of myself as a musician or guitar player *per se*. My guitar is my prop. My guitar is my tool. I am just an entertainer. When people leave the room I hope they are happier than when they came in. The only way I know how to do that is with music."

Joe Perry: Life After Aerosmith

Joe Perry's first appearance in *Guitar World* was in the September 1980 issue. At the time, Perry had made his decision to leave Aerosmith and was in the process of mixing his debut solo album, *Let the Music Do the Talking*. "I was getting stagnant sitting around," Perry told writer John Stix. "It's nothing bad about Aerosmith. It just left me wanting more."

During the interview, Perry gave his five all-time indispensable guitar albums:

1) Chuck Berry—*Chuck Berry Is on Top*
2) The Yardbirds—*Having a Rave Up*
3) The Jimi Hendrix Experience—*Are You Experienced*
4) John Mayall—*A Hard Road*
5) Jeff Beck—*Wired.*

"My guitar is my prop. My guitar is my tool.

DAVE HLUBECK

Molly Hatchet founder Dave Hlubeck doesn't mind if you call his crew a rock band from the South—just don't call them a Southern rock band.

HLUBECK AND COMPANY have been called a Southern rock band in the Allman Brothers/Marshall Tucker mold. Hlubeck rejects this. He has heard it too often. "It's because we're from Jacksonville. We are a rock and roll band that just happens to be from the South. I think we will be a band that changes the stereotype sound of the Southern rock band—that bluesy thing. The title song from our *Flirtin' with Disaster* album is not your typical Southern rock song.

"People come up to us and thank us for coming forth with a refreshing sound from the South instead of, 'Oh baby, I've got the blues / 'bout to have the blues / man, am I going to have the blues if I don't get rid of these blues.' There is nothing wrong with the blues, but man, the 1980 world is bluesy enough for me. There is enough gloom going around to suit me for the rest of my life—poverty, oil shortages and all this political shit overseas. I would like people to be able to forget that crap when they listen. We aren't trying to get people involved in anything. We are just trying to be a successful rock and roll band."

Molly Hatchet's

Dave Hlubeck

Flirtin' with Fortune and Raisin' Hell

by Joel A. Siegel

The Beatles (Don't) Get the Ax

NOV. '80

In our November 1980 issue writer Martin Porter went to the one street in New York City synonymous with musical instrument sales—48th Street—and wrote about the rise of such legendary retail establishments as Manny's, Alex Music, Terminal Music and Sam Ash. During his investigation, Porter interviewed Henry Goldrich, son of Manny's founder Manny Goldrich, who shared this memory of the day three British gentlemen—John Lennon, Paul McCartney and Ringo Starr—strode into the famed guitar shop.

"We were just too busy to take care of them," said Goldrich. "We asked if they would come back but they said they would wait and they sat in the back and amused themselves for about a half hour until we could get a salesman free.

"They wanted a guitar for one of their albums. So we called up the guy who owned the company and told him what they wanted. The guy said, 'I can't give them a guitar but we'll sell it to them for cost.' So Lennon says to me, 'Tell him we'll put it on our next album cover.' I tell him and the guy says, 'Nope, I'm sorry.' And they didn't end up using the guitar after all. Oh, and by the way, the album they were talking about turned out to be *Sgt. Pepper's*."

I am just an entertainer." *—George Thorogood*

icking technique playing country music. It's really wierd."

DiMeola's early music education was also provided by the adrenalin and inspiration pouring out of the clubs and concert halls of nearby New York City. "Living so close to New York, the availability of seeing dif-

was floored. I never screamed at a show in my life. I got so charged up I could feel it in my bones. I learned from that. I carry it over to what I do. I go home, pick up the guitar, and I know something new is gonna come out."

His words took on more than not

a necessity if you want to play this kind of music."

Play it he did. Home for a visit, he met keyboard player Barry Miles in a

"I think I have a good understanding

me, and I got a telegram in Boston asking me to come down and audition." Al joined Barry Miles, filling John Abercrombie's chair.

After six months of sporadic concerts and club dates with Barry, Al was back in Berklee when he got a call to join Chick Corea. It was a Fri-

NOV. 1980

VOL. 1 / NO. 11

Al Di Meola

Guitar World closes out its first year of publication by catching up with the jazz guitar great, who talks about his early influences and the impact of the New York City music scene.

As an aspiring young guitarist,

I used to walk my neighborhood streets fantasizing about what I would do if I had three wishes. Peace on earth could wait, I wanted to play like Jeff Beck. If that was too much, how about being able to play the opening solo from the Byrds' classic "Eight Miles High"? I should have walked around Jersey City, New Jersey, Al Di Meola's hometown. His fantasy to play with Chick Corea became a fact to reflect on by the time he was 19.

Today, seven years later, his four solo albums combined with his output with the group Return to Forever, plus numerous guitar awards in popular polls, make him a likely candidate for the fantasies of other aspiring young guitarists. You can call it luck or fate, but it's the product of hard work and determination.

"I may have been young, but I knew what I wanted a long time ago," says the 26-year-old Di Meola. He picked up his first guitar, a Tempo, at eight. Taking lessons from a jazz player, he learned his scales and theory "right off the bat." He used all four fingers on his left hand, alternately picking with his right, and played melodically instead of using riffs like a rock guitarist. The sounds of Clapton and Hendrix weren't out of the picture, they just weren't a big part of the scene. While I was wishing about Jeff Beck, Di Meola was reading music and working with jazz chords. He wasn't considered a hot player in high school because his sound didn't fit the rock scene; he was looking elsewhere.

"I was so into country music in my early teens," he says. "I used to play pedal steel. I got cowboy clothes, boots—I wanted to move to Nashville. I was into 'Eight Miles High' myself. [*Byrds guitarist*] Clarence White had more than just a bluegrass background. I developed my picking technique playing country music. It's really weird."

Di Meola's early music education was only provided by the adrenalin and inspiration pouring out of the clubs and concert halls of nearby New York City. "Living so close to New York, the availability of seeing different kinds of music was there all the time. All during my teen years I would go to the city almost every week." Be it the Fillmore East, or a small club, live music would provide the energy. His reaction was to go home and play.

"You don't have to teach someone as much as influence them by what you do," he explains. "I can watch Julian Bream play an avant-garde classical piece. I may not know the piece, but because of what I saw, I could sit down and come up with some new ideas. Just from watching him, it was a good feeling, a good experience. I came away from an Earth, Wind and Fire show and I was floored. I never screamed at a show in my life. I got so charged up I could feel it in my bones. I learned from that. I carry it over to what I do. I go home, pick up the guitar, and I know something new is gonna come out."

His words took on more than notable quote status when Al told me he got turned onto jazz by seeing guitarist Larry Coryell on public television. "Larry was combining all these elements, country, rock and jazz into one. That night I knew what my direction was going to be for the next 20 years. I knew it." The 16-year-old Di Meola also listened well beyond his instrument, to the music of Miles Davis, John Coltrane and Chick Corea.

From high school it was a natural for Al to go to Berklee College of Music in Boston. Though he only stayed an intermittent semester and a half, his endorsement of the school is high. "Berklee is the ultimate. It's a necessity if you want to play this kind of music." ✳

Coming Up

EDDIE VAN HALEN, to premier heavy metalsmith, says is for kids—that people over 21 more serious music.

HEAVY METAL CRAS to the fore with groups like A Van Halen, Rush and Def Le leading the way.

KEEPING A GROUP GETHER can be the tou part of the music business—esp for the player who gigs on week We'll examine the problem in de

Eddie Van Halen

Eddie Van Halen's First *GW* Appearance—Oops!
Guitar World concluded its first year of publication with this shocking goof. On the last page of the November issue, in a section previewing the contents of the upcoming issue's cover story with Eddie Van Halen, the accompanying photo, which was identified as Eddie, was actually of singer David Lee Roth. In the years to come, *Guitar World* and EVH would enjoy a fiercely close, loyal relationship...and yet it all started with this blunder.

NINETEEN '81

Guitar World doubles its output in year two
as six issues reach newsstands;
Eddie Van Halen gets his first of 16+ covers.

Dear *Guitar World*,

I purchased the March 1981 issue of *Guitar World* and I may never buy another. I refer to the article on the Pretenders by Van Gosse. His snide way of reporting has no place in a magazine such as yours. Mr. Gosse's remarks on Duane Allman, Dickey Betts and the Grateful Dead ("laid back marijuana music") are best left to cheap rock magazine critics. He even said the Pretenders' drummer looked like "Ginger Baker with teeth." A writer like Van Gosse would last on the staff of any other guitar magazine for about five minutes.

—Bob Cavicchio

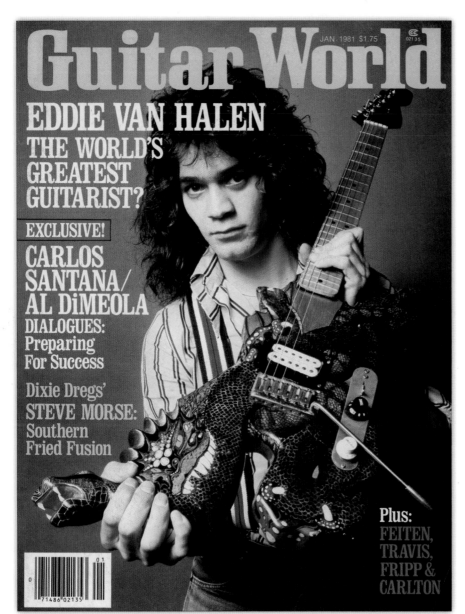

Guitar World

JAN. 1981 $1.75

EDDIE VAN HALEN
THE WORLD'S GREATEST GUITARIST?

EXCLUSIVE!
CARLOS SANTANA/
AL DiMEOLA
DIALOGUES:
Preparing
For Success

Dixie Dregs'
STEVE MORSE:
Southern
Fried Fusion

Plus:
FEITEN,
TRAVIS,
FRIPP &
CARLTON

JANUARY In the first of many Eddie Van Halen cover stories, the new king of hard rock guitar talks about his evolution as a player and whether or not success has gone to his head. "When kids ask me how it feels to be a rock star, I tell them to leave me alone. I'm not a rock star."

COVER STORY BY JOHN STIX; PHOTO BY NEIL ZLOZOWER

   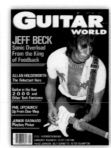

MARCH An inside look at what makes Chrissie Hynde and the Pretenders tick. Among the topics discussed: dealing with sudden notoriety.
COVER STORY BY VAN GOSSE; PHOTO BY EBET ROBERTS

MAY Andy Summers responds to the charges that the Police have hurt reggae music by diluting it for the masses.
COVER STORY BY PETER MENGAZIOL; PHOTO BY JONATHAN POSTAL

JULY Jazz-fusion master John McLaughlin discusses his many philosophies behind his craft. "With music you can touch a lot of people at the same time. But even if you touch only one, it's enough."
COVER STORY BY PETER KEEPNEWS; PHOTO BY CAROL FRIEDMAN

SEPTEMBER Jeff Beck comes clean about his refusal to play the role of guitar superstar. "Becoming a household name with widespread acceptance? No way. I don't want it."
COVER STORY BY JOHN SWENSON; PHOTO BY BOB LEAFE

1981 TOTAL ISSUES: 6

02135   CC NOV 1981 $1.75

GUITAR
WORLD

90 p U.K.

RUSH'S
ALEX
LIFESON
Is He Really
Too Good for
Heavy Metal?

STANLEY
CLARKE
(West) Coasting
on Success

Vintage Centerfold:
JOHNNY
WINTER'S
NATIONAL
STEEL

PLUS: LARRY CORYELL · FRANK ZAPPA
BILL CONNORS · LEO NOCENTELLI
G.E. SMITH · RANDY CALIFORNIA

71486 02135

NOVEMBER A detailed Axology with Rush guitarist Alex Lifeson, who talks about everything he's using on the band's hugely popular *Moving Pictures* tour. Just don't ask him about the double-neck. "I guess I harbor ill will toward it because every time I see a picture of me, it's with the double-neck—but I only use it one song each night!"

COVERY STORY BY JOHN SWENSON; PHOTO BY JONATHAN POSTAL

10 09 08 07 06 05 04 03 02 01 00 99 98 97 96 95 94 93 92 91 90 89 88 87 86 85 84 83 82 81 80

EDDIE VAN HALEN

by John Stix

Just give me some of that rock-and-roll music
Any old way you choose it
Its got a back beat you can't lose it
Any old time you use it
Gotta be rock-and-roll music
If you want to dance with me. *

THE NEW KING OF
HEAVY METAL
GUITAR

Photographer: Mark Leialoha

Chuck Berry wrote those words over twenty years ago. Edward Van Halen, guitarist for the group sporting his last name, couldn't agree more. At 23, you might just say he's respecting his elders. Along with brother Alex on drums, Michael Anthony on bass, and lead vocalist David Lee Roth, the group Van Halen pumps out hard rockin' music that was born in the basement, fused in the bars, and explodes on stage.

Describing himself as a kid "living his rock-and-roll dreams," Eddie Van Halen has been heading there since the fourth grade. He was born in Amsterdam, Holland, where his father, a professional musician, got both brothers to the piano at an early age.

His musical knowhow was born in the classics, but his spirit was in rock-and-roll. "Who wants to sit at the piano!" he exclaimed. "I want to go crazy. Everybody turned me on. I grew up on a lot of early Beatles, DC5, Cream, Clapton, Page, Beck, and Hendrix."

He was ten when the family moved to Los Angeles, "land of opportunity." After the high school dances and diploma, he graduated to the bars and the start of the band that bears his name. "We were all in various bands in the L.A. area, and when we got to the college age everyone started flaking off; wanting to be doctors. We got stuck with each other. There was nobody left that was into it." They played all the bars and all the oldies, including a version of the *Kinks' Your Really Got me* which Eddie calls "a hot tune we turned into a jet plane."

The crowds got bigger and Van Halen were able to draw 3000 people

* Rock & Roll Music. Words and music by Chuck Berry. © 1957 by Arc Music Corp., used by permission.

to a gig they threw themselves. Kiss' Gene Simmons paid for their original demo sessions and Mo Ostin, Chairman of the Board at Warner, and Ted Templemen, V.P. of A&R, caught their act at the Starwood Club. They were signed the next day. Three years ago they played the bar scene, today they headline arenas. "I never imagined that we would get to where we are this quick," Eddie reflects.

Eddie Van Halen is not the arrogant, brash, or angry young man I had imagined. In fact he wears the kind of smile that could sell soft drinks on television. And he wears it well. Because Eddie Van Halen is one happy fella. The explanation is easy. "Everything I did is because I wanted to do it," he says without arrogance. "If I weren't playing this arena, if I were playing a club, I'd still be doing it because that's what I want to do. I love playing the guitar."

More than just playing guitars,

Van Halen builds them. In fact, when we met for this interview, he was surrounded with guitar parts, preparing to put together the instruments for a performance only two hours away. As the pickups, bridges, necks, and strings found their way together, I began to see the picture of a young guitarist whose success in high voltage rock has left his spirit intact and his feet remarkably on the ground. In essence, Eddie Van Halen travels in overdrive while the visions in his rear view mirror remain clear.

"I'm not a rock star. Sure I am to a certain extent because of the situation, but when kids ask me how it feels to be a rock star, I say leave me alone. I'm not a rock star. I'm not in it for the fame, I'm in it because I like to play."

G.W. Were you as good a piano player as you are a guitarist?

V.H. I won first prize four years in a row at Long Beach City College for my category. The piano is a universal instrument. If you start there, learn your theory and how to read, you can go on to any other instrument.

G.W. Sounds like you had a solid foundation in the basics.

V.H. Well, I'm not a good reader. I would read and remember. The one thing I do have is good ears. I don't mean perfect pitch, but ears for picking things up. I developed my ear through piano theory but I never had a guitar lesson in my life, except from Eric Clapton off of records.

G.W. Do you have the ability to think something and play it immediately?

V.H. Not automatically or perfectly, but that's the thing. I don't think when I play. It's spontaneous, it's feeling. It's not calculated or figured out ahead of time. That's why you might say I play off the wall. When I was in junior college at Pasadena City, I took scoring and arranging class with a Dr. Fischer. Frank Zappa had also been his student. Dr. Fischer was very avant-garde and the one thing he taught me was f--k the rules. If it

35

JAN. 1981

VOL. 2 / NO. 1

Eddie Van Halen

In his first *Guitar World* cover story, Eddie Van Halen ponders his rising guitar-hero status.

When Eddie Van Halen first graced *Guitar World*'s cover—the January 1981 issue—he was just 23 but already well on his way to influencing the next generation of guitarists via his two-handed tapping technique. "The World's Greatest Guitarist?" was the question we posed on our cover, but Ed would have none of it. In our interview, which included a discussion of his methods for customizing his guitars, Ed repeatedly shot down suggestions by interviewer John Stix that his head had grown six sizes since the group had released its Platinum-selling 1978 debut, catapulting him to the airy heights of fame. "I'm not a rock star," Ed said. "When kids ask me how it feels to be a rock star, I say leave me alone. I'm not in it for the fame, I'm in it because I like to play."

GUITAR WORLD Did you go through a period of imitation before your own days of invention?

EDDIE VAN HALEN Definitely—and Clapton was it. I knew every note he played. That's what I was known for around home. Me, Alex and another bass player called ourselves Mammoth and we were the junior Cream. It's funny; when I do interviews and tell people Eric Clapton was my main influence, they go, "Who?"

GW Because they're thinking about Clapton doing "Lay Down Sally," not the Bluesbreakers or Cream. Your current trio-and-a-singer format is not much different than Cream. Have you ever thought of working with another guitarist?

VAN HALEN I've never played with another guitarist because I make enough sound on my own. What I loved about Cream is that everybody had to put out. It was three people making all this noise, and you could hear each person. The Allman Brothers feel is something I never got into. Duane was an excellent slide guitarist, but I never cared for Dickie Betts. I found their music too cluttered for my taste.

GW In your Clapton days, I'm sure you did some intense studying on the instrument. Do you still work as hard to improve your playing?

VAN HALEN Yes, but I don't call it practice. This will sound real funny to you, but we tour for eight weeks and then take eight days off. When I'm home on a break, I lock myself in my room and play guitar. After two or three hours I start getting into this total meditation. It's a feeling few people experience, and that's usually when I come up with weird stuff. It just flows. I can't force myself. I don't sit down and say I've got to produce.

GW Can you be specific about how you play better today than, say, when the first *Van Halen* album was released?

VAN HALEN I don't consider myself a better player. I consider myself different. With the technical ability I have, I can play just about as fast as I'd like to play. Any faster at the volume I play and I'd have distortion. So, technically, there's no reason to get any faster.

GW But do you still reach any new plateaus?

VAN HALEN Sure I do.

GW Can you point some out on your records?

VAN HALEN The solo on "Cradle Will Rock" is different. One guitar player who I respect and think is the baddest is Allan Holdsworth. I do one short lick on "Cradle" that came out because I've been listening to this guy. On the second album, I expanded a little more on harmonics.

GW You're talking about hitting false harmonics by using your right hand to hit the fretboard?

VAN HALEN Yes. First I just used my first finger on the right hand to hit a note. Then I discovered the harmonic by hitting the fret an octave above where the left hand is positioned. Now I'm expanding on that by using all the harmonics in between the octave. I also use the slap technique, which I got from black bass players. Jimi Hendrix influenced me on how to hold the pick when I do the harmonics. I saw the Hendrix movie and discovered where the pick goes when it disappears. He holds it between the joints of his middle finger. I pick weird, too. I use the thumb and the middle finger.

GW Have you ever thought you may now be part of the guitar heritage you once studied? Thinking of players like Beck, Page, Clapton and Hendrix, you may be next in line for guitar hero.

VAN HALEN It's very hard to say. That's like me telling you I'm the best. I can't say that. I'm not. I can't say I'm going to influence people, but I know a lot of people are using their right hand on the fingerboard now that never did it before. ✳

G-Force: Another Lizzy member
[...] effort, featuring Gary Moore. His
[...] features a sharper guitar sound
[...] some occasional wah-
[...] cate harmony guitar
[...] on. This also is a
[...] without Phil Lynott's

Iron Maiden: Their single *Sanctuary* from the "Metal For Muthas" album went to No. 1 in England. Basically an updated Deep Purple with progressive overtones. The two guitarists, Dennis Stratton and Dave Murray, both sound like little Blackmores featuring high-energy solos.

[...]: This band features
[...] from the Pink Fairies,
[...]my, and are currently considered
[...] heaviest metal band in the U.K.

Blue Oyster Cult: The East Coast's premiere crunch band has mellowed out on recent albums. Buck Dharma the lead guitarist, sometimes shares

JAN. '81

The Young Guns of Metal

Modern heavy metal was in full swing by the time *Guitar World* reached its January 1981 issue—yet the magazine was still primarily jazz and blues focused. In a nod to the magazine's few headbanging readers, Peter Mengaziol offered a roundup of heavy metal "contenders," writing that Judas Priest's "alleged" lead guitarist K.K. Downing "sounds a bit Clapton-esque at times," Iron Maiden's Dave Murray and Dennis Stratton "sound like little Blackmores" and that Def Leppard is "the hottest new band" with "great potential."

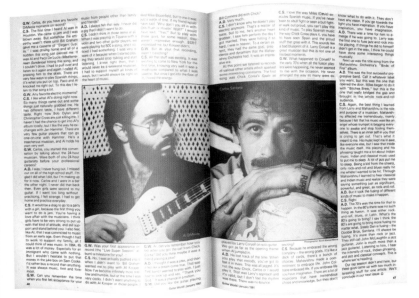

JANUARY / VOL. 2 / NO. 1

CARLOS SANTANA & AL DI MEOLA

Over the course of 30 years, *Guitar World* has built a reputation for bringing together some of the most legendary names in rock guitar: James Hetfield and Tony Iommi (August 1992), Dimebag Darrell and Ace Frehley (August 1993), Jimmy Page and Jeff Beck (October 1999) and numerous others. But the first time the magazine paired up two respected players for a joint interview was in the January 1981 issue, when John Stix met up with Carlos Santana and Al Di Meola—who were on tour together—in a Philadelphia hotel room before a gig.

GUITAR WORLD Did the guitar come easy for you?
CARLOS SANTANA The guitar came easy because all I wanted to do was solo. The first instrument I picked up after the violin was the bass. Then people told me I was playing too many notes. Instead of laying down the foundation, I wanted to wail. So I always think in terms of melody. That's my first and foremost love. So it came very easy to me to get the feeling from blues and think melodically. To me, melody is the most important thing in a tune. If I can't hear a melody, after a while I lose interest.
AL Di MEOLA I feel the same way. If you place too much emphasis on improvisation...
SANTANA It's beautiful for some people.
Di MEOLA Yes it is, but what gets across to everyone is the melody.
SANTANA That's why the Beatles are so heavy. Grandmothers and little children could be sweeping the floor or washing dishes and singing the melody.

"If I can't hear a melody, after a while I lose interest." —Carlos Santana

Tune-Ups

SCHENKER: UFO SIGHTED OFF SATURN

When the lead guitarist and main songwriter Michael Schenker left UFO in 1980 and released the first album under his own name, many fans wondered what was behind such a move. After all, UFO were getting more popular with each album; why leave now?

Michael was frank about his reasons when we met him in New York for the first American tour of the Michael Schenker Band: "I was drinking a lot when I was with UFO. In order to be able to keep going with this group in this kind of atmosphere, alcohol helped. It was depressing. I didn't get along with Phil Mogg, and it was getting to me. I started thinking that if I had to play 200 gigs, I'd have to drink 200 nights and that was too much. I gave two months' notice that I had to go play on the Scorpions' record in Germany, so when I got back to England the British papers were saying I'd been sacked. That made me angry — it wasn't true."

He then told us how his new band debut was delayed because of habits carried over from UFO: "The new band and me did a month and a half of rehearsing for the album and I cracked up because I did a lot of drinking and drugs. I smashed my guitar into a thousand pieces. I cut off my hair and went to a hospital in Germany to get straightened out. I haven't touched drugs or alcohol since.

His band includes Beck veteran drummer Cozy Powell, Paul Raymond from UFO and new vocalist Gary Bart, with Chris Glenn on bass. Michael seems happy with the new line-up: "I wasn't really going 'solo,' I was choosing people I like to play with and using my name because I couldn't think of a group name. At least I knew some people would know my name and that would get some people to the concerts. The new singer has a lot of technique and a different voice from Phil Mogg, so for me now the vocals are twenty times better.

"It's now more or less the same groove as the old UFO, with different players—which gives the music a slightly different character. I've always done the same music, one thing, that I like. I enjoy loud singing, hot guitar with powerful drums. That's the music I like!"
— Peter Mengaziol

BLUES IN A BOTTLE

"I was raised up in the blues," says guitarist Mike Bloomfield. "Now I'm 37, and I'm still a blues man. I'm always gonna be one."

Mike Bloomfield's roots in the blues run deep. He's played with everyone from Chuck Berry ("It Won't Be Me") and Mitch Ryder ("Devil with a Blue Dress") to the Paul Butterfield Blues Band (he's best known for his work on Butterfield's East/West album). Bloomfield co-founded the Electric Flag, participated in two "Super Session" albums with Al Kooper and backed up Dylan on Highway 61 Revisited.

"I met Bob in Chicago at a club called the Bear," Bloomfield explains. "They had cutting contests and I was gonna go down there and burn him. That didn't happen, but we sort of jammed and hung out all day. About a year later he called me up and said, 'Do you want to be on a record?' I said, 'Sure.' Bob said, 'I

MARCH / VOL. 2 / NO. 3

MICHAEL SCHENKER

The former Scorpions/UFO great makes his first appearance in *Guitar World*.

GUITAR WORLD DEBUTED its Tune Ups section—brief news items and profiles on the day's hottest players—in the March 1981 issue with pieces on the Doobie Brothers' Jeff Baxter, blues guitarist Mike Bloomfield, Ten Years After's Alvin Lee and former Scorpions/UFO guitarist Michael Schenker. In his first interview with *Guitar World*, Schenker explained his reasons for his sudden split with the fast-rising UFO the year before. "I was drinking a lot when I was with UFO," the guitarist told Peter Mengaziol. "In order to be able to keep going with this group in this kind of atmosphere, alcohol helped. It was depressing. I didn't get along with [*UFO singer*] Phil Moog, and it was getting to me. I started thinking that if I had to play 200 gigs, I'd have to drink 200 nights and that was too much. I gave two months' notice that I had to go play on the Scorpions' record in Germany, so when I got back to England the British papers were saying I'd been sacked. That made me angry—it wasn't true."

Schenker then proceeded to tell Mengaziol how his new band's debut had been delayed because of habits carried over from UFO: "The new band and I did a month and a half of rehearsing for the album and I cracked up because I did a lot of drinking and drugs. I smashed my guitar into thousands of pieces. I cut off my hair and went to a hospital in Germany to get straightened out. I haven't touched drugs or alcohol since.

"This new band is more or less the same groove as the old UFO, with different players—which gives the music a slightly different character," Schenker added. "I've always done the same music, one thing, that I like. I enjoy loud singing, hot guitar with powerful drums. That's the music I like!"

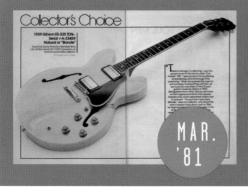

MAR. '81

Collector's Choice Debuts

The March 1981 issue featured the introduction of our "Collector's Choice" gallery of rare guitar finds and famous axes. For our first entry, we chose a "blonde" 1959 Gibson ES-335. It was just one of 73 ES-335s Gibson built that year and one of the few to be issued with a natural finish. The guitar was provided to *Guitar World* by an anonymous private collector who discovered the guitar in a pawn shop in 1965. "The color is its most striking aesthetic aspect," said the proud owner. "Just look at the beautiful contrast created by the combination of woods; that easy low-action mahogany neck and how it joins the natural maple at the twentieth fret."

THE MAKING OF A KILLER SOUND

ALEX LIFESON

By JOHN SWENSON
Photos By JONATHAN POSTAL

November, 1981—Guitar World

The Rush success story is a paradox of rock history. Ten years ago the band was nothing more than a Led Zeppelin copy act playing bars and parties around Toronto. When established record companies all passed on their demo, Rush released a first album privately and its phenomenal grassroots success prompted Mercury records to sign them.

Through the mid-seventies Rush built up a reputation as one of America's top Heavy Metal groups, yet the band was either overlooked or scorned by all but its dedicated fans.

"We had a pretty raw, uncompromising sound," pointed out Rush lead guitarist Alex Lifeson, "and that image really stuck with us."

In the last two years Rush has inched along a painstaking road away from the headbanger tradition toward a sound based more on music than decibel level. The group's *Permanent Waves* lp became the first Rush album to merit extensive radio airplay, while the new album, *Moving Pictures*, became the basis for a whole new sound.

"The idea on this tour," Lifeson said recently after an

50   51

NOV. 1981

VOL. 2 / NO. 11

Alex Lifeson

As Rush continues to tour in support of the great *Moving Pictures* album, Alex Lifeson takes time out to give *Guitar World* the inside scoop on the gear he uses onstage.

The Rush success story is a paradox of rock history. Ten years ago the band was nothing more than a Led Zeppelin copy act playing bars and parties around Toronto. When established record companies all passed on their demo, Rush released a first album privately and its phenomenal grassroots success prompted Mercury Records to sign them.

Through the mid Seventies Rush built up a reputation as one of America's top heavy metal groups, yet the band was either overlooked or scorned by all but its dedicated fans.

"We had a pretty raw, uncompromising sound," says Rush guitarist Alex Lifeson, "and that image really stuck with us."

In the last two years Rush has inched along a painstaking road away from the headbanger tradition toward a sound based more on music than decibel level. The group's *Permanent Waves* album became the first Rush album to merit extensive radio airplay, while the new album, *Moving Pictures*, became the basis for a whole new sound.

"The idea for this tour," Lifeson said recently after an excellent sold-out performance at New York's Madison Square Garden, "was to bring the stage sound down a lot more and really build up the P.A. system. Whatever we needed to hear, rather than having it come from behind, put it in the monitors. If you want to hear the guitar spread across the stage, put it through the monitors rather than cranking it up onstage. I think it's really helped our sound a lot. It's not as blaring off the stage anymore. The whole system sounds different, there's a lot more fidelity to it."

The difference in the group's sound is even better out in the audience. Previous Rush concerts I had heard were pretty much undifferentiated noise, but this night at the Garden everything was crisp and distinct, with Lifeson's many guitar effects sounding particularly good. "I have a lot more control of what I play now," he says. "Everything sounds a lot better. When you hit a chord, the chord sustains a little better, it doesn't break up. The strings are more clearly defined from each other. It makes you tend to play better."

One of the most distinctive features of Rush's sound is Lifeson's intriguing guitar playing, which contrasts fat slabs of bleating chords against searing single line runs and weird, extraterrestrial-sounding fills. For the most part during the set he used a Gibson ES-335 but switched off to several other guitars at different times. "I never really had a lot of luck with guitars I'd use on the road," says Lifeson. "I always stuck with the 335, but at the beginning of this tour I got a Howard Roberts Fusion that I love. It's a great guitar—I use it for 'Hemispheres,' 'Tom Sawyer,' 'Camera Eye' and the medley at the end of the night. It's the dark guitar with the single cutaway—it looks like an oversized hollow-body Led Paul."

At several points in the set Lifeson plays an acoustic guitar fastened to an instrument stand. "I'm using an Ovation Adonis and an Ovation Classic," he says, "not because I think they sound great on their own, but because onstage they're probably the best guitars you can use; the way they have the pickups set up and the controllability of the instrument. When you have a monitor 15 feet away from you and you're playing an acoustic guitar into it, it's really easy for the guitar to pick up the vibration of a certain note and start resonating like crazy. I had an Epiphone Classic that I'd spend hours a day trying to EQ. It was EQ'd like crazy so it didn't go wild onstage. When I got the Ovation Classic, I plugged it in and it was clear, no distortion, it sounded good and was very easy to work with."

The one thing about guitars that drives Lifeson crazy is that people always ask him first about the double-neck guitar he uses onstage. "I use a double-neck on *one* song," he complains. "We were at a point just after the live album when we were deciding whether we wanted to add a fourth member to the band to play keyboards or guitar, or whether we were going to learn to use new instruments, which is what we did do. Geddy [*Lee, vocals, bass and keyboards*] started using a mini moog and I added the double-neck. 'Xanadu,' which we were writing at the time, was a perfect candidate for the 12-string in the chorus, so I used the double-neck. I've used it on a couple of songs in the studio but I only use it in one song in the set, and I don't particularly like playing it. I guess I harbor ill will toward it because every time I see a picture of me with a guitar, it's the double-neck!" ✳

NINETEEN '82

In year three, Neal Schon takes aim at rock
critics and Frank Zappa introduces the world
to his protégé, Steve Vai.

Dear *Guitar World*,

This afternoon I bought the May issue of *Guitar World*, anxiously awaiting the article on the brilliant Randy Rhoads. I read it, appreciating the fact that your magazine was one of the few that realized what a talent he is.

A few short hours later, I heard the first reports of his death. What a loss this is for the guitar players in America—for the music industry as a whole! Randy Rhoads was the best thing to come out of the U.S. since the Les Paul! I feel he was the most innovative and *fresh* musician I had ever heard. His departure has left a deep gap in my music life; but his playing while here has left the greatest influence on me, and I will never forget him. Rest in peace, Randy.

—Mark Yester

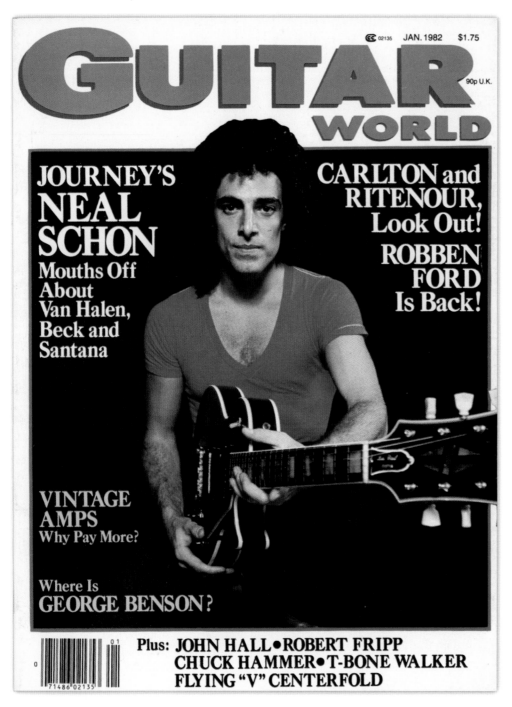

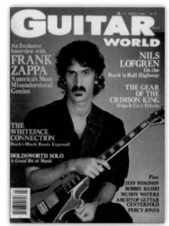

JANUARY A no-holds-barred discussion with Journey's Neal Schon, who takes aim at rock critics. "Columnists and reviewers have their heads shoved so far up their assholes that they can't even see straight!"

COVER STORY BY PETER MENGAZIOL; PHOTO BY MICHAEL PUTLAND

MARCH Frank Zappa holds court on a variety of subjects, including his protégé, a youngster named Steve Vai.

COVER STORY BY JOHN SWENSON
PHOTO BY JOHN LIVZEY

MAY Adrian Belew recalls his musical beginnings...drumming on the floor of his bedroom as a youth.

COVER STORY BY CHIP STERN
PHOTO BY JONATHAN POSTAL

JULY Police frontman and bassist Sting explains his philosophy behind his reserved playing style.

COVER STORY BY PETER MENGAZIOL
PHOTO BY JOHN PEDEN

GUITAR WORLD

SEPT. 1982 $1.75

90p U.K.

STEVE HOWE PLAYS IT
☐ Spellbinding
☐ Outrageous
☐ Awesome
☑ Safe

Five R&B Players On the Tools of the Trade

JEFF BAXTER
The Skunk as Producer

Plus
TAJ MAHAL
JIMI HENDRIX
ELDON SHAMBLIN
SHUGGIE OTIS

SEPTEMBER Steve Howe breaks free from the confines of a being in a single group. "I don't want to be closed in like I was in Yes. It's hard for any one rock group to totally fulfill what I can do on the guitar."
COVER STORY BY PETER MENGAZIOL; PHOTO BY JOHN PEDEN

GUITAR WORLD

EDDIE VAN HALEN On Technique... And Living the Rock 'n' Roll Dream

ALLAN HOLDSWORTH World's Best Kept Secret?

JAMAALADEEN TACUMA Bass Thunder from the 21st Century

Plus: ROY BUCHANAN · MIKE BLOOMFIELD
TODD RUNDGREN · JIMMY WYBLE
JIMMY RANEY · DAN AXELROD

NOVEMBER
Eddie Van Halen comments on the downside of being a guitar superstar. "I miss being able to walk down the street and go shopping, do whatever I want. David Lee Roth doesn't go anywhere without his bodyguard—I don't want to live like that."
COVER STORY BY TIM BRADLEY
PHOTO BY JOHN LIVZEY

1982 TOTAL ISSUES: 6

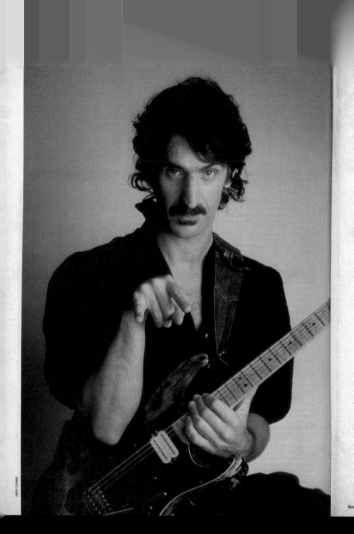

Frank Zappa was at the Palladium in New York for his perennial Pumpkin Day concert celebration with his most loyal fans. The maestro played five illuminating shows, running through a range of material which included an instrumental passage from *200 Motels*, crowd pleasers like "Montana," "Cosmic Debris," "Bobby Brown," "The Illinois Enema Bandit," "I'm the Slime" and "Broken Hearts Are For Assholes," virtually everything from the recent lp's *You Are What You Is* and *Tinseltown Rebellion*, and even a variation on one of the instrumentals from the *Shut Up 'N Play Yer Guitar* mail-order set.

Zappa's crack eight-piece band (himself, Steve Vai and Ray White on guitars, Tommy Mars on keyboards, Bobby Martin on keyboards and horns, Ed Mann on percussion, Scott Thunes on bass and Chad Wackerman on drums) is brilliantly arranged to showcase guitar work, with

FRANK

Z

APPA

THE INTERVIEW By JOHN SWENSON

White pinning down rhythms while Zappa and whiz-kid Vai play breathtaking solo after solo.

There were a few as-yet-unreleased songs thrown in for good measure, including one particularly interesting tune called "Returning Again," an ironic criticism of the wholesale regurgitation of late sixties/early seventies rock moves by current groups. The song could also be considered a Jimi Hendrix tribute (Zappa has a painting of Hendrix in his basement studio).

The ever unpredictable Zappa surprised the hall on several occasions by playing a full encore version of the most-requested tune in rock concert history, "Whipping Post" (that's right, the Allman Brothers tune) in absolutely deadpan sincerity.

Zappa's own soloing was at an all-time peak, a fact which he later attributed to the superb accompaniment his band offered.

MARCH 1982

VOL. 3 / NO. 3

Frank Zappa

Guitar World caught up with Frank Zappa at the Palladium in New York, where the maestro was presenting his perennial Pumpkin Day concert celebration. Zappa had just issued his three *Shut Up 'N Play Yer Guitar* albums, which emphasized his solo and improvisational guitar work, and was bringing his complex compositions to the stage with his latest touring group, for whom he served as "director." (Among the members of his eight-piece band was a young guitarist by the name of Steve Vai, who would go on to grace many *Guitar World* covers himself.) Zappa was in the midst of a boycott on print media interviews, but he agreed to speak with *Guitar World* writer John Swenson, who had reviewed the *Shut Up 'N Play Yer Guitar* albums in the November 1981 issue.

GUITAR WORLD What gets you off as a "director"?

FRANK ZAPPA I enjoy doing anything that is theoretically impossible and making it work. I mean, you saw [*us play*] some things onstage that were impossible and didn't even know it. If you saw what that music was that they were playing, if you saw it on paper and realized these guys were out there doing it with choreography and kind of dancing all over the stage—that was some of the hardest shit anybody in a symphony orchestra would ever be asked to play. They're dancing around and fucking doing it from memory. There's not an orchestra in the world that could have done that. And it looks like, "Hey, we're having a good time." They fucking sweated their nuts off to learn that stuff.

GW How long did you rehearse?

ZAPPA Two months. Minimum of five days a week. Sometimes six days a week. Minimum of six hours a day and sometimes 10 hours a day.

GW Does it ever happen that you put together a band and they seem like the right guys, and then they just can't do it?

ZAPPA Sure, all the time.

GW What do you do then?

ZAPPA Fire them. Get another band.

GW But, obviously, that didn't happen with these guys. The bass player was really great, too.

ZAPPA Great. He's a great guy. His name is Scott T-h-u-n-e-s. And he's really a great guy. He's 21. The drummer, Chad Wackerman, is 21. So is Steve Vai.

GW You know, it would seem almost like an indulgence for you to perform live with a group because it's so expensive and takes so long to work up.

ZAPPA Well, just so you really understand the mathematics involved, what do you think two months of rehearsal costs?

GW Don't know.

ZAPPA A quarter of a million dollars. That's before I buy the airplane tickets and pay for the hotels in advance. That comes out of my pocket before I get a nickel from any ticket [*sales*]. That's what I have to invest to make a band sound like that. And I don't think the audience has the slightest idea what that means. I am not funded from the sky. The money that they spend on a ticket this year turns into somebody's salary next year. Or it turns into airplane tickets. It turns into new equipment. I have been telling people, "I don't stick this up my nose and I don't buy yachts."

GW But in a way it would be much cheaper for you to just record and compose and try to get your things done that way.

ZAPPA Yes and no. But, I mean, look—I love music. I love to play. And I enjoy going onstage and improvising a guitar solo. It's the instant challenge of going against the laws of physics and the laws of gravity and going onstage and playing something nobody ever heard before and nobody would dare to play. That's what I like to do. That's...I mean, that's sex. That takes you into a realm of science. And you can't do that sitting at home and you can't do it in the recording studios. It's not the same feeling. ✳

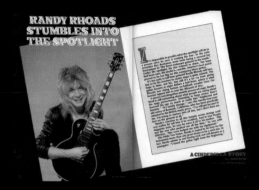

MAY / VOL. 3 / NO. 5

RANDY RHOADS

Randy Rhoads' first appearance in *Guitar World* was in the May 1982 issue, which happened to be on newsstands when the young guitarist died in a plane crash on March 19 of that year. In this frank discussion with John Stix, which was conducted just one week before Rhoads' death while he was enjoying a successful arena tour with Ozzy Osbourne, Rhoads expressed his disappointment with his playing on the still-new *Diary of a Madman* album.

THE RELEASE OF OZZY OSBOURNE'S *Diary of a Madman* is something of an enigma for Rhoads. Coming out at the end of 1981, *Diary* was already in the can before their first American tour to support *Blizzard*. So Randy's newest recording is really old, and from his standpoint, not the best he has to offer. "On the first album none of us had played together, so it was everything at once. We were putting the band together, writing the songs and being in the studio all at the same time. There was an exciting energy on *Blizzard of Ozz*. We turned everything up to 10 and if it felt good we'd play it. We also had time to choose the best parts and record when it felt right.

"Directly after making *Blizzard*, we did a European tour, came back and did *Diary*. There was no break. I didn't have time to sit back and think about What do I want to do? What do I want to accomplish? Therefore, I was really short on ideas that I was interested in pursuing.

"On *Diary* we put a lot more energy into the songwriting. So the songs are happening but my guitar playing isn't. Some parts of the record make me cringe from a guitar standpoint. In fact, on 'Little Dolls' I never got to take a real solo. What you hear on there is actually the guitar track. It's a dummy solo I laid down where I was later supposed to put a real solo."

SEPT. '82

When it comes to his guitars, former Doobie Brother Jeff "Skunk" Baxter goes against the grain.

"I've always been a fan of cheapo guitars because my early musical experiences came from working on 48th Street in New York City," said Baxter in *Guitar World*'s September 1982 issue. "The thing was that I saw kids who made maybe a hundred bucks a week saving up their money and coming in to buy a $1300 guitar they thought would transform them into the next Eric Clapton—to me, that was a real shame. So I sort of started a private campaign of buying and playing instruments that I felt were of excellent quality that just didn't have the reputation that the other ones had. I liked the Harmony Meteor, the Burns Bison Junior and inexpensive Japanese acoustic guitars because they have a nice brightness in the studio."

PHIL LYNOTT: "WHAT'S SO HEAVY ABOUT HEAVY METAL?"

JULY / VOL. 3 / NO. 7

PHIL LYNOTT

Thin Lizzy's bass-playing frontman explains why his band continues to churn out hit songs and play to packed houses in Europe while America sits idle, wondering when the boys will be back in town.

"**I THINK WE'VE NEGLECTED** America to a great extent. For that I'd like to apologize to the Thin Lizzy supporters because the explanation is simple: Success has been our greatest enemy. Like, you can only spread yourself so far. We could tour Germany and make enough money—but if we toured America, we'd break even or lose money. Well, obviously our management tells us it's in our interest to make money, so... We never really died here [*in America*]...most of the shows we've done here were good shows that went well. I'm under the impression that if we had spent as much time or even half as much time as, say, AC/DC have touring, we could have become a lot more popular. It's 'out of sight, out of mind.' I think by hook or crook, whether with Lizzy or myself, like with a standup band, we'll be in America this year."

A second factor contributed to Lizzy's American invisibility in the past few years: radio airplay. The free-form stations that first helped them here no longer have the same musical formats and direction. "It was easy to predict that the American radio would be so controlled," continued Lynott. "Controlled by the number of records they're willing to play. Now all you have to do is look at the English charts—or even European charts—compared to American charts. The American charts almost seem to stagnate. I don't think people hear as much or as varied music as they do, say, in England. You must admit that over the last five years the so-called FM radio stations that used to play free music, whatever they liked, is a lot more controlled via playlists by the powers that be. That is the freedom lost that I am talking about."

Guitar history was made in Los Angeles, whe[re] Van Halen jammed with Holdsworth and acknowledged the Englishman as a champio[n] of the guitar.

NOV. '82

Eddie Van Halen Jams with Allan Holdsworth

In an interview that appeared in our November 1982 issue, Allan Holdsworth talked about how he came to jam onstage with confirmed Holdsworth fan Eddie Van Halen, which took place on April 29, 1982, at the Roxy in West Hollywood, California. "Jeff Berlin and his band were playing with us that night, and we just thought it would be nice if Eddie would play too," said Holdsworth. "Ed's a really great guy, so I asked him to come to the Roxy in the afternoon and play, and we had a bit of a fertile jam session. Then we came up with the idea that we should all get up and play at the end of the show. Eddie worked out this tune [*a cover of AC/DC's "Hells Bells"—Ed.*], and we did it that night in L.A."

There hasn't been an electric guitar innovator who's eclipsed Hendrix. For now,

Eddie Van Halen will have to do

True innovators are rare in rock guitardom. Sure, there is a whole pantheon of pentatonic princes who have taken existing forms and expanded them, usually by making them faster or louder or by patching them through technoid gismos.

But real innovation? Nope. Probably not since Jimi Hendrix. That is, not until one Edward Van Halen fireballed into the guitar star cosmos a scant four years ago, and quickly assumed the stature of hottest and brightest. His style is a synthesis of very fast rock lines and the perfection of a right hand harmonic technique only hinted at in earlier times by the likes of Tal Farlow, Carlos Montoya and Harvey Mandel.

Van Halen's playing is not mere lickery and trickery. It's a carefully worked out approach that, in retrospect, seems to be such an obvious "next level" for rock guitarists that one can easily imagine the applause-like sound across the country of palms slapping foreheads, mixed with exclamations of "Why didn't I think of that" and "How the hell did he do that?"

To talk to Eddie Van Halen is to talk to a man totally consumed by his passion for music in general, and the guitar in particular. The music began with piano lessons for brothers Eddie and Alex after *pater familias* Jan Van Halen, himself an accomplished musician, brought his brood over from Holland some twenty years ago to set up digs in Pasadena.

By TIM BRADLEY
Photographed by JOHN LIVZEY

Guitar World/November, 1982

NOV. 1982

VOL. 3 / NO. 11

Eddie Van Halen

The hottest rock guitarist on the planet gets his second *Guitar World* cover story in as many years. In this conversation with Tim Bradley, Van Halen talks about being unfazed by his newfound riches, as well as the personal frustrations that accompany fame.

No matter what Eddie Van Halen plays, he brings to it such an unfettered ebullience that the listener gets the feeling he's in it more for the yucks than the bucks.

"I have no conception of the money," said Van Halen. "If you asked me right now how much I got, I don't know. I know I have three nice cars that I've always dreamed of having and that's it. I have the guitars I want and the ability to spend the money to put a big production together for a good show. Everything we make we put right back into the show, and if I have to go back to Gazzarri's [*the L.A. club where the band first gained notoriety*], I will not drug out and become depressed and end up in a mental institution and kill myself. I love to play guitar, whether it's in front of two people or eighty thousand. The only benefit of the money is so that we can put it back in and make it better. Not so I can buy a mansion. The house I live in is owned by my wife. The only thing I've done is Alex [*Van Halen, Eddie's brother*] and I retired my father and bought him a nice house and boat. I don't own anything that's typical Beverly Hills rock star 'I'm bitchin' ' type of shit."

That enjoyment of playing for the sake of playing spills out of every Van Halen track. "We go for an attitude, a feeling. We want it to be real, not studio-polished perfect. I have fun playing the way I do and there's never been anything on the albums that I'm unhappy with. There are mistakes that I know I could do better, but the reason I like mistakes is that they have some character to them. It's something you can never do again and sometimes it adds personality. We record live...Ted Templeman, our producer, says, 'Hey, Van Halen, they're the greatest.' All I gotta do is set up two mikes and then play and that's it!' Our last album took about 12 days and cost about 40 grand, which is a piss in the bucket when you compare it with the half million or more some groups spend. We never do more than two or three takes on anything, and usually we keep the first one whether there are mistakes or not, because of the feeling. You play something four times in a row, forget it man. Then you have to think about it. You can't think about it or force yourself to have feeling. It just comes out."

Living the rock and roll dream has not been without its problems and frustrations for Van Halen. There was the guitar manufacturer who put out guitars that were painted like Eddie's. "They were stamping out guitars for $900 to $1200, painting them like mine and using my name to sell them. And the guitars are crap, the worst guitars I've ever seen in my life. I called, my manager called and the attorney, and we all got the same 'Fuck you.' We finally had to go to court to stop them."

And there are the personal frustrations too. "The only thing I do miss is I like to walk down the street and go shopping, do whatever I want. People come up for autographs and it's cool, but there is a point where it really bothers you. Dave [*Lee Roth, vocals*] doesn't go anywhere without Eddie Anderson, his bodyguard. I don't want to live like that.

"I don't know...for some reason...you know, I'm married now [*Van Halen was married to actress Valerie Bertinelli from 1981 to 2007—Ed.*]. I've got to spend a little time with the wife. Her schedule's not as busy as mine at the moment because she's on hiatus. I look tired, right? I stay up till six or seven in the morning every day, because that's the only time I can do anything. I get frustrated sometimes because I want to get into different things, like producing. I'm trying to get the thing going with Allan [*Holdsworth*] and having meetings with Warner Bros. and attorneys and so forth. Then I have to write songs and rehearse and go in the studio and get ready for the tour, so there are like five things going on each day." ✳

Phil Collen: Girl Power

Page 8 of the November 1982 issue featured an advertisement for the Ibanez Destroyer, the guitar of choice for Iron Maiden's Dave Murray and Adrian Smith, and the two guitarists from Girl, an obscure British glam-rock group: Gerry Laffy and a pre-Def Leppard Phil Collen.

NINETEEN '83

Robby Krieger details the origin of the Doors' biggest hits,
Les Paul contemplates life as a one-armed bandit and
Pete Townshend gives birth to the "windmill."

Dear *Guitar World*,

By my calculations, approximately 3.5 percent of *Guitar World* is devoted to musically usable and worthwhile information. The rest is a mindless hodge-podge of equipment and rehashed anecdotes. Find some writers who can probe or some *musicians* who can articulate. Both would be great!

—Bob Chief

JANUARY Doors guitarist Robby Krieger enters a new phase of his musical career, but happily reflects on his glorious past.
COVER STORY BY TIM BRADLEY
PHOTO BY MICHAEL CURTIS

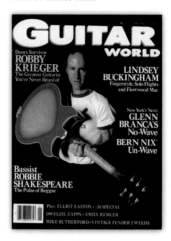

MARCH

Legendary guitar inventor/ tinkerer Les Paul never stopped innovating—even when a 1948 car crash almost cost him an arm. "I figured, if they're going to amputate my arm, I'll play the guitar with *one* hand. To do that, I conceived the synthesized guitar, which you play with your left hand."

COVER STORY BY PETER MENGAZIOL; PHOTO BY JOHN PEDEN

MAY Jaco Pastorius, one of the all-time great bass players, frowns on being called an original.
COVER STORY BY PETER MENGAZIOL
PHOTO BY JONATHAN POSTAL

JULY Dixie Dregs leader Steve Morse talks about his gear, his guitar-playing philosophies, his influences...and his Georgia farm.
COVER STORY BY BILL MILKOWSKI
PHOTO BY JONATHAN POSTAL

SEPTEMBER Toto guitarist and hired gun Steve Lukather offers advice on getting out of a session before it's too late.
COVER STORY BY TIM BRADLEY
PHOTO BY JOHN LIVZEY

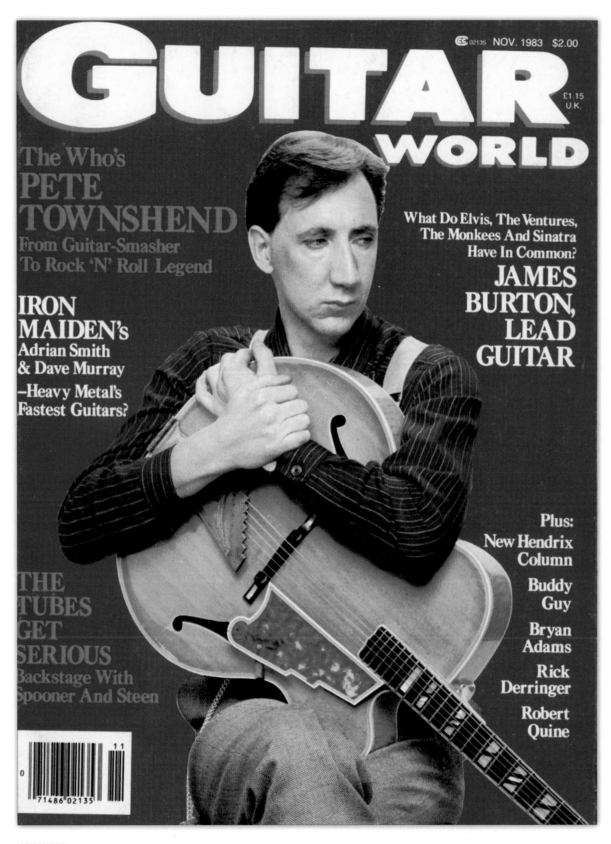

CC 02135 NOV. 1983 $2.00

GUITAR WORLD

£1.15 U.K.

The Who's
PETE TOWNSHEND
From Guitar-Smasher
To Rock 'N' Roll Legend

IRON MAIDEN's
Adrian Smith & Dave Murray
—Heavy Metal's Fastest Guitars?

THE TUBES GET SERIOUS
Backstage With Spooner And Steen

What Do Elvis, The Ventures, The Monkees And Sinatra Have In Common?
JAMES BURTON, LEAD GUITAR

Plus:
New Hendrix Column
Buddy Guy
Bryan Adams
Rick Derringer
Robert Quine

NOVEMBER The Who's Pete Townshend comes clean about where the "windmill" came from. "The first time I swung my arm was after seeing Keith Richards do it the night before. But he must have just done it that one time and never did it again, so it developed into my trademark."
COVER STORY BY JOHN SWENSON; DAVIES/STARR

1983 TOTAL ISSUES: 6

There's More to Life Than Being the Ex-Doors Guitarist
Robby Krieger

The screenplay's almost done. It's called *Fast Times at Heidelberg High* and it chronicles the coming of age (Subtitle: Onan the Barbarian) of American teenagers whose parents were stationed in Germany in 1967 or so. The thrill-a-minute account details, through the music that provided the soundtrack, many a madcap night of banana-gin-and-cokes at the local *gasthaus* and technical virginity tenaciously preserved by all but the friskiest. We (i.e. the characters) were continents away from the back-to-the-garden crowd, so the only music we got was the one hour of Sporty Forty that Armed Forces Network deigned to broadcast each day, usually hosted by some husky voiced female deejay whose sole apparent aim was to keep our boys in uniform humid and tumid. Anything else we got came spiraling in from the BBC or Radio Caroline, the signals fading in and out like some berserk phase shifter. And once in a while, there was this spectral, serpentine music that slithered from the radio into our imaginations, overturning rocks and uncovering our dark little secrets. Yes, people are strange and faces do come out of the rain . . .

The highlight of the movie will be the high school bus trip (yep, in one of Uncle Sam's own olive drab troop transport buses) to Frankfurt to see this weird group called the Doors. This wasn't any old limey blues band or one of those peace-love confections. This was something more menacing, more challenging. And the guitar gang from school didn't really make the trip to see the leather-suited lead singer whose rep had recently expanded from excellent writing and dramatic singing to certain organ recitals, if you catch my drift, wink wink. No way! We came to see Robby!

He didn't sound at all like those Anglo lickmeisters trying to pull off blues cliches at double speed. No, here was something different, more thoughtful, more mysterious. We sat front

By Tim Bradley   *Photo by Michael Curtis*

JAN. 1983
VOL. 4 / NO. 1

Robby Krieger

The Doors guitarist recalls the formation of the legendary California rock band as well as the origin—and subsequent chart-topping success—of "Light My Fire."

After high school came a year at the University of California at Santa Barbara, where Krieger majored in "keeping out of the Army," he told writer Tim Bradley. "By that time, I had gotten more into flamenco and was actually giving lessons at the school."

Krieger made the switch to electric guitar after seeing Chuck Berry perform at the Santa Monica Civic Auditorium. He transferred to UCLA after the year at UC Santa Barbara and decided to major in physics. He had also come to a musical fork in the road. On the one side, he was playing in a band called the Psychedelic Rangers with drummer John Densmore, a buddy from University High School in Los Angeles. And on the other, he was also into Indian music. "They even had an Indian music class at UCLA at the time, which I took. I had a sitar and a sarod and took a lot of lessons on them. I even went to the Ravi Shankar school out here, which was called the Kinnara School. This was during Ravi's heyday. He had about 10 teachers and millions of guys coming in with sitars."

It was this interest in Eastern culture that indirectly led to the construction of the Doors. "John [*Densmore*] and I were doing his meditation class taught by a guy who had been a disciple of the Maharishi's in India. Ray Manzarek, the Doors' organist, happened to be in the class too. At that time, Ray was just forming a group with his brothers called Rick and the Ravens, and Jim Morrison was going to be the singer. They asked John to be the drummer and a couple of weeks later, they decided they needed another guitar player. John brought Jim over to my house and we hit it off good. So we rehearsed and that was it. At first, I never really thought anything would come of it, but after a couple of rehearsals and a couple of gigs, I thought we were incredible! I thought we were as good as anybody out there

and I had no doubt that we would make it."

Because of the overpowering presence of Jim Morrison and Krieger's own mild-mannered and soft-spoken nature, it is not widely realized that many of the band's greatest hits were from the Krieger quill: tunes like "Love Me Two Times," "Touch Me" and one of the all-time greatest songs, "Light My Fire."

"I never even thought about writing until one day Ray said, 'Hey, you guys, we need some songs! Everybody go home and write some songs!' So I went home and wrote 'Light My Fire' and 'Love Me Two Times.' Those are the first two songs I ever wrote, and it's been downhill ever since. [*laughs*] They took about an hour or so. What I had for 'Light My Fire' was just the basic song and Ray added the [*hums the famous organ signature intro*] and we all arranged it together. That's why it said 'written by the Doors' on the albums, because we all sort of worked on the songs together. As soon as we worked up 'Light My Fire' and played it at a few gigs, I knew it was a smash."

With "Light My Fire," the Doors went from being just a club band to being headliners. "It happened so fast that we were booked into a club date at Steve Paul's The Scene in New York for six weeks. We were still in there when the song hit Number One on the charts. We could have been playing giant places and here we were stuck at The Scene making 20 bucks a night. One of the highlights of the whole Doors thing for me was when I was listening to the radio in 1967. They were doing the Top Five countdown and 'Light My Fire' had pushed out the song 'Cherish' [*by the Association*] for Number One. It was a thrill for Elektra Records, too; they'd never had a Number One song. They were going nuts. It climbed very slowly because they didn't have enough records to ship out." ✳

**DWEEZIL LOVES EDDIE;
EDDIE LOVES FRANK;
DWEEZIL LOVES EDDIE'S AX**

Yes, that's thirteen-year-old perfect son-of-the-master, Dweezil Zappa, clutching to his bosom the Kramer Voyager with the patented Eddie Van Halen vibrato bar, given to him by Eddie Van Halen himself. It all started when Eddie attended a performance of Dweezil's band at a school arts festival. Dweezil's ax kept going out of tune, so Eddie offered him this one. "I've radically altered the finish since this photo was taken," says the Dweeze. "I did some painting on it." Dweezil's single will be out by the time you read this. It is called, "My Mother is a Space Cadet."

**REGGAE COMES
TO THOSE
WHO WAIT**

A s Barry Reynolds sits down to be interviewed after etching a razor-sharp series of phrases on Joe Cocker's *Sheffield Steel* to at Compass Point Studios, he is typically ready to dismantle his own growing reputation as a guitar wizard. "Okay, then, as long as there's nothing too technical," he says evenly, cocking a Guiness bottle to hide the mischief in his eyes. "Like how many strings a guitar has, or something." Reynolds avowed ignorance of string gauges and other such specs is in fact a good clue to what makes *Guitar World, January, 1983*

him so special: he's a "feel" player, a thirty-two-year-old white Englishman in the international band that's sometimes called the Compass Point All-tars, and he trusts to instincts honed by years of varied gigging. His name only emerged recently, as a songwriter collaborating with Grace Jones ("I've Done It Again") and Marianne Faithfull ("Guilt"). He's also been writing with Bette Midler lately, and may play on her record (as may Adrian Belew). If it seems that the three ladies who have taken to Reynolds' style share a certain theatricality, that makes sense —he's an expert at spare, but telling, guitar adornments for thoughtful lyrics, perhaps because he is himself a writer with an honest poetic bent. But more to the point is the credits in Reynolds' current

JAN.
'83

Zappa
Plays Van
Halen

Dweezil Zappa was just 13 years old when this photo was taken; in it, he's clutching a Kramer Voyager guitar that was given to him by Eddie Van Halen. It all started when Eddie attended a performance of Dweezil's band at a high school arts festival. Dweezil's ax kept going out of tune, so Eddie offered him this guitar featuring the patented Eddie Van Halen vibrato bar. "I've radically altered the finish since this photo was taken," says Zappa. "I did some painting on it."

MARCH / VOL. 4 / NO. 3

LES PAUL

A *Guitar World* field trip to the master guitar innovator's New Jersey home offers a glimpse into the history of recorded music.

AFTER A FEW EXITS ON Route 17 from New York to northern New Jersey we found Les' secluded estate. Even if you didn't know the exact address there were clues all around that told you which house it was—mainly the stacks of old speakers, the empty cartons with "GIBSON" on them, the old turntable lying in the sun and the unused studio baffle, all out in his back yard.

Les' house is a living archive. In one room is the record cutting lathe that Les fashioned out of an automobile flywheel. That's where he began his experiments with overdubbing via acetates. In another room is a test rig that he still uses to develop guitar pickups. Upstairs lie rows of guitars in cases; some are prototypes, some stock models and some are legends. The living room now houses the first eight-track recording studio ever built, a separate entity from the main recording studio in another part of the building. The house is in controlled disarray; new equipment is being installed and the older, vintage gear Les swears by is being refurbished and incorporated into this new studio. It's a tinkerer's paradise but a suburban housewife's nightmare.

Les' two great loves, music and invention, began when he was nine. "I started out two things in parallel at the same time: electronics and playing the piano, the drums, the saxophone, the harmonica—that was first—and the banjo and the guitar. This came at the same time I built my first crystal set, and from that my first amplifier." So began Les Paul's interest in music and the means for its reproduction.

Before dabbling in "recording," Les tried to produce "multiples," in his own terminology—in a very "acoustic" manner, using the only playback method at his disposal. "By 1928 I was punching holes in my mother's piano roll, making multiples," said Les. "Multiple recordings, sure! Punch a hole in the piano roll and the key goes down. When it was a wrong note, I found the right note. Then I found out that with some tape I could plug the hole back up again, punch it somewhere else. I was making my first multiples *way back*! The first that I've got on disk were about 1933."

"We're not going to let the success of *Pyromania*

TUNE-UPS

seated next to Steve Clark in a New York City conference room. "There's a lot more emphasis on songs now, as opposed to just loud riffs and solos," Clark chimes in. "What we try to do is carefully work a solo into a song. Our fans want to hear the song, not the guitar solo. The solo should be part of the song and not stand out like a sore thumb. Many guitarists have the problem of not knowing when to end the solo. Soloing is a bit like painting—you've got to know when to stop because if you add too much you'll ruin everything."

Soloing is kept to a minimum on

heard Jimmy Page, I said, 'Dad, I want a guitar.' What I liked so much about him was that he played amazing riffs with so much style and feel. From the moment I heard Page, I knew his type of music was what I wanted to play.'

Although Collen's and Clark's favorite rock six-stringers have come from one-guitar groups, both believe a band is better off having two axmen, each playing different riffs. "A lot of guitarists in two-guitar bands play almost exactly the same," Collen asserts, as Clark nods his head in agreement. "The style we adopted on Pyromania is not to play the same parts during a song. If you take one guitar away our music just wouldn't sound proper. When we play different riffs that blend together it improves the sound incredibly."

DEF LEPPARD'S UNMATCHED TWIN LEADS

To hear Def Leppard guitarist Steve Clark tell it. "The band was starting to get a bit lazy" before latching onto its new member, second guitarist Phil Collen. "But now that Phil has joined, his enthusiasm has rubbed off on everybody and has given the band a new lease on life. Our guitar playing is also more adventurous than it was when Pete Willis was sharing guitar duties with me. Pete and I were usually chuggin' along playing the same riffs. Phil has a different approach—we tend to play across each other. While Phil is concentrating on the high end, I will play the low notes and this allows us to get a fuller, richer sound."

Phil Collen and Steve Clark

SEPTEMBER / VOL. 4 / NO. 9

The Def Leppard axman sings the praises of his new partner, Phil Collen.

WHEN *GUITAR WORLD* caught up with Def Leppard's Steve Clark for the first time, Phil Collen had replaced Pete Willis on guitar and the band's third album, *Pyromania*, was a chart-topping success fueled by its three Top 40 singles, "Photograph," "Rock of Ages" and "Foolin'."

"The band was starting to get a bit lazy," Clark told writer Joe Lalaina, "but now that Phil has joined, his enthusiasm has rubbed off on everybody and has given the band a new lease on life. Our guitar playing is also more adventurous than it was when Pete was sharing guitar duties with me. Pete and I were usually chuggin' along playing the same riffs. Phil has a different approach—we tend to play across each other.

"The style we adopted on *Pyromania* is not to play the same parts during a song. If you take one guitar away our music just wouldn't sound proper. When we play different riffs that blend together it improves the sound incredibly."

Also evident on *Pyromania* is the newfound approach to guitar harmonies adopted by Clark and Collen. "Guitar harmonies are a bit dated now, which is why we didn't want to do them on *Pyromania*," says Clark. "We did them on the last album, but we didn't want to get in a rut of being a guitar harmony band. So on the current album we do them on the chords instead—I think that's taking the harmony thing a step further."

When asked about his influences, Clark had one very specific answer. "When I heard Jimmy Page, I said, 'Dad, I want a guitar.' What I liked so much about him was that he played amazing riffs with so much style and feel. From the moment I heard Page, I knew his type of music was what I wanted to play."

As for what the future holds for Def Leppard, Clark commented, "Maybe we'll add a keyboard player for our next tour. But no matter what happens, we're not going to let the success of *Pyromania* get to our heads—no way."

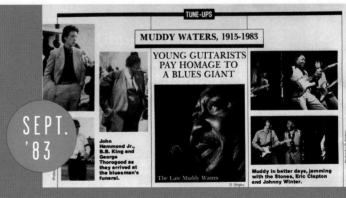

Muddy Waters Dies; Blues Legends Pay Respect

SEPT. '83

Delta blues legend Muddy Waters died on April 30, 1983, and *Guitar World* writer Rafael Alvarez was among those at the funeral chapel on Chicago's South Side where the great bluesman lay in rest during the first week of May. Among the many musicians who attended was George Thorogood, who commented, "It's a great loss, of course." In the parking lot behind the chapel, a visibly shaken Johnny Winter—"too depressed to talk," according to his manager—sat in the back of a black limousine before being ushered into the chapel for the start of the 7 P.M. service on May 4. At the Restvale Cemetery burial service the following morning, B.B. King offered these words: "It's like losing your father. It's going to be years and years before most people realize how great he was to American music."

Reflections on a Rock and Roll Lifetime
PETE TOWNSHEND:
The One-Time Guitar-Smasher Looks Back

BY JOHN SWENSON

Pete Townshend has been one of the most charismatic and influential guitarists ever to work in a rock and roll format. His understanding of the dynamics of the instrument in live performance, its relation to the various forms of amplification that have existed over the years, the ability to combine playing with effective theatrics and his synergistic combination of variously unrelated styles has made him a pioneer in the application of rock guitar techniques to both live and recorded formats.

Townshend is a complex and often contradictory personality; perhaps the greatest irony in a career filled with irony is that this celebrated guitarist started out playing banjo. Though his grandmother bought him his first guitar when he was twelve, Townshend abandoned that instrument for the banjo, which he would practice playing jazz with. He went to Acton Grammar School in London, where he met John Entwistle, who at the time was already an accomplished musician on trumpet, bass and french horn. Townshend and Entwistle played in Dixieland-style "trad jazz" bands together, Townshend on banjo and Entwistle on trumpet.

Townshend recalls getting interested in guitar again around 1957 when he heard recordings by Cliff Richard and the Shadows, which featured the stinging lead guitar of Hank Marvin. Even after he began playing guitar full-time, however, traces of his banjo-oriented techniques kept cropping up.

The most successful group at Acton Grammar School was the Detours, a band run by guitarist Roger Daltrey. Daltrey hired Entwistle to play bass for the Detours, and John in turn urged Daltrey to bring in Townshend to play rhythm guitar. At first Entwistle recalls Townshend playing the guitar somewhat like a banjo, but as the band changed its repertoire to include mostly blues material, Townshend began to adjust his style accordingly.

While still a member fo the Detours, Townshend graduated

November, 1983/Guitar World

from Acton Grammar School and enrolled in Ealing Art College, where a lot of his musical influences and aesthetic concepts were formularized. In addition to his interest in jazz players like Charlie Parker and Charlie Christian, he developed an avid love of blues, listening to Mose Allison (whose "Young Man Blues" was later recorded by the Who), Ray Charles, Jimmy Reed, John Lee Hooker and others. "The guy who really influenced the sound I did," Townshend points out, "was John Lee Hooker. That really impressed me. Although I was listening to a lot of jazz and playing jazz at the time, I preferred Hooker."

The training in conceptual art Townshend received at Ealing was equally important in developing his style. He learned that

Guitar World/November, 1983

music was a lot more than just the technical mastery of an instrument, that valid artistic statements could be made in completely unconventional ways. Townshend's art school training enabled him to combine his musical instincts with artistic and sociopolitical concepts. It also helped him to learn how to make a guitar do things it's not supposed to.

The Detours eventually adopted an association with the mod movement in England, and became the High Numbers. They augmented the blues material with Tamla/Motown r&b. The band's first recording, "I'm the Face"/"Zoot Suit" showed Townshend playing in a strict r&b mode. Daltrey stopped playing guitar, switching to vocals, Keith Moon became the drummer,

37

NOV. 1983
VOL. 4 / NO. 11

Pete Townshend

Guitar World's first cover story with the Who legend sees him reflecting on his many trademarks: feedback, windmilling and smashing guitars.

The Detours—the school band

led by Roger Daltrey and featuring John Entwistle on bass and Pete Townshend on guitar—eventually adopted an association with the mod movement in England, and became the High Numbers. Soon after, Daltry stopped playing guitar and switched to vocals, Keith Moon became the drummer and the name changed again to the Who. The group steadily improved, developing a style centered around the astonishing instrumental technique of Townshend, Entwistle and Moon. Townshend experimented with rhythm guitar patterns, using feedback and distortion ingeniously.

"As the level went up," said Townshend, "as people started to use bigger amps and we were all still using semi-acoustic instruments, feedback started to happen quite naturally." He played a Rickenbacker guitar because the Beatles used it and "I liked the look of it." His strange, almost non-musical approach to sound sculpture became tremendously influential.

Though his use of feedback was a trademark he developed on his own, much of Townshend's visual style was patched together from a number of influences. He was a shrewd observer of the pop world and when he saw something that looked good he would often adapt it to his own style. Even his windmill chord-playing style, where he would swing his arm in an exaggerated circle above his head, and which earned him the nickname "Birdman," was picked up from something he noticed Rolling Stones guitarist Keith Richards doing one night.

"The first time I swung my arm," said Townshend, "was after seeing Keith the night before swinging his arm like a windmill. I thought I was copying him, so when we did a gig with them later I didn't do it all night, and I watched him and he didn't do it all night either. 'Swing me what?' he said. He must have just gotten into it as a warming-up thing that night, but he didn't remember and it developed into my sort of trademark.

"There's a lot we've pinched from the Stones—absolutely nothing from the Beatles, funnily enough—but the Stones were a local band for us. I saw some of their first gigs at Richmond, and all the girls I was going out with at the time were in love with one or the other of them. I was just a Rolling Stones substitute."

Then one night something happened which was to change the course of history for both Townshend and the Who. The band was playing at the Railway Tavern, which had a low ceiling, and during one of his follow-throughs Townshend accidentally struck the neck of his guitar against the ceiling, cracking it. At first he was saddened by the loss of his costly instrument. Then he got mad. "I proceeded to make a big thing out of breaking the guitar," he said. "I pounced all over the stage with it and I threw the bits on the stage and I picked up my spare guitar and carried on as if I had really meant to do it."

Townshend's guitar demolition quickly became the focal point of the group's kinetic stage presentation. An early fan, Speedy Keen, who later went on to play in the Townshed-produced group Thunderclap Newman, recalled the Who's impact at that time. "The Who had become legendary. Townshend would go into the local music store and buy 10 Rickenbackers—in those days a Rickenbacker guitar meant real class; they cost about three hundred quid and anyone who owned one stood apart—and he would bust them all up in a week, then take 'em back without paying for 'em. This caused quite a stir at the time, for a guy to get three grand worth of guitars and bust them up."

The basis of the live sound that would make the Who famous was established, but Townshend was still working out songwriting strategies, composing at home by multi-tracking on tape recorders. Townshend was less interested in becoming a great guitar player than in coming up with a great sound for the Who. His attitude toward the guitar was more of a composer's than a soloist's. "At the beginning, it was really more of a situation where I felt that the only way I was ever, ever going to make myself felt was through writing. So I really got obsessed with writing rock songs, and I probably concentrated far more on that than on any other single thing in my life." ✳

NINETEEN '84

Eddie Van Halen, Judas Priest, Angus Young and Quiet Riot's Carlos Cavazo lead *Guitar World*'s heavy metal charge.

Dear *Guitar World,*

I've never seen a more pathetic record
review than the one Bruce Malamut wrote
on Stevie Ray Vaughan's *Texas Flood* in
the November 1983 issue. By referring
to Stevie and Double Trouble's music as
"tremeloed Texarkana Blooze," it shows
that Mr. Malamut tries to make his reviews
look good by using his own language which
could only be useful to a "heavy metal"
enthusiast. By calling Stevie's album
boring he only shows his bad taste in
music even further.

—Dave Gogo

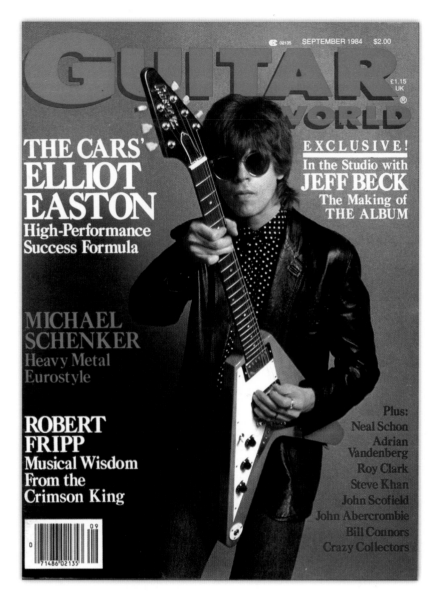

JANUARY Eddie Van Halen gives a preview of the groundbreaking album the world would soon come to know as *1984*. "I think this next one is going to be a hellified record. There's a fast boogie called 'Hot for Teacher,' a song called 'Panama' with a live solo and a song called 'Jump.' I've been getting into keyboards lately—and if people don't like it, that's too bad."
COVER STORY BY STEVEN ROSEN; PHOTO BY GLEN LA FERMAN

MARCH AC/DC's Angus Young shoots back at those who consider him a lead guitar master. "People tend to see me as a soloist. Poor people. You'd think they'd have something better to do. I mean, there's a lot of comedy on TV worth watching."
COVER STORY BY STEVEN ROSEN; PHOTO BY GLEN LA FERMAN

MAY ZZ Top's Billy Gibbons reflects on what he learned touring with Jimi Hendrix in 1968. "He taught me how to combine effects pedals. Back then it was one thing to use a fuzz pedal, but it was a Jimi Hendrix thing to hook up five of them."
COVER STORY BY BILL MILKOWSKI; PHOTO BY AGAPITO SANCHEZ JR.

JULY Judas Priest's K.K. Downing recalls his introduction to singer Rob Halford. "Our bassist, Ian Hill, was dating this girl, and Rob was her brother. She used to tell Ian, 'Oh, you should hear my brother sing. He's really quite good.' Once we heard him, we kicked out our old singer and hired Rob."
COVER STORY BY BILL MILKOWSKI; PHOTO BY C. GASSIAN/P. TERRASSON

SEPTEMBER The Cars' master mechanic Elliot Easton has definitive ideas on what a song is. "It's like a mini-capsule form of any art, such as life or a brook. It comes in and it goes out, like a little movie."
COVER STORY BY BOB DAVIS; PHOTO BY JONATHAN POSTAL

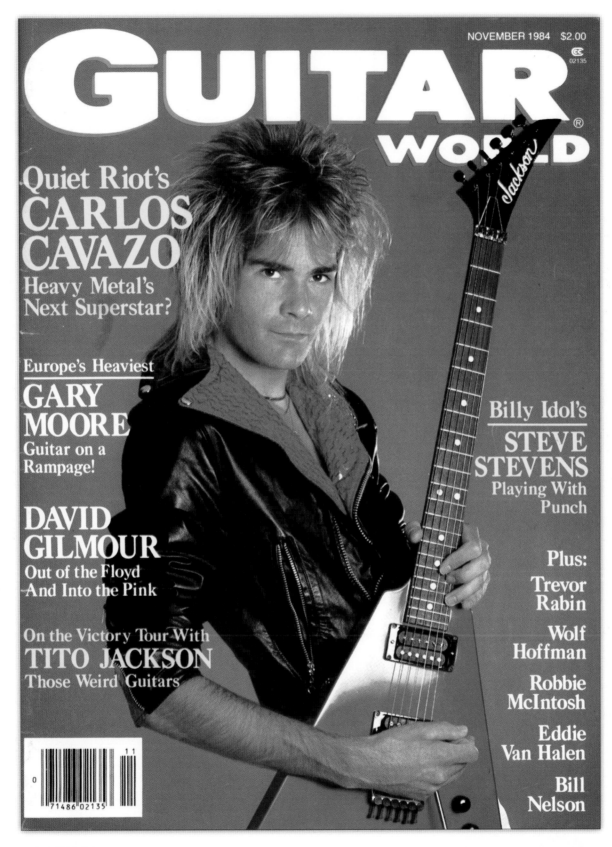

BILLY GIBBONS

Blazes His Way to the Top

The bearded collossus plays the hard-drivin'est blues-boogie north of the Rio Grande.

Agapito Sanchez Jr.
Stylist: JoDe Romano

It was just a little more than fourteen years ago that Billy Gibbons joined forces with drummer Frank Beard and bassist Dusty Hill to create perhaps the most formidable blues-based rock group to ever come out of Texas—ZZ Top.

As Gibbons recalls: "We met on February 10 of 1970, that's our official anniversary celebration. We threw a jam session together that fateful day. We started off with a shuffle in C and didn't quit for a couple of hours. We decided that it was so much fun that we kept on cookin'. And that same lineup has remained intact to this day. It's not only phenomenal that we've managed to stay together this long, but it's still a lot of fun." The boys are still thoroughly immersed in basic three-chord blues patterns, albeit a bit crunchier-sounding than blues of their Texas colleagues.

But it's this stripped-down heavy metal approach to the blues that has won ZZ Top a huge international following. And with their slick videos of "Sharp Dressed Man" and "TV Dinners" seeing heavy rotation on MTV and winning favor with call-in voters on NBC's *Friday Night Videos*, it seems that ZZ Top is destined for even greater success in the coming year.

"1983 was just a banner year for us," says Billy. "It's remarkable that we're now selling records in numbers far beyond our wildest dreams. Promotional efforts for the band have been monumental, and as a result, *Eliminator* has just surpassed the three million mark in sales."

The advent of MTV has had no small effect on ZZ's quantum leap in album sales, as Billy readily concedes. "Without a doubt, it's had an effect. Personally, I feel that the videos have been instrumen-

tal in popularizing the image of the group. For one thing, I can't drive that hot rod (which appears in the "Sharp Dressed Man" video clip) around anymore without being recognized. But beyond that, I think MTV is offering an added dimension that has certainly extended the popularity of modern music and has certainly stimulated record sales."

Of course, 1983 wasn't entirely rosey for the Texas trio. At the outset of their *Eliminator* tour, which began in May, 1983, tragedy struck. "The second night out we came up missing an entire semi-load of equipment. All the amps, guitars, basses, drums, accessories, including our lasers —all gone. Everything we had prepared for the tour had suddenly disappeared."

Luckily, Dean Guitars of Houston came to their rescue, quickly supplying Gibbons and Hill with a matched set of instruments. Says Billy, "We were quite pleased with the instruments. They were both equipped with one Seymour Duncan and one EMG pickup. And I tellya, it was quite a challenge to show up three days later with an entirely new set of guitars to work out on. That'll really make you learn fast."

Fortunately, Gibbons had his trusty '59 Les Paul (which he had christened Pearly Gates) safely under lock and key at the time of the theft. Gibbons has such a close personal relationship with that particular ax that it's doubtful he would survive if that beauty ever got ripped off. He tells the tale of Pearly Gates' origins:

"It was back in 1969, just before ZZ formed. What happened was, I gave a car to a young lady who was auditioning for a part in a movie and she had no way to get out to California, so I gave her my 1939 Packard to drive. Well, she did indeed get the part, so we named the car Pearly Gates because it had divine connections to get her in the movies. She drove the thing for a few months and then one afternoon a check arrived for me in the mail. She called me up that day and explained that she had sold the car for $450 and wanted me to have the money, which was great because

in the meantime I had found this guitar I wanted—this '59 Les Paul. So I immediately cashed the check and went out to buy that guitar. She called me back the next day and said, 'We're going to name the guitar Pearly Gates because you'll be playing some divine music on it.' So Pearly Gates it was. It's the instrument pictured on the cover of the first ZZ Top album, leaning up against the door jam of a '49 Chevrolet sitting in a bed of polk salad."

BILLY'S ONGOING INFATUATION WITH the world of guitars was initially sparked by two significant events that occurred when he was an impressionable twelve-year-old. One was seeing Elvis Presley on TV. The other was hearing two kids down the block playing their electric guitars in the house every day. "Bobby and Mickey . . . the two of them had a teen combo that was outa sight," says Billy, recalling a time when he was a mere beardless youth. "One guy had a '61 Les Paul and the other had a Fender Jazzmaster. And it was just impossible to ignore because even though they lived down the block, you could hear them for miles. That was a great source of inspiration. That's what really turned me onto the electric guitar."

His first instrument, a Gibson Melody Maker, arrived Christmas day just after he had turned thirteen. "It was a great surprise because the guitar appeared and the tissue wrapping had gotten caught up on the controls, so I thought it was just an acoustic, which would've been good enough for me. But I peaked around the corner and saw a little Fender Champ amp sitting next to it . . . and I knew then it was time to burn."

Rather than taking lessons right away, Billy locked himself in his bedroom with two records—"What'd I Say" by Ray Charles and "Found Love" by Jimmy Reed. Aside from scrutinizing those two, he was also an avid listener of radio station KYOK in Houston, which piped a constant flow of r&b music into his home.

His first organized band was a garage

outfit called The Saints. Their first gig was a beer party sponsored by Hoffa High Ronka, one of the unauthorized social clubs during his high school days. The gig paid five dollars a man. Billy adds, "We were not only rewarded financially but the experience proved to be memorable inasmuch as the party was raided halfway through the night, which sent us scrambling over the back fence, holding onto our guitars and amps, getting cut and bruised up, but smiling all the way as we beat it out of there. So we were stung after that. We were definitely hooked. It was the beginning of what has now resulted in the same kind of thing, actually."

The Saints eventually became The Coachmen, which led up to a dynamite r&b horn band with the hot handle of Billy G & His Ten Blue Flames. "It was very loose," recalls Gibbons. "Strictly white r&b with a little blues thrown in. We actually had only eight pieces but each night somebody would inevitably sit in, so we'd wind up with a dozen or so. We were only about seventeen years old at the time and just having a lot of fun."

Around that time, the local Texas music scene was undergoing some radical changes. By 1967 a new psychedelic scene was emerging—a curious blend of white r&b with mind-frying crunch-power. This new Texas movement was being spearheaded at the time by The 13th Floor Elevators. "They became such a local favorite that they were soon inspiring bands to start trying out new sounds and experimenting with different kinds of musical stylings," says Gibbons, who quickly jumped onto the psychedelic bandwagon with a group called The Moving Sidewalks. The lineup featured Tommy Moore on keyboards, B.F. Summers on bass, D.M. Mitchell on drums and Billy Gibbons on guitar. They cut one notorious album, which was recently reissued from Paris (Eva Records) containing all the cuts that were on the orginal album plus the two singles they later released.

A highpoint of Billy's Moving Sidewalks

MAY 1984

VOL. 5 / NO. 5

Billy Gibbons

Before he formed ZZ Top, Texas boogie-blues great Billy Gibbons spent the summer of 1968 opening for Jimi Hendrix. Here, Gibbons recalls the experience

By 1967 a new psychedelic scene

was emerging in Texas—a curious blend of white R&B with mind-frying crunch-power. This new Texas movement was being spearheaded at the time by the 13th Floor Elevators. "They became such a local favorite that they were soon inspiring bands to start trying out new sounds and experimenting with different kinds of musical stylings," said Billy Gibbons, who quickly jumped onto the psychedelic bandwagon with a group called the Moving Sidewalks. The lineup featured Tommy Moore on keyboards, B.F. Summers on bass, D.M. Mitchell on drums and Gibbons on guitar.

A highpoint of Billy's Moving Sidewalks phase was the summer of 1968 when they toured for six months as an opening act for Jimi Hendrix. "That was a real eye-opener, to say the least," said Gibbons. "We were all of about 18 years old and here we were opening for Jimi. We got to be running buddies during that time. He and Mitch Mitchell and Noel Redding...they were great players, man. I can't say enough about them because that was the definitive trio for us. We were still working a four-piece with the Sidewalks, but what they were able to do with just the trio was phenomenal."

Gibbons was especially awed by Hendrix's unorthodox technique. "It was just wild. He knew all the tricks—five-way position on the toggle switch before it was five-way, bending the wang-bar up so that it'd go down farther, immobilizing the strings...it was just great to be near him to see all this stuff he was doing instinctively. I remember one night he came ripping into the hotel room and said, 'Um, do you know this?' and he'd slap down a lick that would last for 10 minutes. I'd shake my head and say, 'Uh, no. Could you run through it maybe once more?'"

Besides being in awe of Jimi at the time, the fledgling Gibbons came away from that experience with some valuable insights as well.

"Things that were really awesome to me then are fairly common now...like hammer-ons. But I did learn a thing or two from Jimi about attack and a few showmanship things, like playing behind your head. He had all the tricks down. He just embodied the sound and the spirit of that time. He took the guitar into Martianland.

"Another important thing was he taught me how to combine effects pedals. Back then it was one thing to use a fuzz pedal, but it was a Jimi Hendrix thing to hook up five of them. He used to have these things called Fuzz Faces and he'd figure out a way to hook five of them in sequence. He would say, 'If you wanna use 'em, you gotta learn how to dance with 'em first.' So I picked up things like that from him. But as far as sitting down and studying with him, there was rarely any academic exchange. It just wasn't a part of the times as much as it might be today, where two guitar players will sit down and share ideas or talk shop. It was always more like, 'Hey bro, what's happening? Let's jam.' And besides, Hendrix was more interested in chasing women than talking guitars."

Gibbons then takes the opportunity to share another tale from his band's touring stint with Hendrix. "Part of the Sidewalks' act was a fluorescent rainfall. It was a water-based fluorescent liquid that we used in a trough above the stage, and it would rain purple raindrops at the end of the set. Well, Hendrix was intrigued by it. He really thought it was neat. So one night after one of the shows, he had attached a great big sponge to the end of his guitar neck and he said to me, 'I've got something for the act.' He had set up three washtubs with different colored fluorescent paints and he had this huge white backdrop installed. And he started doing paintings with his Strat! He tied a sponge onto my guitar and said, 'Come on, let's do it!' So here it was, three o'clock in the morning, and the hall manager was trying to kick us out. We had eight Marshalls turned up to 10, doing fluorescent paintings on a huge backdrop. We never got to work it into the act, but for one night it was great fun." ✳

JAN. '84

The Guitars of Randy Rhoads

The Collector's Choice centerfold in the January 1984 issue featured two of Randy Rhoads' personal Jackson guitars: his white 1980 prototype model and his black 1981 Custom. The white guitar was designed by Randy with Charvel Guitars president Grover Jackson. Wrote Bob Davis: It came equipped with a maple through-the-body neck and ebony slab fingerboard and Les Paul–type inlays. The wings of the body are maple, and it is finished in a white ivory with custom pin-striping. The guitar is equipped with a Seymour Duncan distortion humbucking pickup in the bridge and a jazz model in the neck position. The streamlined black Custom came about because Randy felt the earlier model looked too much like a V. Grover developed the offset design you see here. It also has a maple neck-through-the-body design and an ebony fingerboard, with custom inlays designed by Randy. The wings of the body are poplar. Replacing the tremolo is a tunamatic bridge with strings coming through the body, V-fashion. The electronics consist of two volumes, one tone and a pickup selector. All the hardware is brass, for that extra-sleek effect.

JULY / VOL. 5 / NO. 7

BO DIDDLEY

He may have pioneered rock and roll guitar in the Fifties and Sixties, but in the Eighties Bo Diddley had a battle with youth on his hands. Backstage at the Bottom Line in New York City before a Diddley performance, *Guitar World* writer Howard Mandel got the story.

"**I'M WHAT YOU CALL A HAS-BEEN,**" said Bo Diddley in this 1984 interview. "See, when you reach a certain age everybody starts lookin' at you sideways, you understand, and it don't make any difference whether you're a genius at what you're doin'—it's just 'Move him out of the way, a new thing is comin' and he ain't gonna change.' Nobody asked me if I would change, or whether I'm interested in doin' this new thing. Which is *not* rock and roll.

"That term—rock and roll—has been misused. You got DJs comin' up now, bein' told that this is rock and roll, what the kids do today. A guy in the audience the other night, he kept buggin' me: 'Play some rock and roll!' But I looked at him, pulled him off to the side, and said, 'Can I explain somethin' to you? I had to school him. Because I was playin' the only thing I knew how, *my* type of rock and roll—which is where it came from, because I was the beginning. He wanted me to play some screamin' guitar, and I said, 'I don't play that stuff. I'm not against it, but that's not my bag. I'm into writing songs that might be national hits—like the song 'Bo Diddley'—that grow on you.

Bo prefers to not dwell on this past much, but had this to say when asked about his musical upbringing: "I played all the time when I was a youngster. Kids today don't have to play in their neighborhoods, up and down the street, but I think what's what they should start at. Not because I started there, but because it was good experience for me; it taught me about the stage, it taught me how to work an audience, and that's very important. Back then I had a raggedy guitar, a washtub bass, a dude 'sanding' on a sheet of paper, and Jerome Green had maracas, shakin' 'em, and man...it was lovely."

"Nobody asked me if I would change, or whether

DAVID GILMOUR: OUT OF THE PINK AND INTO ETERNITY

After years of Floyd obscurity, the man with the humongous Fender steps out on his own.

BY BILL MILKOWSKI

DAVID GILMOUR

The very first time David Gilmour spoke to *Guitar World*, the Pink Floyd guitarist opened up about his friend and former bandmate Syd Barrett, "one of the great rock and roll tragedies."

DAVID GILMOUR JOINED PINK FLOYD on February 18, 1968, and for about seven weeks he and Syd Barrett played together. But it was only a matter of time before Syd left, leaving Gilmour as lead guitarist.

"I knew Syd since I was 15," recalled Gilmour. "My old band, Jokers Wild, used to open for Pink Floyd on gigs. I knew them all well. Syd was one of the great rock and roll tragedies. He was one of the most talented people and could have given a fantastic amount. He really could write songs and if he had stayed right he could've been a great one today.

"I actually haven't seen Syd since 1975, but I have a couple of friends who do see him once in a while and I talk to them about how he is and stuff. Syd is being looked after by his mother now. He can't look after himself. He's not the sort of figure that most people imagine he is, sort of sitting around being wonderful, getting ready to make another record or something. He's just a sick human being who can't look after himself and has to be looked after, and he'll probably wind up institutionalized when his mother can't look after him any longer. Nothing very glamorous or pleasant."

Gilmour also recalled being slightly intimidated by the prospect of replacing Barrett in the group. "It took a long time for me to feel part of the band after Syd left. It was such a strange band and it was very difficult for me to know what we were doing. People were very down on us after Syd left. Everyone thought Syd was all the group had, so they dismissed us. They were hard times. Even our management believed in Syd more than the band. It was an insecure time for us all and it really didn't start coming together until *Saucerful of Secrets*."

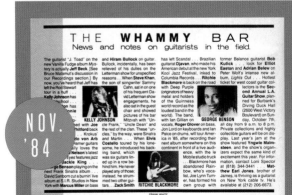

NOV. '84

The Whammy Bar Debuts

1984 saw the debut of the Whammy Bar section in *Guitar World*, a ticker-tape of news and notes from the guitar community. A sampling from the November issue encapsulates the events surrounding the rock and metal scene from that period: *The guitarist "J. Toad" on the new Vanilla Fudge album* Mystery *is actually **Jeff Beck**. By now you've heard that Jeff has left the **Rod Stewart** tour in a huff...**Kelly Johnson** has left Girlschool...**Mark Norton** has replaced **Vinnie Vincent** in Kiss...the original Aerosmith has reformed with **Joe Perry** and **Brad Whitford** back together again...Ritchie Blackmore has abandoned Rainbow and is back on the road with **Deep Purple**. Rainbow vocalist **Joe Lynn Turner** has formed his own group with former Balance guitarist **Bob Kulick**.*

GUITAR SAFARI AT THE POWER STATION:
BECK RECORDS A SMOKIN' NEW ALBUM

Nile and Jeff bounce the aural ideas in the studio. [below,] Jeff gets down on some heavy air guitar. Note the special air guitar tuning pegs and invisible string-bender.

Beck is back in force—the arbiter of rock guitar style for the last two decades arrived in New York this April 30 (just before GW press time) to work with producer Nile Rodgers at the Power Station on his most exciting album yet, by the sound of it so far. "I'm not holding back this time," Jeff told GW after laying down the first batch of tracks for the long-awaited album. "People are going to hear me play my ass off." With Nile producing and co-writing much of the material, as well as holding down the rhythm guitar parts, Beck seems to have finally found the proper counterpart to spur his seething talent and coax it onto vinyl. Being a perfectionist, Beck had already made a couple of false starts on the album that he has stored away as unreleasable. With Nile on, the magic seems to be happening as Jeff brings tapes of their outrageous funkifying to pals like Rod Stewart as soon as they're finished laying them down.

Jeff and Nile have been bouncing aural ideas back and forth like so many hot potatoes. For example, Jeff had brought in a tape of some out-of-control soloing he did for a British TV Commercial. It's Jeff playing notes like bulldozers and army tanks for sixty seconds in a humongous powerdrive "cultured noise" effect. Nile heard the track and said, "Boom, let's do something like that on the album." So it looks like we'll get to hear Jeff re-creating World War II somewhere on the platter.

No sooner did the legend arrive on these shores than he began to accept numerous calls for special guest shots on albums by his superstar cohorts: he recorded some parts of Rod Stewart's next one as well as appearing on Rod's video; then there was the session with Tina Turner, wherein the former Ikette scratched her name on the finish of Jeff's brand-new pink Charvel-Jackson "soloist." "I sort of let her do it," said Jeff soon afterwards. As soon as the major work was finished at the Power Station, he guested on Diana Ross' album, then Beck flew down to the Bahamas to lay some track on Mick Jagger's solo venture.

That's not all. Beck brought with him an album's worth of tunes from a reunion of former Yardbird members known as *Box of Frogs*. The album should be out about the time you read this, from Beck's longtime label, Epic, and it includes some bluesy harmonizing with such artists as Chris Dreja, Jim McCarty, Paul Samwell-Smith, John Fiddler, Jeff Beck, Eric Clapton and Rory Gallagher.

Of course, the coolest in this series of events is the next Jeff Beck album. Nile will appear on Synclavier II, also used as a drum machine, as will be some special guest vocalists like T. Turner. The rhythm tracks will include such luminaries as Jamaaladeen Tacuma and (probably) Fernando Saunders on bass. Tony Thompson will hold down the tubs with Dave Weckal.

News of Beck's arrival has rolled over the music biz like a tank—especially among guitar heavies. Billy Gibbons, Adrian Belew and Les Paul have all called to get close to the action, but at press time, we still don't know who else has done so, or who has gotten together with the man who loves guitars and cars. While in town, Jeff did a lot of hanging out, working at the Power Station with Nile during the day and venturing into the big city at night. This little report is only a preview of the shape of things to come.

Beck, for one, ain't superstitious. He's at the peak of his powers, on a roll. He seems to be taking on all comers, excited by the energy his own music is creating and anxious for the world to hear his current sound. This first report on the current wave of Beck-mania is only a taste of our further exploration of Beck the man and his legend. We'll give you the Blow By Blow next issue in our exclusive encounter with the man who can't stop rockin'. Stay tuned.

—*Bob Davis*

"Sounds a bit of alright," says the champ. Later, at a party at the Hard Rock, Beck can't wait to play the tapes for his former vocalist.

JULY 1984

VOL. 5 / NO. 7

Jeff Beck

The recording of his 1985 album *Flash* brought the legendary British guitarist to New York City, where *Guitar World* got the inside scoop on the long-awaited record.

Beck is back in force—the arbiter of rock guitar style for the last two decades arrived in New York on April 30 to work with producer Nile Rodgers at the Power Station on his most exciting album yet. "I'm not holding back this time," Beck told *Guitar World* after laying down the first batch of tracks for the long-awaited album. "People are going to hear me play my ass off." With Rodgers producing and co-writing much of the material, as well as holding down the rhythm guitar parts, Beck seems to have finally found the proper counterpart to spur his seething talent and coax it onto vinyl. Being a perfectionist, Beck had already made a couple of false starts on the album that he has stored away as unreleasable. With Rodgers on, the magic seems to be happening as Beck brings tapes of their outrageous funkifying to pals like Rod Stewart as soon as they're finished laying them down.

Beck and Rodgers have been bouncing aural ideas back and forth like so many hot potatoes. For example, Beck had brought in a tape of some out-of-control soloing he did for a British television commercial. It's Beck playing notes like bulldozers and army tanks for 60 seconds in a humongous powerdrive "cultured noise" effect. Rodgers heard the track and said, "Boom, let's do something like that on the album." So it looks like we'll get to hear Beck re-creating World War II somewhere on the platter.

No sooner did the legend arrive on these shores than he began to accept numerous calls for special guest shots on albums by his superstar cohorts: he recorded some parts of Rod Stewart's next one and also appeared in a video for Stewart's "People Get Ready;" then there was the session with Tina Turner wherein the former Ikette scratched her name on the finish of Beck's brand-new pink Jackson Soloist. "I sort of let her do it," said Beck soon afterward. As soon as the major work was finished at the Power Station, he guested on Diana Ross' album, then Beck flew down to the Bahamas to lay some tracks on Mick Jagger's solo venture.

That's not all. Beck brought with him an album's worth of tunes from a reunion of former Yardbirds members known as Box of Frogs. The album should be out around the time you read this, from Beck's longtime label, Epic, and it includes some bluesy harmonizing with such artists as Chris Dreja, Jim McCarty, Paul Samwell-Smith, John Fiddler, Beck, Eric Clapton and Rory Gallagher.

Of course, the coolest in this series of events is the next Jeff Beck album. Rodgers will appear on Synclavier II, also used as a drum machine, as will be some special guest vocalists like Tina Turner. The rhythm tracks will include such luminaries as Jamaaladeen Tacuma and (probably) Fernando Saunders on bass. Tony Thompson will hold down the drums with Dave Weckl.

News of Beck's U.S. arrival has rolled over the music biz like a tank especially among guitar heavies. Billy Gibbons, Adrian Belew and Les Paul have all called to get close to the action, but at press time, we still don't know who else has done so, or who has gotten together with the man who loves guitars and cars. While in town, Beck did a lot of hanging out, working at the Power Station with Rodgers during the day and venturing into the big city at night. This little report is only a preview of the shape of things to come.

Beck, for one, ain't superstitious. He's at the peak of his powers, on a roll. He seems to be taking on all comers, excited by the energy his own music is creating and anxious for the world to hear his current sound. This first report on the current wave of Beck-mania is only a taste of our further exploration of Beck the man and his legend. We'll give you the blow by blow next issue in our exclusive encounter with the man who can't stop rockin'. Stay tuned. ✳

NINETEEN '85

Blues, classic rock and rockabilly set the tone as
Jeff Beck, Stevie Ray Vaughan, Ron Wood and
Brian Setzer provide revealing interviews.

Dear *Guitar World*,

You guys throw around compliments like they're Frisbees! On your covers recently you've used such phrases as "Still the Greatest Guitarist" (Jeff Beck), "The World's Greatest Guitarist?" (Eddie Van Halen), "World's Greatest Bass Player?" (Jaco Pastorius) and "Heavy Metal's Fastest Guitars?" (Iron Maiden's Adrian Smith and Dave Murray). Sure, most of the players covered in *Guitar World* are fine musicians, but let's keep things in proportion and eliminate the sensationalism. By the way, I'm willing to audition for the title of "World's Slowest White Heavy Metal Guitarist with a College Degree Between the Ages of 20 and 26" if you are interested.

—Paul Johnson

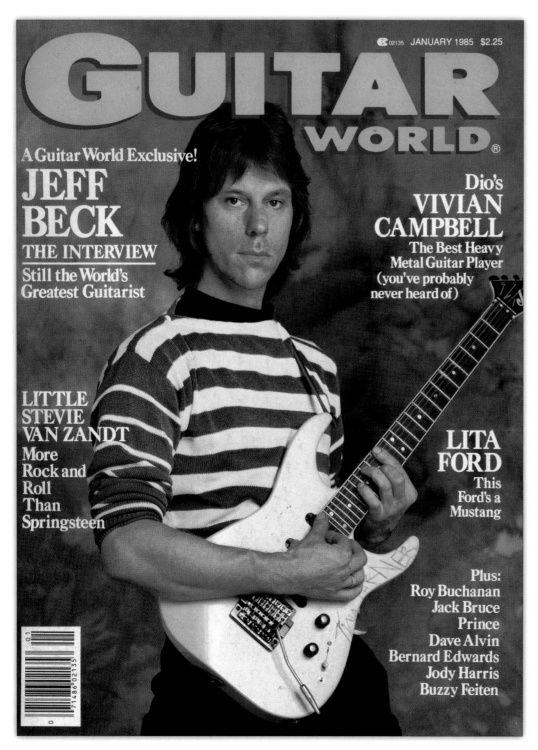

GUITAR WORLD®

CC 02135 JANUARY 1985 $2.25

A Guitar World Exclusive!

JEFF BECK
THE INTERVIEW
Still the World's Greatest Guitarist

Dio's
VIVIAN CAMPBELL
The Best Heavy Metal Guitar Player (you've probably never heard of)

LITTLE
STEVIE
VAN ZANDT
More Rock and Roll Than Springsteen

LITA
FORD
This Ford's a Mustang

Plus:
Roy Buchanan
Jack Bruce
Prince
Dave Alvin
Bernard Edwards
Jody Harris
Buzzy Feiten

JANUARY Guitar icon Jeff Beck recalls the legendary 1983 ARMS Charity Concerts. "Because it was Jimmy Page, Eric Clapton and myself playing for Ronnie Lane, the whole thing seemed to really *mean* something."
COVER STORY BY GENE SANTORO; PHOTO BY MICHAEL PUTLAND

MARCH Ron Wood admits to giving the Rolling Stones a "huge kick in the ass," but freely admits to being a yes man.
COVER STORY BY GENE SANTORO
PHOTO BY JONATHAN POSTAL

MAY Former Stray Cat Brian Setzer explains his transformation to rockabilly rebel.
COVER STORY BY GENE SANTORO
PHOTO BY JONATHAN POSTAL

JULY Eddie Van Halen talks about having a family one day, and whether he would want his son to follow in his footsteps.
COVER STORY BY STEVEN ROSEN
PHOTO BY GLEN LA FERMAN

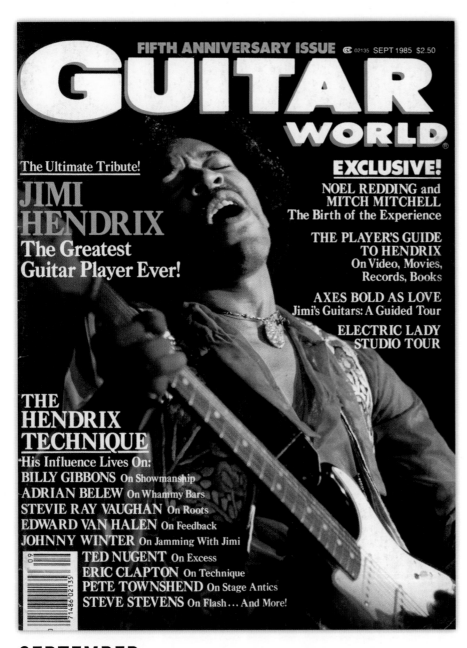

FIFTH ANNIVERSARY ISSUE 02135 SEPT 1985 $2.50

GUITAR WORLD

The Ultimate Tribute!

JIMI HENDRIX
The Greatest Guitar Player Ever!

EXCLUSIVE!

NOEL REDDING and MITCH MITCHELL
The Birth of the Experience

THE PLAYER'S GUIDE TO HENDRIX
On Video, Movies, Records, Books

AXES BOLD AS LOVE
Jimi's Guitars: A Guided Tour

ELECTRIC LADY STUDIO TOUR

THE HENDRIX TECHNIQUE
His Influence Lives On:
BILLY GIBBONS On Showmanship
ADRIAN BELEW On Whammy Bars
STEVIE RAY VAUGHAN On Roots
EDWARD VAN HALEN On Feedback
JOHNNY WINTER On Jamming With Jimi
TED NUGENT On Excess
ERIC CLAPTON On Technique
PETE TOWNSHEND On Stage Antics
STEVE STEVENS On Flash...And More!

GUITAR WORLD

The Making Of A Guitar Hero

STEVIE RAY VAUGHAN
On Fame, Fortune And Living The Blues

EDWARD VAN HALEN
Hanging Out On Bourbon Street

RITCHIE BLACKMORE
The Secrets Of His Mystery Riff

U2's THE EDGE
Sharp Sounds From The New Frontier

Autograph's
STEVE LYNCH
Two Hands On The Neck Are Better Than One

PLUS:
Johnny Winter
Slickee Boys
Blackie Lawless
Arto Lindsay
Tommy Shaw
Randy Hansen
Psychedelic Axmen

NOVEMBER Stevie Ray Vaughan understands he has demons, and is doing his best to cope. "I haven't resolved all my problems, but I'm working on it. I can *see* the problems, at least, and that takes a lot of the pressure off. I've been running from myself too long, and now I feel like I'm walking with myself."
COVER STORY BY BRUCE NIXON; PHOTO BY IAN CAMPBELL

SEPTEMBER *Guitar World*'s Fifth Anniversary issue is a cover-to-cover celebration of Jimi Hendrix, including tributes by such rock luminaries as Ted Nugent, Paul Stanley, Johnny Winter and Stevie Ray Vaughan. "He played rock like nobody had ever heard it," said SRV, "because he was just made to do it."
STORIES BY GENE SANTORO, JON TIVEN AND NOEL REDDING; PHOTO BY JIM MARSHALL

1985 TOTAL ISSUES: 6

JOHN BELLISSIMO

Woody socks it to Tina and Mick.

MICHAEL PUTLAND/RETNA

We caught Ron on the way to party

...AND/RETNA

MARCH 1985

VOL. 6 / NO. 3

Ron Wood

The Rolling Stones guitarist opens up about a range of subjects, including bass theft, getting a dog from Jimi Hendrix and the demise of the first Jeff Beck Group.

GUITAR WORLD I heard you copped your first bass by just walking out with it from a music store.

RON WOOD Yeah, I went to Selmer's [*in London*] because we were rehearsing around the corner from there. I picked out this Fender Jazz Bass, which I've still got, and I filled out all the papers, but I was too young, so my parents had to be guarantors for the payment. So we left it that they would come down the following day and I would borrow the bass for an hour. I went down and paid them six years later. [*laughs*] I also used a Danelectro six-string for a while. I liked them because they were easily replaceable. Townshend used to go through them like crazy. [*laughs*]

GW Who did you listen to to help you make the transition from guitar to bass?

WOOD Mostly Paul Samwell-Smith. I used to go down to the Crawdaddy Club in Richmond [*England*] and watch the Yardbirds every week, almost. I used to love Eric Clapton's guitar playing and would try to copy him. In fact, at the time he was going out with the girl who ended up being my first wife. [*laughs*] But I also learned a lot on the bass just sticking with Jeff Beck's licks. "Let Me Love You Baby," for instance—that was great to do.

GW What was Beck like to work with?

WOOD I always got along with him fine. He turned me on to the whole series of Chicago blues people. Buddy Guy is still one of my favorites—I just gave him a guitar, one of my Strats. He also turned me on to the Vanilla Fudge, who had a lot to offer when they first came out with that beautiful version of "You Keep Me Hangin' On." But as far as my bass lines, Jeff used to just let me go, because he knew that I was nice enough to stop playing guitar. He could've gotten a few bass players, mind you, but they weren't very inventive.

I always used to play with wirewound strings and a hard pick, though I remember I played with an English penny once in Detroit—on someone else's guitar, because mine got lost. [*laughs*] It was still a great show: the Grande Ballroom with foot-long hot dogs. We did all those 2,000-3,000 seaters: the Kinetic Playground in Philadelphia,

Boston Tea Party, Fillmore East and West. In fact, that first appearance at the Fillmore East is what built the Beck Group's reputation. They Xeroxed the write-up Robert Shelton gave us [*in the* New York Times] and bang, the rest of the country was intrigued. Of course, Jeff *was* playing great, and Rod Stewart *was* singing great, though those two had more of a thing of not talking to each other. I got on so well with Rod that I joined in the fun as well, but I wouldn't let it go too far because I respected Jeff's more-or-less purist approach to being a great manipulator of his guitar. Last time I saw him, a couple of months ago, he told me he still practices a couple of hours a day, and I can well believe it. But me, I practice when I'm onstage. [*laughs*] No, I keep my chops together, but lately I've been doing more painting than anything else. It'll never take over for the guitar, though; when Keith Richards is in town, I'm *always* playing with him.

GW You met Jimi Hendrix while you were playing with Beck.

WOOD Yeah, he gave me a dog once, a Bassett Hound. He also gave me his original B.B. King *Live at the Regal* album. He used to give me a chance to play solo bass stuff. Of course, I always used to do a bass solo with the Beck Group, but when Jimi and I jammed—once at the Scene, once out on Staten Island—he'd say, 'Hey Jeff, let the bass player go, he's got a good feel for it.' I saw him the night he went as well; he was in Ronnie Scott's. *That* was pretty shattering.

GW So what finally ended the Beck Group?

WOOD Well, besides Rod and Jeff not getting along, there was a nice amount of hate between [*keyboardist*] Nicky Hopkins and Jeff, though I suppose a lot of that went into the music. Nicky would always come with the briefcase and the mack. [*laughs*] When there was the final drummer with the group, Tony Newman—a *real* businessman. [*In mocking tone*] You mean you're getting paid *what*? [*Producer*] Mickey Most is doing *what*? You need somebody to get organized! And on and on. And so, two weeks before Woodstock, we all erupted and broke up. ✳

Much of Dio's recent popularity can be traced to an Irish lickmaster who could play 'em faster, but won't.

Viv Campbell: Form Follows Feeling

BY JOE LALAINA

VIVIAN CAMPBELL

The Irish-born shredder comes into his own as Ronnie James Dio's protégé—and talks about how the recording of *Holy Diver* nearly ruined him.

"I WASN'T SURE WHAT the best playing approach was when I first came to Los Angeles and started rehearsing with the band," the Irish guitarist told *Guitar World*'s Joe Lalaina. "Since there are so many fast guitarists in L.A., it totally disrupted my way of thinking. And since I never had much experience in the studio, I had to rely on Ronnie [*James Dio*]'s guidance. My playing is a lot more liberal on the new album, *The Last in Line*, though. Ronnie developed more confidence in my ability so he gave me a lot more freedom. I also became more relaxed with everybody in the band, so I voiced my opinion more. For the last album, *Holy Diver*, I was so happy to be a part of a major band that I didn't speak out as much.

"Although my playing has considerably improved on *The Last in Line*, I'm still not completely happy with it. For example, I especially like the solo I played on the title track, but it's not the sort of thing I'm going to listen to over and over. Once I've played something I'm happy with, I know I can do a lot better. I don't glory in my playing and say, 'Wow, what a brilliant solo.' I just play the best I can and refuse to analyze it.

Later in the interview Campbell recalled the 1983 *Holy Diver* recording experience, and how the pressure of working in such a high-profile situation at a young age nearly got to him.

"My hands started shaking as soon as I began recording. I mean, we weren't talking about it or rehearsing—we were actually *doing it*. It was the first time I was ever in a professional situation of this sort, and the pressure was getting to me."

CHARVEL/JACKS GUITARS

MAR. '85

Charvel/Jackson Advertisement: A Motley Crew

This full-color ad from Charvel/Jackson Guitars appeared on the inside back cover of numerous *Guitar World* issues in 1985 and featured a colorful group of some of the company's hottest endorsees. Among the participants are Steve Vai (Alcatrazz), Jake E. Lee (Ozzy Osbourne), Marc Ferrari (Keel), Michael Sweet & Oz Fox (Stryper) and Vinnie Vincent. Can you identify the rest?

MAY / VOL. 6 / NO. 5

GEORGE LYNCH

Dokken was on a fast track to success in 1985—
but that didn't keep the occasional disaster from
happening. Guitarist George Lynch explains.

DOKKEN'S CURRENT TOUR, in support of the band's latest album, *Tooth and Nail*, has been very eventful both on and off stage. In Albuquerque, guitarist George Lynch passed out during a performance. "It was a sold-out show," Lynch told writer Tim Bradley, "general seating and real hot onstage, but it was hot for everybody, not just me—so I don't know what it was. I just blacked out at the end of the last song. I think it was lack of chocolate milk...do we have any here? There have been all kinds of disasters on this tour. They found one of the truck drivers dead in his truck a few weeks ago. Thirty years old. Natural causes, they said."

Similarly, the group's hot video, "Into the Fire," seemed jinxed in the making. "It was done in London," said Lynch. "The actual filming took two days, one day outside by the River Thames and one day in the studio doing the cutaway scenes. We envisioned it differently from how it turned out. We wanted a set that looked outdoors but was really indoors with an *Escape from New York* look. But we just couldn't get our ideas together with the director.

"When I was doing my solo, I had these boots on that I'd never worn before and it was real slippery onstage. My legs started spreading apart by themselves. In the video, it looks like I'm doing it on purpose. I was in pain!"

And then there was the matter of the helicopter in the video, which caused three stacks of Marshall cabinets to tumble over "in sequence, like dominoes," said Lynch. "These were real Marshalls that we rented; they fell and bounced and broke. The helicopter was over the river the whole time and kept blowing water on us. The guy who flew the helicopter was killed the next day filming another video."

The *Guitar World* Buyer's Guide Debuts

The bi-annual *Guitar World Buyer's Guide* issue is known for many things: hundreds upon hundreds of instrument listings and specs, gorgeous images of guitars, amps and effects—and, yes, photos of some of the world's most beautiful women showing off the hottest instruments on the market. But when the *Buyer's Guide* debuted in the July 1985 issue, it was anything but sexy. The 15-page pull-out section was all black and white and contained only listings for electric guitars: among them, the Dean Mach V, the Carvin V220T, the Washburn HM-20 and the Lacey Rocket Ship One, a $2500 spacecraft-shaped guitar that featured a body made from something called "NASA-approved mahogany."

The EDGE

"I'm sick of conventional approaches to guitar," says U2's guitarist, "so I experiment with new sounds constantly."

BY BRUCE NIXON

The Edge is part of a new and rather unique generation of guitar players. These are individuals who have developed within a single band—who haven't served the traditional apprenticeship or built their chops in endless strings of groups or jam sessions. Quite often, their styles aren't constructed on the blues, or on any traditional rock and roll sound. Instead, their approach is based on a single context, and because of the unique demands of that sort of situation, they are expanding the vocabulary of the instrument—but they probably couldn't climb on stage and jam with a Lonnie Mack or a Stevie Ray Vaughan. They're stylists in the truest sense; pioneers, in a way.

Around particular needs of U2, the Edge (David Evans in real life) has designed an original, idiosyncratic sound that is neither rhythm nor lead, but, at the same time, is a lot of both. *War*, U2's third album, released in mid-1983, consolidated the band's following in the United States. It was music of purpose and intent that also happened to be very good rock and roll. The album seemed to represent a blossoming of U2's sound, and it announced the arrival of an important young band. *The Unforgettable Fire*, which appeared late last year, seemed to suggest that U2 would be around for the long haul.

The Unforgettable Fire, which was produced by soundscapist Brian Eno, has the sense of urgency, awareness and commitment that made *War* such a compelling record, but the guitar takes a very different kind of textural role: the edgy, clanging, high-strung guitar did create much of the texture and personality of *War*, but on the more recent album, Edge's trademark harmonic effects have taken on a softly-chiming, gossamer quality, and his three- and four-string chord-leads are either funky, fast, loose-wristed, thin-sounding and Talking Heads-like, or they're laid down in rich textured layers. If *War* was like an artfully-constructed documentary film in black & white, full of spare, clean-toned, slashing guitar images, *The Unforgettable Fire* continues the same story in soft, swirling color. U2's follow-up tour, which

November, 1985 Guitar World

Guitar World-November, 1985

began in Dallas during the last week in February, was triumphant, a kind of event: U2 has become the people's champ.

The Edge himself is a slightly-built chap, thoughtful and soft-spoken in conversation, given to long, carefully-drawn answers, sitting back in his chair like a mild-mannered professor meeting with one of his students. He's a kind of foil, perhaps, to Bono, U2's vocalist, who is as ebullient and as gregarious off-stage as he is on. But the Edge seems rather a different fel-

low on stage, too: intense, intent, the image of concentration. It's clear from listening to U2's records that the Edge works particularly well off drummer Larry Mullen; at the same time, bassist Adam Clayton serves a function similar to that of a rhythm guitarist, often playing chords to fill out the spaces in the Edge's style. The remarkable workability of all these combinations—musically and personally—may be a key to U2's chemistry.

"We never sat down and decided how

we would sound," the Edge said. "We've developed an intuitive kind of thing. We never contrived anything. That's something Eno said—this band's weaknesses have turned out to be its strengths in the sense that the limitations of our technical capabilities and our various ineptitudes have been instrumental in developing our style. The kinds of compromises that are required have spawned benefits. Making the most of what you've got can be the best course of action, in other words.

NOV. 1985

VOL. 6 / NO. 11

The Edge

The Edge spoke to *Guitar World* about *The Unforgettable Fire* and his band's constant need to push sonic boundaries.

The Edge is a slightly built chap, thoughtful and soft-spoken in conversation, given to long, carefully drawn answers, sitting back in his chair like a mild-mannered professor meeting with one of his students. He's a kind of foil, perhaps, to Bono, U2's vocalist, who is as ebullient and as gregarious offstage as he is on. But the Edge seems rather a different fellow onstage, too: intense, intent, the image of concentration. It's clear from listening to U2's records that the Edge works particularly well off drummer Larry Mullen; at the same time, bassist Adam Clayton serves a function similar to that of a rhythm guitarist, often playing chords to fill out the spaces in the Edge's style. The remarkable workability of all these combinations—musically and personally—may be a key to U2's chemistry.

"We never sat down and decided how we would sound," the Edge told *Guitar World* writer Bruce Nixon. "We've developed an intuitive kind of thing. We never contrived anything. That's something Eno [*Brian Eno, producer of* The Unforgettable Fire] said—this band's weaknesses have turned out to be its strengths in the sense that the limitations of our technical capabilities and our various ineptitudes have been instrumental in developing our style. The kinds of compromises that are required have spawned benefits. Making the most of what you've got can be the best course of action, in other words.

"What's strange about the group is that our influences are very subliminal. We've drawn from so many sources. We even try to contain what we listen to sometimes—there have been certain things we've consciously stayed away from at different times. We have no tradition to draw from, so we're constantly redefining what U2 is, musically. We're not like the Beatles or the Rolling Stones, drawing from roots. We're drawing from each other. This is a very close group, and my guitar style may sound sophisticated or evolved to some, but I think it's just been a case of having a good ear and the people I ended up playing with. It came naturally. I didn't *decide* on a particular idea to explore. I've taken a lot of happy accidents and built on them. Maybe what you do with the happy accidents says whether you're good or not."

The Edge is extremely pleased with *The Unforgettable Fire*. He thinks it's U2's best record to date, that it contains his best playing, and that it will be the most enduring of the band's first four albums. *War*, he remarked, was burdened by its political overtones, which served to lock the music into a particular geography and time. *The Unforgettable Fire*, he felt, may have the kind of timelessness that he himself considers a characteristic of good music. He still seemed a little enchanted by all the sounds on the record.

"The material was significantly different from anything we'd done before," he said, "so we knew it would sound different. We were pleased with *War*, of course, but we also didn't want to return to that sound and have it become too familiar to people. We wanted to broaden our horizons and leave ourselves some freedom.

"On this album I tried to do things I hadn't done before; using the guitar to get sounds that would produce a different sort of approach. On *War*, there was an attempt on some tracks—'Sunday Bloody Sunday,' 'Like a Song...,' 'Two Hearts Beat As One'—to go for a totally clean, unaffected sound. But when people start talking about a 'classic' Edge sound, I start worrying it slightly. I prefer to have personality to what I do, but I want to do different things too.

"The band influences what I do—on 'Pride,' the guitar playing makes the song what it is rhythmically. The song is a classic melody, and it didn't offer anything out of the ordinary until the guitar was added. That song was a case of the band being back together and rehearsing again after a while, and we had a really good day. I was playing less guitar, and doing more textural work, and that subordinate role served the song very well, Things like 'Wire' are very tight, no guitar excesses and little overdubbing. I consider that my best guitar playing, even though it's a lot less ostentatious to the listener." ✱

NINETEEN '86

In its final year as a bi-monthly publication, *Guitar World* pays tribute to Jimmy Page and Led Zeppelin as Yngwie Malmsteen and Steve Stevens show where guitar in the Eighties is headed.

Dear *Guitar World*,

What a hatchet job you guys did on Jimmy Page in the July issue! First, you bill him as the Ultimate Guitar Hero, then you proceed to explain precisely why he is not. Perhaps if certain people listened to more than "Whole Lotta Love" and "Stairway to Heaven" they would understand that the key to Page and Led Zeppelin is the emotional intensity behind the playing, not technical virtuosity. I loved how Vivian Campbell blew Jimmy off because he wears his guitar low—a surefire way to tell if a player is serious or not. Give me a break! And Steve Rosen's interview with Jimmy was going fine until Steve started pushing Eddie Van Halen into Jimmy's face and consequently aggravated the hell out of him, Steve, let Eddie be Eddie and just do your job, okay?

—Pete Gerace

JANUARY In his first *Guitar World* cover story, Yngwie Malmsteen shoots from the lip on a range of subjects, including his take on speed playing.
COVER STORY BY JOE LALAINA; PHOTO BY JOHN LIVZEY

MARCH Keith Richards acknowledges the instantly recognizable factor in "Satisfaction," "Start Me Up" and countless other Rolling Stones songs.
COVER STORY BY GENE SANTORO; PHOTO BY JOHN PEDEN

MAY Billy Idol guitarist Steve Stevens has played with the Thompson Twins, Nile Rodgers and even performed on a remix of a Diana Ross-Michael Jackson duet. But don't call him a session musician.
COVER STORY BY GENE SANTORO; PHOTO BY JOHN PEDEN

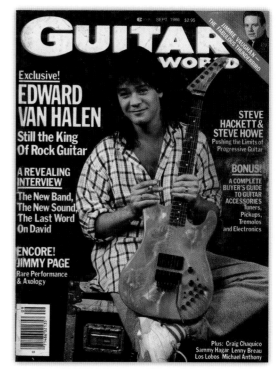

JULY Jimmy Page speaks candidly on a range of subjects in this cover-to-cover tribute issue, including Led Zeppelin's Live Aid performance. "I was so worried about forgetting this chord and that chord because I hadn't played the numbers for years. But to be part of Live Aid was wonderful."
COVER STORY BY STEVEN ROSEN; PHOTO BY NEAL PRESTON

SEPTEMBER David Lee Roth is out and Sammy Hagar is in as lead vocalist of Van Halen, and Eddie Van Halen has no regrets. "It was a blessing in disguise," said Van Halen. "When we get nominated for a Grammy and win I'm going to thank Dave. [*laughs*] I'm serious!"
COVER STORY BY STEVEN ROSEN; PHOTO BY PAUL NATKIN

CC 02 NOV. 1986 $2.95

JAKE E. LEE—THE WIZARD OF OZZY

GUITAR WORLD®

ZZ TOP's BILLY GIBBONS
A Guitar Genius Conquers The World

Bonus! MIDI A Complete Buyer's Guide To Hardware

EDWARD VAN HALEN Interviews LES PAUL

YNGWIE MALMSTEEN Declares Marshall Law

ROBERT FRIPP Sittin' In With The Professor Of Guitar

Plus: LARRY CARLTON · MIKE STERN
CHUCK BERRY · ZENO ROTH
ROBERT JOHNSON
RON WOOD

0 71486 02135 11

NOVEMBER For the recording of ZZ Top's *Afterburner*, Billy Gibbons took a few cues from Eddie Van Halen—specifically, when it came to setting up a home studio. "Eddie told me he has this hut behind his house where they make records now," said Gibbons. "That to me is important—close proximity, body language, all those elements."

COVER STORY BY STEVEN ROSEN; PHOTO BY JOHN PEDEN

1986 TOTAL ISSUES: 6

YNGWIE MALMSTEEN:

Like Him Or Not, He Demands Your Attention

BY JOE LALAINA

Either you love him or hate him—that's the way it is with Yngwie Malmsteen. Either way, it doesn't phase him. "I'd rather have people dislike my style than change it," he says. "If someone says, 'Hey, Yngwie, you play too damn much'—I don't care. The way I play is the way I like to play. If people like it—great. If they don't, it's still fine with me.

"I want to say something very clearly. I can understand that I'm a self-confident person who might come off with the wrong attitude sometimes, but I don't mean to. I just believe in certain things and I know exactly what I want. I've always sacrificed things in order to become the best musician I could be. My will power has always been very strong. If I want something, I'll get it. I've had no trouble keeping my head on my shoulders," and, he adds angrily, "nor do I have any chips on there."

That last comment is a reference to the story contributing editor Steven Rosen did in Guitar World in the July '84 issue. The title was "The God With The Chip On His Shoulder," and Malmsteen is upset about

it. "That's not the way I am," he says. "That story described me as being a big-headed guy who sucks up attention, which is totally wrong. The biggest mistake people make about me is that they see me as some sort of God-like figure with a big ego. If I see a button or a t-shirt that says 'Yngwie Is God,' I just look at it as a complimentary way of people telling me they like me. Although it's very flattering, it doesn't change the way I look at myself. I'm just a normal person completely devoted to my art as a guitarist and musician."

That confidence and singularity of vision are precisely why he has become so musically accomplished today. Since emigrating from his native Sweden in February, 1983, Malmsteen has become the fastest-rising—and most controversial—guitarist of the eighties. Much of the bad press he's received can be attributed more to a lack of understanding his intentions than to his so-called big ego. It's not the ego, folks, it's rock and roll careerism. Malmsteen's sole objective has always been the advancement of Yngwie Malmsteen. He used

the two previous bands he was in, Steeler and Alcatrazz, merely as stepping stones to return to the Rising Force project he initiated in Sweden seven years ago.

"I wanted to leave Alcatrazz a lot sooner than I actually left," says Malmsteen, who stayed in the band for nearly a year and a half and in Steeler for just four months. "There was always a subliminal disliking between me and the rest of the guys in the band. We couldn't agree upon things and my influences and beliefs were totally different from theirs. We tried to be as nice as we could to one another, but it was an uncomfortable atmosphere. They probably feel the same way about me."

Maybe so, but you can be sure Malmsteen's former band members are not knocking his staggeringly unconventional playing style or his rapid ascension toward the top of the guitar world. What made Malmsteen so successful so fast? A total obsession with the instrument and a craving to develop a style quite unlike his contemporaries—that's what. "If guitar players just listen to other guitar players

it's almost impossible to avoid sounding like them," says Malmsteen, who acknowledges only Jimi Hendrix and Ritchie Blackmore as guitar influences. "I try to achieve a style that is a lot different from what other guitarists sound like. If you listen to other instruments like violin, flutes or keyboards you will break away from the cliches of guitar playing."

Malmsteen, as you know, is most influenced by classical music, especially the unorthodox work of violin virtuoso Niccolo Paganini and the more sedate compositions of J.S. Bach. "Classical is the peak of the development of music," says the guitarist, "and Bach is the most influential classical composer of all. Beethoven, Chopin and Liszt all took from Bach. Mozart even took from Bach; he was a little kid when Bach died. Classical is the source of music; it's like a religion, almost.

"Paganini is probably my biggest classical influence. I got turned on to him through a tv show in Sweden. This guy was playing Paganini and I freaked, so I went out and bought Paganini's 'Twenty-Four Caprices,' which is my all-time favorite thing to listen to. Paganini did with his instrument what few people have ever come close to doing. He was a rock and roller—very wild and very extreme."

Extreme is one of the many words used to describe Malmsteen's guitar style—an ear-searing combination of heavy metal bombast and classical beauty. Although this approach is readily apparent on most of his recorded work, it was the Rising Force album which gave Malmsteen's career a quick boost right after leaving Alcatrazz. Originally released only in Japan on Polygram, the album sold so many copies as an import that U.S. Polygram went on to release it . . . a good move. At its peak the album went as high as number 60 on the Billboard chart—an uncommon achievement for a predominantly instrumental album with no airplay.

...and the monster of the Marshalls is waving his Strat at posterity.

JAN. 1986

VOL. 7 / NO. 1

Yngwie Malmsteen

It was the first time the Swedish phenom appeared on a *Guitar World* cover—and he took the opportunity to set the magazine straight about a few things.

Either you love him or hate him—that's the way it is with Yngwie Malmsteen. Either way, it doesn't phase him. "I'd rather have people dislike my style than change it," he told writer Joe Lalaina. "If someone says, 'Hey, Yngwie, you play too damn much'—I don't care. The way I play is the way I like to play. If people like it, great. If they don't, it's still fine with me.

"I want to say something very clearly," the guitarist continued. "I can understand that I'm a self-confident person who might come off with the wrong attitude sometimes, but I don't mean to. I just believe in certain things and I know exactly what I want. I've always sacrificed things in order to become the best musician I could be. My will power has always been very strong. If I want something, I'll get it. I've had no trouble keeping my head on my shoulders. Nor do I have any *chips* on there."

Yngwie is referring to an article that appeared in the July 1984 issue of *Guitar World* that was titled "The God with the Chip on His Shoulder." "That's not the way I am," he responded. "That story described me as being a big-headed guy who sucks up attention, which is totally wrong. The biggest mistake people make about me is that they see me as some sort of God-like figure with a big ego. If I see a button or T-shirt that says, 'Yngwie Is God' I just look at it as a complimentary way of people telling me they like me. Although it's very flattering, it doesn't change the way I look at myself. I'm just a normal person completely devoted to my art as a guitarist and musician."

In addition to his self-assuredness, Yngwie has earned a reputation for playing demonically fast. So what is it about speed that appeals to him? "It's not playing fast in itself that appeals to me," he says. "Speed can be very dramatic if you do it together with playing slow—it's a great contrast. It's also important to me that what I play fast will also sound good if the same notes are played at a slower speed. The reason I concentrate mostly on fast licks is because that's what my audience wants to hear, to a certain extent.

"I don't consider myself to be a very fast player. I'm sure there are other guitarists who can play faster. What I do that a lot of other guitarists don't do is I don't play things that are rubbish. If you would slow down the fast licks that a lot of other guitarists do, people would puke. I play classical runs, arpeggios and broken chords that if played at a slower speed would sound very nice as well. But if you do it very fast and very clean, but not necessarily as fast as someone else, you will appear much faster because what you're playing actually makes more sense.

"I developed a fast technique simply because I didn't want to be limited. I was obsessed with the fact of always improving. Just because I would play a certain thing in a particular way one day, it doesn't mean I couldn't improvise and play it better the very next day. I approached the guitar that way for a real long time."

As for how he developed his technique, Malmsteen offered this explanation: "I had two cassette decks that I used to tape my music on—one at the rehearsal studio and one at home. The one at the rehearsal studio was slower than the one at home. So when I went home and listened back to the tape I recorded at the rehearsals, my guitar sounded so much faster than I actually played it. I said, 'Wow—I can't believe how fast I sound.' And since my goal was to improve on everything I would play the day before, I developed a lot of speed and I began playing faster and faster and faster. It's a weird story, but it's the truth." ✱

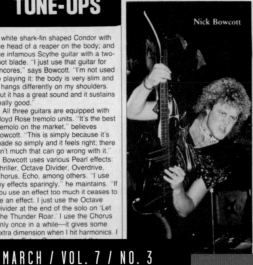
NICK BOWCOTT

Guitar World readers know Nick Bowcott as the author of many Dimebag Darrell, Zakk Wylde and Kirk Hammett lessons and columns over the years, but before his byline ever appeared in the magazine, he was featured as a Tune Up celebrating the release of *Fear No Evil*, the second album from his Eighties metal band, Grim Reaper.

L IKE MANY MID-EIGHTIES rock guitarists, Grim Reaper axman Nick Bowcott is much influenced by Edward Van Halen. "I use a lot of his two-handed tricks," admits the 26-year-old native of Droitwich, England, "but I do them in my own way. Although he popularized the technique, guitarists shouldn't shy away from using it. You should learn from other people. Since the two-handed technique gives you an extra span on your fretboard hand, it makes you do things your hands are not used to playing. Every solo on our new album has some form of two-handed playing on it."

The album Bowcott is referring to is *Fear No Evil*, a vast improvement from Grim Reaper's lackluster debut, *See You in Hell*. "That first album took less than five days to record," says Bowcott. "It was one of the first times we were ever in a 24-track recording studio. *See You in Hell* has a rough and ready sound to it. And there are some really bad mistakes on it, but I'd rather not point them out in case people haven't spotted them yet."

Unlike most guitarists, Bowcott plays lefty. "I was born left-handed," he says. "Gary Moore and Rik Emmett are left-handed guys who learned how to play righty—I tried to do that, but it just didn't feel right."

Bowcott has been playing guitar since his middle teens. "I used to play piano," he reveals, "but then I became attracted to the sound of the guitar. One of the first guitarists I copied from was Ace Frehley. Kiss' *Alive!* is a great album to learn from; it's like a library of acceptable guitar clichés."

Although Bowcott is a big Edward Van Halen fan, he is equally enamored of the late Randy Rhoads. "His death was one of the biggest tragedies of the Eighties. Randy had a great feel for heavy metal and his use of the tremolo bar was brilliant.

"I may never make it as big as either of those guys," he adds. "I just love playing guitar and want to keep getting better. As long as people enjoy my playing, I'll be happy."

R FINGERS DO THE ROCKIN'

re cele-
occurred
is past
hen Ed-
and Les
rst time.

Eddie Van Halen Meets Les Paul

One of rock's more celebrated moments occurred in Hollywood on November 13, 1985, when Edward Van Halen and Les Paul met for the first time. Ed, Les and other music notables were on hand to have their handprints frozen for posterity as part of the new Guitar Center Rock Walk—a rock and roll answer to the Grauman's Chinese Theatre feet-in-cement sidewalk. This photo of the event appeared in the May 1986 issue, with a full interview featuring both guitar tinkerers appearing in the November issue. "We had a mutual friend and he used to bring Eddie's records over to the house," said Les, "so I heard Eddie before Eddie knew I was listening to him."

"Why shouldn't the three of us get

Rock 'n' Roll Royalty

The parties were legendary, the hotels trashed regularly, the hangers-on flowed constantly when the Zep cruised the skyways.

Rodney at one of the many happening evenings in the fast lane.

talent in the band.

"You knew they were going to be something because of all the talent in the band. Because some of these people were like studio musicians for Herman's Hermits and P. J. Proby and people like that."

This was during the period when all visiting English bands stationed themselves at the playground known as the Continental Hyatt House, a hotel which catered to the whims and fanciful desires of the working musician. And Led Zeppelin were among the leaders of the whimsical.

"These guys were party animals, beyond party animals. I went to a birthday party for Andy Taylor of Duran Duran recently and Rod Stewart was there and Adam Ant and all these different people. And I was saying 'Gee, the parties today are different than they were in seventies.' In the seventies, the parties were real wild: there were like orgies and drugs. Nowadays people are real polite. They'll actually come up and meet your date and you don't have to worry if they're going to snatch your date away."

out there frequently. In fact there were times when they'd arrive in Los Angeles and have the limousines pick them up. And the luggage would still be in the limousines and before checking into the hotel they would go directly to my club. With all the luggage still in the limos. Because there was English beer there and English rock 'n' roll and of course that's where

Rodney [inset] with The Man. [above,] Partaking of the rock 'n' roll nectar, backstage

The Jimmy and Bill Show

By William Burroughs

When I was first asked to write an article on the Led Zeppelin Group, to be based on attending a concert and talking with Jimmy Page, I was not sure I could do it, not being sufficiently knowledgeable about music to attempt anything in the way of musical criticism thirteenth row. Over a relaxed dinner before the concert, a Crawdaddy companion had said he had a feeling that something bad could happen at this concert. I pointed out that it always can when you get that many people together—like bullfights where you buy a straw hat at the door to protect you from bottles and other missiles. I was displacing possible danger

JULY / VOL. 7 / NO. 7

JIMMY PAGE

Broaching the subject of a Led Zeppelin reunion with Jimmy Page is never easy, as *Guitar World*'s Steven Rosen finds out.

IN THE *GUITAR WORLD* archives, there is but one copy of our July 1986 issue. The reason for its scarcity becomes obvious once you see its cover: the entire issue is devoted to Jimmy Page. From front to back, we packed the 114-page magazine with Page-related articles, including reminiscences from his band mates in the Yardbirds and Led Zeppelin, photo essays of Page and his gear, and transcriptions of his "six hottest solos" (with handwritten tab!). At its center was a lengthy new interview with Page, conducted by writer Steven Rosen. Though averse to interviews due to previous hatchet jobs, Page had granted us a rare opportunity to question him at length. Despite Rosen's attempts not to rouse the Dark Lord's wrath, Page's patience with the interview process ran out when the subject turned to the future of Led Zeppelin, as this all-too-brief excerpt demonstrates.

GUITAR WORLD Have you been doing some writing with Robert [Plant]?
JIMMY PAGE Yeah, we have been. We've been playing together, yeah.
GW What does it feel like?
PAGE Well, it feels like playing with old friends. So it's good. Well, we all know everyone is into different things. I must admit at first it was kind of odd. Not odd but a big smile and slightly tense the first day. The second day was great, and we were all close

together. It was great, fantastic.
GW Obviously, *Coda* was not the last album you wanted to make with Led Zeppelin.
PAGE Of course not, no. But if you knew how many bootlegs there were out on Zeppelin. Those were all the studio recordings left from amassing all the Zeppelin tapes.
GW And what about *In Through the Out Door*, the last real Zeppelin studio album?
PAGE What? *Out the In Door*? It was the last album as such where we were all together in the studio to be playing. What can I say? It's a tragedy that John Bonham passed away. I think that at that point in time, *In Through the Out Door* could have been a very interesting transitional stage to what would have been happening after that. I think it really would have been interesting to see what came after that. But I don't know. Maybe we would have split up. I don't know. I don't think so.
GW Without trying to be too inquisitive...
PAGE You can be as inquisitive as you want in the right areas, providing you only print those areas.
GW Okay. Is there any other information you can give about your work with Robert Plant and John Paul Jones?
PAGE Well, what do you want to know? What do you want to know, for fuck's sake?
GW Will Led Zeppelin get together?
PAGE Is that what you wanted to know? Okay, fair enough. The guys, the band, is get-

ting back together and playing maybe every six months or every year. That's all. If I can do so without it being public knowledge, that would be great. But I can't do it, obviously. That's the truth, too. It's difficult, or it appears to be. It would be nice to play together just as friends.
GW Or maybe just make some music together.
PAGE Just as friends, that's it. I mean, who knows? I think everyone has their own thing going on separately. If you've had a friendship in the past, there's no reason why you shouldn't get together. I played with Robert in the Honeydrippers thing [*Plant's star-studded 1981 R&B album project*], and I'm playing with John on the *Scream for Help* album [*Jones' soundtrack for the 1985 film of the same name*]. So why not? Why shouldn't the three of us get back together and see what happens? And have a good smile at the end of the day, hopefully, and that's it.
GW I get the impression that you would have felt comfortable as a street musician on some corner, say, in Morocco.
PAGE Maybe not quite on a street corner or whatever. Just to be able to have a play with other guys and not have a to-do about it. If I'd never played the guitar, I'd probably be a juvenile...well, I wouldn't be a juvenile delinquent at 42, would I? I don't know what I would have been. Mass murderer.

back together and see what happens?" —*Jimmy Page*

JAKE E. LEE

HOW TO SUCCEED WITHOUT REALLY WHAMMYING

By Steven Rosen

Virginia-born Jake E. Lee stands virtually alone in the arena of electric guitar players. The lanky guitarist for Ozzy Osbourne is one of the very few guitar gladiators confronting the beast of heavy metal without a vibrato bar. Armed solely with his modified Fender Stratocaster and 10 digits, Jake reproduces sounds and effects others could attempt only with a whammy bar and like David against Goliath, he has proven that one need not go into battle wielding the steel straw. A listen to *Bark At The Moon* or the more recent *The Ultimate Sin* displays his unique use of finger vibrato, neck-bending and beyond-bridge tweaking to make up for the absence of bar. And even Ozzy—originally an unbeliever—was instantly converted once he heard Jake's whammy-less approach. Now holding the chair once hallowed by the late Randy Rhoads, one of the more apt students of the shimmy bar, Jake has had a difficult case to prove.

But the verdict is in and the thumbs are up and Jake E. Lee is making heads turn. Lee began playing at age 13, when he picked up his sister's "beat-up acoustic." The first song he learned was the Guess Who's "No Time" and in no time he was fronting his own original bands in his stomping ground of San Diego. There was a notion that this city lying 120 miles south of Los Angeles was too far from the musical mainstream and, packing his guitar, he moved north. Ratt, a one-time local band in San Diego, were just breaking into the L.A. club circuit and within a month of his arrival, Lee had a gig. But this was relatively short-lived.

"Stephen [Pearcy] was mainly why I quit Ratt. He was getting ridiculously drunk onstage and announcing songs we'd just played and forgetting words. He was embarrassing."

Consequently, Jake referred Pearcy to Warren DeMartini, also from San Diego, and Lee went through a series of local bands. Ultimately he joined Rough Cutt—for all the wrong reasons: "I felt bad about that because I didn't like the band that much and I only joined because of the Dio connection and because I wasn't doing anything. I hated to see another guitarist lose a gig."

Rough Cutt, too, failed to keep his attention and when the audition for Ozzy's band landed in his lap he—reluctantly—traded licks with the rest of the hopefuls. He has since gone on to become a major light, his playing consistently exciting, inventive and sleek. His only lacking quality is knowing what time of day it is—he was 45 minutes late to the Ozzy audition, late for the first flight of his first date on Ozzy's American

Guitar World • November, 1986

NOV. 1986

VOL. 7 / NO. 11

Jake E. Lee

Ozzy Osbourne's guitarist on *Bark at the Moon* and *The Ultimate Sin* talks about the making of those two classic albums, how he got the gig and what it was like being

GUITAR WORLD You had far more input on *The Ultimate Sin* than you did with *Bark at the Moon*. Did you want to become more involved or was that just a natural process?

JAKE E. LEE It was thrust upon me, more or less. I wanted more input. Every band I've ever been in I had almost complete control over. Except for Ratt, which was almost a partnership between me and [*singer*] Stephen Pearcy, but I had control over the music. It was like a Van Halen/David Lee Roth thing. Steve had control over the clothing and the show and I had control over the music. So I was used to being in control of the music in a band. And I wanted it that way.

GW How much input did you have on *Bark at the Moon*?

LEE Most of the music was mine—"Rock 'N' Roll Rebel," "Bark at the Moon," "Now You See It (Now You Don't)," "Waiting for Darkness" and "Slow Down" were mine.

GW How easy or difficult is it working with Ozzy in regards to presenting him with material?

LEE On *Bark at the Moon* I approached it really cautiously because I was the new guy and I could be out at any second. So I just played him riffs and if he liked the riff then the whole band would work on it. When I write a riff, I don't just write a riff—I write a verse and a chorus and everything around it. And Bob Daisely [*bassist on* Bark at the Moon] might change a part here or there and Ozzy might change a part and that was it really. I didn't argue too much if I didn't like the way something was coming out. I'd go, "I don't really like this" and they'd go, "Well, what do you know?" And I'd go [*in sheepish voice*] "I don't know anything, let's change it."

The strings on "Bark at the Moon" I hated; "So Tired" I hated. Actually, I didn't mind that when it was done as a four-piece band but then they schmaltzed it up with all the strings and I hated it.

So I'd present something and they'd fight, debate, say it sucked or whatever. Everybody contributed a little bit and it didn't necessarily come out the way I imagined it would. On *The Ultimate Sin*, while Ozzy was in the Betty Ford Clinic, I got a drum machine, one of those mini-studios, a bass from Charvel—a really shitty one—and I more or less wrote entire songs. I didn't write melodies or lyrics because Ozzy is bound to do a lot of changing if I was to do that, I just write the music. I write the riff and I'll come up with a chorus, verse, bridge and solo section, and I'll write the drum and bass parts I had in mind. I put about 12 songs like that down on tape and when he got out of the Betty Ford Clinic it was, "Here ya go, here's what I've got so far." And I'd say half of it ended up on the album.

GW How did you get the gig playing for Ozzy?

LEE Someone contacted me about it and at first I said no because I didn't want to step into Randy Rhoads' shoes. It's hard enough trying to replace a good guitar player—and I don't want this to sound callous—but when they die they turn into a legend. And that's really tough; I didn't want that. I'd make it on my own and I didn't want to be compared to somebody else for the rest of my life. But I went down there anyway and I think there was a list of 12 guitar players and we all spent 15 minutes in the studio, each doing whatever we wanted to do. We had our pictures taken and they were given to Ozzy and he picked three of us: George Lynch was one of them and he was flown to England and given first crack at it. And there was me and Mitch Perry left in Los Angeles. Ozzy came down and we auditioned at S.I.R. and I got it. And I was 45 minutes late! The guy who found the guitar players said that Ozzy had almost walked out the door; he said, "Fuck it, if this guy doesn't care enough to show up on time *and* he's going to be this kind of problem, forget it. I don't care how good he is." But this guy kept him there. ✳

NINETEEN '87

Joe Perry gets sober, Steve Vai and Billy Sheehan team up with David Lee Roth and Randy Rhoads is honored with a special collector's edition.

Dear *Guitar World*,

My wife and I have to number as one of our great thrills in our son Steve's musical career the cover story of your March 1987 issue. Both of your interviews—Steve's and Billy Sheehan's—were outstandingly written. You people are absolutely great. We have had the pleasure of meeting David Lee Roth, Billy *and* Greg Bissonette—we would take them as "sons" any day. We are very proud that our son Steve is in such fine *and* great company. Frank Zappa is a friend of ours, too—and it was he who told us that Steve was great. Steve was only 19 then. But, of course, you know that when Frank speaks, the music world stands up and listens. We read your magazine faithfully, picking up copies at Focus II Guitars. Thank you for your respect—we hope someday to meet you.

—Theresa and Johnny Vai, Carle Place, NY

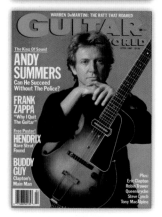

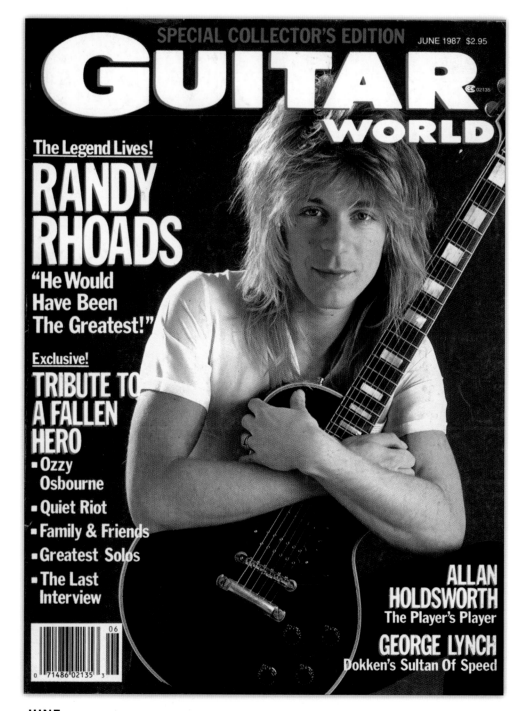

JANUARY As his *Trilogy* album hits store shelves, Yngwie Malmsteen takes time out to talk gear, his approach to guitar, and the impact of his playing on a generation of new guitarists.
COVER STORY BY JOE LALAINA
PHOTO BY JOHN PEDEN

MARCH Bassist Billy Sheehan and guitarist Steve Vai join forces and provide a shedderific foundation for David Lee Roth's *Eat 'Em and Smile* album.
COVER STORIES BY BILL MILKOWSKI
AND JOE LALAINA
PHOTO BY GLEN LA FERMAN

APRIL Police guitarist Andy Summers breaks out with *Quark*, his first solo album—his latest in a string of guitar-playing activities.
COVER STORIES BY GENE SANTORO
PHOTO BY JOHN PEDEN

JUNE *Guitar World*'s first ever tribute to Randy Rhoads features reminiscences from Sharon Osbourne, former Quiet Riot bandmates and pictures from the guitarist's last photo shoot. On the subject of the newly discovered *Tribute* live album, Ozzy Osbourne says, "When we found the tapes, we were devastated. The tape was only on for a minute or so and all I could say was, 'My God!' It's that good."
COVER STORIES BY JOSEPH BOSSO, JOE LALAINA, BILLY CIOFFI AND JOHN STIX; PHOTO BY JOHN LIVZEY

1987 TOTAL ISSUES: 8

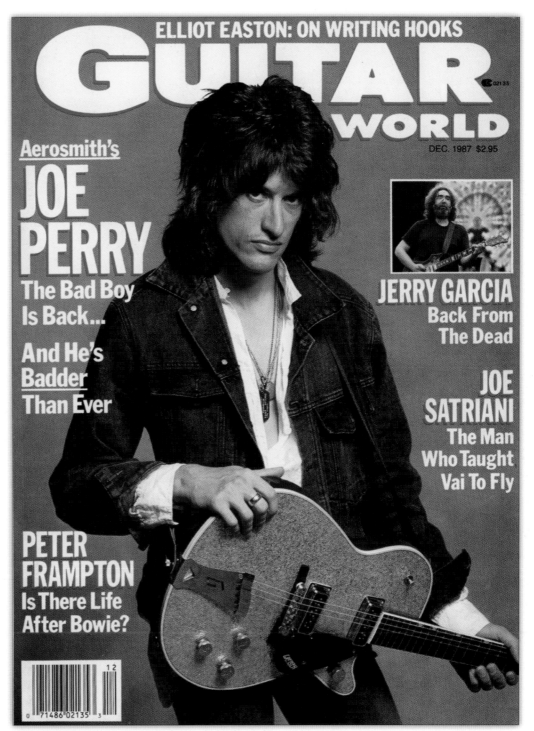

JULY As *The Joshua Tree* propels U2 to new levels of rock superstardom, The Edge talks to *Guitar World* about the progression from *The Unforgettable Fire* to the new album.
COVER STORY BY JOSEPH BOSSO
PHOTO BY ANTON CORBIJN

SEPTEMBER Yes bassist Chris Squire sings the praises of Trevor Rabin, the South African hotshot who revitalized the Yes formula in the mid Eighties, and reflects on the success of "Owner of a Lonely Heart."
COVER STORY BY BUD SCOPPA
PHOTO BY NEAL PRESTON

NOVEMBER With Dire Straits on top of the world, Mark Knopfler takes time out to reflect on his band's recent mass success and various side projects, including performing with Eric Clapton.
COVER STORY BY GENE SANTORO
PHOTO BY ANN SUMMA

DECEMBER Aerosmith return after four years with *Permanent Vacation*, their strongest album in years and the first to reflect a newly clean and sober Aerosmith. "I'm so much more aware now, so much freer," says Joe Perry. "Drinking blocked so many areas, and though I could occasionally 'throw a few back' and get to that place, the more you drink the harder it gets. There were things I felt that I couldn't tap into, but I can now."
COVER STORY BY STEVEN ROSEN; PHOTO BY GLEN LA FERMAN

ve You Seen These Guitars?: Most of the guitars in this photo re stolen, including (left to right); featured in Dave's video (partly obscured by Steve); an oriental blue Stratocaster by Performance, with three humbuckers; a '59

JAN. 1987

VOL. 8 / NO. 1

Steve Vai

ith the David Lee Roth world tour just weeks away, Steve Vai falls victim to a major itar and amp robbery. *Guitar World* spreads the word about the missing gear with

It is late July 1986. Los Angeles. At Steve Vai's recording studio. The same studio that produced the solo albums that have haunted guitarists since their release. Through the glass I could see Steve playing furiously and I was in a position to do my hero a favor. I entered the room and heard the squealing licks that filled the air. I listened, awestruck, and hesitated to interrupt. I wasn't simply an admirer; I had a purpose as well. I then presented Steve with the custom 30-fret Guild I had designed for him.

Rumor had it that all his equipment had been stolen just three weeks before the 12- to 18-month world tour began. Speaking to Steve, I found rumor to be fact: nearly all his gear had been stolen from the theater in Pasadena where the David Lee Roth band had been rehearsing. He was in trouble and somehow I was there at the right time to be of some help. Steve smiled, and immediately began introducing his fingers to their new friend. Vai unleashed his maniacal licks on the ax and seemed at home with his new mistress. It sounded like the trouble just disappeared. He turned the whole bad scene into something to get inspired about. Although, in later conversation, he was evidently apoplectic about his stolen harem of axes.

Missing were five custom guitars and two custom amplifiers. All of the axes are easily recognizable and two were featured in the band's video, "Yankee Rose." Both Steve and his longtime guitar tech, Elwood Francis, filled me in on the details of each missing ax.

First up was the eyeball, or "Steve Eye," yellow Jackson Soloist. The finish has Steve's personal design of a pyramid with an eye in the middle and the number seven on each outside corner. Loaded with a Floyd Rose tremolo and custom-wound DiMarzio pickups, this is one of the axes seen in the "Yankee Rose" video.

The second was a custom-designed green Swiss-cheese guitar built for Steve by his childhood friend Joe Despagni. The body was metallic green with holes carved through the body of various sizes and colors. There's a handle carved in the body as well, to enable Steve to hold the ax and play with one hand. Loaded with a gold Floyd Rose and one humbucker, this beauty also shares spotlight in the "Yankee Rose" video.

Third: a pink and black tiger-striped Guild 284 Avatar with left-handed headstock. The ax had a Floyd Rose, two EMG humbuckers and one EMG single-coil in the middle position. The serial number is HC100788.

Fourth: a white Guild 281 Flyer, serial number HC101025. This guitar was built for Steve to use while touring with Alcatrazz. It's loaded with a Floyd Rose, two EMG humbuckers and one EMG single-coil.

Fifth: an Ibanez two-humbucker Strat-styled ax with a fluorescent snakeskin print for a finish. No further descriptions were given. This ax was used as a backup.

Steve's custom rebuilt Marshalls were missing as well. Two 100-watt heads rebuilt by Jose Arredondo. Says Vai, "Those amps were especially loud, but they had a great tone; they won't be easily replaced."

"We want that gear back," says tech Elwood Francis. "I can't imagine what someone's doing with that gear except playing it in their house and looking at pictures of Steve. That gear is so recognizable, there's no way it could be used by anyone else. I mean, who else would play anything like that except Steve Vai?"

Steve was not alone this past summer. Stevie Ray Vaughan, Missing Persons and Kiss' Bruce Kulick had the exact same misfortunes. Further details of each incident will be published in *Guitar World*. If anyone knows of any further information concerning the location of any of the missing gear, please contact the magazine. ✳

UPDATE In June 2010 we asked Steve to comment on the guitars that were stolen in 1986. Here is his response:

"The Jackson 'eyeball' guitar actually showed up a few months later. For some reason it was taken from the venue prior to the theft and was not actually stolen; it is now the property of the Hard Rock Café. In general, the guitars that were stolen didn't mean that much to me, with the exception of the 'Swiss-cheese' guitar. Joe Despagni was my best friend since before Kindergarten and he made that guitar for me from scratch. The other guitars were spares and I got them all for free, and even collected $20,000 in insurance money after the theft, which I felt weird about.

"While I was on the *Skyscraper* tour with David Lee Roth in 1988 I had two other valuable guitars stolen. One was a 1967 Sunburst Stratocaster and the other was the first floral pattern Jem ever made. The Strat was the first very expensive guitar I ever purchased—I had looked forward to getting one for like 20 years—and the Jem was a tremendous ax. They were both priceless to me. A year or so later we got a call from someone who found the Jem and bought it for $1,500 just so he could return it to me. I arranged for him to meet me so I could verify that it was my darling floral guitar, and I ended up letting him keep it because I felt bad about him paying for it just to get it back to me. I even canceled the insurance claim. I felt a lot of karma was cleaned up through this whole thing, and I'm at peace with it all now."

Two necks are better than one

Chicago-native Michael Batio has been causing quite a stir within environs of Los Angeles. The lead guitarist of rock outfit Holland h... his stuff on an asymmetrical double-necked custom Dean Guitar b...

Michael Angelo Batio Makes His *GW* Debut

Before joining Nitro and becoming known to the *Headbangers Ball* masses for his quadruple-neck guitar pyrotechnics, Michael Angelo Batio was a relative unknown playing with the Chicago metal band Holland. *Guitar World* took notice of the up-and-coming shredder in its January 1987 issue, noting that the guitarist "has been strutting his stuff on an asymmetrical double-necked custom Dean guitar by playing both necks simultaneously, criss-crossing hands and Lord-knows-what! Michael, the *GW* staff acknowledges your talents and applauds your handy fretwork." In the following issue, the magazine acknowledged that the guitar ace was misidentified as Michael Batio "due to the insidious rattlings of an overzealous proofreader, who dug into the guitarist's discology to produce his given name rather than his stage name."

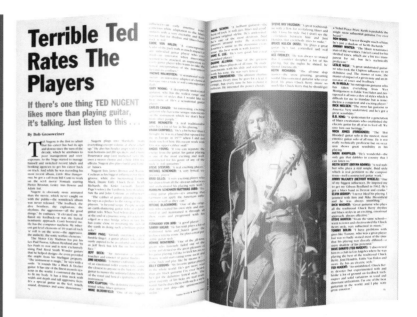

MARCH / VOL. 8 / NO. 3

TED NUGENT

The Motor City Madman takes aim and fires at a slew of his contemporaries.

Jeff Beck: "An innovator—a master toucher and emoter of guitar fluidity."

Jimmy Page: "Grossly overrated, a real fumble-finger, a guitar player who obviously aspired to be as colorful and lyrical as Jeff Beck but fell flat on his stoned face."

Jimi Hendrix: "A master craftsman, a pilot of an emotional roller coaster who came the closest to anyone in the history of the guitar to master the unlimited dimensions of the tonal and lyrical capabilities of the instrument."

Eddie Van Halen: "A contemporary leader of the pack with as much impact as any individual guitar player who ever lived—an innovator when innovation seemed to be attacked, an inspiration to every guitar player who wants to take the lyrical interpretation of the instrument beyond its confines."

Billy Gibbons: "My favorite guitar player in the whole world. He's got more soul than any black guitarist I've ever heard."

Stevie Ray Vaughan: "I love his style, but I don't see the correlation between him and Jimi Hendrix that everybody tries to make."

Ace Frehley: "He was always so stoned that I couldn't decipher a lot of his playing. But the nights he shined, he shined fantastically."

Keith Richards: "The all-time slop master—the most grunting, groaning, soulful, blues-oriented guitarist who ever lived. He plays Chuck Berry music so much like Chuck Berry that he should get a Nobel Peace Prize. Keith Richards is probably the single most influential guitarist I've ever heard."

Jake E. Lee: "He's very good, but a real standard player."

Ted Nugent: "An uninhibited, Chuck Berry devotee but experimented with and broke a lot of ground on feedback techniques and solid variations in tonal and dissonant utilizations. I'm one of the best guitarists in the world, and I play with great emotion."

"Keith Richards is the all-time slop master—the most grunting,

APRIL / VOL. 8 / NO. 4

BUDDY GUY

The blues legend recounts the night he performed with Jimi Hendrix in New York City—as word of Dr. Martin Luther King's assassination shook the world.

"THE MOST MEMORABLE night I had with Jimi was the night Dr. King got assassinated," Guy told Gene Santoro. "I was playing down in the Village in a place called the Generation Club, and all of a sudden they say Dr. King got shot. Then a few hours or so later they say he's dead. Then the mayor closed all the bars because the rioting was really starting to tee off. So B.B. King couldn't play, 'cause where he was playing they served booze, and Janis Joplin was there 'cause she had to close. And Hendrix was there. At the time I didn't know who he was; my manager knew him, y'know. So I was up onstage *really* putting on this show when somebody came up and whispered right behind and said, 'Just don't quit doing what you doing; can I tape it?' So that night I had the chance to play with Hendrix, B.B. King and Janis Joplin. If I just only had any kind of tape of that...

"That was one of those nights, I think we were all primed, too, playing blues on a sad day—it was a good mixture. After that Hendrix used to come in whenever I was playing: I remember on several occasions he'd have a gig somewhere and find out I was playing in New York and cancel. He'd come tell me, 'I canceled a gig just to catch you, man.' Oh yeah, he was a good guy."

Guitar Sam Begins His Long *GW* Career

MAR. '87

Of all the departments that have graced the pages of *Guitar World* throughout the years, our *Guitar Sam* comic strip by Jim Ryan was among the most beloved and longest running. The strip featured the amusing misadventures of Sam Barker, an uncomplicated but musically consumed young dude who wandered through life clinging to his one true love, his guitar. *Guitar Sam* debuted in the March 1987 issue and appeared in the magazine until the September 2004 issue, coming to an end with Sam being goofed on by yet another female for his six-string infatuation. For 16 years of loyal service, Jim Ryan, we salute you.

career, I can say that I got to play 'Rumble' with Link Wray, I got to play 'Got My Mojo Workin' ' with Muddy Waters, I got to play 'Johnny B. Goode' with Chuck Berry and I got to play 'Rock 'n' Roll Hootchie Koo' with Johnny Winter.

Originally from Milwaukee, Wisconsin, where he headed up a sixties power trio called Ox, Paris moved to New York City in 1975 to

Scott Johnson
Guitar meets Stravinsky

As a classical music student at the University of Wisconsin during the early seventies, Scott Johnson came up against some strong taboos. "You couldn't do anything in classical

night, and I had a good time doing it," he says. "But eventually I started having less of a good time because the musical forms of the blues weren't complicated enough to interest me,

METALLICA: THE BASHERS NEXT DOOR

JAMES HETFIELD and KIRK HAMMETT have conquered America with their down-home looks and their killer hooks.

Metallica's guitarists might be the Mutt & Jeff of metal. James Hetfield, 23, who writes most of the music, all of the lyrics and sings is a huge blond hulk who gutters in half-sentences and sound effects and beats his ax like a drum. Kirk Hammett, 24, is a small, dark angelic figure who whispers reverentially about guitars and the players he worships. But what they share is a vision. When it comes to

the current generation of American metal, there is Metallica and there is everyone else.

Metallica was there first. *Kill 'Em All* and *Ride The Lightning*, their two independent albums' worth of punk/metal/ European thrash fusion and anti-glam/ ripped jean image spawned an entire brave new underground. Metallica still outstrips the competition—Megadeth, Anthrax, Slayer, et al—not only in number of records sold, arenas filled, but in sheer breadth and originality. *Master Of Puppets*, their first album for a major label (Elektra), sold 700,000 copies in the United States alone, without catering to radio or video. Charged with rampaging time signatures, dramatic interplay of acoustic filigree and nuclear power assault topped by Hetfield's terse, evoca-

tive world view, *Puppets* was generally hailed as a landmark album that may change hard rock forever. But just as Metallica got their first taste of the arenas, their meteoric rise was marked by tragedy. Last October, their tour bus skidded off an icy road en route to Copenhagen, killing bassist Cliff Burton. Instead of falling apart, the band drew closer together and finished their 11-month world tour with a new bassist, Jason Newsted. But no sooner did the band return to their San Francisco home base in February to write their fourth album, than they suffered another setback. James Hetfield, who'd broken his left wrist in a skateboarding accident last summer, shattered his left arm in another spill. His fretting hand and arm immobilized in a cast after surgery, his skateboard now wears a "for sale" sign. Both Hetfield and Hammett had spare time to discuss Metallica's past and future.

James Hetfield grew up in Downey, a suburb south of Los Angeles. His mother sang light opera, his older brothers played guitar and drums. At his mother's insistence, he took piano lessons, his only formal training. "There was always stuff hangin' 'round the house," he remembers. "I just liked bashin' all this stuff, particularly the drums," which may explain the empathy between himself

By Deborah Frost

SEPT. 1987

VOL. 8 / NO. 9

Metallica's James Hetfield & Kirk Hammett

Guitar World's first coverage of Metallica appeared in the September 1987 issue. In the following excerpt, the two guitarists talk to writer Deborah Frost about the circumstances surrounding Hammett's hiring.

By 1984, Metallica had relocated to San Francisco, where they became kings of a burgeoning metal scene. After crossing the country in a U-Haul, they were ready to record their debut album, *Kill 'Em All*, for Megaforce Records in New York, when they decided lead guitarist Dave Mustaine had to go. "We wanted someone with more feeling," explains James Hetfield. Enter Kirk Hammett, lead guitarist for Exodus, whose former manager was Metallica's soundman.

"If Kirk hadn't worked out," says Hetfield, "I don't know what we would have done. We flew him out and we had no money to send him home. I look back now, it's like, *whoa*. He plugged in, me and Lars [*Ulrich, drums*] just looked at each other and said, 'Yeah! It's a lead instead of that doodling.' Dave always seemed to go on and on."

For Hammett, Metallica's offer was "a huge risk that paid off," says Hammett. "I never was 100 percent sure I'd get the success we have now." A pre-schooler in San Francisco during the Summer of Love, Hammett was surrounded by the music of his teenaged brother. "I knew all about Jimi Hendrix and Cream and Santana, the Beatles, Grateful Dead, Rolling Stones, Jethro Tull, Moby Grape, Jefferson Airplane. All that music was very influential to me." Then, Hammett says, in a confession that may blow all of the PMRC theories straight to hell, "I started listening to all this stuff that kids listened to back then—the Partridge Family, Jackson Five, the Osmonds." At 15, he traded a Kiss album and 10 bucks for "some Montgomery Ward special that had weird gold cellophane pickups."

Unlike Hetfield, whose family was his first fan club, Hammett was discouraged from playing.

"When I started to cut school, they associated it with my guitar playing. They thought it was going nowhere. It was a constant battle. All the equipment I ever got, I had to pay for by working in places like Burger King and washing dishes."

Eventually he scrounged up enough money to buy a white Stratocaster. "I used to have a poster on the wall of Hendrix. I even took off the back plate because he did. I never knew when I first started playing guitar why he did that. The reason I do it now is because it's easier to change strings. I played that for a while. It used to have a different pickup in it every other month."

When he first heard UFO's "Mother Mary," he was "blown away" and soon traded the Strat for a Flying V. In addition to Hendrix and UFO guitarist Michael Schenker, he listened to Pat Travers, Ritchie Blackmore, Jimmy Page, Jeff Beck, Eric Clapton, Eddie Van Halen and Blue Öyster Cult's Buck Dharma.

In 1980, Hammett was wandering around a record store with his friend John Marshall (who became his guitar roadie in Exodus and Metallica, eventually playing onstage when Hetfield broke his wrist) and was attracted to the illustration on the cover of the first Iron Maiden record. "All the heavy stuff that was out—UFO, Judas Priest, Scorpions—was a bit faster, the guitar changes were heavier, the vocals raunchier," says Hammett. Like Lars Ulrich in his native Denmark, Hammett became obsessed with the New Wave of British Heavy Metal and English bands like Angel Witch and the Tygers of Pan Tang.

When he formed his "first real professional band," Exodus, he wanted it to sound like a combination of his favorites—Motörhead, Tygers, Iron Maiden and UFO. He had learned to read music and played Bach and Haydn in a classical guitar trio in high school. But just before joining Metallica, he took lessons from Joe Satriani (who also taught Steve Vai), whom Hammett describes as "absolutely brilliant. He's the best guitar player I know. He taught me a lot about scales, three-octave scales, arpeggios, basic theory, modes, cycle of fifths and how to make a guitar solo harmonically tight, basically how to fit in best with the chords I'm working with."

Instead of continuing lessons, as he would have liked, Hammett flew to New York, had a week of rehearsals and played his first gig with Metallica. Three weeks later, he was in a recording studio for the first time in his life—and, as he adds, "to make an album, on top of that."

"I was extremely nervous when it came time to put down leads," says Hammett. "I found that I couldn't play with headphones on, so I had to come into the booth and play all my leads with the backing tracks coming through the monitors."

Despite his obvious facility, Hammett doesn't see himself as a guitar hero. "Jimi Hendrix is like a god to me. I don't see myself in the same light; I'm just another guitar player." ✳

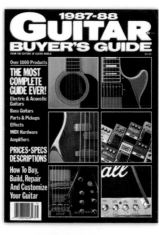

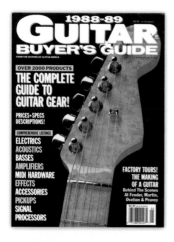

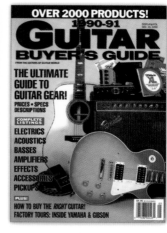

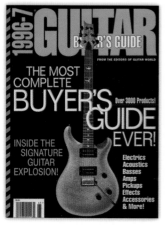

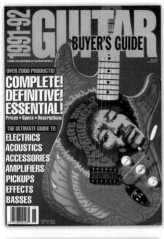

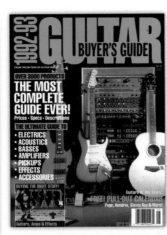

NINETEEN

'88

Guitar World goes to 11! Issues per year, that is.

Dear *Guitar World*,

Why do you guys always have wimps like Eric
Clapton and Jeff Beck in your rag? All I hear
about is how great these two dudes are. I
listened to both of these guys at a buddy's pad
the other day and almost puked. Those dudes suck
and they play wimp-ass music. They aren't a hair
on Yngwie Malmsteen's ass. I'm 19 years old and
I've been around, and I know.

I used to listen to Van Halen when I was
younger. When I found out that Yngwie was faster,
I threw away my Van Halen records. You'd never
catch Yngwie playing with a wimp like Michael
Jackson. I think they should have some kind of
speed test and get all the guitar players in the
world to take it. Then everyone will know that
Yngwie is the best.

—Kevin Augustino

JANUARY Michael Schenker speaks candidly about his tumultuous career, including the time he briefly departed UFO.
COVER STORY BY S.L. DUFF
PHOTO BY GLEN LA FERMAN

MARCH *Guitar World* devotes its second special issue in three years to Jimi Hendrix.
COVER STORIES BY BILL MILKOWSKI AND S.L. DUFF
PHOTO BY JEAN-PIERRE LELOIR

APRIL #1 (LYNCH) Dokken's George Lynch reflects on his time teaching at the California music school owned by Delores Rhoads.
COVER STORY BY MATT RESNICOFF
PHOTO BY MARK WEISS

APRIL #2 (RUSH) Rush's Geddy Lee and Alex Lifeson look back on their career and acknowledge the profound impact they've had on progressive rock music.
COVER STORY BY JOHN SWENSON AND MATT RESNICOFF
PHOTO BY JONATHAN POSTAL

MAY Steve Vai offers his thoughts on what it's like to be famous...or not.
COVER STORY BY GENE SANTORO
PHOTO BY JOHN LIVZEY

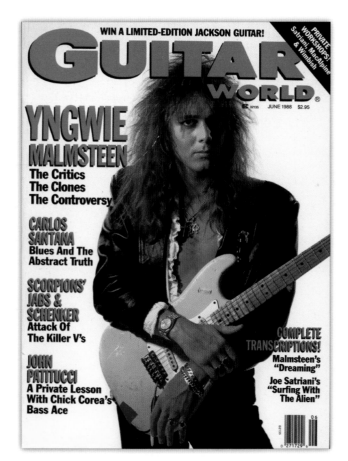

JUNE Yngwie Malmsteen discusses his *Odyssey* record, which was delayed by three months after the Swedish phenom was involved in a near-fatal car accident. "It was horrible. I had a brain hemorrhage, was in a coma and when I woke up I had a paralyzed right arm. My picking hand wasn't even capable of holding a glass of water."
COVER STORY BY MATT RESNICOFF; PHOTO BY JONNIE MILES

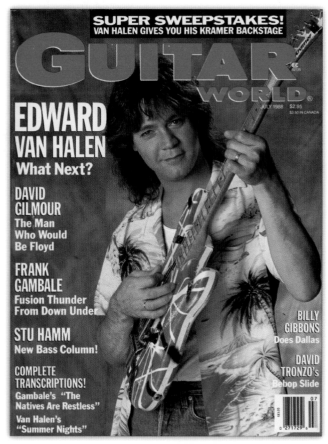

JULY Eddie Van Halen opens up about his band's transition between David Lee Roth and new frontman Sammy Hagar. "I don't think our first six albums were bad, but we have a different quarterback now so we're running different plays. We won the Super Bowl last year—and we're gonna be the first ones to do it twice in a row."
COVER STORY BY BUD SCOPPA; PHOTO BY JOHN LIVZEY

1988 TOTAL ISSUES: 11

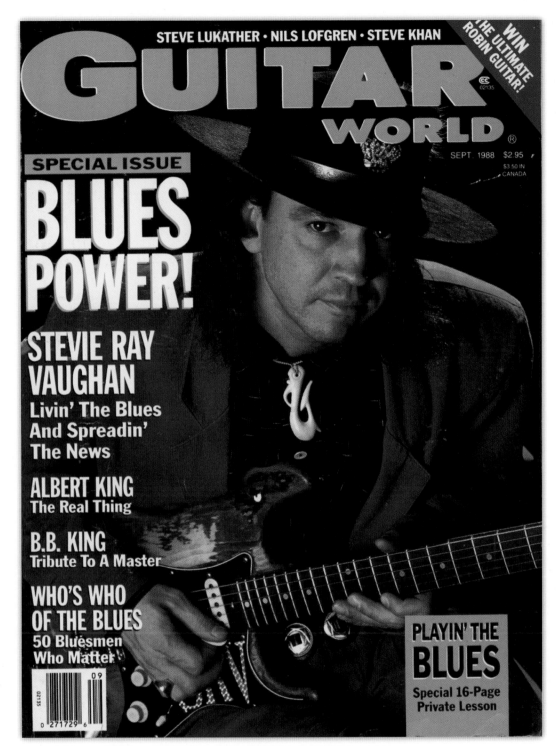

GUITAR WORLD

STEVE LUKATHER • NILS LOFGREN • STEVE KHAN

WIN THE ULTIMATE ROBIN GUITAR!

SEPT. 1988 $2.95
$3.50 IN CANADA

SPECIAL ISSUE

BLUES POWER!

STEVIE RAY VAUGHAN
Livin' The Blues And Spreadin' The News

ALBERT KING
The Real Thing

B.B. KING
Tribute To A Master

WHO'S WHO OF THE BLUES
50 Bluesmen Who Matter

PLAYIN' THE BLUES
Special 16-Page Private Lesson

SEPTEMBER A clean and sober Stevie Ray Vaughan gets honest about his past indiscretions. "Between the coke and the alcohol, it got to the point where I no longer had any idea what it would take to get drunk. One day I could drink a quart and the next day all I had to do was drink one sip and I'd get completely smashed."

COVER STORY BY BILL MILKOWSKI; PHOTO BY JONNIE MILES

OCTOBER Jimmy Page feels Led Zeppelin's 1988 reunion performance at Atlantic Records' 40th anniversary concert spectacular was triumphant—though he has less than complimentary words for the soundman.
COVER STORY BY BUD SCOPPA
PHOTO BY PETER ASHWORTH

NOVEMBER Kirk Hammett has no problem with his band being metal—just don't lump Metallica in with those *other* metal bands.
COVER STORY BY JEFF SPURRIER
PHOTO BY GLEN LA FERMAN

DECEMBER Keith Richards expresses mixed feelings about going solo with *Talk Is Cheap.*
COVER STORY BY JOSEPH BOSSO
PHOTO BY TIMOTHY WHITE

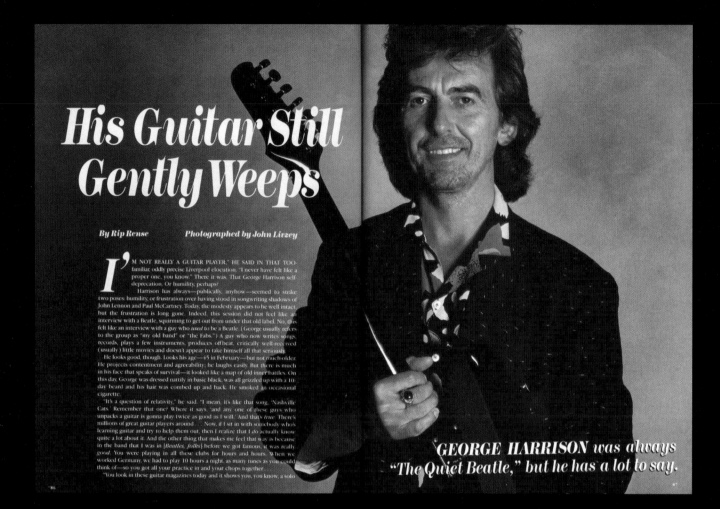

His Guitar Still Gently Weeps

By Rip Rense   Photographed by John Livzey

I'M NOT REALLY A GUITAR PLAYER," HE SAID IN THAT TOO-familiar, oddly precise Liverpool elocution. "I never have felt like a proper one, you know." There it was. That George Harrison self-deprecation. Or humility, perhaps?

Harrison has always—publically, anyhow—seemed to strike two poses: humility, or frustration over having stood in songwriting shadows of John Lennon and Paul McCartney. Today, the modesty appears to be well intact, but the frustration is long gone. Indeed, this session did not feel like an interview with a Beatle, squirming to get out from under that old label. No, this felt like an interview with a guy who *used* to be a Beatle. (George usually refers to the group as "my old band" or "the Fabs.") A guy who now writes songs, records, plays a few instruments, produces offbeat, critically well-received (usually) little movies and doesn't appear to take himself all that seriously.

He looks good, though. Looks his age—45 in February—but not much older. He projects contentment and agreeability; he laughs easily. But there is much in his face that speaks of survival—it looked like a map of old inner battles. On this day, George was dressed nattily in basic black, was all grizzled up with a 10-day beard and his hair was combed up and back. He smoked an occasional cigarette.

"It's a question of relativity," he said. "I mean, it's like that song, 'Nashville Cats.' Remember that one? Where it says, 'and any one of these guys who unpacks a guitar is gonna play twice as good as I will.' And that's *true*. There's millions of great guitar players around . . . Now, if I sit in with somebody who's learning guitar and try to help them out, then I realize that I *do* actually know quite a lot about it. And the other thing that makes me feel that way is because in the band that I was in [*Beatles, folks*] before we got famous, it was really good. You were playing in all these clubs for hours and hours. When we worked Germany, we had to play 10 hours a night, as many tunes as you could think of—so you got all your practice in and your chops together.

"You look in these guitar magazines today and it shows you, you know, a solo

GEORGE HARRISON *was always* "The Quiet Beatle," *but he has a lot to say.*

APRIL 1988

VOL. 9 / NO. 4

George Harrison

Guitar World writer Rip Rense provides a thoughtful analysis of George Harrison's playing style in this excerpt from the former Beatle's first appearance in the magazine.

"I'm not really a guitar player,"

he said in that too-familiar, oddly precise Liverpool elocution. "I never have felt like a proper one, you know." There it was. That George Harrison self-deprecation. Or humility, perhaps?

Harrison has always—publicly, anyhow—seemed to strike two poses: humility, or frustration over having stood in the songwriting shadows of John Lennon and Paul McCartney. Today, the modesty appears to be well intact, but the frustration is long gone. Indeed, this session did not feel like an interview with a Beatle, squirming to get out from under that old label. No, this felt like an interview with a guy who *used* to be a Beatle. (George usually refers to the group as "my old band" or "the Fabs.") A guy who now writes songs, records, plays a few instruments, produces offbeat, critically well-received (usually) little movies and doesn't appear to take himself all that seriously.

He looks good, though. Looks his age—45 in February—but not much older. He projects contentment and agreeability; he laughs easily. But there is much in his face that speaks of survival—it looks like a map of old inner battles. On this day, George was dressed nattily in basic black, was all grizzled up with a 10-day beard and his hair was combed up and back. He smoked an occasional cigarette.

"It's a question of relativity," he says. "I mean, it's like that song, 'Nashville Cats' [*by the Lovin' Spoonful*]. Remember that one? Where it says, 'And any one that unpacks his guitar could play twice as better than I will.' And that's *true*. There are millions of great guitar players around. Now, if I sit in with somebody who's learning guitar and try to help them out, then I realize that I *do* actually know quite a lot about it. And the other thing that makes me feel that way is because in the band that I was in [*Beatles, folks*], before we got famous, it was really *good*. You were playing in all these clubs for hours and hours. When we worked Germany, we had to play 10 hours a night, as many tunes as you could think of—so you got all your practice in and your chops together..."

"You look in these guitar magazines today and it shows you, you know, a solo by George Benson or Chet Atkins or something like that, all written down in these nice tidy little notes—well, I mean, I wouldn't *mind* seeing one of my solos transcribed and looking like that, too, but it wouldn't be of any use for me because I don't even read that sort of stuff."

Indeed, Harrison never has read music (except for some Indian script when he learned sitar), and he hardly ever does anything that could be called practicing. Despite all this, and the criticism and snickering he has been targeted for by "serious," studied guitarists, the man knows his own special way around strings and frets. There's a definite style here. Reviewing his solos over the years, it seems that George is as "good," as dexterous as he wants to be. *Somewhat* like the similarly criticized drumming of Ringo Starr, Harrison is always as solid and dependable as his inspiration. Doubt it? Listen to some of his own favorite recorded leads, on Lennon's "Gimme Some Truth" or "How Do You Sleep?" No, that's not Clapton. Neither is the very expressive break on "Something." And he sustains lovely lyricism in acoustic moments like "Learning How to Love You" from *Thirty Three & 1/3* and "Dark Sweet Lady" from *George Harrison*. His slide work is nothing for Ry Cooder (another humble one) to sneeze at ("The Light That Has Lighted the World" and Ringo's "Early 1970"), and some of the early BBC recordings of the Beatles—more so than the band's released albums of the era—find George *Chuck Berrying* with the best of them. But he's not interested in compliments...

"You know, I started playing guitar because of this thing which was called 'skiffle' in England in the late Fifties, and I think it was based on folk, country, blues, that kind of thing. Lonnie Johnson, Leadbelly. All you had to know was two or three chords and you just thrashed away on it, with a washboard and a tea chest bass. That's how we got started. Skiffle. At the moment, as a guitar player, I feel more like I play *posh* skiffle. As opposed to being a classic guitarist." ✱

Zakk Wylde
Ozzy's new wizard

Zakk Wylde's dream has come to life: he is now in his idol's band. "Ozzy told me he just happened to pick up my tape out of the pile of tapes that he had," explains Zakk excitedly as he prepares for a GW photo shoot. "I was up against *so many* other people, but he picked *me*.

"I auditioned twice in L.A.," says Zakk, who was born and raised in New Jersey. "I didn't meet Ozzy the first time I auditioned; I just jammed with the guys in his band. I went back home

friends were into Lynyrd Skynyrd, but I was totally into Sabbath. They'd

Zakk's smashing Les Paul probably won't be on Ozzy's new lp.

MARTY FRIEDMAN, JASON BECKER & ZAKK WYLDE

A ménage-a-shred as *Guitar World* introduces the guitar community to three up-and-coming hotshots.

OUR MAY 1988 ISSUE featured a number of first appearances in its Tune Ups section, including Marty Friedman and Jason Becker, who had just launched their Cacophony project on Shrapnel Records, and Zakk Wylde, a skinny blonde kid from New Jersey who had recently landed the gig of a lifetime as Ozzy Osbourne's new guitarist.

"I was up against *so many* other people," Wylde told writer Joe Lalaina, "but he picked *me*." Zakk then talked about how Ozzy frequently mentions Randy Rhoads during rehearsals: "He'll just mention Randy to help push me to play my best. Ozzy will never say something like, 'Oh, Randy would never have played that guitar part like that.' He'll just say, 'It took Randy many hours to get the solo right on "Flying High Again."'" Ozzy wants the guitar solos to be individually constructed pieces, not a bunch of fast licks pasted together."

As for Friedman and Becker, writer Bill Milkowski put the two shredders in their rightful place among the best of the best: "How fast are Friedman and Becker? Don't ask. Both are destined to take their place alongside such big guns as Uli Roth and Yngwie Malmsteen. Cacophony's *Speed Metal Symphony* is their important first step." Said Jason Becker at the time, "I'm still working on getting my own style. There's always something new to listen to and learn, so you keep developing your own vocabulary. I mean, too much of that fast Paganini stuff can be a drag."

Marty and Jason currently use Hurricane LTD's.

specialized in Indian classi "From there I began listeni Japanese and Korean music to incorporate those styles onto the guitar."

In 1982 Marty formed a guitar-oriented group, Haw year later recorded an albu brought the band cult pop Europe. That year, he was Dutch Aarschok magazine's Guitarist poll.

Marty left the band in 19 on what he had hoped wou world's heaviest guitar-orie Soon after, Varney introduc Jason and the two went to *Speed Metal Symphony*. W the world's heaviest is ope (How does one measure su Count the number of note scales? Weigh the album?) heavy metal will certainly l by the facility and ferocity

(introduced to each other by Varney)

A Tale of Two Covers

As you'll see in the coming pages of this book, *Guitar World* has pulled off many unique stunts with its covers over the years, including star-studded gatefolds, 3D images and gleaming foil stamps. There have also been numerous instances of something we call a "split cover," where half the magazines in a given month have one artist on the cover, and the other half have a different artist on the cover. The first time such an experiment was undertaken was the April 1988 issue, which featured Rush's Geddy Lee and Alex Lifeson on one cover and Dokken's George Lynch on the other cover. More often than not in these situations, one cover outsells the other by a significant margin. Which do you think sold better?

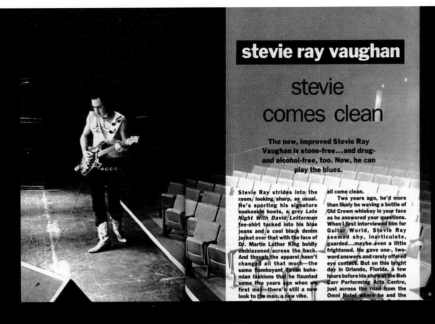

SEPTEMBER / VOL. 9 / NO. 9

STEVIE RAY VAUGHAN

Fresh out of rehab, the newly sober blues ace recounts his brush with rock bottom.

"I WAS RUNNING OUT OF gas and there were no pumps inside," Stevie told writer Bill Milkowski in the summer of 1988. "It was getting to a point where, you know, you can't give somebody a dollar if you ain't got one. This was around the time we were mixing the *Live Alive* album. It was a real crazy period for all of us, because for a long time we had a schedule that was just completely out of hand. And the only reason we put up with it was because we thought we were superhuman, partly from the situation we were in and partly from doing too much coke.

"We had spread ourselves way too thin, tried to put our finger in too many parts of the pie at the same time. It was taking its toll, and the only way we could see to deal with that was, 'Oh, you're too tired? Well, here, snort some of this.'

"And between the coke and the alcohol, it had gotten to the point where I no longer had any idea what it would take to get drunk. I passed the stage where I could drink whatever I wanted to and hold my liquor, so to speak. One day I could drink a quart and then the next day all I'd have to do was drink one sip and I'd get completely smashed. I would wake up and guzzle something just to get rid of the pain I was feeling. Whiskey, beer, vodka, whatever was by me. And it got to the point where I'd try to say hi to somebody and I would just all apart, crying and everything. It was like...solid doom."

"Scarified" Ushers In the Transcription Era

JAN. '88

Guitar World has been printing transcribed music since its inception in one form or another, starting out with brief instructional segments in various how-to columns and eventually moving on to bits and pieces from popular songs (the solo from Charlie Christian's "Solo Flight" in the January 1982 issue may be the first instance of actual tablature in the magazine). The first complete guitar and bass transcriptions—the somewhat odd pairing of Racer X's "Scarified" and Michael Hedges' "Ragamuffin"—appeared in the May 1988 issue, establishing *Guitar World* as a force to be reckoned with in the burgeoning world of guitar tabs. Since that issue, *Guitar World* has published nearly 1300 complete transcriptions [turn to page 96 for the complete list].

EEEEEEYYAAAARGHHHHHH!!!!!!!!

BY JEFF SPURRIER

To any Metallica maniac, the chain of events that occurred during the band's set at the L.A. Coliseum Monsters of Rock show was about as predictable as the clichéd ham-fisted riffs heard from the other acts on the bill. During the third song, an estimated fifteen thousand fans suddenly breached the wire barricades set up around the floor of the arena. Under a blistering mid-afternoon sun, the metal militia battered down the fence and rushed up to the front of the stage in a lemming-like onslaught that left the yellow-jacketed security guards running for cover, shaking their heads in futility.

"AlcoholicA," read a banner unfurled in the mass of bodies. "Drink 'Em All," referring to the band's debut lp, Kill 'Em All as well as the group's dipsomaniac reputation.

Throughout Metallica's per-formance, objects rained in from the crowd: shoes, hats, plastic spritzer bottles, shirts. At one point, drummer Lars Ulrich leaned over his drum riser at the rear of the stage and made a one-handed catch of a thong sandal lofted towards him. He held it up like a trophy, grinned devilishly and gave a thumbs-up sign before throwing it back.

As the band played on, the frenzy of the audience shifted into over-drive, and soon pieces of plastic chairs (which had been used for seating on the arena's floor) were being passed up over heads toward the stage. Pieces of the chairs came flying in with the shoes and hats until finally a whole chair was thrown, nearly hitting singer James Hetfield. At that moment, the PA system conveniently gave out and the band retired quickly to the rear while efforts were made to

PHOTOGRAPHED BY GLEN LA FERMAN

METALLICA'S KIRK HAMMETT

NOV. 1988

VOL. 9 / NO. 11

Kirk Hammett

When it comes to recording, says Metallica's lead guitarist in his first *Guitar World*

Ever since the release of *Master of Puppets* in 1986, we knew the time was right for a Metallica cover. The album was the group's first to go Gold, and the subsequent tour proved they had broken out of the underground to become the reigning kings of thrash-based metal. By the time guitarist Kirk Hammett sat for his November 1988 *Guitar World* cover, the band had suffered the death of founding bassist Cliff Burton and recorded its fourth full-length album, *...And Justice for All*. In this cover feature excerpt, Hammett discusses the challenges of making the album while he offers a glimpse into the modesty and mastery behind his influential guitar work.

During the *...And Justice for All* sessions, Metallica were getting ready for the Monsters of Rock tour, and rather than enjoying his usual relaxed schedule to work on his solos, Hammett found himself working long hours trying to make things work.

"From a technical point of view, this album was a nightmare," he says, grimacing. "There were so many tempo changes. James [*Hetfield*] would come up with a rhythm background, and the only scale that would fit would be a minor pentatonic scale with a flatted fifth. Trying to be melodic in an altered scale like that was a nightmare. In 'Blackened,' there are four different tempo and rhythm background changes, and for me to make it smooth all the way through was really challenging. To this day I don't think I did it successfully. People tell me differently, but in my head I know otherwise.

"There's something about being in the studio, in the heat of the moment when the red light goes on, that just makes you want to change things around. After playing to rehearsal tapes for three months, where it's slightly out of tempo and the recording isn't the best, and then you're in there hearing perfect drum tracks, perfect guitar tracks—everything is picture perfect—it's really bothering to me. I literally did all my leads for the album in seven days because I *had* to. The Monsters tour was coming up. When you do stuff that quickly, you settle for something, and when you go back and listen to it, you may discover it's not happening; things sound forced. I was working 16 hours a day doing solos, and when you work that long it shows in your perspective. Your ear goes down the drain."

However, there was one aspect to the *Justice* recording that was not a nightmare for Hammett: getting the tone he wanted from his guitar. For the *Master of Puppets* album, he spent three days in the studio trying to get the right sound.

"I knew what I wanted this time," he says. "During *Master*, I wasn't 100 percent sure. There's nothing more discouraging than working on something for eight hours and at the end of the session knowing it's crap. I think the guitar tones on this album are some of the better lead tones I've gotten. The rhythm sound that James got is amazing. We didn't have time to do anything super weird—which I wanted to do. I wanted to experiment a lot more."

Like his band mates, Kirk Hammett doesn't believe in setting himself up on a pedestal, removed from the fans. Metallica's following has been built by word of mouth, not hype or MTV or radio play. There was some discussion before *Justice* was completed about recording shorter songs—the shortest song from *Master of Puppets* is longer than five minutes, others exceed eight minutes—but the ultimate decision was to go with what they like, and demographically, Kirk says, "People who listen to the radio probably aren't our type of crowd."

Similarly, jumping on bandwagons or following trends is simply not the Metallica way. After some persistent probing, Hammett admits that he does have some classical influences, but he doesn't like talking about them.

"Everyone says, 'Oh, I'm a heavy metal guitarist, but I'm classically influenced,' " he groans. "It's so trendy that I hate to talk about it. But one of my favorite all-time albums is *Christopher Parkening Plays Bach*. I love that. I went to see him with some friends of mine seven months ago, and he was brilliant."

But is Kirk Hammett as brilliant in his chosen field? It's hard to say just yet. There's no doubt that the *technical* prowess is there. But as he himself concludes, that's not all there is to it.

"It's weird," he says, somewhat wearily. "I've found that with all this study of technique, when you get right down to it, you throw all that out the window and go with what works best. I believe you have to have [*the technique*], but it's also good to detach yourself from all of it and go with what feels good. Just because you know umpteen billion scales, it doesn't mean you have to use them all in a solo."

It's just such an awareness that filters out the technicians from the artists, and Kirk Hammett seems to have the humility and love of his instrument to propel him into genuine stardom. He's only 25, so who knows? ✳

TRANSCRIPTIONS

A year-by-year, month-by-month breakdown of every song ever transcribed in *Guitar World*.

1988

May
Racer X "Scarified"
Michael Hedges "Ragamuffin"
June
Yngwie Malmsteen "Dreaming"
Joe Satriani "Surfing with the Alien"
July
Frank Gambale "The Natives Are Restless"
Van Halen "Summer Nights"
September
Bill Doggett "Honky Tonk Part 1"
October
Led Zeppelin "The Rain Song"
John Scofield "Tell You What"
November
Robben Ford "Getaway"
Tommy Bolin "Savannah Woman"
December
Greg Howe "Kick It All Over"

1989

January
Robert Cray "Too Many Cooks"
Danny Gatton "Notcho Blues"
February
Night Ranger "Man in Motion"
Barry Finnerty "Unh!"
March
Allman Brothers Band "Jessica"
Johnny Winter "Ain't That Just Like a Woman"
May
Allan Holdsworth "City Nights"
Ratt "Way Cool Jr."
July
Badlands "Winter's Call"
September
White Lion "Little Fighter"
October
The Cult "Sun King"
November
Joe Satriani "One Big Rush"
December
Eric Clapton "Let It Rain"
Cream "Tales of Brave Ulysses"

1990

January
Jeff Beck "Big Block"
February
Michael Jackson "Beat It"
Stevie Ray Vaughan "Texas Flood"
Whitesnake "Still of the Night"
March
Aerosmith "Monkey on My Back"
April
Whitesnake "Slip of the Tongue"
May
Stevie Ray Vaughan "Tightrope"

June
Black Sabbath "War Pigs"
September
Jimi Hendrix "Red House"
October
Winger "Loosen Up"
November
Lynch Mob "Street Fighting Man"
December
Stevie Ray Vaughan "Pride and Joy"

1991

January
Led Zeppelin "The Song Remains the Same"
Led Zeppelin "Ramble On"
February
Deep Purple "Highway Star"
March
ZZ Top "Doubleback"
Poison "Something to Believe In"
The Black Crowes "Hard to Handle"
April
Stevie Ray Vaughan "Superstition"
Cinderella "Shelter Me"
Extreme "Pornograffitti"
May
AC/DC "Money Talks"
The Doors "Roadhouse Blues"
Steppenwolf "Born to Be Wild"
June
The Eagles "Hotel California"
Van Halen "Ice Cream Man"
Jimi Hendrix "Changes"
July
The Allman Brothers Band "Statesboro Blues"
Robert Johnson "Traveling Riverside Blues"
Bulletboys "Talk to Your Daughter"
August
Megadeth "Hangar 18"
Warrant "Uncle Tom's Cabin"
Queen "We Will Rock You"
Chris Isaak "Wicked Game"
September
Extreme "Hole Hearted"
Jane's Addiction "Been Caught Stealing"
Tom Petty "Refugee"
October
The Beatles "Blackbird"
Yes "Yours Is No Disgrace"
Metallica "Escape"
November
The Vaughan Brothers "D/FW"
Steve Vai "The Reaper"
Led Zeppelin "Stairway to Heaven" (live)
December
Lynyrd Skynyrd "Free Bird"
Primus "Tommy the Cat"
Mötley Crüe "Looks That Kill"

1992

January
Guns N' Roses "Live and Let Die"
Extreme "More Than Words"
Queensrÿche "Jet City Woman"
February
Nirvana "Smells Like Teen Spirit"
The Who "Won't Get Fooled Again"
Neil Young "Hey Hey, My My"
March
Van Halen "Finish What Ya Started"
Rush "Roll the Bones"
Aerosmith "Dream On"
April
Mr. Big "To Be with You"
Pink Floyd "Shine on You Crazy Diamond"
Spinal Tap "Big Bottom"
Spinal Tap "(Tonight I'm Gonna) Rock You Tonight"
May
Jimi Hendrix "Angel"
Red Hot Chili Peppers "Under the Bridge"
Ozzy Osbourne "Flying High Again"
June
Eric Clapton "Tears in Heaven"
Ugly Kid Joe "Everything About You"
Joe Walsh "Rocky Mountain Way"
July
Queen "Stone Cold Crazy"
Testament "So Many Lies"
Gary Moore "Cold Day in Hell"
August
Led Zeppelin "The Lemon Song"
The Black Crowes "Remedy"
Black Sabbath "Paranoid"
September
The Beatles "Sgt. Pepper's Lonely Hearts Club Band"
Megadeth "Skin O' My Teeth"
U2 "Mysterious Ways"
October
Eric Clapton "Wonderful Tonight"
Bruce Springsteen "Born to Run"
Crosby, Stills & Nash "Suite: Judy Blue Eyes"
November
Damn Yankees "Don't Tread on Me"
The Romantics "What I Like About You"
Mountain "Mississippi Queen"
Steve Vai "The Audience Is Listening"
December
Extreme "Stop the World"
Red Hot Chili Peppers "Breaking the Girl"
Eric Clapton "Layla" (acoustic)
AC/DC "Highway to Hell"

1993

January
Pearl Jam "Even Flow"

Stevie Ray Vaughan "Shake for Me"
Helmet "Unsung"
The Allman Brothers Band "Whipping Post"
February
R.E.M. "Drive"
Saigon Kick "Love Is on the Way"
Sepultura "Arise"
Pink Floyd "Comfortably Numb"
March
Pantera "This Love"
Temple of the Dog "Say Hello 2 Heaven"
Soul Asylum "Somebody to Shove"
Jimi Hendrix "Little Wing"
Skid Row "Little Wing"
April
Def Leppard "Let's Get Rocked"
Living Colour "Leave It Alone"
Poison "Stand"
Stevie Ray Vaughan "Wham!"
May
Van Halen "Won't Get Fooled Again"
Rush "The Spirit of Radio"
Dream Theater "Pull Me Under"
June
Ugly Kid Joe "Cat's in the Cradle"
Neil Young "Harvest Moon"
Alice in Chains "Angry Chair"
Lynyrd Skynyrd "Sweet Home Alabama"
July
Led Zeppelin "Kashmir"
Coverdale/Page "Pride and Joy"
Anthrax "Only"
August
Aerosmith "Eat the Rich"
Stone Temple Pilots "Plush"
Cream "White Room"
September
The Allman Brothers Band "Blue Sky"
Ted Nugent "Stranglehold"
Porno for Pyros "Pets"
October
Kansas "Dust in the Wind"
Santana "Black Magic Woman"
Megadeth "Angry Again"
Radiohead "Creep"
November
Blind Melon "No Rain"
Nirvana "Heart-Shaped Box"
Pantera "Cemetery Gates"
The Cure "Just Like Heaven"
December
Led Zeppelin "Ten Years Gone"
Sepultura "Territory"
Smashing Pumpkins "Cherub Rock"

1994

January
Eric Clapton "Stone Free"
Rush "Stick It Out"
Bob Marley "Get Up Stand Up"
February
Guns N' Roses "Hair of the Dog"

Megadeth "99 Ways to Die"
The Beatles "Help!"
The Beatles "Paperback Writer"
March
Pearl Jam "Black"
Primus "DMV"
The Doors "People Are Strange"
ZZ Top "Cheap Sunglasses"
April
Pink Floyd "Wish You Were Here"
Metallica "Am I Evil?"
STP "Creep"
Smashing Pumpkins "Disarm"
May
Pantera "I'm Broken"
James Taylor "Fire and Rain"
Joe Satriani "Mighty Turtle Head"
Tom Petty "Breakdown"
June
The Who "Pinball Wizard"
Beck "Loser"
Nirvana "All Apologies"
Jimi Hendrix "Hear My Train A Comin' " (acoustic)
Candlebox "You"
July
Danzig "Twist of Cain"
Boston "More Than a Feeling"
Allman Brothers Band "Midnight Rider"
Cracker "Low"
August
The Rolling Stones "Beast of Burden"
Collective Soul "Shine"
Spin Doctors "Cleopatra's Cat"
Stone Temple Pilots "Vasoline"
September
Green Day "Longview"
The Eagles "Life in the Fast Lane"
Helmet "Milquetoast"
Pink Floyd "Take It Back"
October
Candlebox "Far Behind"
John Mellencamp "Wild Night"
Stone Temple Pilots "Interstate Love Song"
Rick Derringer "Rock and Roll Hoochie Koo"
November
Pantera "Planet Caravan"
Jane's Addiction "Mountain Song"
The Doors "Love Her Madly"
James Brown "Sex Machine"
Beavis & Butt-head "Theme Song"
December
Danzig "Until You Call on the Dark"
Jimi Hendrix "Voodoo Child (Slight Return)"
Weezer "Undone—The Sweater Song"
Eric Clapton "I'm Tore Down"

1995

January
Nirvana "About a Girl"
Led Zeppelin "Gallows Pole"
Dream Theater "Erotomania"
R.E.M. "What's the Frequency, Kenneth?"
February
AC/DC "Back in Black"
Soundgarden "Fell on Black Days"
Bob Seger "Night Moves"
Queensrÿche "Bridges"
March
Stevie Ray Vaughan "Pride and Joy" (acoustic)
The Eagles "Hotel California" (acoustic)
Tom Petty "You Don't Know How It Feels"
Van Halen "Hot for Teacher"
April
The Allman Brothers Band "In

Memory of Elizabeth Reed"
Hole "Doll Parts"
Weezer "Buddy Holly"
Yes "The Clap"
May
R.E.M. "It's the End of the World As We Know It"
Metallica "Creeping Death"
Nirvana "The Man Who Sold the World"
Van Halen "Eruption"
June
White Zombie "More Human Than Human"
Sheryl Crow "Strong Enough"
Stone Temple Pilots "Pretty Penny"
Bruce Springsteen "Glory Days"
July
Jimi Hendrix "All Along the Watchtower"
Dave Matthews "What Would You Say"
Led Zeppelin "Thank You"
King Crimson "21st Century Schizoid Man"
August
Blues Traveler "Run-Around"
Soul Asylum "Misery"
Neil Young "Old Man"
Creedence Clearwater Revival "Fortunate Son"
Bush "Little Things"
September
The Grateful Dead "Friend of the Devil"
The Velvet Underground "Sweet Jane"
The Rembrandts "I'll Be There"
Stevie Ray Vaughan "The House Is Rockin' "
October
Collective Soul "December"
Better Than Ezra "Good"
Pink Floyd "Money"
Van Morrison "Brown Eyed Girl"
November
Metallica "Nothing Else Matters"
The Eagles "Take It Easy"
Alanis Morissette "You Oughta Know"
AC/DC "Hard As a Rock"
December
Red Hot Chili Peppers "My Friends"
Slayer "Seasons in the Abyss"
Lenny Kravitz "Rock & Roll Is Dead"
Elvis Costello "Alison"

1996

January
Smashing Pumpkins "Bullet with Butterfly Wings"
Foo Fighters "I'll Stick Around"
The Rolling Stones "Angie"
Presidents of the U.S.A. "Lump"
The Beatles "Here Comes the Sun"
February
Led Zeppelin "Over the Hills and Far Away"
Live "Lightning Crashes"
Goo Goo Dolls "Name"
Toadies "Possum Kingdom"
March
Metallica "One"
Jimi Hendrix "Red House"
Ozzy Osbourne "Crazy Train"
Bush "Glycerine"
April
Everclear "Santa Monica"
Aerosmith "Dream On"
Joan Osborne "One of Us"
Beastie Boys "(You Gotta) Fight for Your Right (To Party!)"
Korn "Shoots and Ladders"
May
Oasis "Wonderwall"

Alice in Chains "Heaven Beside You"
Van Halen "Can't Stop Lovin' You"
The Allman Brothers Band "Jessica"
June
Led Zeppelin "Stairway to Heaven"
Foo Fighters "Big Me"
Kiss "Deuce" (live)
R.E.M. "Driver 8"
The Nixons "Sister"
July
Metallica "Enter Sandman"
Soundgarden "Black Hole Sun"
Stone Temple Pilots "Big Bang Baby"
Pantera "Drag the Waters"
August
Deep Purple "Smoke on the Water"
The Sex Pistols "God Save the Queen"
Marilyn Manson "Sweet Dreams"
Green Day "Brain Stew/Jaded"
Jimi Hendrix "Purple Haze"
September
Led Zeppelin "Rock and Roll"
Alice in Chains "Rooster"
Tracy Bonham "Mother Mother"
Lynyrd Skynyrd "Free Bird"
October
Nirvana "Lake of Fire"
Van Halen "Runnin' with the Devil"
Red Hot Chili Peppers "Give It Away"
Metallica "King Nothing"
Nada Surf "Popular"
November
311 "Down"
Jimi Hendrix "Hey Joe"
Rage Against the Machine "Bombtrack"
Tom Petty "The Waiting"
The Doors "Love Me Two Times"
December
Smashing Pumpkins "Tonight, Tonight"
Bush "Machinehead"
Oasis "Champagne Supernova"
Rush "Tom Sawyer"

1997

January
Metallica "Hero of the Day"
Tool "Stinkfist"
Nirvana "Aneurysm"
Van Halen "You Really Got Me"
Bush "Swallowed"
February
Van Halen "Can't Get This Stuff No More"
The Beatles "Mother Nature's Son"
Korn "No Place to Hide"
Sheryl Crow "If It Makes You Happy"
Marilyn Manson "The Beautiful People"
March
The Beatles "I Want You (She's So Heavy)"
Smashing Pumpkins "Thirty Three"
Silverchair "Abuse Me"
Red Hot Chili Peppers "Love Rollercoaster"
April
Pink Floyd "Brain Damage"/"Eclipse"
Cake "The Distance"
David Bowie "Ziggy Stardust"
U2 "One"
May
No Doubt "Just a Girl"
Cheap Trick "Surrender"
Live "All Over You"
ZZ Top "Tush"
June
The Wallflowers "One Headlight"
The Verve Pipe "The Freshmen"
Black Sabbath "Supernaut"
The Offspring "Self Esteem"

July
Nine Inch Nails "Head Like a Hole"
Foo Fighters "Monkey Wrench"
U2 "Staring at the Sun"
Jimi Hendrix "Dolly Dagger"
August
Fleetwood Mac "Go Your Own Way"
Blur "Song 2"
Blue Öyster Cult "(Don't Fear) the Reaper"
Beck "The New Pollution"
Live "Freaks"
September
Steve Miller Band "The Joker"
311 "Transistor"
Jethro Tull "Aqualung"
Korn "A.D.I.D.A.S."
October
Sugar Ray "Fly"
Mighty Mighty Bosstones "The Impression That I Get"
Pantera "Walk"
The Police "Every Breath You Take"
November
Smash Mouth "Walking on the Sun"
Fleetwood Mac "The Chain" (live)
Reel Big Fish "Sell Out"
Ted Nugent "Cat Scratch Fever"
December
Elton John "Candle in the Wind" (piano, guitar & bass)
The Rolling Stones "Tumbling Dice"
Days of the New "Touch, Peel and Stand"
AC/DC "Dirty Deeds Done Dirt Cheap"

1998

January
Led Zeppelin "Communication Breakdown"
Led Zeppelin "Dancing Days"
Tool "Aenima"
Green Day "Good Riddance (Time of Your Life)"
February
Alice in Chains "Would?"
Bob Dylan "Like a Rolling Stone"
Deftones "Be Quiet and Drive (Far Away)"
The Police "Roxanne"
Sam & Dave "Soul Man"
March
Blink-182 "Dammit (Growing Up)"
Guns N' Roses "November Rain"
Matchbox 20 "Push"
Van Halen "Ain't Talkin' 'Bout Love"
April
Radiohead "Karma Police"
Van Halen "Without You"
John Fogerty "Centerfield"
Big Wreck "The Oaf"
May
Sublime "Santeria"
Eric Clapton "I Shot the Sheriff"
Pantera "Floods"
Pink Floyd "Hey You"
Primus "South Park Theme"
June
Led Zeppelin "Achilles Last Stand"
Led Zeppelin "Kashmir"
Metallica "Devil's Dance"
Page & Plant "Most High"
Bob Dylan "Tangled Up in Blue"
July
Metallica "Seek & Destroy"
Fastball "The Way"
Chicago "25 or 6 to 4"
Marcy Playground "Sex and Candy"
Creed "Torn"
August
Smashing Pumpkins "Ava Adore"
Ozzy Osbourne "Mr. Crowley"

Limp Bizkit "Counterfeit"
Cherry Poppin' Daddies "Zoot Suit Riot"
Journey "Any Way You Want It"
September
Radiohead "Paranoid Android"
Jimi Hendrix "All Along the Watchtower"
Van Halen "Eruption"
Eve 6 "Inside Out"
October
Brian Setzer "Jump Jive An' Wail"
Guns N' Roses "Paradise City"
Barenaked Ladies "One Week"
Korn "Got the Life"
November
Marilyn Manson "The Dope Show"
The Beatles "Something"
Smashing Pumpkins "Perfect"
Stevie Ray Vaughan "Texas Flood"
Jefferson Airplane "Somebody to Love"
Fear Factory "Edge Crusher"
December
Goo Goo Dolls "Iris"
Stray Cats "Stray Cat Strut"
Metallica "Of Wolf and Man"
Aerosmith "Back in the Saddle"
Sheryl Crow "My Favorite Mistake"

1999

January
Limp Bizkit "Faith"
Creed "What's This Life For"
Pink Floyd "Us and Them"
Wild Cherry "Play That Funky Music"
U2 "Where the Streets Have No Name"
T.Rex "Bang a Gong (Get It On)"
February
Metallica "Turn the Page"
John Lennon "Imagine" (guitar arrangement)
Korn "Freak on a Leash"
Yes "I've Seen All Good People (Your Move)"
Everlast "What It's Like"
March
The Offspring "Pretty Fly (For a White Guy)"
Rob Zombie "Dragula"
Paul McCartney & Wings "Band on the Run"
Alice in Chains "Down in a Hole"
Stray Cats "Rock This Town"
April
Jimi Hendrix "Machine Gun"
Creed "One"
Pink Floyd "Another Brick in the Wall (Pt. II)"
Bad Company "Can't Get Enough"
May
The Offspring "The Kids Aren't Alright"
The Eagles "One of These Nights"
Third Eye Blind "Jumper"
Deep Purple "Highway Star"
June
The Beatles "Get Back"
Creedence Clearwater Revival "Proud Mary"
Cream "Badge"
Crosby, Stills & Nash "Helplessly Hoping"
The Stooges "1969"
Orgy "Blue Monday"
July
Sugar Ray "Falls Apart"
Everclear "Father of Mine"
Guns N' Roses "Welcome to the Jungle"
Def Leppard "Photograph"
Red Hot Chili Peppers "Under the Bridge"

August
Limp Bizkit "Nookie"
Alice Cooper "I'm Eighteen"
Blink-182 "What's My Age Again?"
Ricky Martin "Livin' La Vida Loca"
Queen "Crazy Little Thing Called Love"
Fear Factory "Cars"
September
Kid Rock "Bawitdaba"
Smash Mouth "All Star"
The Guess Who "American Woman"
Godsmack "Whatever"
Poison "Talk Dirty to Me"
Pat Benatar "Hit Me with Your Best Shot"
October
Buckcherry "For the Movies"
Jimi Hendrix "The Wind Cries Mary"
Led Zeppelin "Good Times Bad Times"
Red Hot Chili Peppers "Around the World"
Van Halen "Jamie's Cryin'"
Pennywise "Alien"
Dave Matthews & Tim Reynolds "Ants Marching" (live)
November
Creed "Higher"
Days of the New "Enemy"
Lynyrd Skynyrd "Saturday Night Special"
Powerman 5000 "When Worlds Collide"
Coal Chamber "Notion"
ZZ Top "La Grange"
December
Limp Bizkit "Re-Arranged"
Santana with Everlast "Put Your Lights On"
Rage Against the Machine "Guerrilla Radio"
Doobie Brothers "Listen to the Music"
Kenny Wayne Shepherd "In 2 Deep"
Nine Inch Nails "We're in This Together"

2000

January
Santana "Smooth"
The Doors "L.A. Woman"
Korn "Falling Away from Me"
Red Hot Chili Peppers "Scar Tissue"
Wilson Pickett "In the Midnight Hour"
311 "Come Original"
February
Filter "Take a Picture"
The Rolling Stones "Shattered"
Guns N' Roses "Mr. Brownstone"
Santana "Evil Ways"
Static-X "Push It"
Buffalo Springfield "For What It's Worth"
March
Pink Floyd "Comfortably Numb"
Pink Floyd "Run Like Hell"
Kid Rock "Only God Knows Why"
Slipknot "Wait and Bleed"
AC/DC "Rock and Roll Ain't Noise Pollution"
Lou Reed "Walk on the Wild Side"
April
Smashing Pumpkins "The Everlasting Gaze"
The Who "Baba O'Riley"
Foo Fighters "Stacked Actors"
Stevie Ray Vaughan "Mary Had a Little Lamb"
System of a Down "Sugar"
Incubus "Pardon Me"
May
Staind "Home"
The Black Crowes "Hard to Handle"
Led Zeppelin "Heartbreaker"

Stroke 9 "Little Black Backpack"
Godsmack "Voodoo"
Pantera "Revolution Is My Name"
June
Rage Against the Machine "Sleep Now in the Fire"
Limp Bizkit "Break Stuff"
Pearl Jam "Yellow Ledbetter"
Lynyrd Skynyrd "That Smell"
Live "Run to the Water"
Korn "Blind"
July
Led Zeppelin "Stairway to Heaven"
Metallica "One"
Steely Dan "Kid Charlemagne"
Kittie "Brackish"
P.O.D. "Southtown"
Bloodhound Gang "The Bad Touch"
August
Limp Bizkit "Take a Look Around"
Stone Temple Pilots "Sour Girl"
Led Zeppelin "What Is and What Should Never Be"
Metallica "Sad But True"
Deftones "Change (In the House of Flies)"
September
Papa Roach "Last Resort"
Pink Floyd "Young Lust"
Black Sabbath "Sabbath Bloody Sabbath"
Korn "Somebody Someone"
Dynamite Hack "Boyz-N-The Hood"
U.P.O. "Godless"
October
A Perfect Circle "Judith"
3 Doors Down "Kryptonite"
Everclear "Wonderful"
Red Hot Chili Peppers "Californication"
Norman Greenbaum "Spirit in the Sky"
Vertical Horizon "Everything You Want"
November
Creed "Are You Ready?"
Jimi Hendrix "Purple Haze"
Jimi Hendrix "Little Wing"
SR-71 "Right Now"
Fuel "Hemorrhage"
Queens of the Stone Age "The Lost Art of Keeping a Secret"
December
Godsmack "Awake"
Green Day "Minority"
3 Doors Down "Loser"
The Eagles "Life in the Fast Lane"
Zebrahead "Playmate of the Year"
Orgy "Fiction (Dreams in Digital)"

2001

January
The Offspring "Original Prankster"
Disturbed "Voices"
The Beatles "Revolution"
Marilyn Manson "Disposable Teens"
The Doors "Riders on the Storm"
Linkin Park "One Step Closer"
Cat Stevens "Peace Train"
February
Limp Bizkit "Rollin' (Air Raid Vehicle)"
Rage Against the Machine "Renegades of Funk"
Creed "With Arms Wide Open"
Collective Soul "Why Pt. 2"
Modern English "I Melt with You"
Joan Jett "I Love Rock N Roll"
Billy Idol "White Wedding"
March
Aaron Lewis & Fred Durst "Outside"
Metallica "Fade to Black"
Led Zeppelin "Black Dog"

Van Halen "Mean Street"
Alice in Chains "Man in the Box"
Ozzy Osbourne "Flying High Again"
April
Crazy Town "Butterfly"
Black Sabbath "War Pigs"
Deftones "Back to School"
Papa Roach "Between Angels and Insects"
Eric Clapton & B.B. King "Riding with the King"
B.B. King "The Thrill Is Gone"
May
Coldplay "Yellow"
Aerosmith "Walk This Way"
Aerosmith "Jaded"
At the Drive-In "One Armed Scissor"
Ozzy Osbourne "Over the Mountain"
Fuel "Innocent"
June
Staind "It's Been Awhile"
The Eagles "Take It Easy"
Fear Factory "Linchpin"
Cold "No One"
Oleander "Are You There?"
Van Halen "Dance the Night Away"
Korn "A.D.I.D.A.S."
July
Mudvayne "Dig"
American Hi-Fi "Flavor of the Weak"
Black Sabbath "Iron Man"
Black Sabbath "Sweet Leaf"
Bruce Springsteen "Badlands"
Train "Drops of Jupiter" (guitar arrangement)
August
Linkin Park "Crawling"
Weezer "Hash Pipe"
Led Zeppelin "The Ocean"
AC/DC "You Shook Me All Night Long"
Alien Ant Farm "Smooth Criminal"
The Beatles "Ticket to Ride"
Static-X "This Is Not"
September
Staind "Outside" (electric version)
3 Doors Down "Be Like That"
Thin Lizzy "The Boys Are Back in Town"
311 "You Wouldn't Believe"
Rush "Tom Sawyer"
U2 "Pride (In the Name of Love)"
Queen "We Will Rock You"
October
Nirvana "All Apologies"
Lifehouse "Hanging By a Moment"
Drowning Pool "Bodies"
Fuel "Bad Day"
Creedence Clearwater Revival "Bad Moon Rising"
Puddle of Mudd "Control"
Eve 6 "Here's to the Night"
November
Nickelback "How You Remind Me"
Tool "Schism"
Staind "Fade"
P.O.D. "Alive"
Afroman "Because I Got High"
Van Halen "Jump"
Adema "Giving In"
The Allman Brothers Band "Midnight Rider"
December
Incubus "Drive"
Weezer "Island in the Sun"
Drowning Pool "Sinner"
Pink Floyd "Wish You Were Here"
Blink-182 "Rock Show"
Dave Matthews Band "The Space Between"
Kittie "What I Always Wanted"
"Star Spangled Banner"
"America the Beautiful"

2002

January
Creed "My Sacrifice"
Sum 41 "Fat Lip"
Led Zeppelin "Hey Hey What Can I Do"
Puddle of Mudd "Blurry"
Lit "Lipstick and Bruises"
The Doors "Love Her Madly"
Sevendust "Praise"
February
Tool "Lateralus"
Linkin Park "In the End"
Blink-182 "Adam's Song"
Kid Rock "Forever"
Slipknot "The Heretic Anthem"
Sublime "The Wrong Way"
Journey "Lights"
March
Ozzy Osbourne "You Can't Kill Rock and Roll"
System of a Down "Toxicity"
Metallica "Harvester of Sorrow"
Sum 41 "In Too Deep"
Staind "For You"
Fugazi "Waiting Room"
Dead Kennedys "Too Drunk to Fuck"
Black Flag "TV Party"
April
Creed "Bullets"
Nickelback "Too Bad"
Lynyrd Skynyrd "Free Bird"
The Beatles "Something"
Incubus "Nice to Know You"
Jimmy Eat World "The Middle"
May
Blink-182 "Stay Together for the Kids"
Trik Turner "Friends & Family"
Pink Floyd "Time"
Ted Nugent "Stranglehold"
Adema "The Way You Like It"
Def Leppard "Pour Some Sugar on Me"
June
The White Stripes "Fell in Love with a Girl"
Hoobastank "Crawling in the Dark"
Metallica "The Call of Ktulu"
Mudvayne "Death Blooms"
Rush "Freewill"
Unwritten Law "Seein' Red"
July
Korn "Here to Stay"
The Eagles "Hotel California"
Staind "Epiphany"
Alien Ant Farm "Attitude"
ZZ Top "Sharp Dressed Man"
Stevie Ray Vaughan "Lenny"
AC/DC "Shoot to Thrill"
August
P.O.D. "Youth of the Nation"
Godsmack "I Stand Alone"
Moby "We're All Made of Stars"
Rob Zombie "Never Gonna Stop (The Red, Red Kroovy)"
The Beatles "Blackbird"
Van Halen "Unchained"
Hoobastank "Running Away"
September
Korn "Thoughtless"
Jimmy Eat World "Sweetness"
Phish "You Enjoy Myself"
Aerosmith "Last Child"
David Bowie "Ziggy Stardust"
Yes "Long Distance Runaround"
October
The Rolling Stones "Brown Sugar"
The Rolling Stones "Honky Tonk Women"
New Found Glory "My Friends Over You"
The White Stripes "Dead Leaves and the Dirty Ground"

The Vines "Get Free"
Trust Company "Downfall"
Charlie Christian "Flying Home"
November
Disturbed "Prayer"
Grateful Dead "Truckin' "
Chad Kroeger "Hero"
Stone Sour "Brother"
Thursday "Understanding in a Car Crash"
System of a Down "Spiders"
December
Puddle of Mudd "She Hates Me"
Pink Floyd "Have a Cigar"
Sparta "Cut Your Ribbon"
The Doors "Light My Fire"
Lynyrd Skynyrd "Simple Man"
Queens of the Stone Age "No One Knows"

2003

January
Audioslave "Cochise"
Disturbed "Remember"
Good Charlotte "Lifestyles of the Rich & Famous"
Mudvayne "Not Falling"
Ramones "Blitzkrieg Bop"
Iron Maiden "Wrathchild"
Steve Vai "Head-Cuttin' Duel" (from *Crossroads*)
February
Weezer "Dope Nose"
Chevelle "The Red"
Pantera "This Love"
Guns N' Roses "It's So Easy"
Santana "America"
Taproot "Poem"
Elvis Presley "Jailhouse Rock"
March
Van Halen "Beautiful Girls"
Van Halen "And the Cradle Will Rock…"
Van Halen "Eruption"
The Vines "Outtathaway"
Fleetwood Mac "Landslide"
Black Label Society "Bleed for Me"
The Allman Brothers Band "Melissa"
April
Led Zeppelin "When the Levee Breaks"
Red Hot Chili Peppers "By the Way"
Black Sabbath "Paranoid"
AC/DC "Highway to Hell"
Stevie Ray Vaughan "Tightrope"
Alice in Chains "Them Bones"
The MC5 "Kick Out the Jams"
May
Coldplay "Clocks" (arranged for guitar)
Audioslave "Like a Stone"
Godsmack "Straight Out of Line"
Foo Fighters "Everlong" (electric & acoustic)
Yngwie Malmsteen "Black Star"
AFI "Girl's Not Grey"
Motörhead "Ace of Spades"
June
The Clash "London Calling"
Good Charlotte "Anthem"
Linkin Park "Somewhere I Belong"
Down "Ghosts Along the Mississippi"
All-American Rejects "Swing, Swing"
ZZ Top "I'm Bad, I'm Nationwide"
July
Led Zeppelin "Dazed and Confused"
Led Zeppelin "Immigrant Song" (live)
Staind "Price to Play"
White Stripes "Seven Nation Army"
Trapt "Headstrong"
The Used "The Taste of Ink"
Simple Plan "I'd Do Anything"

August
Evanescence "Going Under"
Linkin Park "Faint"
Red Hot Chili Peppers "The Zephyr Song"
Cold "Stupid Girl"
Finch "What It Is to Burn"
Queen "Bohemian Rhapsody" (piano arranged for guitar)
September
The Ataris "The Boys of Summer"
Pink Floyd "Breathe"
Lynyrd Skynyrd "Gimme Three Steps"
Shadows Fall "Destroyer of Senses"
AFI "The Leaving Song Pt. II"
Vendetta Red "Shatterday"
Joe Satriani "Cool #9"
October
Nirvana "You Know You're Right"
Killswitch Engage "Fixation on the Darkness"
Smile Empty Soul "Bottom of a Bottle"
Metallica "For Whom the Bell Tolls"
Grateful Dead "Friend of the Devil"
Cheap Trick "I Want You to Want Me"
Rancid "Fall Back Down"
November
Pearl Jam "Jeremy"
Smashing Pumpkins "Bullet with Butterfly Wings"
Ozzy Osbourne "I Don't Know"
Judas Priest "Electric Eye"
Thrice "All That's Left"
Steve Miller "The Joker"
December
Korn "Did My Time"
Iron Maiden "The Number of the Beast"
Brand New "The Quiet Things That No One Ever Knows"
Sublime "Santeria"
The Strokes "Last Nite"
The Rolling Stones "Sympathy for the Devil"

2004

January
Slayer "South of Heaven"
Rush "Limelight"
Jet "Are You Gonna Be My Girl"
The Beatles "Let It Be"
The Cure "Fascination Street"
Coldplay "God Put a Smile Upon Your Face"
Lamb of God "Ruin"
February
Metallica "St. Anger"
Blink-182 "Feelin' This"
Arch Enemy "We Will Rise"
Stevie Ray Vaughan "Riviera Paradise"
The Cars "My Best Friend's Girl"
Rage Against the Machine "Bulls on Parade"
March
Black Sabbath "Black Sabbath"
Linkin Park "Numb"
Metallica "Welcome Home (Sanitarium)"
Poison "Nothin' But a Good Time"
Megadeth "Holy Wars...The Punishment Due"
Black Label Society "The Blessed Hellride"
April
Stevie Ray Vaughan "Pride and Joy"
Finger Eleven "One Thing"
Led Zeppelin "The Lemon Song"
Dream Theater "As I Am"
Damageplan "Save Me"
Jimi Hendrix "Red House"
May
Trapt "Echo"
Hatebreed "This Is Now"

The Vines "Ride"
White Stripes "I Just Don't Know What to Do with Myself"
Red Hot Chili Peppers "Soul to Squeeze"
Steppenwolf "Born to Be Wild"
The Darkness "I Believe in a Thing Called Love"
June
The Allman Brothers Band "Statesboro Blues"
Cream "Crossroads"
Robert Johnson "Sweet Home Chicago"
Yellowcard "Ocean Avenue"
In Flames "Episode 666"
AFI "Silver and Cold"
July
Led Zeppelin "Houses of the Holy"
New Found Glory "All Downhill from Here"
Guns N' Roses "Sweet Child O' Mine"
Los Lonely Boys "Heaven"
Simple Plan "Perfect"
Drowning Pool "Step Up"
August
Modest Mouse "Float On"
Incubus "Megalomaniac"
Metallica "The Four Horsemen"
Nickelback "Figured You Out"
Killswitch Engage "Rose of Sharyn"
Maroon 5 "This Love"
The Who "Happy Jack"
September
Story of the Year "Until the Day I Die"
Bob Seger "Rock & Roll Never Forgets"
Soundgarden "Black Hole Sun"
Coheed and Cambria "A Favor House Atlantic"
Judas Priest "Hell Bent for Leather"
Black Sabbath "Supernaut"
October
Phish "Stash"
Van Halen "It's About Time"
Alice in Chains "Them Bones"
Franz Ferdinand "Take Me Out"
Green Day "When I Come Around"
The Ramones "Sheena Is a Punk Rocker"
The Pixies "Here Comes Your Man"
November
Velvet Underground "Fall to Pieces"
Led Zeppelin "Trampled Under Foot"
Children of Bodom "Needled 24/7"
The Darkness "Get Your Hands Off My Woman"
Jet "Rollover D.J."
Free "All Right Now"
December
The Beatles "Helter Skelter"
Pink Floyd "Money"
Lamb of God "Laid to Rest"
No Doubt "It's My Life"
Shadows Fall "The Power of I and I"
Ten Years After "I'd Love to Change the World"
Holiday
Green Day "American Idiot"
Jimmy Eat World "Pain"
Korn "Word Up"
Metallica "Enter Sandman"
Creedence Clearwater Revival "Fortunate Son"
Jimi Hendrix "Voodoo Child (Slight Return)"

2005

January
AC/DC "Back in Black"
Ozzy Osbourne "Crazy Train"
Interpol "Slow Hands"
Pearl Jam "Alive"
Social Distortion "Ball and Chain"

Simple Plan "Welcome to My Life"
February
Metallica "Master of Puppets"
Santana "Black Magic Woman"
Ozzy Osbourne "No More Tears"
Green Day "Boulevard of Broken Dreams"
Van Halen "Atomic Punk"
March
Blue Öyster Cult "(Don't Fear) The Reaper"
Pantera "Cemetery Gates"
Kansas "Dust in the Wind"
My Chemical Romance "I'm Not Okay (I Promise)"
Foghat "Fool for the City"
April
David Lee Roth with Steve Vai "Shyboy"
Mötley Crüe "Girls Girls Girls"
The Killers "Mr. Brightside"
Marilyn Manson "Personal Jesus"
Mahavishnu Orchestra "Birds of Fire"
May
Nirvana "Come As You Are"
Green Day "Holiday"
Mastodon "Blood and Thunder"
Led Zeppelin "Bron-Yr-Aur"
Queen "Stone Cold Crazy"
The Mars Volta "The Widow"
June
Nirvana "Smells Like Teen Spirit"
Lamb of God "Ashes of the Wake"
Slipknot "Before I Forget"
Janis Joplin "Piece of My Heart"
Pink Floyd "Shine on You Crazy Diamond"
July
My Chemical Romance "Helena"
System of a Down "Aerials"
Killswitch Engage "The End of Heartache"
Steely Dan "Josie"
The Offspring "Come Out and Play"
Weezer "Beverly Hills"
August
Shadows Fall "Inspiration on Demand"
The Who "Pinball Wizard"
Led Zeppelin "The Song Remains the Same"
Billy Idol "Rebel Yell"
Joe Walsh "Rocky Mountain Way"
September
U2 "Vertigo"
U2 "Pride (In the Name of Love)"
Led Zeppelin "The Wanton Song"
Soundgarden "Outshined"
Fall Out Boy "Sugar, We're Goin Down"
The Doors "Love Me Two Times"
October
Pink Floyd "Us and Them"
Hawthorne Heights "Ohio Is for Lovers"
Megadeth "Symphony of Destruction"
Iron Maiden "Aces High"
John Petrucci "Bite of the Mosquito"
November
The Rolling Stones "Start Me Up"
The Rolling Stones "Jumpin' Jack Flash"
As I Lay Dying "Confined"
Bon Jovi "Living on a Prayer"
Joy Division "Love Will Tear Us Apart"
Green Day "Wake Me Up When September Ends"
December
Blind Melon "No Rain"
AC/DC "Have a Drink on Me"
Cream "Born Under a Bad Sign"
INXS "I Need You Tonight"
Pantera "5 Minutes Alone"
Holiday
Audioslave "Be Yourself"

Bob Dylan "Like a Rolling Stone"
Avenged Sevenfold "Bat Country"
Weezer "We Are All on Drugs"
Neil Young "Southern Man"

2006

January
Metallica "Disposable Heroes"
Nickelback "Photograph"
Papa Roach "Scars"
Creedence Clearwater Revival "Bad Moon Rising"
Thin Lizzy "Jailbreak"
The Beatles "Hey Jude"
February
Led Zeppelin "Stairway to Heaven"
White Stripes "Blue Orchid"
Coheed and Cambria "The Suffering"
Korn "Twisted Transistor"
Deep Purple "Lazy"
March
Fall Out Boy "Dance Dance"
Johnny Cash "Folsom Prison Blues"
Green Day "Jesus of Suburbia"
Eric Johnson "Cliffs of Dover"
Ozzy Osbourne "Crazy Train"
April
Jimi Hendrix "Purple Haze"
Joe Satriani "Satch Boogie"
10 Years "Wasteland"
Disturbed "Stupify"
Trivium "A Gunshot to the Head of Trepidation"
May
Foo Fighters "Best of You"
Eric Clapton "Cocaine"
Mastodon "Seabeast"
Guns N' Roses "Don't Cry"
Pink Floyd "Another Brick in the Wall, Pt. II"
June
Tool "Schism"
ZZ Top "Tush"
Atreyu "Ex's and Oh's"
All-American Rejects "Dirty Little Secret"
Radiohead "Just"
July
Red Hot Chili Peppers "Under the Bridge"
Thursday "Counting 5-4-3-2-1"
The Beatles "Paperback Writer"
Matisyahu "King without a Crown"
Disturbed "Stupify"
August
Led Zeppelin "Misty Mountain Hop"
Def Leppard "Bringin' on the Heartbreak"
Rebel Meets Rebel "Get Outta My Life"
Robin Trower "Bridge of Sighs"
The Raconteurs "Steady, As She Goes"
Avenged Sevenfold "Beast and the Harlot"
September
Lacuna Coil "Our Truth"
AFI "Miss Murder"
Slayer "Dead Skin Mask"
Journey "Don't Stop Believin' "
Pearl Jam "Betterman"
October
Boston "More Than a Feeling"
Kiss "Detroit Rock City"
Rush "Freewill"
ZZ Top "Sharp Dressed Man"
Pearl Jam "World Wide Suicide"
November
Pantera "Hollow"
Jimi Hendrix "Foxey Lady"
Ted Nugent "Cat Scratch Fever"
Alice in Chains "Dam That River"
AC/DC "Let There Be Rock"
December
Audioslave "Original Fire"

The Allman Brothers Band "Midnight Rider"
Children of Bodom "Are You Dead Yet?"
Megadeth "Hangar 18"
Black Sabbath "Heaven and Hell"
Holiday
My Chemical Romance "Welcome to the Black Parade"
Avenged Sevenfold "Seize the Day"
Ozzy Osbourne "Diary of a Madman"
The Doors "Peace Frog"
Led Zeppelin "Since I've Been Loving You"

2007

January
Trivium "Entrance of the Conflagration"
The Who "My Generation"
Dio "Rainbow in the Dark"
Wolfmother "Joker & the Thief"
OK Go "Here It Goes Again"
Jerry C. "Canon Rock"
February
Jimi Hendrix "Hey Joe"
Jimi Hendrix "The Wind Cries Mary"
Jimi Hendrix "All Along the Watchtower"
Panic! At the Disco "I Write Sins Not Tragedies"
Killswitch Engage "My Curse"
Slipknot "Surfacing"
March
Van Halen "Top Jimmy"
Van Halen "Oh, Pretty Woman"
Buckethead "Jordan"
Red Hot Chili Peppers "Snow (Hey Oh)"
The Mars Volta "Viscera Eyes"
April
Ozzy Osbourne "Flying High Again" (live)
Pantera "Revolution Is My Name"
The Allman Brothers Band "Trouble No More" (live)
Iron Maiden "Hallowed Be Thy Name"
Death "Pull the Plug"
May
AC/DC "For Those About to Rock (We Salute You)"
Black Sabbath "The Mob Rules"
Stevie Ray Vaughan "Pride and Joy" (live)
My Chemical Romance "Famous Last Words"
The Shins "Phantom Limb"
June
The Beatles "All You Need Is Love"
Mötley Crüe "Dr. Feelgood"
Derek and the Dominos "Layla"
Disturbed "Down with the Sickness"
Korn "Freak on a Leash" (*Unplugged*)
July
Guns N' Roses "November Rain"
Jimi Hendrix "Spanish Castle Magic"
Mastodon "Colony of Birchmen"
Atreyu "Shameful"
Godsmack "The Enemy"
August
Rush "Working Man"
Lynyrd Skynyrd "Simple Man"
White Stripes "Icky Thump"
Ozzy Osbourne "Bark at the Moon"
Daughtry "It's Not Over"
The Grateful Dead "Truckin' " (*Unplugged*)
September
AC/DC "You Shook Me All Night Long"
Plain White T's "Hey There Delilah"
Pantera "Primal Concrete Sledge"
Van Halen "Jamie's Cryin' "

The Rolling Stones "19th Nervous Breakdown"
October
Stone Sour "Through Glass"
Ozzy Osbourne "I Don't Wanna Stop"
Steve Vai "For the Love of God"
Death "Crystal Mountain"
Silversun Pickups "Lazy Eye"
Extreme "More Than Words" (*Unplugged*)
Journey "Don't Stop Believin' " (*Unplugged*)
November
Fall Out Boy "Thnks Fr the Mmrs"
Boston "Foreplay/Long Time"
Accept "Balls to the Wall"
Behemoth "Prometherion"
My Chemical Romance "Teenagers"
Amy Winehouse "Rehab" (*Unplugged*)
December
AC/DC "T.N.T."
Mountain "Mississippi Queen"
Pink Floyd "Pigs (Three Different Ones)"
Atreyu "Becoming the Bull"
Van Halen "Somebody Get Me a Doctor"
Holiday
Yngwie Malmsteen "Evil Eye"
Linkin Park "Bleed It Out"
Nickeback "Rockstar"
Jimi Hendrix "Killing Floor" (live)
Slayer "Chemical Warfare"

2008

January
Led Zeppelin "No Quarter"
Led Zeppelin "Celebration Day" (live)
Stevie Ray Vaughan "Lenny"
Kid Rock "So Hott"
Dio "Holy Diver"
"Silent Night"
February
Metallica "Ride the Lightning"
Jimi Hendrix "Little Wing"
Lynyrd Skynyrd "Tuesday's Gone"
Hellyeah "Alcohaulin' Ass"
Rodrigo y Gabriela "Tamacun"
March
Smashing Pumpkins "Cherub Rock"
Nirvana "The Man Who Sold the World"
Pantera "Floods"
Seether "Fake It"
The Charlie Daniels Band "The Devil Went Down to Georgia"
April
Van Halen "Little Dreamer"
Quiet Riot "Metal Health"
Soundgarden "Pretty Noose"
Thin Lizzy "Whiskey in the Jar"
Daughtry "Home"
May
DragonForce "Through the Fire and Flames"
Metallica "The Call of Ktulu"
Stevie Ray Vaughan "Texas Flood"
Motörhead "Ace of Spades"
June
Children of Bodom "Lake Bodom"
Dethklok "Thunderhorse"
Avenged Sevenfold "Almost Easy"
Foghat "Slow Ride"
Heart "Barracuda"
July
Testament "Practice What You Preach"
The Black Crowes "Remedy"
Blue Öyster Cult "Godzilla"
Iron Maiden "Powerslave"
Atreyu "Falling Down"
August
Led Zeppelin "Achilles Last Stand"

Disturbed "Inside the Fire"
Buckcherry "Sorry"
Black Sabbath "Hole in the Sky"
Stone Temple Pilots "Interstate Love Song"
September
Jimi Hendrix "Voodoo Child (Slight Return)"
Lynyrd Skynyrd "Sweet Home Alabama"
Opeth "The Grand Conjuration"
Ram Jam "Black Betty"
Rimsky-Korsakov "Flight of the Bumblebee"
October
Bullet for My Valentine "Scream Aim Fire"
Megadeth "Tornado of Souls"
Mötley Crüe "Too Young to Fall in Love"
Stevie Ray Vaughan "Pride and Joy"
Yes "Clap"
November
Aerosmith "Train Kept a Rollin' "
Avenged Sevenfold "After Life"
Dream Theater "The Test That Stumped Them All"
B.B. King "The Thrill Is Gone"
Radiohead "Creep"
December
Trivium "Down from the Sky"
Metallica "...And Justice for All"
Skid Row "18 and Life"
Survivor "Eye of the Tiger"
Underoath "Writing on the Walls"
Holiday
Black Sabbath "Iron Man"
Buckethead "Soothsayer"
Alice Cooper "School's Out"
Fleetwood Mac "Big Love" (acoustic)
Nirvana "Heart-Shaped Box"

2009

January
AC/DC "Hells Bells"
AC/DC "Who Made Who"
All That Remains "Two Weeks"
Ozzy Osbourne "Mr. Crowley"
Trans-Siberian Orchestra "Christmas Eve/Sarajevo 12/24"
February
Children of Bodom "Blooddrunk"
Kansas "Carry on Wayward Son"
Kiss "Shout It Out Loud"
Metallica "Trapped Under Ice"
Michael Jackson "Beat It"
March
Carcass "Heartwork"
Led Zeppelin "Babe I'm Gonna Leave You"
Nickelback "Gotta Be Somebody"
Pink Floyd "Brain Damage"/"Eclipse"
Saving Abel "Addicted"
April
Coheed and Cambria "Welcome Home"
Jimi Hendrix "Crosstown Traffic"
Racer X "Scarified"
Savatage "Hall of the Mountain King"
Tool "The Pot"
May
Black Sabbath "Into the Void"
Gojira "Toxic Garbage Island"
Jason Mraz "I'm Yours"
David Lee Roth "Yankee Rose"
Steve Vai "The Attitude Song"
June
Alter Bridge "Blackbird"
Sammy Hagar "I Can't Drive 55"
Metallica "All Nightmare Long"
Stevie Ray Vaughan "Superstition"
July
AC/DC "Thunderstruck"

The Allman Brothers Band "In Memory of Elizabeth Reed"
Cannibal Corpse "A Cauldron of Hate"
Slipknot "Duality"
Triumph "Lay It On the Line"
August
Green Day "Know Your Enemy"
Jane's Addiction "Three Days"
Killswitch Engage "This Is Absolution"
Soundgarden "Spoonman"
Black Label Society "New Religion"
September
Led Zeppelin "Ten Years Gone"
Mastodon "Divinations"
Ratt "Round and Round"
Suicide Silence "Bludgeoned to Death"
Ten Years Gone "I'm Going Home" (live)
October
Bring Me the Horizon "Chelsea Smile"
Heart "Crazy on You"
Metallica "Broken, Beat & Scarred"
Nickelback "If Today Was Your Last Day"
Neil Young "Cinnamon Girl"
November
Killswitch Engage "Reckoning"
Rush "YYZ"
Shinedown "Second Chance"
Slayer "War Ensemble"
Steve Oimette "Dueling Banjos"
December
Alice in Chains "Man in the Box"
Doobie Brothers "Listen to the Music"
Kiss "Shock Me"
Megadeth "Peace Sells...But Who's Buying?"
Dream Theater "Rite of Passage"
Holiday
Jace Everett "Bad Things"
Living Colour "Cult of Personality"
Lynyrd Skynyrd "Free Bird"
Nile "Papyrus"
George Thorogood "Who Do You Love?"

2010

Anniversary
Kings of Leon "Use Somebody"
Metallica "Creeping Death"
Muse "Uprising"
Nirvana "Lithium"
Van Halen "Everybody Wants Some!!"
January
Eric Clapton "Tears in Heaven" (*Unplugged*)
Creed "Higher"
Foo Fighters "Everlong" (acoustic)
James Gang "Funk #49"
Pantera "A New Level"
Suicide Silence "Wake Up"
February
Atreyu "Storm to Pass"
Jeff Beck "Going Down"
John Mayer "Waiting on the World to Change"
Megadeth "44 Minutes"
Stevie Ray Vaughan "Cold Shot"
March
Lamb of God "Set to Fail"
Led Zeppelin "Black Dog"
Ozzy Osbourne "Over the Mountain"
Slipknot "Psychosocial"
Them Crooked Vultures "New Fang"
April
Jimi Hendrix "Stone Free"
Iron Maiden "Flight of Icarus"
AC/DC "Shoot to Thrill"
Devil Wears Prada "Danger: Wildman"
Zac Brown Band "Toes"

May
Guns N' Roses "Paradise City"
Yes "Starship Trooper"
Jeff Beck "People Get Ready"
Megadeth "Dialectic Chaos"
Creedence Clearwater Revival "Green River"
June
The Rolling Stones "Tumbling Dice"
The Beatles "Dig a Pony"
Peter Frampton "Show Me the Way" (live)
Dillinger Escape Plan "43% Burnt"
Vampire Weekend "Cousins"
July
Stevie Ray Vaughan "Couldn't Stand the Weather"
Killswitch Engage "My Obsession"
Johnny Winter "Rock and Roll Hoochie Koo"
Megadeth "Rust in Peace...Polaris"
Dokken "Mr. Scary"
August
Black Sabbath "Neon Knights"
Morbid Angel "Chapel of Ghouls"
Bullet for My Valentine "Your Betrayal"
Muse "Knights of Cydonia"
Steve Miller Band "Rock 'N Me"
September
Avenged Sevenfold "Scream"
Django Reinhardt "Minor Swing"
Drowning Pool "Bodies"
Stray Cats "Rock This Town"
AC/DC "Highway to Hell"
October
Slipknot "Sulfur"
Children of Bodom "If You Want Peace...Prepare for War"
Metallica "That Was Just Your Life"
Journey "Wheel in the Sky"
Derek and the Dominos "Bell Bottom Blues"

GUITAR WORLD
Celebrity Columnists
1980–2010

Trey Anastasio
Matt Bachand & Jon Donais (Shadows Fall)
Michael Angelo Batio
Reb Beach
Corey Beaulieu & Matt Heafy (Trivium)
Adrian Belew
Dickey Betts
Joe Bonamassa
Nick Bowcott
Chris Broderick
Billy Corgan
Dimebag Darrell
Brad Delson
Tom Dumont
Elliot Easton
Michael Fath
Michael Lee Firkins
Robben Ford

Marty Friedman
Frank Gambale
Paul Gilbert
Buddy Guy
Marten Hagstrom & Frederick Thordendal (Meshuggah)
Stu Hamm
Kirk Hammett
Frank Hannon
Juliana Hatfield
Warren Haynes
Scott Henderson
Jimmy Herring
Gary Hoey
Jerry Horton
Ihsahn
Tony Iommi
Randy Jackson
Eric Johnson
John Paul Jones
John Jorgenson
Tom Keeley & Steve Pedulla (Thursday)
B.B. King
Kerry King
Richie Kotzen
Alexi Laiho
Will Lee
Richard Lloyd
Jeff Loomis
Steve Lynch
Tony MacAlpine
Benji Madden & Billy Martin (Good Charlotte)
Yngwie Malmsteen
Wolf Marshall
Brian May
Tom Morello
Steve Morse
Mark Morton & Willie Adler (Lamb of God)
Mike Mushok
Dave Mustaine
Joe Perry & Brad Whitford (Aerosmith)
Eric Peterson
John Petrucci
Teisco Del Ray
Arlen Roth
Tony Rombola
Joe Satriani
John Scofield
James Shaffer & Brian Welch (Korn)
Billy Sheehan
Kenny Wayne Shepherd
Alex Skolnick
Slash
Steve Stevens
Robin Trower
Steve Vai
Doug Wimbish
Zakk Wylde
Angus Young
J. Yuenger

NINETEEN '89

As the Eighties come to a close, *Guitar World* talks to Stevie Ray Vaughan for the final time and recognizes Joe Satriani as the new king of shred guitar.

Dear *Guitar World*,

I really don't know how your staff could give a front cover to Slash and Izzy Stradlin [*March 1989*]. Granted, they do have a very successful album and I'm sure life is good for them now. But those two have got to be the *worst* cover story *ever*. They absolutely do not contribute anything logical, or helpful for that matter, in guitar knowledge.

I beg you gentlemen: please, please give the cover story to someone deserving. Life is sometimes hard enough to cope with by itself, but those two sound like someone playing with two broken arms.

Maybe if we all changed our names to Smashed and Dizzy, we could all be on your cover.

—W.P. Apolinar

JANUARY Robert Cray is making the blues popular to the MTV generation but takes his inspiration from old-schoolers like Albert King.
COVER STORY BY BILL MILKOWSKI
PHOTO BY JEFF KATZ

FEBRUARY Brad Gillis and Jeff Watson's virtuosity lays the foundation for Night Ranger's slick rock sound, but writing songs is another story.
COVER STORY BY MATT RESNICOFF
PHOTO BY GLEN LA FERMAN

MARCH Guns N' Roses have become the world's most dangerous rock band, but guitarist Izzy Stradlin isn't having any of it.
COVER STORY BY JOSEPH BOSSO
PHOTO BY GLEN LA FERMAN

APRIL In this heady discussion between bass gods Jack Bruce and Billy Sheehan, Sheehan takes time out to promote his upcoming project with Paul Gilbert.
COVER STORY BY CHRIS JISI
PHOTO BY JOHNNIE MILES

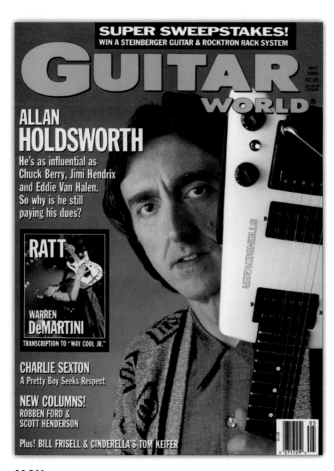

MAY Jazz guitar maestro Allan Holdsworth is at the top of his game, but has a surprisingly casual attitude about his craft. "All I'm doing is rearranging notes—and I don't feel I do it very well. It's just an approach to the guitar, that's all."

COVER STORY BY MATT RESNICOFF; PHOTO BY ANN SUMA

JUNE Zakk Wylde is flying high as Ozzy Osbourne's new six-string star, and in his first *Guitar World* cover story he recalls his pre-fame days. "I was giving guitar lessons for 10 bucks an hour. I was making more money doing construction, but I almost fell off a roof a few times; I said, 'The hell with this!' and got into guitar teaching."

COVER STORY BY JOE LALAINA; PHOTO BY BOB LEAFE

1989 TOTAL ISSUES: 11

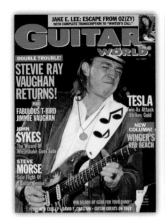

JULY 34-year-old blues ace Stevie Ray Vaughan speaks to *Guitar World* for the final time in his life.
COVER STORY BY DAN FORTE
PHOTO BY RICK GOULD

SEPTEMBER White Lion guitarist Vito Bratta is making a name for himself in hair-metal circles, but can't deny the ever-present influence of his heroes.
COVER STORY BY BRAD TOLINSKI
PHOTO BY GLEN LA FERMAN

OCTOBER After seven years as Billy Idol's axman, Steve Stevens forges ahead on his own.
COVER STORY BY BILL MILKOWSKI
PHOTO BY LARRY DIMARZIO

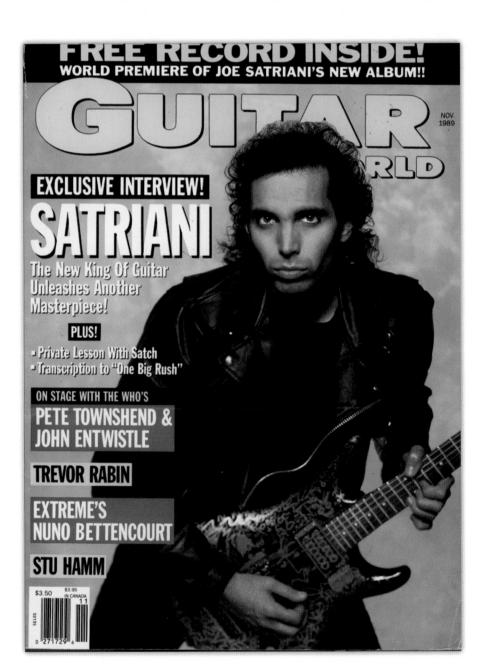

NOVEMBER Joe Satriani is fast becoming the world's preeminent shredder, but still finds time to seize the occasional guest-star opportunity. "The position I filled touring with Mick Jagger was based on the fact that Mick asked me. Mick Jagger is not like any other band. There's only one Mick, and that's all there was to it."
COVER STORY BY JOSEPH BOSSO;
PHOTO BY NEIL ZLOZOWER

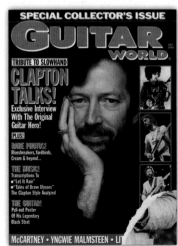

DECEMBER In this tribute to Eric Clapton, Slowhand responds to the accusations that he's mellowing with age.
COVER STORY BY DAN FORTE; PHOTO BY TERRY O'NEILL

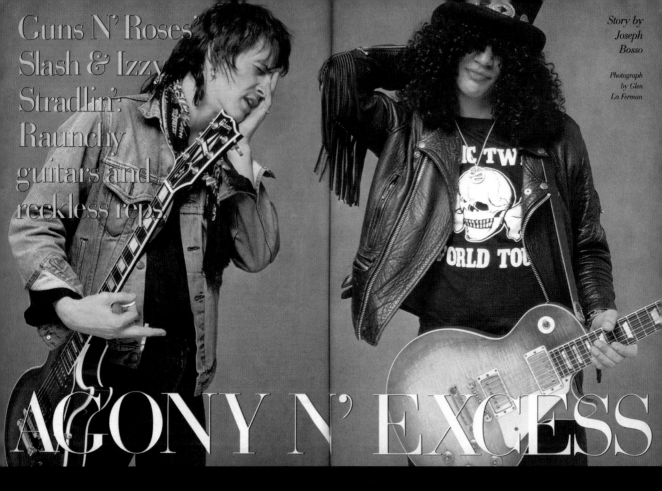

Guns N' Roses'
Slash & Izzy
Stradlin?
Raunchy
guitars and
reckless reps.

Story by
Joseph
Bosso

Photograph
by Glen
La Ferman

AGONY N' EXCESS

MARCH 1989

VOL. 10 / NO. 3

Slash & Izzy Stradlin

**Guns N' Roses' dynamic duo reflect on the band's lean years and talk about how
hardship led them to write some of the band's most successful songs.**

It's another perfect wreck of a Sunday afternoon in downtown Los Angeles. While thousands of dazed denizens attempt to piece together fragments of the previous night's misadventures for either themselves or some like-minded compatriots, the very object of many of their fantasies is polishing off his morning cocktail. For the man known as Slash, Guns N' Roses' volatile, rakish lead guitarist, living the crude values extolled on the band's debut, *Appetite for Destruction*, has become something of a fulltime occupation.

Sleep—an increasingly rare indulgence for Slash—is a welcome but impractical notion. In just a few hours, Guns N' Roses is due to convene its first rehearsal in a month, a preparation for its maiden voyage to Japan. New Zealand will quickly follow. And then there's the business of writing and recording the follow-up to *Appetite for Destruction*, the raging slab of backstreet howls and disillusionment that came from nowhere and managed to sell over six million copies in the United States alone (ranking it behind *Whitney Houston* and *Boston* as the third largest-selling debut of all time).

"Yep, the pressure's kind of on," Slash admits sheepishly. "Still, it's nothing we can't handle. What I try and do is act as if nothing has really happened. So we sold a lot of records—big deal. It's not going to change the way we live or the way we try to make our music. Surface things will take a different course, sure, but the important thing for us is to just ignore it."

Slash's humble assertions notwithstanding, the fact is that indifference is something none of the members of Guns N' Roses appear particularly adept at. Pain and outrage have inspired some of rock and roll's finest moments, from Elvis Presley right on through to the Sex Pistols. In that spirit, Guns N' Roses' memory of a more squalid existence—at one point, the band shared guitarist Izzy Stradlin's ratty studio apartment, its members relegated to floor space—served as fuel for the dozen compositions that became *Appetite for Destruction*.

To all appearances, they were just one more ragged bunch of losers, going nowhere fast. But, as Slash says, there was a method to their madness. "We basically junked

a lot of our lives at that point to work on the band, to work on the music. Sure, it might not have worked, but that was the chance we had to take. We didn't know any other way, nor were we particularly interested in any alternatives. I guess we were sort of...fearless."

Holed up in Izzy's one-room digs, the band eked out songs on whatever equipment they happened to own that week, viewing their desperate situation as necessary fodder for their compositions.

"Some of the best stuff can be written out of dire times," Izzy states matter-of-factly. "Slash and I would throw riffs back and forth, which is certainly one of his major strengths. I write on anything—I did then, and I still do. I think that I wrote much of the stuff on *Appetite* on an old Harmony. It was pretty hilarious. Stevie would set up this suitcase and drum on it. Pretty crude. I would tape-record the whole thing on this little micro-cassette recorder. It sounded real good; that's how we wrote. I think maybe one day I'll press that stuff. So it doesn't matter what you write on: PortaStudios, eight-tracks. If you have a song that can cut it, it doesn't matter."

Guns N' Roses' impact is manifest on the dozens of L.A. stages brimming with chest-pounding, bandana-wrapped posers who parade their "streetwise" selves. Ironically, the more these wannabe's huff and puff, the more the public seems to respond to the band they perceive as the real thing.

"It could be said that we have a pretty nasty history," admits Stradlin. "The thing is, I don't give a fuck about the image that everyone buys. It's all been blown out of proportion, the 'bad-boy' thing, how much we drink, how much drugs we do or don't do. It's boring. While everyone's talkin' about what we did or *supposedly* did yesterday, we're already working *today* on the music they're gonna hear tomorrow."

Slash, for his part, sees the humorous side: "The image tag is an easy thing to finger us on. None of us are model citizens, I guess. But the musical end of it can get funny. Why, I'm already hearing people pulling out those wah-wah pedals, slipping 'em onto tracks, and subliminally sounding a lot like us. That's a compliment, but it's kind of missing the point, isn't it?" ✳

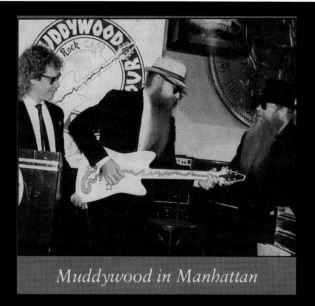

Muddywood in Manhattan

THE "MUDDYWOOD" GUITAR COMES TO NEW YORK CITY

Billy Gibbons and ZZ Top present the one-of-a-kind ax, built from a piece of Muddy Waters' destroyed home, to the Hard Rock Café. Harold Steinblatt reports.

IT WAS 10 A.M., TOO EARLY for the usual gaggle of rubes to be camped outside. But on Tuesday morning, December 12, 1988, New York's Hard Rock Café was the site of a legitimate happening. The "Muddywood" guitar—the unique electric built from a beam taken from Muddy Waters' Mississippi home—was officially presented to the Hard Rock by ZZ Top's Billy Gibbons, Dusty Hill and Frank Beard. The Muddywood is on a Hard Rock–coordinated world tour to raise funds for the Delta Blues Museum in Clarksdale, Mississippi. It remained in New York until January 10, when it was shipped to London. Its ultimate destination is Clarksdale, in the Delta.

Billy Gibbons, resplendent in fishing hat, shades and serious beard, played a brief, Muddy-esque riff prior to the presentation. Gibbons himself designed the gleaming white Muddywood, which was built by Pyramid Guitars of Memphis. The "Muddy" has contours suggesting the Telecasters favored by Waters, and a black, squiggly line traversing its body. "That represents the power and mystery of the Mississippi River," explained Gibbons.

ZZ Top, who played on tour with Muddy Waters several times in the late Seventies, have championed the Delta Blues Museum since their first visit there in September 1987. Waters' cabin at nearby Stovall's Plantation had some time previously been partially destroyed by a tornado. Gibbons took a beam as a souvenir, later deciding to turn it into a guitar for the benefit of the museum. When it was suggested to him at the Hard Rock that Clarksdale, Mississippi, is an inaccessible, if historically appropriate, location for the institution, Gibbons replied, "That's the beauty of it. To get there, you've either got to go to Memphis and head south for a couple of hours or go to Jackson and head north for two hours. That ensures that you'll discover for yourself what you *can't* get from a record bin."

New Blood

1989 was a significant year in *Guitar World*'s history for a number of reasons, two of which cannot be overlooked. In the spring, the first issue of *Guitar School* magazine hit newsstands, and in the September issue of *GW*, Brad Tolinski, the magazine's current and longest-running editor-in-chief, made his debut as associate editor. Spearheaded by editor-in-chief John Cerullo, *Guitar School* was aimed at young players looking to improve their playing through instructional columns and multiple transcriptions in every issue. The April 1989 issue was the magazine's first, and featured Steve Vai on the cover with full transcriptions to nine songs, including Led Zeppelin's "Heartbreaker," Van Halen's "I'm the One," and Vai's "Headcuttin' Duel" *tour-de-force* from the movie *Crossroads*. *Guitar School* thrived for many years as the instructional guitar magazine of choice, but fell on hard times in 1998 after changing its name to *Maximum Guitar*. The August 1998 issue, a Southern Rock–themed affair, would be the magazine's swan song.

"Ozzy's great when he's sober and ugly

JAKE E. LEE

He rose to six-string superstardom alongside Ozzy Osbourne during the mid Eighties, and now Jake E. Lee is ready take his Badlands project to the hard rock masses. Here, the gifted guitarist reflects on his frustrating relationship with his former boss.

GUITAR WORLD The Badlands record doesn't sound anything like your work with Ozzy. How has your approach to recording changed?
JAKE E. LEE I don't know how to answer that. I've always played what's inside my head, but Badlands is purer because I didn't have to filter my ideas through Ozzy. Ozzy encouraged a flashier, trick-oriented style. Badlands is definitely more blues-based. When we got together we started by playing old Cream, Free, Led Zeppelin—the things we all grew up on. When we started writing songs, it carried over.

I naturally went back to my pre-Ozzy approach. Our bassist, Greg Chaisson, says he's relieved. He used to see me in my club days when I was playing in Ratt and Rough Cutt, and he said I was his favorite. When he heard *Bark at the Moon*, he was disappointed.
GW I heard that Ozzy prohibited certain ideas in his music.
LEE Yeah, when he didn't like something he called it "Frank Zappa on acid." He would've cringed at the middle solo of "Winter's Call." Even the band argued about it. The riff is in E and I come in on an E. Everyone did a double-take and asked me if that's what I meant to do. I even caught some hell from the record company, but I put my foot down.
GW What caused the split between you and Ozzy?
LEE I think it was because we were almost living together for a while. It pushes a relationship to the limit. Basically, I like Ozzy, but he does a lot of things I don't like. He's great when he's sober and ugly when he's drunk—a real Jekyll and Hyde.

Guitar World Slips a Disc

Guitar World broke new ground in the November 1989 issue when a six-inch "flexi disc" (or "sound sheet," as it was also known) of the Joe Satriani song "The Mystical Potato Head Groove Thing," from the guitarist's *Flying in a Blue Dream* album, was included inside every copy of the magazine. The one-sided, 33 1/3 RPM disc was sandwiched between pages 50 and 51 (the opening spread of the issue's cover story on Satriani). "For best results," read the instructions, "place over an LP record, and set coin here."

clapton

SEATED IN HIS opulent but tasteful London office, Eric Clapton listens intently to a tape he's just been introduced to. "That's beautiful," he sighs, as the Turtle Island String Quartet sound a long minor chord. The tempo abruptly quickens, and Clapton finds himself listening to an oddly familiar arrangement of "Crossroads," a song, and theme, that has circumscribed his 25-odd years as the guitar community's resident hero. "Is that all charted out from the original Cream version?" he asks, as a solo he improvised onstage 20 years ago is echoed by a cello, two violins and a viola. "I always thought everyone overrated that version of 'Crossroads.' I've heard about guitar players learning the solo note for note, but until I heard *this*...It sounds better as a transcription—just to hear fiddles play those lines—than it did with Cream."

The notion of hearing bits of his legacy analyzed and replayed by would-be guitarslingers by the thousands, and now a string quartet is, in Clapton's words, "mind-boggling." The same could be said for a large chunk of that legacy. By the time Clapton encountered the MTV generation, and vice versa, his short but profound stints with the Yardbirds and John Mayall's

PHOTOGRAPH BY VIRGINIA LOHLE/STARFILE

INTERVIEW BY DAN FORTE

FEB. 1989

VOL. 10 / NO. 2

Eric Clapton

In this special collector's tribute to Eric Clapton, Slowhand talks about the making of his recent *Journeyman* album and how being labeled a guitar hero is a source of motivation.

GUITAR WORLD Nearly all of the material on *Journeyman* came from outside sources.

ERIC CLAPTON I was really having a difficult time writing, this last year or two. Nothing came until halfway through the sessions. I had a week's rest in England, and going back to New York I caught the flu. I knew Robert Cray was going to be in, and suddenly I was faced with the fact that we didn't have anything to do—which is how "Before You Accuse Me" came about. "Let's do that. It's simple and we both know it." That's Robert and me intertwining all through the song. He plays the second solo. Then I was in my hotel room just playing around with a riff, and it ended up being "Old Love." Robert wrote the turnaround and the bridge. He takes the first solo and the ride at the end, and I kind of chip in here and there. I wrote "Bad Love" right at the very end, because Warner Bros., as is their wont, came in and said, "Well, where's 'Layla'?" [*laughs*] I methodically thought about it and said, "Well, I'll get a riff, I'll modulate into the verse, and there'll be a chorus where we go into a minor key with a little guitar line. Then there'll be a breakdown and I'll put 'Badge' in for good measure."

GW There's a lot of wah-wah on this record.

CLAPTON Yeah, I've always liked wah-wah, but I was scared of it for a while because it became very fashionable in the Philadelphia sound and then sort of burned out. So I thought, Stay clear of this for a bit. I've always liked the Hendrix wah-wah stuff, and I was in the avant-garde of that, too, with "Tales of Brave Ulysses." I bought my wah-wah at Manny's in 1967, and I did "Tales of Brave Ulysses" in New York, I think, the same day—just experimenting with it.

GW The magnitude of the 1988 *Crossroads* box set reinforces something you, in certain respects, have tried to downplay: the Clapton-is-bigger-than-life Guitar Hero. Not only in terms of yourself, but in general, how do you view the so-called Guitar Hero? Do you think it's a valid thing, a taste-less exercise...

CLAPTON No, I think it's very admirable, and I think it strengthens a belief that kept me going for years—that you have to have an ideal. And if I have to be a hero, even to myself, it's worth it because it's something to strive for. I quite like having my mettle tested in that way. I didn't like it not so long ago; I tried to avoid it, to play it down, and tried to *destroy* it. And that process nearly destroyed me, too—as a human being. I found that one went with the other: in order to be a growing human being you have to keep pushing yourself to the limit. To try to go inward or backward is actually very, very destructive. I find now that I'm actually quite happy to try and perpetuate this myth, even to myself. I mean, I was in Africa this last tour, where I had to fill out all these forms each time we changed countries. And where it said "Occupation," I put "Legend." [*laughs*] I couldn't have done that 10 years ago; I took it all far too seriously.

GW You must be aware that certain critics will inevitably slag you because "this has all been done" and "the days of guitar heroes are over." Does that ever inspire you to go out and say, "I'll show them who's washed up!"

CLAPTON Oh, it does even now. On this record I was determined to make each solo as outside my capabilities as possible, to push myself as far as I could—even if it was just in terms of how many frets you can bend. "Anything for Your Love" has got Robert playing on it, and when I did the solo on that, I looked at him, and he was amazed that I had this one note—I just push it—at the end of a phrase. He was just blown away. So if I can do that to him...

And that really reflects on what I think about critics. I don't think they have much experience to talk from, except for listening. It's my peers that count, and if I get criticism from them, if they think I'm going in the wrong direction or not living up to my capability, then I'll take it onboard. The last time that something hurt me involved Elvis Costello. I mean, I consider him a peer because we're in the same business. I'm not that well acquainted with this music or anything, but I consider him to be very serious. And he wrote me off. It had to do with the beer-commercial syndrome and all that. [*In the mid Eighties, Clapton recorded the J.J. Cale song "After Midnight" for a Michelob beer commercial. Clapton had previously recorded the track for his self-titled 1970 solo debut.*]. He's got a bit of a soapbox about that, you know. He said that he could understand certain people who've got something to say doing it, but as far as he was concerned, I'd said it all and had nothing left to offer. So that, coming from a peer, is hurtful. But that will make me strive more than anything a critic will say. When a musician runs me down, then I want to prove something to him. ✳

TUNE UPS

SOUNDGARDEN'S
KIM THAYIL

SOUNDGARDENING TIPS

**Grunge
Infiltrates
*Guitar World***

1989 was coming to a close, and so was the era of spandex-wrapped, teased-hair shred demons. Grunge rock was waiting patiently in the wings, ready to kick commercial metal into irrelevance with its crunching detuned riffs and flannel outerwear—and *Guitar World* was there to report on the shifting climate. On page 12 of the December 1989 issue, Soundgarden became the first official grunge band to receive ink in the magazine. "It's sweater-snagging rock and roll," said guitarist Kim Thayil in describing his band's *Louder Than Love* album to Jeff Gilbert. "It's loud, and it's heavier and it rocks more than anything else you see on MTV; it's a waterbed album!"

NINETEEN '90

Steve Vai, Eddie Van Halen, Jeff Healey, Reb Beach and others come to *Guitar World*'s 10th birthday party.

Dear *Guitar World*,

Guitar World's 10th Anniversary issue
[*July 1990*] is like getting two pizzas
with everything, delivered by Susan Anton
wearing a bikini. What a blast!

—The Blazer

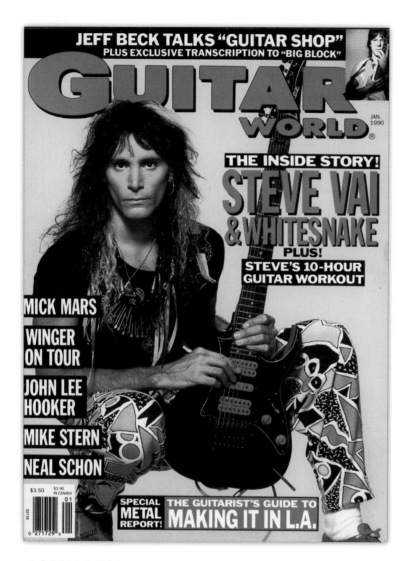

JEFF BECK TALKS "GUITAR SHOP"
PLUS EXCLUSIVE TRANSCRIPTION TO "BIG BLOCK"

GUITAR WORLD

JAN. 1990

THE INSIDE STORY!
STEVE VAI & WHITESNAKE
PLUS!
STEVE'S 10-HOUR GUITAR WORKOUT

MICK MARS

WINGER ON TOUR

JOHN LEE HOOKER

MIKE STERN

NEAL SCHON

$3.50 $3.95 IN CANADA   01

SPECIAL METAL REPORT! **THE GUITARIST'S GUIDE TO MAKING IT IN L.A.**

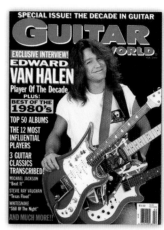

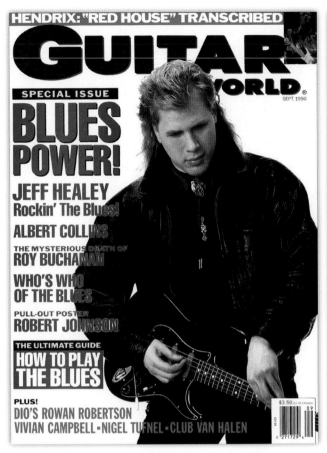

SEPTEMBER A tribute to the blues with Jeff Healey, who has no interest in being labeled a blues musician.

COVER STORY BY HAROLD STEINBLATT, PHOTO BY JONNIE MILES

OCTOBER Winger's Reb Beach makes his second *Guitar World* cover appearance in five months and extols the virtues of dumbed-down songwriting.

COVER STORY BY JOE BOSSO; PHOTO BY JOHN PEDEN

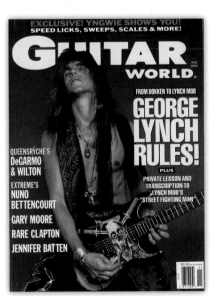

NOVEMBER With his new band Lynch Mob, former Dokken ace George Lynch hopes to right a few wrongs. "Dokken made some big mistakes, and I wanted to learn from them. The biggest problem was the lack of chemistry between band members; I wanted to ensure that the people in Lynch Mob were compatible in every way."

COVER STORY BY BRAD TOLINSKI; PHOTO BY JONNIE MILES

DECEMBER *Guitar World* closes out the year with a touching tribute to one of its favorite subjects, Stevie Ray Vaughan, the blues titan who died on August 27. "As a bluesman, he was as good as anybody," recalls Buddy Guy. "Ever."

COVER STORY BY BILL MILKOWSKI; PHOTO BY JONNIE MILES

1990 TOTAL ISSUES: 11

The Monster of Rock

The guy couldn't help it. He did what came naturally, and look what happened. He's **Edward Van Halen**, player of the decade.

BY JOSEPH BOSSO

"Look at this mess!" Eddie Van Halen takes in the barren and dusty confines of what used to be 5150, his beloved recording studio/clubhouse. Where most men find rest and rumination in neighborhood bars, Eddie has for years sought not-so-quiet refuge in this, his hangout-joint to end all hangout-joints. Here he stays up late, pours back some Buds with his buds, and plays his vids. Here, too, he cranks it to hell and back, capturing bits of genius on two-inch tape.

But at this moment he couldn't nail a solo banjo track in here, let alone the monstrous sonic booms that are part-and-parcel of all VH recordings. 5150 is being remodeled, so everything's been stripped away, sawed-off, gutted. Amps, effects racks, consoles, you name it—they're outta here! Construction will surely take a

Editorial research assisted by Greg Di Benedetto

Photograph by Larry DiMarzio

FEB. 1990

VOL. 11 / NO. 2

Eddie Van Halen

Guitar World's **Player of the Decade** shares his views on the Van Halen album catalog.

Van Halen (1978)

"Party. That was a lot of fun. We just played the way we played onstage, and that was great. It didn't feel like we were making a record. We just went in, poured back a few beers and played. We did demos with Gene Simmons about a year earlier and I tried to overdub, but just didn't know how. It's like you have to play to yourself, and I was like, 'How the hell do I do this?' I hadn't even played with another guitarist, let alone play with myself. So when we got signed to Warned Bros., I begged Donn [*Landee, engineer*] and Ted [*Templeman, [producer*], 'Please, just let me play the way I play live.' "

Van Halen II (1979)

"I remember not liking the studio very much. It was some place on Wilshire Boulevard. We wound up doing overdubs at Lion's Share, I think. God, I don't know. I just remember not liking the studios."

Women and Children First (1980)

"I remember playing 'And the Cradle Will Rock...' for Ted. It was on a Wurlitzer electric piano that I played through my Marshalls. I just pounded on the lower registers and put it through an MXR flanger to get that weird sound. Ted went, 'Wow! What the *fuck* is that?' [*laughs*] 'Oh, nothing, just me, fucking around.' So we recorded it."

Fair Warning (1981)

"It's kind of a dark album. I remember that was kind of when I wanted to start doing things my way, and we all kinda butted heads—like me versus them. I remember sneaking down in the studio around four o'clock in the morning with Donn and doing what I wanted to do, and the next day they'd walk in and go, 'Hey, that's great! When'd you do that?' It was funny because the stuff I did when they weren't there, they would think that they *were* there. It's kind of a cheap thing to do, I guess, but I had to do *something* to get what I wanted."

Diver Down (1982)

"My least favorite album. It's half cover tunes. I don't think a lot of people even know that half the songs aren't ours. The album pisses me off, because at the time I had enough music of my own. You know that Mini-Moog riff that opens 'Dancing in the Street'? I said, '*What*?' So that's why I built my own studio. Put it this way: I'd rather bomb with my own songs than make it with someone else's."

1984 (1984)

"That's the first record we did at [*Edward's home studio*] 5150. We did it on the 16-track, recorded, mixed and everything. I thought it was a good record. But it was the beginning of doing things my way, or at least as a band, meaning Mike [*Anthony, bass*], my brother [*Alex, drums*] and I, our way of wanting to do things. The beginning of the new Van Halen."

5150 (1986)

"Lots of jokes! Sammy [*Hagar, vocals*] has to be one of the funniest guys on the face of the planet. After putting in maybe an honest 45 minutes of work, we'll be standing around just laughing, doing anything, eating ribs, and then we'll go, 'Should we go in and try one? *Nahhh*!' We spend so much time doing nothing, it's silly. It's hard to call it work. But it was a very inspired record. A lot of the tunes are real fresh. There's a lot of soul on that record."

OU812 (1988)

"That album reflects that Sammy and I are more comfortable with each other. We're neighbors out at the beach now. It was easier. Not to say that *5150* was hard, but we were just feeling each other out on that one. This record was more comfortable, more relaxed. It was like opening the doors and letting it out. It's more mature too."

Guitar World Editors Pick the 50 Best Guitar Records of the Eighties

1) Van Halen—*1984*
2) Joe Satriani—*Surfing with the Alien*
3) Stevie Ray Vaughan & Double Trouble—*Texas Flood*
4) Yngwie Malmsteen—*Rising Force*
5) AC/DC—*Back in Black*
6) Ozzy Osbourne—*Blizzard of Ozz*
7) U2—*War*
8) David Lee Roth—*Eat 'Em and Smile*
9) Price and the Revolution—*Purple Rain*
10) Danny Gatton—*Unfinished Business*
11) ZZ Top—*Eliminator*
12) Jimi Hendrix—*Live at the Winterland*
13) Sonic Youth—*Daydream Nation*
14) Metallica—*Master of Puppets*
15) Jimi Hendrix—*Radio One*
16) Stevie Ray Vaughan & Double Trouble—*Couldn't Stand the Weather*
17) Joe Satriani—*Not of This Earth*
18) John Hiatt (with Ry Cooder)—*Bring the Family*
19) Stanley Jordan—*Magic Touch*
20) David Lindley—*El Rayo-X*
21) The Dregs—*Industry Standard*
22) Allan Holdsworth—*Allan Holdsworth, I.O.U.*
23) Frank Zappa—*Shut Up N' Play Yer Guitar*
24) Jeff Beck—*Guitar Shop*
25) The Clash—*London Calling*
26) King Crimson—*Discipline*
27) R.E.M.—*Murmur*
28) Eric Clapton—*Crossroads*
29) The Police—*Synchronicity*
30) Jeff Beck—*There and Back*
31) Steve Morse—*The Introduction*
32) Guns N' Roses—*Appetite for Destruction*
33) Allan Holdsworth—*Road Games*
34) Steve Vai—*Flex-able*
35) U2—*The Unforgettable Fire*
36) Stevie Ray Vaughan & Double Trouble—*In Step*
37) Van Halen—*Fair Warning*
38) Whitesnake—*Whitesnake*
39) John Fogerty—*Centerfield*
40) Jimmy Page—*Outrider*
41) Michael Hedges—*Aerial Boundaries*
42) Deep Purple—*Perfect Strangers*
43) Dire Straits—*Brothers in Arms*
44) David Lindley & El Rayo-X—*Very Greasy*
45) Son Seals—*Chicago Fire*
46) The Cult—*Sonic Temple*
47) XTC—*Oranges & Lemons*
48) Van Halen—*Women and Children First*
49) Eric Johnson—*Tones*
50) (tie) Yngwie Malmsteen—*Trilogy*/Steve Morse—*High Tension Wires*
51) (honorary) Spinal Tap—*This Is Spinal Tap*

GUITAR WORLD'S FIRST READERS POLL

Nowadays, generating a Readers Poll is a piece of cake—just put up an online poll and ask your loyal followers to click a few choices and hit "submit." But when we first asked our readers to give their best-of-the-year selections, we did it the hard way: tabulating, by hand, thousands of submission cards that were mailed to the magazine's offices. The work was painstaking and brutal, but we asked for it. Here are the results of the very first *Guitar World* Readers Poll.

MVP
1) **Joe Satriani**
2) Steve Vai
3) Edward Van Halen
4) Eric Clapton
5) Yngwie Malmsteen

Best New Artist
1) **Reb Beach**
2) Vernon Reid
3) Jeff Healey
4) Paul Gilbert
5) Nuno Bettencourt

Rock Guitarist
1) **Steve Vai**

2) Joe Satriani
3) Edward Van Halen
4) Eric Clapton
5) Jeff Beck

Pop Guitarist
1) **Richie Sambora**
2) The Edge
3) Neal Schon
4) Reb Beach
5) Eric Clapton

Worst Guitarists
1) **C.C. DeVille**
2) "Not a good category," "Me," "No reply"

3) Mick Mars
4) Yngwie Malmsteen
5) The Great Kat

Heavy Metal Guitarist
1) **Kirk Hammett**
2) Yngwie Malmsteen
3) Steve Vai
4) George Lynch
5) Paul Gilbert

Thrash Guitarist
1) **Kirk Hammett**
2) Alex Skolnick
3) Dan Spitz

4) Dave Mustaine
5) James Hetfield

Jazz/Fusion Guitarist
1) **Stanley Jordan**
2) Jeff Beck
3) Joe Satriani
4) Larry Carlton
5) Frank Gambale

Rock Bassist
1) **Billy Sheehan**
2) Stuart Hamm
3) Geddy Lee
4) John Entwistle

5) Muzz Skillings

Jazz Bassist
1) **Stuart Hamm**
2) Stanley Clarke
3) Jeff Berlin
4) John Patitucci
5) Jaco Pastorius

Blues Guitarist
1) **Stevie Ray Vaughan**
2) Eric Clapton
3) Jeff Healey
4) B.B. King
5) Robert Cray

HURRICANE
Slave To The Thrill
ENIGMA

WILL INDUCE vomiting.
—HAROLD STEINBLATT

(Dis)Like a Hurricane

JUN. '90

Guitar World always took pride in its thoughtful, thorough record reviews—but all that went sailing out the window with Harold Steinblatt's June issue review of pop-metal band Hurricane's third album, 1990's *Slave to the Thrill*. Steinblatt gave the album the only negative-one-star rating in the magazine's history, and kept his review to a brief "Will induce vomiting." Reader responses to Steinblatt's review ranged from supportive high-fives ("Harold hit the nail on the head!") to pure disgust ("I can't believe you're managing editor. If Joe Bosso were smart, he'd put you in charge of licking mailing labels instead of reviews.").

CLAPTON. BECK. PAGE. Richards, Van Halen, Vaughan. It would be hard to name a major rock guitar hero who hasn't influenced Nigel Tufnel. From his skiffle and blues beginnings, to his metal and mega-boogie present—including flirtations with psychedelia (1967's "(Listen To The) Flower People") and light pop (1965's "Cups And Cakes")—the Spinal Tap guitarist has, in his words, "exonerated" the styles of the greats and near-greats to forge one of the loudest styles in rock and roll.

After nearly two decades of mixed success in the United Kingdom, Tap—Tufnel, rhythm guitarist David St. Hubbins, bassist Derek Smalls, keyboardist Viv Savage and the late Mick Shrimpton on drums—came to the attention of American ears in 1983, when filmmaker Martin di Bergi documented their first tour of the States. The resulting "rockumentary," *This Is Spinal Tap*, featured such Tap staples as "Hell Hole," "Big Bottom," "Stonehenge" and "Tonight I'm Gonna Rock You Tonight," and still ranks as perhaps the definitive filmed account of life on the road with a rock band. It also offered a unique insight into the creative mind of Tufnel the guitarist (his memorable unaccompanied twin-guitar solo, in which he plays one instrument conventionally, the second with his foot), composer (the lyrical "Lick My Love Pump" from his as-yet-unfinished trilogy, "Clam Caravan"), and collector (his coveted Fender 6-string bass, which he never plays but is never without).

Also introduced in the film was one of the secrets to the Tufnel wall of sound: his customized Marshall amp, with all controls going that "one extra" to 11. This modification in turn inspired Marshall engineers to design the new JCM 900, which goes to 20. The reclusive but congenial bandleader recently hosted the unveiling of the 900 at Hollywood's

DEC. '90

GW Welcomes Diamond Darrell

Until his death in 2004, Pantera/Damageplan guitarist "Dimebag" Darrell Abbott was as much a *Guitar World* family member as anyone. Cover stories, instructional lessons, columns, photo shoots, video shoots, you name it—Dimebag was happy to oblige whenever we called upon him, and for that we are forever indebted. Dimebag's history with the magazine dates back to the October 1990 issue, when editor-in-chief Joe Bosso gave a three-and-a-half-star record review to Pantera's *Cowboys from Hell* album. "A band, and a player, worth checking out," wrote Bosso. The first time the guitarist, who was known as Diamond Darrell back then, was profiled in the magazine was in the December 1990 issue, in which he enthusiastically told writer Joe Lalaina, "We're like fine-tuned, clean-cutting machinery. After listening to *Cowboys from Hell*, you'll view the world with a bigger pair of balls."

SEPTEMBER / VOL. 11 / NO. 9

SPINAL TAP'S NIGEL TUFNEL

Teisco Del Rey catches up with the "Lick My Love Pump" composer and talks about his life post-Tap.

GUITAR WORLD Did you form a new band and play any solo gigs?

NIGEL TUFNEL No, I did some solo things, where I'd get pre-taped stuff that I'd do and take it onstage. All the drums, all the bass, the keyboard stuff—and the guitars and the vocals.

GW Would you do any of it live?

TUFNEL No. That was the interesting thing—it was *all* taped. It didn't go over that well, to be honest. So I retreated back into myself again.

GW There were rumors that you had gotten a bit more philosophical and were a member of, would you call it a sect or a cult?

TUFNEL Well, I would call it that, yeah.

GW What was the overriding philosophy?

TUFNEL "Sleep late" was the main thing. What would happen is, you'd go to bed late and sleep late. That's what the guru said to do, and I did—for about three or four months, actually.

GW Hadn't you already been doing that, more or less, when you were with the band?

TUFNEL Yes, but I didn't realize it until after the fact.

GW Is Spinal Tap currently affiliated with a major label?

TUFNEL Well, *Christmas with the Devil* was on Demon Records, and the *Spinal Tap* record was just re-released in London about a year ago. I was talking to Windham Hill Records for a while, but they seemed to say something about not being right for the label. I didn't really know what they meant.

GW They're mostly folk music.

TUFNEL Oh, is that why?

GW And, of course, volume, has always been one of your fortes.

TUFNEL See, that's probably why they nixed it. My idea was to do very loud acoustic music. Like what's happening with all the guitar stuff—what they call "new age"—but to make it loud and exciting, rather than quiet, you know?

GW How would you make an acoustic guitar louder?

TUFNEL Play on an electric.

THE GOOD TEXAN

The musical life of **Stevie Ray Vaughan**, who rose from obscure beginnings to become a blues titan in his own lifetime.

BY BILL MILKOWSKI
PHOTOGRAPH BY ALDO MAURO

DEC. 1990

VOL. 11 / NO. 12

Stevie Ray Vaughan

Bill Milkowski chronicles the events in Austin and Dallas in the days after Stevie Ray Vaughan's August 27, 1990, death.

Monday, August 27, 1990: The first flash comes over the Associated Press wire around 7 A.M.: "Copter crash in East Troy, Wisconsin. Five fatalities, including a musician." Keen-eyed staffers at the Austin *American Statesman* catch the item and begin to put two and two together as the AP updates the story every half hour. The mysterious "musician" soon becomes "a member of Eric Clapton's entourage," then "a guitarist." By 9:30, rumors have spread that Stevie Ray Vaughan, Austin's favorite son, was aboard the doomed craft.

At 11:30, Clapton's manager confirms the worst: Vaughan was indeed among the passengers in the five-seat helicopter, which slammed into a fog-shrouded hillside near southeastern Wisconsin's Alpine Valley ski resort. Stevie Ray had boarded the aircraft after performing in an enormous blues show at the resort and taking part in an all-star finale jam featuring Eric Clapton, Robert Cray, Jimmie Vaughan and Chicago blues legend Buddy Guy, all of whom ripped it up before an ecstatic crowd of 25,000.

The caravan of blues stars departed from Alpine Valley at two-minute intervals. The first, second and fourth copters landed without incident at Chicago's Meigs Field. The third, bearing members of Clapton's entourage and Stevie Ray, never made it. Poor visibility due to dense fog is prominent among factors blamed for the disaster. (The Austin *American-Statesman* later reports that Federal Aviation Administration records show that the pilot, Jeffrey William Brown, had two previous helicopter accidents.)

By noon, the capital city of Texas is in shock. Vaughan's death is the most devastating blow to the Lone Star State's music community since Lubbock's Buddy Holly died in an Iowa plane crash 31 years earlier. Throughout the afternoon, merchants post signs and banners outside their stores, proclaiming "We Love You Stevie" and "So Long Stevie." Plumbing stores, Tex-Mex restaurants, musical instrument stores, donut shops—all fly the flag of grief in this central Texas town, where Little Stevie Vaughan, the skinny kid from Oak Cliff, became Stevie Ray Vaughan, hometown hero and Austin's musical ambassador to the world.

As night falls, fans begin converging on Zilker Park, where, 10 years earlier, mourners gathered for a candlelight vigil on the night John Lennon was murdered. Now they sit side by side in the darkness—tattooed Chicano bikers, lawyers in Brooks Brothers suits and crystal-wielding New Agers—and weep openly as disc jockey Jody Denberg of Austin's KLBJ radio pumps a steady stream of SRV through a makeshift P.A.

Even as the mourners gather at Zilker Park, others instinctively head to the club Antone's, a focal point of the Austin blues scene throughout the mid Seventies and a favorite hangout of the Vaughan brothers over the years. Local TV stations begin converging on the club, their cameras and microphones focused on SRV intimates, such as club owner Clifford Antone, a close friend to both Vaughan brothers. "I met Stevie when I was 22 and he was 17," he sobs. "I mean, he was my friend, just this little guy who played guitar. The rest is the world's trip, you know?"

Four days later, on Friday, August 31, Stevie's family and friends gather at Laurel Land Memorial Park in Dallas to say their goodbyes. Among those in attendance are Double Trouble's Chris Layton and Tommy Shannon, Bonnie Raitt, Jackson Browne, Stevie Wonder, Jeff Healey and his band, Charlie Sexton, Dr. John, Buddy Guy and ZZ Top's Billy Gibbons, Dusty Hill and Frank Beard.

First to emerge is Stevie Wonder. A hush comes over the crowd as he is led to a sheltered reviewing stand near the grave. The casket is placed in a white hearse, which slowly drives to the site; the mourners follow behind on foot. Jimmie and his mother, Martha, walk with the late guitarist's fiancé, Janna Lapidus. Strolling behind them, heads bowed, are Chris Layton, Tommy Shannon and Kim Wilson. Behind them are Jeff Healey and his band, a tearful Charlie Sexton, Dr. John, ZZ Top's Billy Gibbons, Dusty Hill and Frank Beard, Mark Pollack of the Charley's Guitars store in Dallas, Colin James and Charlie Comer, Stevie Ray's personal friend and publicist for the past eight years. Buddy Guy, overcome with grief, slips out of the chapel into a nearby car.

Bonnie Raitt, Jackson Browne and Stevie Wonder lead the crowd in a sing-along of "Amazing Grace." Bonnie carries the melody as the other two harmonize. When Raitt says, "Take it, Stevie," the magnificent Wonder voice, swooping and swirling around the notes with awesome, emotionally charged power, causes many in the crowd to lose control. Tears flow as his voice soars.

Outside, more than 3,000 of the faithful converge, braving 100-degree temperatures. As the service ends and family and friends depart, the mourners enter the chapel.

One by one, the mourners pass the casket, leaving behind flowers, religious artifacts and guitar picks. Last to come forward is Doug Castor, a young wheelchair-bound fan from Pittsburgh who'd flown to Austin two days ago, only to discover the funeral was in Dallas, 200 miles away. He wheels himself up to the casket and pays his respects to Stevie Ray Vaughan. ✳

NINETEEN '91

Guitar World goes monthly with issues devoted to celebrity lessons, best-album lists and classic rock gods like Page, Blackmore and Beck.

Dear *Guitar World*,

Is Jeff Gilbert an idiot? Why would he think Ratt could rehearse with a bunch of chicks hanging out? Forget it, man. My band tried to rehearse in a rented house with our girlfriends hanging out all the time. After three weeks, the girls made our lives so miserable with their nagging and comments about our music that we broke up with them. And then the band broke up! My new band is doing things my way—*no chicks allowed!*

—Rog Grant

JANUARY In this ultimate tribute to Led Zeppelin Jimmy Page details the making of his band's greatest songs, including the mother of them all, "Stairway to Heaven." "We knew it was really something when we wrote it. I remember we played it at the Los Angeles Forum before the record had even come out, and there was like this standing ovation."

COVER STORIES BY ALAN DI PERNA, JOE BOSSO AND ROBERT GODWIN; PHOTO BY NEAL PRESTON

1991 TOTAL ISSUES: 12

FEBRUARY Ritchie Blackmore gives *Guitar World* a rare, in-depth interview chronicling his entire career—and foreshadows a bit of his future by looking into the past.
COVER STORY BY MORDECHAI KLEIDERMACHER
PHOTO BY BY LORINDA SULLIVAN

MARCH With *Recycler*, ZZ Top look to the future—by going back to their roots. Billy Gibbons explains what first attracted him to the blues.
COVER STORY BY HAROLD STEINBLATT AND BRAD TOLINSKI
PHOTO BY ANN SUMMA

APRIL Steve Vai isn't afraid to blaze new trails—be it on guitar or a new fad called Bungee jumping.
COVER STORY BY BRAD TOLINSKI; PHOTO BY LORINDA SULLIVAN

MAY Mr. Big's Paul Gilbert and Billy Sheehan talk about their new album, *Lean Into It*—and hope that, one day, people will remember a little ballad called "To Be with You."
COVER STORY BY ALAN DI PERNA; PHOTO BY ANN SUMMA

JUNE The 25 Greatest Rock Guitar Records, as selected by the *Guitar World* editors. Among the honorees are the usual suspects, like *Are You Experienced*, *Van Halen* and *Layla*, and a healthy dose of the not-so-obvious, like Elvis Presley's *Sun Sessions*, *The Velvet Underground and Nico* and the Mahavishnu Orchestra's *Birds of Fire*.
COVER STORY BY BRAD TOLINSKI, HAROLD STEINBLATT AND JEFF GILBERT; PHOTO BY BARON WOLMAN

JULY A celebration of blues power with Joe Louis Walker, B.B. and Albert King and a historic joint interview with Jeff Beck and Buddy Guy.
COVER STORY BY CHARLES SHAAR MURRAY
PHOTO BY KEVIN WESTENBERG

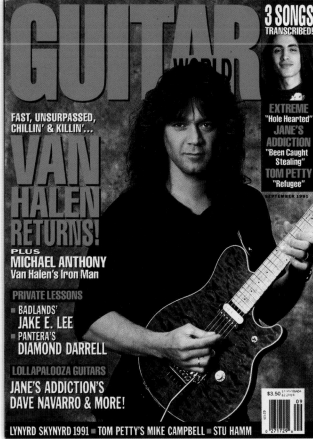

AUGUST After the multi-Platinum success of their debut album, Skid Row crank up the volume on their follow-up, *Slave to the Grind*. "We had four months off before we started working on this record," says Scotti Hill. "All this energy started to build up. I sat home, listened to Pantera's *Cowboys from Hell* and literally went crazy. I was ready to kill."

COVER STORY BY BRAD TOLINSKI; PHOTO BY MARK WEISS

SEPTEMBER Eddie Van Halen tells all about the recording of *For Unlawful Carnal Knowledge*—and how going with the flow is his preferred approach to music. "Whenever I try to plan something out, it never seems to work out. So why plan? It only seems to lead to disappointment."

COVER STORY BY BRAD TOLINSKI; PHOTO BY ANN SUMMA

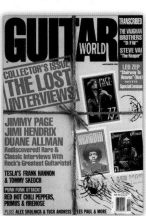

OCTOBER Metallica get set to release the Black Album—shorter songs and all—on an unsuspecting world.
COVER STORY BY JEFF GILBERT AND BRAD TOLINSKI
PHOTO BY ROSS HALFIN

NOVEMBER *Guitar World* uncovers lost interviews with three legends: Jimmy Page, Jimi Hendrix and Duane Allman.
COVER STORIES BY DAVE SCHULPS, JAY RUBY AND
ELLEN MANDEL; PHOTOS BY BOB GRUEN, SCOTT MCDOUGALL,
CARL SMOOL AND LORINDA SULLIVAN

DECEMBER An issue devoted to playing rock, blues and thrash, with Megadeth's Dave Mustaine and Marty Friedman, Johnny Winter, Zakk Wylde and Anthrax's Danny Spitz as guest instructors. For Mustaine, the key to Megadeth's soloing approach is economy. "Less is more—if you play too much, it just sounds like the guitar player's got hornets in his brain."
COVER STORY BY CARLO SEKA; PHOTO BY NEAL PRESTON

LED ZEP LIVES!
Led Zeppelin's "quiet man," **JOHN PAUL JONES** spoke volumes with his masterful bass riffs and eclectic contributions on keyboards and other instruments.

Steady Rolling Man
BY ALAN di PERNA

PHOTOGRAPH BY NEAL PRESTON

JAN. 1991

VOL. 12 / NO. 1

John Paul Jones

In this interview with Alan di Perna, Led Zeppelin bassist John Paul Jones talks about how he worked with his fellow bandmates to create some of the most legendary music in history.

GUITAR WORLD Can you recall the first songs you ever played with Led Zeppelin?

JOHN PAUL JONES The idea for the band was Jimmy Page's, meaning that he came in with the first tunes. He had "Dazed and Confused" and we played "Train Kept a Rollin'." That was the first thing we ever played, actually, at the first rehearsal we ever had—the "try out," as it were.

GW There was certainly a sense at the time that Led Zeppelin was "Jimmy Page's new band." Wasn't it even called the New Yardbirds, initially?

JONES I think we had to be the New Yardbirds for a little while, because there were some contractual obligations to be fulfilled. So we sort of went in as the New Yardbirds on some of the dates that I think maybe the old Yardbirds had already booked.

GW So many archetypal heavy metal moves seem to date from the early period of Led Zeppelin. Like all those riffs where the bass doubles what the guitar's doing, as on "Heartbreaker." Where did that stuff come from?

JONES Jimmy and I both liked blues riffs. You say the bass doubles the guitar. In some cases, of course, it was the guitar doubling the bass. [*laughs*] Things like "Black Dog" are my riffs. Basically we just felt that a particularly effective way of bringing a riff across was to have two instruments doubling it.

GW What prompted Led Zeppelin's interest in odd time signatures around the time of *Houses of the Holy*?

JONES Jimmy and I were always interested in odd time signatures. But it was like we had a "let's do an odd time signature" day. Some songs were just formed that way. Some of them came from Bonzo [*drummer John Bonham*] as well. We'd just find a pattern he would like which would just happen to be in an odd time signature. And then we would write the riff around that. Great fun they were, too.

GW That's the way "The Crunge" came about, I guess.

JONES Oh yes. "The Crunge" is brilliant. "The Crunge" is very tight, really, when you think about it. It's one of my favorites. All the synthesizer lines were done monophonically from an old VCS3.

GW Do you think people tend to fixate, retrospectively, on certain aspects of Led Zeppelin? The heavy rock aspects, for example?

JONES That's right. Especially the heavy rock aspects. I mean, by the third album everybody was saying, "Aww, they've got an acoustic number; they've gone soft." Not realizing that there were two acoustic numbers on the first album. It seems very short sighted. People remember the heaviness and immediately assume that it was created today—which is with a very loud drum sound and lots of electric guitars banging away. But "Babe I'm Gonna Leave You" was an acoustic number, and yet it was heavy. Which was one of the things that was part of Jimmy's vision—using an acoustic guitar in a heavy manner.

GW To what extend did Bonzo's drum style determine what you were doing on bass?

JONES To quite a large extent. Bass players and drummers tend to grow together; it's kind of a marriage, really. You have to listen to each other very carefully. And we did. Bonzo was one of the finest drummers I've ever come across. A joy to play with. And very inspiring. I hope perhaps I inspired him a bit.

GW He was perhaps the most unrelentingly *solid* drummer ever. Was that a very liberating thing for you on bass, in terms of what you could play rhythmically and tonally?

JONES Yes. But then again, I used to enjoy locking into the drums very tightly—I suppose it was my session background. A good session was one where the rhythm section really locked together. In Led Zeppelin, I would listen to the bass drum and be very careful not to cross it or diminish its effectiveness. I really wanted the drums and bass to be as one unit—that's what drove the band along—so for Jimmy and Robert [*Plant, vocals*] there would be a really solid foundation between the bass and the drums that would leave them more free. Robert always used to say that onstage I should stand much nearer the front—get some light on me and all that, from the visual angle. And I would try. I would start at the front and I would just move backward and backward. I would always end up in my favorite position, which was as close to the bass drum as possible. ✳

MAR. '91

FEBRUARY / VOL. 12 / NO. 2

RITCHIE BLACKMORE

In this rare interview—his first in a decade, actually—the Deep Purple/Rainbow legend gives his true feeling about two modern masters, Yngwie Malmsteen and Eddie Van Halen.

GUITAR WORLD What do you think of Yngwie Malmsteen? He's often credited you as an influence.

RITCHIE BLACKMORE He's always been very nice to me, and I always get on very well with him. I don't understand him, though—his playing, what he wears. His movements are also a bit creepy. Normally you say, "Well, the guy's just an idiot." But, when you hear him play, you think, This guy's *no* idiot. He knows what he's doing. He's got to calm down. He's not Paganini—though he thinks he is. When Yngwie can break all of his strings but one, and play the same piece on one string, then I'll be impressed.

In three or four years, we'll probably hear some good stuff from him.

GW What do you think of tapping?

BLACKMORE Thank goodness it's come to an end. The first person I saw doing that hammer-on stuff was Harvey Mandel, at the Whisky a Go-Go in 1968. I thought, What the hell is he doing? It was so funny, [*laughs*] Jim Morrison was carried out because he was shouting abuse at the band. Jimi Hendrix was there. We were all getting drunk. Then Harvey Mandel stars doing this stuff [*mimes tapping*]. "What's he doing?" everybody was saying. Even the audience stopped dancing. Obviously, Eddie Van Halen must have picked up a few of those things.

GW What do you think of Eddie?

BLACKMORE It depends on my mood. He is probably the most influential player in the last 15 years 'cause everybody's one of those, what does he play, Charvel, Carvel...

GW Kramer, with the locking nut.

BLACKMORE Yes, with the locking nut! And everyone's gone hammer-on crazy! So he's obviously done something. He's a great guitar player, but I'm more impressed by his recent songwriting and keyboard work.

The 25 Ultimate Blues CDs

Guitar World's resident blues experts Bill Milkowski and Harold Steinblatt round up the genre's best.

Blind Blake—*Ragtime Guitar's Foremost Fingerpicker*
Clarence Gatemouth Brown—*The Original Peacock Recordings*
The Paul Butterfield Blues Band—*The Paul Butterfield Blues Band*
Albert Collins—*Cold Snap*
Buddy Guy—*A Man and the Blues*
John Lee Hooker—*The Detroit Lion*
Howlin' Wolf—*More Real Folk Blues*
Mississippi John Hurt—*1928 Session*
Elmore Jame—*Shake Your Money Maker*
Blind Lemon Jefferson—*King of the Country Blues Singers*
Blind Willie Johnson—*Praise God I'm Satisfied*
Lonnie Johnson—*Steppin' on the Blues*
Robert Johnson—*The Complete Recordings*
Albert King—*Let's Have a Natural Ball*
B.B. King—*Across the Tracks*
B.B. King—*Live at the Regal*
Freddy King—*Just Pickin'*
Magic Sam—*West Side Soul*
Blind Willie McTell—*1927 - 1933 The Early Years*
Little Milton—*The Sun Masters*
Hound Dog Taylor and the Houserockers—*Beware of the Dog*
Stevie Ray Vaughan and Double Trouble—*In Step*
T-Bone Walker—*The Complete Recordings 1940 - 1954*
Muddy Waters—*The Chess Box*
Johnny Winter—*3rd Degree*

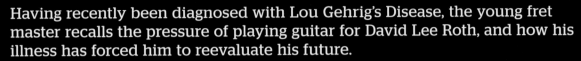

The Young Lion

When he joined forces with **David Lee Roth.**

JASON BECKER successfully wrestled with the giant shadows of Steve Vai and Eddie Van Halen. Now, a brilliant album behind him, he faces even greater battles ahead.

JASON BECKER

Having recently been diagnosed with Lou Gehrig's Disease, the young fret master recalls the pressure of playing guitar for David Lee Roth, and how his illness has forced him to reevaluate his future.

GUITAR WORLD What were your feelings on stepping into a guitar slot that had formerly been occupied by people like Steve Vai and Eddie Van Halen?

JASON BECKER It was great. I couldn't think about it too much, because I'd just go crazy, thinking, Wow, am I playing as well as Vai? Am I playing as well as Van Halen? The only thing I could do to keep sane was just keep saying, They hired me because they liked what I do, so I'm just going to go ahead. No one held Vai or Van Halen over my head, either.

GW After the record, *A Little Ain't Enough*, was finished, you had to turn down touring with Dave because of your condition.

BECKER Yeah. It wasn't like I would have under any other circumstances. I was just forced to. It's really hard for me to walk. I need a cane, and that barely works. So I couldn't put that physical strain on myself. And with Dave, it would have to be a show. So that was really too bad. We were both bummed about that. But I think I'll work with Dave again, maybe on his next record. We're still friends.

GW When did your illness begin?

BECKER I first started feeling it maybe half a year before the Dave thing.

GW Is this something that's eventually going to affect your playing?

BECKER That's a good question. I'm not going to think about it. I'm just going to do as much as I can. I have to work on taking care of it. It has a lot to do with the mind, I think. I'm kind of approaching it that way. But it's all right. I don't feel too bad. It definitely won't affect my songwriting, put it that way.

Bosso Moves On; Tolinski Moves In

The May 1991 issue marked the most significant editorial change in *Guitar World*'s history—the promotion of Brad Tolinski to editor-in-chief. The previous editor, Joe Bosso, took on an A&R position at Polydor Records, where he signed the post-hardcore band Quicksand (and has since returned to the *Guitar World* family as a writer). Brad came to *Guitar World* in the September 1989 issue as associate editor after a short stint as editor of **GW**'s then-sister publication *Keyboard Magazine*, and has reigned atop the masthead ever since the May '91 issue. It is Brad's unwavering vision and commitment to *Guitar World* that has not only kept the magazine thriving all these years, but has broadened the franchise to include DVD products, online efforts and digital ventures.

MAY '91

PUBLISHER
...y R. Harris

...E PUBLISHER
...s S. Page

...LISHER/ADVERT
Greg Di Benedetto

EDITOR-IN-CHIEF
Brad Tolinski

DESIGN DIRECTOR

ZAKK KNOWS.

ROCK HARDER and SHRED FASTER in your GUITAR WORLD T-Shirt! ONLY $12.95!

DARE TO BE WYLDE!

AUG. '91

Holy Shirt!

In 1991, *Guitar World* went into the business of selling T-shirts—and when we needed a model to pose in the advertisement, which debuted in the August issue, we knew it had to be a skinny blonde. But instead of using some hot babe from an agency, we called on our friend Zakk Wylde (when he could still fit into a medium T-shirt and 30-inch jeans) to help us sell our wares.

Jeff Hanneman/Slayer

Scott Ian/Anthrax

Kerry King/Slayer

Dave Mustaine/Megadeth

AUG. 1991

VOL. 12 / NO. 8

Jeff Hanneman, Dave Mustaine & Scott Ian

As the Clash of the Titans tour continues its history-making trek across the U.S., three kings of thrash sit with *Guitar World*'s Jeff Gilbert for a shocking conversation that's sure to ruffle a few feathers across the rock and metal scenes.

GUITAR WORLD Do you object to the use of the term "thrash" to describe your music?

DAVE MUSTAINE Speaking for myself, I think we're a little deeper than just thrash.

SCOTT IAN Yeah, we're all titans now. [*laughter all around*] A certain element of our music is thrash—but that doesn't tell the whole story. If it did, we wouldn't even have to play—we could just turn a speed drill on and record it. That would be the ultimate thrash record.

JEFF HANNEMAN Also, there's a shitload of thrash bands out there that mean nothing. I don't even know what thrash is anymore.

GW What would you consider to be the worst trend in thrash metal right now?

IAN There are so many bands out there who sound like that, and they sell a ton of records, but I just don't understand—it makes me sick. Of course, in any type of music, there are always clones. We've been on tour with bands who might as well have looked exactly like us. They might as well have been wearing goatees.

MUSTAINE Everybody is copying one particular band—and I think we all know who we're talking about. I listen to the radio and everybody sounds like this singer, everybody does the same chord chunk. It's cool to be safe and dance in somebody's footsteps in paint-by-numbers steps on the floor. Granted, Scott's band and my band play a lot of the same chord progressions, but a lot of bands rip that off *exactly*. And they rip off...I'll call them "M." It blows me away. Why not just call your band "Metallibabies"?

IAN None of the three bands represented here sound like Metallica—or each other. I can't name four or five bands outside those four who don't sound like at least one of us. Sometimes we write a riff and think, That sounds like Metallica. So we don't use it.

MUSTAINE It's like those Bullet fags [*Bullet Boys*] that sound just like David Lee Roth.

IAN And Cinderella. You can listen to their records and literally pick out the riffs they took from AC/DC's *Highway to Hell*.

GW So who do you think is the worst band in metal?

IAN Metallica. [*laughs*]

MUSTAINE I hate to point fingers, but Queensrÿche are fag yuppie metal now. It's the same way with Guns N' Roses. I hate those mothers, though *Appetite for Destruction* is a great album. Slash is absolutely one of the better blues-based guitarists on the rock scene.

GW So who are the new children of thrash?

MUSTAINE I don't have any children that I know of. [*laughs*]

GW What about Testament?

MUSTAINE Who? You mean the guys who are ripping off our drum riser and stage moves, and copying all of Metallica's sounds and singing like James Hetfield?

IAN And with dance steps laid out on the stage on how to have stage presence. But we didn't mention the name. You did.

MUSTAINE This magazine called them the Lennon and McCartney of thrash, but aren't they more like Simon and Garfunkel?

IAN All I've got to say is, where would they be without these three bands and Metallica? I just find Testament hard to even take seriously. Whatever they do, I suppose they do it well, but it just isn't them. Every time you hear them on the radio, you think Metallica.

HANNEMAN I heard them the other day and I could have sworn it was Metallica.

GW With thrash metal getting tons of mainstream acceptance—meaning Grammy nominations, big money tours, TV show appearances—do you think the genre is in danger of becoming too respectable?

MUSTAINE I don't really think respect is something that we're really looking to achieve. As soon as we get approval, we're going to screw it right back up by doing something else to piss you off. That's the nature of the beast. We like to keep people on their toes. We get respect by doing our jobs and not confirming. Yeah, it was kind of depressing to have to alter the length of "Hangar 18" to get on Arsenio Hall's show, but I don't think that any of these three bands have made any major, obvious compromises. ✳

METAL DETECTOR

When Marc Sides and Keith Whitman, two teen-age metal devotees from New Jersey, read a glowing review of Marc Ribot's avant garde Rootless Cosmopol-

appropriately hostile compl offices. We contacted the t pissed off" readers and re, yeah? Let's see you do the agreed, with the following everything we send them m and heavy. This is the first in their review column.

SKRAPP METTLE *Sensitive* (I joke! Maybe if these guys los ons, they could make some ★ (for showing up)

DEVASTATION *Idolatry* (Co nite arm-twisting, bone-crus in-your-brain double bass w metal grooves. Yes, this is a

THE COUP DE GRACE *The Cou* (Red Decibel Records) A de hard-hitting heavy metal, w stylings from a cornucopia influences. ★★★½

NINETEEN '92

Slash and Nuno dominate the covers as *Guitar World* continues to celebrate guitar legends of the past, present and—hello, Diamond Darrell and Kim Thayil—future.

Dear *Guitar World*,

Randy Rhoads, Jimi Hendrix, Cliff Burton and Duane Allman are just a few of the many great musicians who died relatively early in their careers. My esteemed colleagues and I have therefore calculated that Nelson will live forever.

—Jeremy Simmons

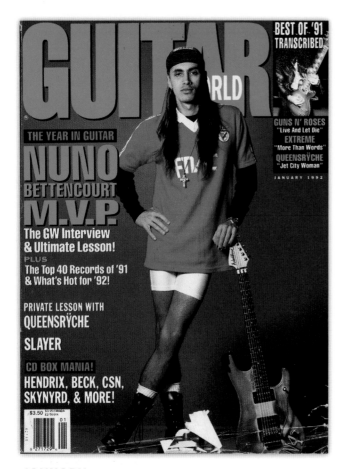

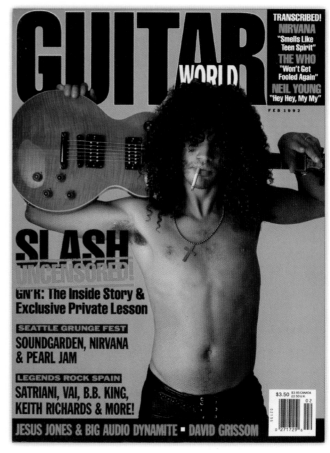

JANUARY *Guitar World*'s Player of the Year, Nuno Bettencourt, comments on the Red Hot Chili Peppers, who once accused Extreme of ripping them off. "Who's that? Oh yeah, those are the guys that had a hit with that Stevie Wonder tune. I don't usually buy records by bands that aren't able to write their own material."

COVER STORY BY BRAD TOLINSKI; PHOTO BY LORINDA SULLIVAN

FEBRUARY As the sprawling *Use Your Illusion* records race up the charts, Slash comments on the mysterious departure of his co-guitarist, Izzy Stradlin. "I just can't understand how he could let something like this just fall apart. I mean, the guy didn't want to tour or do videos; he hardly wanted to record. I just never thought he was one of those guys that this would happen with."

COVER STORY BY ALAN DI PERNA; PHOTO BY ANN SUMMA

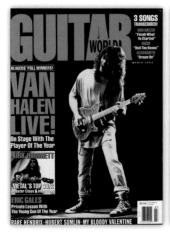

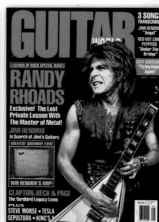

MARCH In this rare interview with all four members of Van Halen, the rockers discuss the ins and outs of playing live. As far as Eddie is concerned, onstage happiness is a matter of math.
COVER STORY BY BRAD TOLINSKI
PHOTO BY LARRY DIMARZIO

APRIL Spinal Tap's David St. Hubbins, Derek Smalls and Nigel Tufnel engage in an enlightening discussion about the changeover from vinyl to CDs, and how to solve the problem of not being able to play a CD in reverse to hear backward messages.
COVER STORY BY TEISCO DEL RAY
PHOTO BY ANN SUMMA

MAY *Guitar World* uncovers a Seventies-era private lesson with Randy Rhoads.
COVER STORY BY WOLF MARSHALL; PHOTO ILLUSTRATION BY FRANCISCO CACERES/PAUL NATKIN

JULY Joe Satriani recalls how the recording of *The Extremist* nearly ended his studio career.
COVER STORY BY ALAN DI PERNA
PHOTO BY ALDO MAURO

AUGUST Black Sabbath's Tony Iommi, the Godfather of Metal, and Metallica's James Hetfield, thrash pioneer, meet face to face for the first time in this historic *GW* interview. In a moment Hetfield will never forget, Iommi shows him which fingertips were damaged in a factory accident in the Sixties.
COVER STORY BY BRAD TOLINSKI AND ALAN PAUL; PHOTO BY LORINDA SULLIVAN

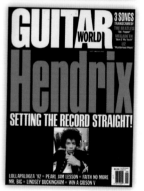

SEPTEMBER The inside story of the recording of Jimi Hendrix's *Axis: Bold As Love* and *Electric Ladyland*.
COVER STORY BY JOHN MCDERMOTT AND EDDIE KRAMER; PHOTO BY TONY GALE

JUNE *Guitar World* celebrates the new generation of hard rock with a roundtable discussion between members of Soundgarden, Skid Row and Pantera. Soundgarden's Kim Thayil comments on his unorthodox style of lead playing. "It's hard to trace where my lead playing comes from. Even though I'm Indian, I didn't grow up listening to Ravi Shankar or anything. My playing just evolved from experimentation."

COVER STORY BY BRAD TOLINSKI; PHOTO BY KEVIN WESTENBERG

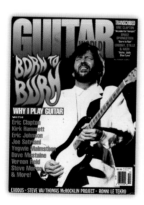

OCTOBER A host of legendary guitarists explain why they are "born to burn."
COVER STORY BY JENNY BOYD, PH.D., HOLLY GEORGE-WARREN AND HAROLD STEINBLATT; PHOTO BY PHILIP OLLERENSHAW

NOVEMBER Gilby Clarke becomes a permanent member of the Guns N' Roses family.
COVER STORY BY BRAD TOLINSKI; PHOTO BY ROBERT JOHN

DECEMBER Extreme's Nuno Bettencourt closes out 1992 with his second *Guitar World* cover story of the year—only this time, he elects to pose without his guitar.
COVER STORY BY BRAD TOLINSKI; PHOTO BY LORINDA SULLIVAN

1992 TOTAL ISSUES: 12

t enough. People can relate to

easonable enough, consider-
evermind, the Seattle trio's
l debut, has become one of
t out-of-the-box albums in the
eled by the contagious hit sin-
ls Like Teen Spirit," the spir-
turned gold a mere five weeks
lease, and leaped past both
ses' *Illusions* just one month
heir sudden, platinum-bound
probably has more to do with
infectious, dirty riffs and wry
oks than with the roughly
ut-of-tune guitars, of which
so proud.
nd like the Bay City Rollers
sault by Black Sabbath," con-
guitarist in his nasty smoker's
," he expectorates, "we vom-
better than *anyone!*"
began their career with
each (Sub Pop), an intensely
nelange of untuned metal,
and Seventies pop, written
erspective of a college drop-
bum's *other* notable distinc-
hat it was recorded in three
600. *Nevermind*, costing con-
ore than six bills, is Nirvana's
I, power-punk/pop master-
sh in slashing, ragged guitar
d lyrics and more teen spirit

FEB. 1992

VOL. 13 / NO. 2

Kurt Cobain

**As grunge begins to pose a major threat to hard rock and metal, Kurt Cobain tries
to explain to *Guitar World*'s Jeff Gilbert why Nirvana, third-hand guitars and all, is**

"We're just musically and rhythmically retarded," asserts Kurt Cobain, guitarist, vocalist and chief songwriter for Nirvana. "We play so hard that we can't tune our guitars fast enough. People can relate to that."

Seems reasonable enough, considering that *Nevermind*, the Seattle trio's major label debut, has become one of the hottest out-of-the-box albums in the country. Fueled by the contagious hit single, "Smells Like Teen Spirit," the spirited album turned Gold a mere five weeks after its release, and leaped past both volumes of Guns N' Roses' *Use Your Illusion* just one month later. But their sudden, Platinum-bound popularity probably has more to do with the band's infectious, dirty riffs and wry lyrical hooks than with their roughly played, out-of-tune guitars, of which Cobain is so proud.

"We sound like the Bay City Rollers after an assault by Black Sabbath," continues the guitarist in his nasty smoker's hack. "And," he expectorates, "we vomit onstage better than anyone!"

Nirvana began their career with 1989's *Bleach* (Sub Pop), an intensely physical mélange of untuned metal, drunk punk and Seventies pop, written from the perspective of a college dropout. The album's other notable distinction was that it was recorded in three days for $600. *Nevermind*, costing considerably more than six bills, is Nirvana's major-label, power-punk/pop masterpiece, awash in slashing, ragged guitar riffs, garbled lyrics and more teen spirit than you can shake a Kiss record at.

GUITAR WORLD MTV thinks Nirvana is a metal band.

KURT COBAIN That's fine; let them be fooled! I don't have anything against *Headbanger's Ball*, but it's strange to see our faces on MTV.

GW Metallica's Kirk Hammett is a huge Nirvana fan.

COBAIN That's real flattering. We met him recently and he's a real nice guy. We talked about the Sub Pop scene, heavy metal and guitars.

GW Speaking of guitars, you seem to favor low-end models.

COBAIN I don't favor them—it's just that I can afford them. [*laughs*] I'm left-handed, and it's not very easy to find reasonably priced, high-quality left-handed guitars. But out of all the guitars in the whole world, the Fender Mustang is my favorite. I've only owned two of them.

GW What is it about the Mustang that works for you?

COBAIN They're cheap and totally inefficient, and they sound like crap. They are also very small and don't stay in tune, and when you want to raise the string action on the fretboard, you have to loosen all the strings and completely remove the bridge. You have to turn these little screws with your fingers and hope that you've estimated it right. If you screw up, you have to repeat the process over and over until you get it right. Whoever invented that guitar was a dork.

GW Is the Mustang your only guitar?

COBAIN No, I own a '66 Jaguar. That's the guitar I polish and baby—I refuse to let anyone touch it when I jump into the crowd. [*laughs*] Lately, I've been using a Strat live, because I don't want to ruin my Mustang yet. I like to use Japanese Strats because they're a bit cheaper, and the frets are smaller than the American version's.

GW The acoustic guitar you play on "Polly" sounds flat.

COBAIN That's a 20-dollar junk shop Stella—I didn't bother changing the strings. [*laughs*] It barely stays in tune. In fact, I have to use duct tape to hold the tuning keys in place.

GW Considering how violently you play the guitar, you probably use pretty heavy-duty strings.

COBAIN Yeah. And I keep blowing up amplifiers, so I use whatever I can find at junk shops—junk is always best.

GW What was the last amp you blew up?

COBAIN A Crown power amp that was intended for use as a P.A., but which I used for a guitar head because I can never find an amp that's powerful enough—and because I don't want to have to deal with hauling 10 Marshall heads. I'm lazy—I like to have it all in one package. For a preamp I have a Mesa/Boogie, and I turn all the mid-range up. And I use Radio Shack speakers.

GW Ever get the urge to use a twang bar?

COBAIN No. Anybody that plays guitar knows that only Jimi Hendrix was able to use the standard tremolo and still keep it in tune. Those things are totally worthless. I do have one on a Japanese Strat, but I don't use it.

GW Your first album, *Bleach*, was recorded for $600; how much did *Nevermind* run you?

COBAIN [*laughs*] I don't remember; I've got Alzheimer's. And don't ask us how much our video cost; that's a hell of an embarrassment. ✱

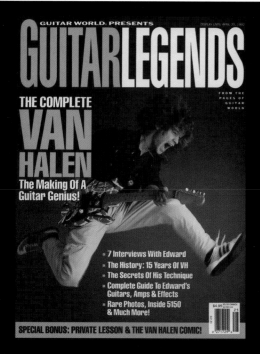

MARCH / VOL. 13 / NO. 3

THE PREMIERE OF
GUITAR LEGENDS

Eddie Van Halen is the first to get the royal treatment in *Guitar World*'s new sister publication.

IN THE 18 YEARS SINCE its debut, *Guitar Legends* magazine has been the gold standard for special issues dedicated to a single artist or genre. Over the years we've devoted issues of *Guitar Legends* to a wide range of subjects, including Stevie Ray Vaughan, Randy Rhoads, Kiss, Dimebag Darrell, Iron Maiden, southern rock, punk rock, thrash metal and grunge. Each issue contains interviews and articles from the pages of *Guitar World*, plus guitar and bass transcriptions to some of the world's best-known songs.

For Volume 1, Number 1 of this new publication, the *Guitar World* editors went with Eddie Van Halen as the cover-to-cover subject. Across 98 pages, the issue offered numerous interviews with the King, articles on his primary gear, a timeline history of the events leading to Van Halen's formation and rise to rock power, and even a private lesson in which EVH demos some of his trademark licks.

But perhaps the issue's most unique piece of content was the seven-page comic book in the middle chronicling Eddie's legendary guest solo appearance on the Michael Jackson song "Beat It" (and how, in the end, Eddie received a big-fat nothing as payment). The comic, scripted by Brad Tolinski and illustrated by comic artist Stan Shaw, depicted the story of Eddie receiving a phone call from producer Quincy Jones, who called to ask Ed if he would play on a Michael Jackson song, and Ed going into the studio with Quincy, Michael— and Bubbles, Jackson's pet chimp—to lay down the "Beat It" solo.

MAY '92

Hometown Hero: Jeff Loomis

Regular readers of *Guitar World* should be well familiar with the name Jeff Loomis. The Nevermore guitarist has been in the magazine numerous times in recent years, served as a columnist on two occasions, and even filmed a successful *Guitar World* instructional DVD in 2009 called *Super Shred Guitar*. Jeff's history with the magazine actually dates back to 1992, when he was featured as a Hometown Hero in the May issue. To be a Hometown Hero, players had to submit a cassette tape showcasing their six-string abilities along with a bio and a black-and-white photo, and the best of the best would make it to the magazine each month. Loomis' three-song tape wowed the editors, prompting them to give the 20-year-old Seattle native the recognition he so deserved.

Guitarists from MORBID ANGEL, OBITUARY and DEATH celebrate death metal's rise from the depths of obscurity.
THE LOST BOYS
BY JEFF KITTS
PHOTOGRAPHY BY ALEX MCKNIGHT
LETTERING BY STEVEN CERIO
CHUCK SCHULDINER OF DEATH
RICHARD BRUNELLE OF MORBID ANGEL
ALLEN WEST OF OBITUARY

NOVEMBER / VOL. 13 / NO. 11

FLORIDA DEATH METAL SUMMIT

Members of Death, Obituary and Morbid Angel join forces in a historic roundtable; Deicide declines the invitation.

WHEN *GUITAR WORLD* FIRST proposed convening a death metal roundtable, those close to the bands responded with pure skepticism: "It'll never happen—they all hate each other."

The "they" in question were key members of Death, Obituary, Morbid Angel and Deicide, the unchallenged kings of the Florida death metal scene. And it was true that no such gathering of the gods of grind had previously been attempted. But in death metal, as in life, there's a first time for everything. *Guitar World* extended the invitations, hoping that the bands could overcome their reported animosities—their hatred—to engage in a nice, guitar-related chat about death metal, past, present and future.

Death, Obituary and Morbid Angel accepted our invitation, while Deicide declined. The meeting took place in the summer of 1992 at Tampa's Morrisound Studios, the most important death metal recording facility in the world. On hand were Death's Chuck Schuldiner, Obituary's Allen West, Morbid Angel's Richard Brunelle and *Guitar World* contributing editor Jeff Kitts.

"This coverage is a good opportunity for bands like ours," said Schuldiner. "It does a lot for the genre, and it means we're starting to be taken seriously. If Glen [*Benton, Deicide's bassist/vocalist*] doesn't want to be here, that's his right. But by not being here, he's only feeding a negative vibe that already exists in the public eye. He should learn to put personal things aside, and get together with the rest of us. Maybe it would change the way people look at the scene."

Cat and Mouth

DEC. '92

Cat Fight!

Dave Mustaine and Brian Setzer bare their claws in the December issue.

When Megadeth's Dave Mustaine learned that his partner, Marty Friedman, had taken lessons from the Stray Cats' Brian Setzer, he had this to say: "If Setzer's coaching Marty, he's doing a damn good job. But it sure doesn't show in his own playing. I think he better have another dose of hairspray." Setzer responded thusly: "Marty came over a few months ago, and although I don't give lessons, it definitely *was* a lesson. If Dave can't handle that, who cares? He was thrown out of Metallica, and admits that his entire group has to go to therapy to deal with him. He's spent the last three years in a coma. And I think we all know who the hair farmer is..."

Jingle Bell Rock

SOON it Will Be Christmas, and Guitar Heroes everywhere will Be making A List and checking it Twice. Below, some of the Fellas Reveal THEiR Favorite gift Ideas. Yule Love it!

EVERY YEAR, MOST of us spend the weeks before December 25 engaged in a peculiarly Hellish activity: choosing and buying X-mas gifts. We at Guitar World thought we might make things easier for our readers by looking into how some of their favorite players deal with their gift-giving blues. Each guitarist was asked to respond to the following two questions:

1) If he had to select a single album to give to a friend for X-mas, what would it be?

2) What would he want in return? (Answers to this question were not limited to albums; anything—stuffed animals, bowling ball bags, Steakum—was deemed acceptable.)

We'd like to thank the artists for cooperating in our little survey, and for providing all of us with gifts galore the entire year round.

ILLUSTRATIONS BY Danny Hellman

JOE SATRIANI
1) *Dirt*—Alice In Chains
2) The deed to Electric Lady Studios.

DIAMOND DARRELL (PANTERA)
1) *Plaid*—Blues Saraceno
2) Some time alone in my eight-track studio.

ROBBY KRIEGER
1) *Giant Steps*—John Coltrane
2) *Milagre*—Santana

PAUL STANLEY (KISS)
1) *Led Zeppelin*—Led Zeppelin
2) A 1959 Sunburst Les Paul

BRUCE KULICK (KISS)
1) *Beckology*—Jeff Beck
2) Jimi Hendrix's entire Woodstock performance.

GENE SIMMONS (KISS)
1) *Meantime*—Helmet
2) Your mother.

DAVE "THE SNAKE" SABO (SKID ROW)
1) *Pandora's Box*—Aerosmith
2) A sulfuric acid enema from Slymenstra Hymen (GWAR).

SCOTTI HILL (SKID ROW)
1) *Back In Black*—AC/DC
2) Either a) to be Ruler Of The Universe, or b) a train set.

LEMMY (MOTÖRHEAD)
1) Little Richard's Greatest Hits
2) A Rolls-Royce.

ALBERT COLLINS
1) *Showdown*—Albert Collins, Johnny Copeland and Robert Cray
2) A video camera.

PAUL GILBERT (MR. BIG)
1) *Ingenue*—K.D. Lang
2) Some mangoes.

BILLY SHEEHAN (MR. BIG)
1) The Everly Brothers Greatest Hits
2) *Blood Rock*—Blood Rock, on CD.

K.K. DOWNING (JUDAS PRIEST)
1) *Tyr*—Black Sabbath
2) A Yamaha snowmobile.

PAGE HAMILTON (HELMET)
1) *A Love Supreme*—John Coltrane
2) A violin.

ADRIAN LEGG
1) The Bach Double Violin Concerto
2) A hit record!

TREY AZAGTHOTH (MORBID ANGEL)
1) *Baptism*—Laibach
2) To jam with Eddie Van Halen.

TED NUGENT (DAMN YANKEES)
1) *Don't Tread*—Damn Yankees
2) A year off with my family.

BEN SHEPARD (SOUNDGARDEN)
1) *Dry Lungs* - 2 CD compilation (to George Bush)
2) If I want it, I already have it.

JACK BLADES (DAMN YANKEES)
1) *White Album*—The Beatles
2) *There's A Riot Going On*—Sly Stone

TOMMY SHAW (DAMN YANKEES)
1) *Abbey Road*—The Beatles
2) Anything from Bobby Moore and the Rhythm Aces.

EDWARD VAN HALEN
1) Anything by Van Halen.
2) Anything by Van Halen.

GARY HOLT (EXODUS)
1) *Double Live Gonzo*—Ted Nugent
2) A 1959 Les Paul.

DECEMBER 1992/GUITAR WORLD

DEC.1992

VOL. 13 / NO. 12

Jingle Bell Rock

A bevy of guitar heroes reveal their favorite gift ideas for the 1992 holiday season.

Every year, most of us spend the weeks before December 25 engaged in a particularly hellish activity: choosing and buying Christmas gifts. We at *Guitar World* thought we might make things easier for our readers by looking into how some of their favorite players deal with their gift-giving blues. Each guitarist was asked to respond to the following two questions:

1) If he had to select a single album to give to a friend for Christmas, what would it be?
2) What would he want in return?

Joe Satriani
1) *Dirt*—Alice in Chains
2) The deed to Electric Lady Studios

Diamond Darrell
1) *Plaid*—Blues Saraceno
2) Some time alone in my eight-track studio

Robby Krieger
1) *Giant Steps*—John Coltrane
2) *Milagro*—Santana

Paul Stanley
1) *Led Zeppelin*—Led Zeppelin
2) A 1959 Sunburt Les Paul

Gene Simmons
1) *Meantime*—Helmet
2) Your mother

Lemmy Kilmister
1) *Little Richard's Greatest Hits*
2) A Rolls-Royce

Paul Gilbert
1) *Ingenue*—k.d. lang
2) Some mangoes

K.K. Downing
1) *Tyr*—Black Sabbath
2) A Yamaha snowmobile

Trey Azagthoth
1) *Baptism*—Laibach
2) To jam with Eddie Van Halen

Ted Nugent
1) *Don't Tread*—Damn Yankees
2) A year off with my family

Edward Van Halen
1) Anything by Van Halen
2) Anything by Van Halen

Kim Thayil
1) *Badmotorfinger*—Soundgarden
2) My two front teeth

Eric Johnson
1) *Letter from Home*—Pat Metheny
2) Peace and tranquility

Zakk Wylde
1) *Dreams*—The Allman Brothers Band
2) A one-year supply of dog food for five dogs and a one-year supply of diapers

Ritchie Blackmore
1) Any Christmas selection of or by Mannheim Steamroller and "Snoopy vs. the Red Baron" by the Royal Guardsman
2) See number 1

Warren Haynes
1) *The Otis Redding Story* to a non-guitar player; *Blow by Blow*—Jeff Beck, to a guitar player
2) George Bush out of the White House

Steve Morse
1) A compilation tape featuring the greatest solos of Jeff Beck, Eric Clapton, Jimmy Page, Eddie Van Halen, Joe Walsh, Buddy Guy, B.B. King and a whole lot of other guys.
2) The ability to look forward to every new day

Scott Ian
1) *It Takes a Nation of Millions to Hold Us Back*—Public Enemy
2) Madonna

Carlos Santana
1) *Sketches of Spain*—Miles Davis
2) *Band of Gypsys*—Jimi Hendrix

Rocky George
1) *Tribal Tech*—Scott Henderson
2) A 1963 mint-condition Corvette

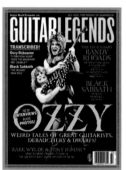

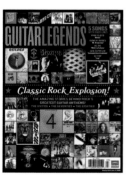

GUITAR LEGENDS 1992–2010

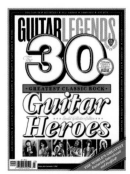

NINETEEN '93

The magazine makes bass lines a standard of every transcription, grants ample space to the guitar stars of tomorrow (welcome, Tom Morello and Billy Corgan) and compiles greatest-album lists galore.

Dear *Guitar World*,

It was a day like any other. We were
flipping through the January 1993 issue
and savoring each picture—until we
shrieked in horror as we glanced at Angus
Young's butt. After we tore out the page
and burned it, the rest of the magazine
was perfect.

—Josh Johnson and Chat Dressen

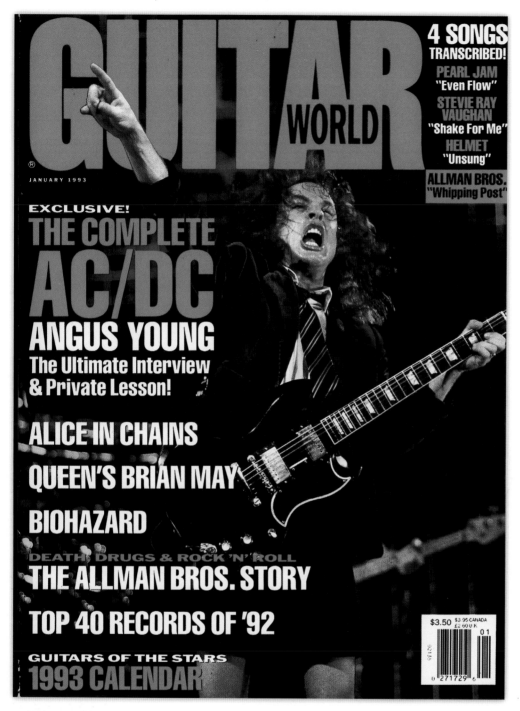

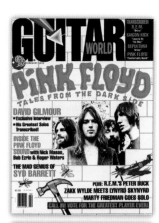

JANUARY Angus Young and AC/DC are certainly known for putting their all into their live show—sometimes more than they'd like. "I've had my pants fall off," says Young. "All of a sudden my wedding tackle was out there for all to see."

COVER STORY BY ALAN DI PERNA; PHOTO BY BOB LEAFE

1993 TOTAL ISSUES: 12

FEBRUARY Impeccable Pink Floyd guitarist David Gilmour offers a retrospective look at the band's remarkable, quarter-century career.
COVER STORY BY ALAN DI PERNA
PHOTO BY MICHAEL OCHS

MARCH In a roundtable of rage celebrating the guitar stars of tomorrow, *Guitar World* unites three thunderous players behind the industrial strength sounds of Ministry, Helmet and Sepultura.
COVER STORY BY BRAD TOLINSKI
AND JEFF KITTS
PHOTOS BY LORINDA SULLIVAN,
JOE GIRON AND LARRY DIMARZIO

APRIL Living Colour's outspoken guitarist sits down with Robert Fripp, the father of progressive rock guitar, for a provocative, wide-ranging conversation.
COVER STORY BY ROBERT FRIPP
PHOTO BY KRISTINE LARSEN

MAY Jimmy Page and David Coverdale—two of English rock's most respected squires—unite for a surprisingly vital and original album.

COVER STORY BY BRAD TOLINSKI WITH GREG DI BENEDETTO; PHOTO BY NORMAN SEEFF

JUNE *Guitar World* examines the delicate art of playing acoustic guitar and finds out what makes acoustic masters like Eric Clapton and Neil Young tick.

COVER STORIES BY ALEX COLETTI AND GARY GRAFF; PHOTOS BY BRIAN RASIC AND JAY BLAKESBERG

JULY
On *The Sound of White Noise*, Anthrax's Scott Ian and Danny Spitz crank out another helping of heavy duty, blue-collar riffs even as they prepare for blue-chip super-stardom.
COVER STORY BY ALAN DI PERNA
PHOTO BY LORINDA SULLIVAN

AUGUST
Pantera's Dimebag Darrell and Skid Row's Dave "The Snake" Sabo come face to face with Ace Frehley and engage in some serious guitar-hero worship.
COVER STORY BY JEFF KITTS
PHOTO BY LORINDA SULLIVAN

SEPTEMBER
He has a new band (Vai), a new singer (Devin Townsend) and a new album (*Sex and Religion*). But Steve Vai remains his same old, obsessed, guitar hero self.
COVER STORY BY ALAN DI PERNA
PHOTO BY LARRY DIMARZIO

OCTOBER
Guitar World goes classic rock mad with this issue devoted to the real stories behind legendary songs like "Light My Fire," "Free Bird," "Stairway to Heaven" and more, plus the 25 most influential albums of all time.
COVER STORIES BY VARIOUS

NOVEMBER
Joe Satriani assesses the development and current state of rock guitar, and answers the question, "Is shred really dead?"
COVER STORY BY ALAN DI PERNA
PHOTO BY MICHAEL SEXTON

DECEMBER
Led Zeppelin's legendary guitarist Jimmy Page discusses the magic, mystery and music of one of rock's most enduring bands.
COVER STORY BY BRAD TOLINSKI WITH GREG DI BENEDETTO
PHOTO BY NEIL ZLOZOWER

ALICE IN CHAINS' JERRY CANTRELL CLEANS UP HIS ACT AND HITS PAY DIRT

RAIN MAN

BY JEFF GILBERT
PHOTOGRAPH THIS PAGE CHRIS CUFARO
PHOTOGRAPH THAT PAGE MARTY TEMME

JAN.1993

VOL. 14 / NO. 1

Jerry Cantrell

Alice in Chains' moody guitarist discusses how the band exorcised some of its most

GUITAR WORLD With a new album, two hit songs, "Would?" and "Them Bones," and the *Singles* movie out at the same time, you certainly are in an enviable position. Talk about hitting the ground running...

JERRY CANTRELL Exactly. It couldn't be any better for us; we're in a real good spot right now. A lot of it was planned, but most of it was luck—it all came together at the right time. And *Singles* is a great movie, real nice and pleasant. I'm totally in love with Bridget Fonda.

GW Same here. So let's begin with your new album, *Dirt*.

CANTRELL It turned out so damn good...

GW Was it any more difficult in the studio for you this time around, especially in terms of any extra pressure your success with *Facelift* may have created?

CANTRELL No. It was a lot easier because we really didn't think about how we wanted the songs to go down. We went in with the basic idea, but stayed more true to the demo tapes than we did the first time. This album was a lot more free-form, like, "Let's just throw out some ideas, and just put something down." We kept doing it. All of these ideas kept piling up, and by the time it was done, it was just so fucking massive it blew me away. I was really proud to be in this band and playing with Layne [*Staley, singer*], Sean [*Kinney, drummer*] and Mike [*Starr, bassist*]. They rock.

GW *Dirt* is heavier than *Facelift* and quite a bit darker. Some of the song titles—well, they might lead people to draw certain conclusions about the band. If nothing else, the album seems very personal.

CANTRELL You're right. It is very personal, especially the songs on the second half—"Junkhead," "God Smack" and "Sickman." They were written as a trilogy-type thing, actually a story, all the way from "Junkhead" to "Angry Chair." "Junkhead" is a pretty blatant song—it sounds like we're flying the flag for drug use. But the whole point is that a lot of people believe that it's great to go out and get fucked up; they reflect the attitude of somebody who's partying and using. "God Smack" starts getting into the realization of what the fuck is really up, and the story moves all the way down into "Angry Chair" and "Hate to Feel," where you realize that this is not the right way to live. Taken as a whole, it's a really positive thing, but a lot of people will probably take it out of context.

GW It sounds like you're purging a lot of internal poisons with these songs.

CANTRELL That's the whole thing. Without getting too heavy into this whole drug thing, our music has always been an outlet for feelings that we can't or won't express verbally. People hold things in, and we do, too; we're no different than anybody else. Holding those bad feelings in will just eat you away. We're lucky to have an outlet that we can put this stuff into, and I think that's why a lot of people can relate to our music—it really means something to us. It's an exorcising of demons. I think the majority of our fans understand that, and by listening to us, purge some stuff themselves. Something doesn't have to be physical to be addictive.

GW What would you say is most distinctive about Alice in Chains? Layne's vocals are unique, as is your approach to the guitar and sound.

CANTRELL I think both of those things are distinctive—and they go hand in hand. Our music has grown more because we've grown more. The guitar riffs on "Hate to Feel" and "Angry Chair" are some of the sickest riffs on the album, and those are Layne's songs—he wrote those on guitar and he plays them live.

GW Layne plays guitar?

CANTRELL Totally. We're all growing as players, including Layne. And he's helped me grow as a singer. Powerful back-up vocals have been something that we've really lacked live, and that's something I'm working on. As for those things we're known for—our trademarks—the reason they're so much more immense this time is that we've really just naturally evolved.

GW You did a fair amount of the lead vocals on the 1992 EP *Sap*. On *Dirt*, you take that two steps further.

CANTRELL Yeah, I did, and it's really cool. And it happened because of some elbowing from Layne. I write some of the lyrics, and singing them can be difficult for Layne. At the same time, writing for someone else from his point of view—even if that someone is like your brother, as Layne is—will sometimes mean that you fall short in interpretation. Fortunately, I've been able to write stuff that we can all relate to. But I've also written some things where Layne said, "Well, why don't you sing it, man?"

GW *Sap* serves as a bridge between *Facelift* and *Dirt*. The new album has strong elements of both records.

CANTRELL You're exactly right. I'm at a loss for adjectives to describe *Dirt*. Basically, by reaching into the depths, we went lower, musically, than we've ever been. At the same time we also found some really cool and good things about ourselves. At first, going through the whole experience of having a successful first album was kind of hard to accept. It's like, "I'm not worthy!" [*laughs*] It's easy to beat yourself up about it because it's so fake. You're just this thing on a tape and a face on a piece of paper. People forget you're a person, and you forget you're a person. But there came a realization that, yes, I am worth this. I do deserve this. I've worked hard and I'm good. ✱

FEBRUARY / VOL. 14 / NO. 2

ZAKK WYLDE MEETS LYNYRD SKYNYRD

Ozzy Osbourne's wild man comes face to face with his heroes, Gary Rossington and Ed King, at the Four Seasons Hotel in Philadelphia—and *Guitar World* is there to document the historic occasion.

ZAKK WYLDE Did you ever imagine that 20 years down the line "Free Bird" would still be played constantly on the radio?

GARY ROSSINGTON Believe me, that was beyond our wildest dreams.

ED KING But I knew "Sweet Home Alabama" was a classic the minute we wrote it. The same goes for "Saturday Night Special." I played Ronnie [*Van Zant, singer*] this riff one day in rehearsal, and he just nodded. Ronnie never wrote down or recorded anything. So the next day I was bummed because the groove was lost, but Ronnie called me over and sang a song in my ear based on that lost riff—and it was "Saturday Night Special."

ROSSINGTON Ronnie felt that if you had to write something down, it wasn't worth remembering. Hell, I wish we had recorded all those early songs, because we'd have a lot more material now. [*laughs*]

WYLDE If it's a good idea, it'll always come back to you. What was cool about those days was that every band sounded different. You had Skynyrd, Jethro Tull, Deep Purple, Led Zeppelin, Black Sabbath—and no one sounded like the others. Ozzy says that nowadays, all you have to do to get a record deal is grow your hair long—but back then, only the good bands made it.

ROSSINGTON You can watch MTV and close your eyes, and you probably won't be able to tell one band from the other. All these rock bands sound the same, and all these guitarists are just jerkin' off. I love Eddie Van Halen—he's so good he's a freak of nature—but once you've heard him play one song you've heard just about every fuckin' note there is to play. What's left?

Derek Trucks & Joe Bonamassa: The Kids Are Alright

MAR. '93

If you think 31-year-old Allman Brothers guitarist Derek Trucks still has a bit of a baby face today, take a look at him at age 13, when he first appeared in *Guitar World*! Sitting on the edge of his bed at home, the nephew of ABB drummer Butch Trucks could probably pass for eight or nine back in 1993—although his playing was clearly becoming the envy of even the most seasoned professionals. "He's the real thing," said Joe Walsh in our March issue. He reminds me of Duane and Eric and myself, but I'm mostly impressed that he's developing on his own." Trucks, however, was at a loss when it came to acknowledging his own talent. "I'm starting to round out my playing," he said. "But I've still got a long ways to go."

Interestingly, the article above the Derek Trucks piece featured another teen-aged phenomenon—Joe Bonamassa, who was just 15 when *Guitar World* profiled his band, Bloodline, which also featured the sons of Robby Krieger, Berry Oakley and Miles Davis.

GENE SIMMONS VS. RAGE AGAINST THE MACHINE

Guitar World premiers the Picks & Pans section, where every month one musician critiques the work of their peers. First up is Kiss bassist Gene Simmons, who offers his views on the debut album from Rage Against the Machine.

I T'S ALWAYS INTERESTING to hear white boys trying to rap and play funky, and while the music of Rage Against the Machine may not be very convincing in that respect, it is rather intriguing. The band has a strong sense of groove, and when they find a good riff, they play it to death—and they do this quite well.

"Although I had a difficult time finding anything memorable on the album, I did like the fact that the band tends to forsake traditional A-B-A song structures. No one ever said we had to follow the verse, chorus, verse pattern all the time, and Rage Against the Machine certainly take advantage of that.

"They have tremendous energy and, at times, make you feel like you're being run over by a truck. Music like this is important—at least to make sure that the rest of us here in pop hell don't rest too much."

The summer of 1993 also saw *Guitar World* branch out with two new products: *Country Guitar* magazine and the German edition of *GW*. *Country Guitar* eventually morphed into *Guitar World Acoustic* and existed until 2007, while the German edition lasted a little more than a year before being *hinrichten*.

The Essential Unplugged
Guitar World's guide to great unplugged albums and songs of the past and present.

JUN. '93

Rock on Wood
1) Crosby, Stills and Nash—*Crosby, Stills and Nash*
2) Grateful Dead—*American Beauty*
3) Led Zeppelin—*Led Zeppelin III*
4) The Beatles—*The Beatles*
5) Guns N' Roses—*GN'R Lies*
6) Eric Clapton—*Unplugged*
7) Neil Young—*Harvest*
8) Violent Femmes—*Violent Femmes*
9) Alice in Chains—*Sap*
10) Bob Dylan—*Freewheelin' Bob Dylan*

Wood Ol' Boys
1) Various Artists—*Pioneers of the Jazz Guitar*
2) Blind Blake—*Ragtime*
3) Robert Johnson—*The Complete Recordings*
4) Django Reinhardt—*The First Quintet Hot Club of France Recordings, 1934–35*
5) The Kentucky Colonels with Roland & Clarence White—*Appalachian Swing!*
6) Doc Watson—*Southbound*
7) Richard Thompson—*Small Town*

8) The Nitty Gritty Dirt Band and Guests—*Will the Circle Be Unbroken*
9) John Renbourn—*The Hermit*
10) Michael Hedges—*Aerial Boundaries*

The Wood, the Bad and the Ugly
1) Black Sabbath—"Children of the Sea" (*Heaven and Hell*)
2) Metallica—"Nothing Else Matters" (*Metallica*)
3) Chris Cornell—"Seasons" (*Singles* soundtrack)

4) Led Zeppelin—"Stairway to Heaven" (*Led Zeppelin IV*)
5) Van Halen—"Spanish Fly" (*Van Halen II*)
6) Extreme—"Hole Hearted" (*Extreme II: Pornograffitti*)
7) Exodus—"No Love" (*Bonded by Blood*)
8) Ozzy Osbourne— "Revelation (Mother Earth)" (*Blizzard of Ozz*)
9) Morbid Angel—"Desolate Ways" (*Blessed Are the Sick*)
10) Death Angel—"A Room with a View" (*Act III*)

Photograph by Bill Baker   Photograph by Bob Gruen/Starfile

KISS AND TELL

ACE FREHLEY IS PISSED OFF, and with good reason. It's May 18th, the day his former Kiss bandmates are to be honored by the city of Los Angeles and Hollywood's Rock Walk association for 20 years of rock and roll greatness. So where is Ace? At Guitar World's New York City headquarters, explaining why he isn't at the ceremony. Did he just refuse to join current Kiss members Gene Simmons and Paul Stanley in immortal-

HE'S HOTTER THAN HELL AND HE'S NOT GOING TO TAKE IT ANYMORE! AFTER TEN YEARS OF GRITTING HIS TEETH, ACE FREHLEY, GUITAR HERO OF US ALL, BARES HIS KISS SOUL. BY JEFF KITTS

izing his hand prints in the Rock Walk's wet cement? Hardly. Ace simply wasn't invited.

"It doesn't surprise me that they don't want me there," says Frehley. "But they're only hurting themselves. I have fans constantly telling me that they've lost all respect for Paul and Gene because of the way they've been treating me lately. It only makes me realize how much I made the right choice when I left the band 10 years ago."

AUG. 1993

VOL. 14 / NO. 8

Ace Frehley

With the feud between he and his former Kiss bandmates escalating to ugly proportions, the legendary lead guitarist comes to *Guitar World* HQ to tell Jeff Kitts his side of the shocking story.

Ace Frehley is pissed off, and with good reason. It's May 18, 1993, the day his former Kiss bandmates are to be honored by the city of Los Angeles and the Hollywood Rock Walk association for 20 years of rock and roll greatness. So where is Ace? At *Guitar World*'s New York City headquarters, explaining why he isn't at the ceremony. Did he just refuse to join current Kiss members Gene Simmons and Paul Stanley in immortalizing his hand prints in the Rock Walk's wet cement?

Hardly. Ace simply wasn't invited.

"It doesn't surprise me that they don't want me there," says Frehley. "But they're only hurting themselves. I have fans constantly telling me that they've lost all respect for Paul and Gene because of the way they've been treating me lately. It only makes me realize how much I made the right choice when I left the band 10 years ago."

It is difficult to believe that Stanley and Simmons chose to see Kiss honored without acknowledging the towering contributions of their first lead guitarist or original drummer, Peter Criss. But there have been other slights. Frehley has been verbally slapped in the face, without provocation, by Stanley and Simmons on numerous occasions just this past year, usually via the media.

"I was in Canada a few weeks ago, and Gene called me a moron in one of the local magazines," says Frehley. "What the hell is his problem? But if they want to put me down all the time, that's fine. They're just making assholes of themselves."

Mabye so. But *why* would Gene and Paul want to attack their former comrade now, 10 years after his voluntary departure from Kiss? Ace believes it's because his exit left scars that apparently still have not healed.

"Let's face it—when I left the group, Kiss got a musical vasectomy. I was the original and I was the best, and they'll never be able to replace me. But they don't want to face that. I think they're tired of hearing about Ace Frehley all the time, and they just want to get on with their careers without giving me the recognition I'm due.

"I guess they want to put the past behind them and prove that they can make it on their own without me," adds Ace. "They've been able to do it to a certain extent—but they'll never be able to recapture the chemistry and success we once had."

Of course, few bands—even today's most popular artists—ever attain the kind of success Kiss enjoyed in the late Seventies, when they rose from being an unknown New York City bar band to the status of worldwide phe-

nomenon in less than five years. By 1978, Kiss was the biggest rock band in the world—and Ace, a punk kid from the tough Bronx, had more money than he could handle.

"I always had at least $5,000 in cash on me," says Ace. "I would walk into toy stores and spend $2,000 on the most ridiculous shit, like radio controlled helicopters, $3,000 telescopes—all the shit I could never afford as a kid. And having all that money really screws you up."

But the financial rewards of their astounding success paled next to the tremendous impact the band was to have on an entire generation of American youngsters. And Ace Frehley, despite his lack of critical recognition, has proven himself to be one of the most influential players in rock history. His dizzying vibrato, memorable studio lead work, cosmic image and legendary onstage guitar solos—during which his heavily modified Les Paul would emit an ungodly amount of smoke—were directly responsible for many of today's hottest players taking up the guitar.

"It's flattering to know that I've had such an impact," says Frehley. "But I had no idea at the time."

After ruling the universe for five years, the Kiss empire began crumbling at the dawn of the Eighties. The band's popularity, record sales and musical firepower reached an all-time low with the 1981 release of the bizarre concept album, *Music from "The Elder,"* the first without drummer Peter Criss, whose ever-mounting personal problems had caused an irreparable rift between he and his bandmates. With his closest companion gone, Frehley, already a serious drinker, turned to the bottle with alarming regularity. He soon made the decision to leave the band for good. By the next Kiss album, the band had stopped wearing their trademark makeup and started writing limp pop-rock tunes. It was official: the Kiss that had been an all-consuming obsession for so many youngsters throughout the Seventies was gone.

It's been 10 years since Ace left Kiss, and while his former bandmates celebrate the band's 20th anniversary without him, the Spaceman appears to be on the verge of making a great comeback. He's sober, touring constantly and playing the guitar with the same innocent passion he displayed when he first joined the band. Ace is definitely on the right track.

"I know that Paul and Gene want me to fail," says Ace. "They want me to become a drunk again and disappear into the fucking mist. But that's not gonna happen—in fact, I'm only gonna get bigger. I'm like a bad rash that won't go away." ✳

NINETEEN '94

Guitar World celebrates rock facial hair with the scruffy (Billy Gibbons, Dimebag Darrell, Kim Thayil) and the neatly trimmed (Stone Gossard, Chris Cornell, Prince).

Dear *Guitar World*,

I'd like to take the person who came up with
the idea for the ZZ Top cover [*March 1994*] and
conk him over the head with my Les Paul. How
could you guys allow such a thing to happen
when women are fighting so hard for their
rights in the sexist world of guitar playing?
If what you want is "titillation," then maybe
you should start a guitar column in *Penthouse*.
If and when I ever get to be on the cover of
your magazine, I hope you'll allow me to be
surrounded by Chippendales dancers.

—Antonia Simigis

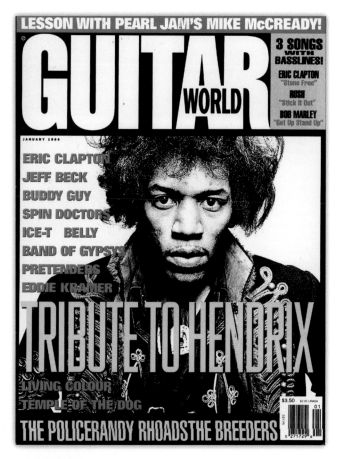

JANUARY A behind-the-scenes look at the making of the *Stone Free: A Tribute to Jimi Hendrix* album, including commentary from such rockers as Jeff Beck, Slash, Chrissie Hynde and Eric Clapton about the tracks they chose to record. "I wanted to do a tribute, and not just imitate Jimi, so I couldn't do one of my real favorites, like 'Machine Gun' or 'If Six Was Nine,' " says Slash. "I just couldn't play those songs without trying to cop his feel, so we chose 'I Don't Live Today.' "

COVER STORY BY JOHN MCDERMOTT; PHOTO BY GERED MANKOWITZ

FEBRUARY Pearl Jam's Stone Gossard, Mike McCready and Jeff Ament spill their guts in their most revealing interview ever. "Speaking of creative accidents," says McCready, "I had quite a wet fart onstage last night. I just looked over at Dave [*Abbruzzese, drummer*] during 'Garden' and suddenly..."

COVER STORY BY VIC GARBARINI; PHOTO BY LANCE MERCER

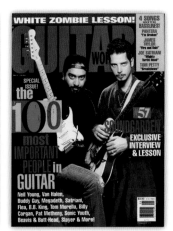

MARCH Texas bluesmen or MTV fabrications? *Guitar World* investigates the weird world of ZZ Top's Billy Gibbons and Dusty Hill.
COVER STORY BY ALAN DI PERNA
PHOTO BY JAMES BLAND

APRIL Dimebag Darrell, the world's most dangerous guitarist, lives up to his reputation on Pantera's vicious new album, *Far Beyond Driven*—and lands his first solo *Guitar World* cover.
COVER STORY BY BRAD TOLINSKI
PHOTO BY LORINDA SULLIVAN

MAY As Soundgarden releases a new album, Kim Thayil and Chris Cornell prepare to blast off into the *Superunknown*.
COVER STORY BY JEFF GILBERT
PHOTO BY KARJEAN NG

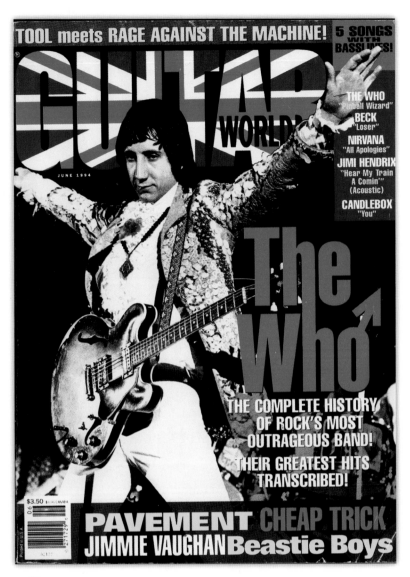

TOOL meets RAGE AGAINST THE MACHINE!

5 SONGS WITH BASSLINES!

GUITAR WORLD

JUNE 1994

THE WHO
"Pinball Wizard"

BECK
"Loser"

NIRVANA
"All Apologies"

JIMI HENDRIX
"Hear My Train
A Comin'"
(Acoustic)

CANDLEBOX
"You"

The Who

THE COMPLETE HISTORY
OF ROCK'S MOST
OUTRAGEOUS BAND!

THEIR GREATEST HITS
TRANSCRIBED!

$3.50

PAVEMENT CHEAP TRICK
JIMMIE VAUGHAN Beastie Boys

JUNE *Guitar World* celebrates Pete Townshend and the Who with this detailed history of the musical barrier–smashing group. Commenting on the first time he smashed a guitar, Townshend says, "It banged against the ceiling and smashed against a whole in the plaster, and the guitar head actually poked through the ceiling. When I took it out, the top of the neck was left behind. I couldn't believe what had happened."

COVER STORY BY ALAN DI PERNA; PHOTO BY BARON WOLMAN

KURT COBAIN: 1967–1994

GUITAR WORLD

SOUTHERN ROCK LIVES!
THE ALLMAN BROTHERS
PLUS! DUANE ALLMAN TRIBUTE
SCREAMIN' CHEETAH WHEELS, BROTHER CANE, CRY OF LOVE & MORE!

ZAKK WYLDE
Les Claypool BIOHAZARD

JULY
Allman Brothers Band guitarist Dickey Betts and his trusty sidekick Warren Haynes explain how they keep their Southern-fried sound sizzling on the long and dusty road.
COVER STORY BY ALAN PAUL
PHOTO BY DANNY CLINCH

GUITAR WORLD

SURVIVING THE GRUNGE WARS: STONE TEMPLE PILOTS' PURPLE REIGN

STP

EAGLES REUNION

YNGWIE
Danzig PHISH
Death Metal Mega Lesson

AUGUST
Stone Temple Pilots' DeLeo brothers, Dean and Robert, laugh away the incessant Pearl Jam comparisons but are deadly serious about their new album, *Purple*.
COVER STORY BY ALAN DI PERNA
PHOTO BY LISA JOHNSON

STEVIE RAY VAUGHAN IN THE STUDIO

GUITAR WORLD

PINK FLOYD RETURNS!
Exclusive Interview With David Gilmour

STEVE MORSE Helmet WOODSTOCK
LYNYRD SKYNYRD SUPER LESSON!

SEPTEMBER
David Gilmour discusses Pink Floyd's newest album, *The Division Bell*, and the band's groundbreaking world tour.
COVER STORY BY BRAD TOLINSKI
ART BY MICHAEL CHATHAM

GUITAR WORLD

CLASSIC ROCK SPECIAL!

THE ROLLING STONES
EXCLUSIVE INTERVIEWS WITH KEITH & MICK
THE WHO THE LAST WORD FROM PETE TOWNSHEND
DINOSAUR JR Slayer ALEX SKOLNICK

CANDLEBOX ZZ TOP

5 SONGS WITH BASSLINES!

PANTERA

GUITAR WORLD

EXCLUSIVE INTERVIEW! The Funked-Up Genius Of

THE HISTORY OF HARDCORE
Black Flag
Agnostic Front,
Bad Brains
& More!

DREAM THEATER LIZ PHAIR

4 SONGS WITH BASSLINES!

GUITAR WORLD

A Man And His Blues

EXCLUSIVE! Inside The Cradle Sessions

CLAPTON REMEMBERS: Jim Hendrix, Cream, Bluesbreakers & More!

SPECIAL REPORT: The Making Of Layla

ROBERT PALMER On Clapton's Blues

BLUES POWER '94
CARLOS SANTANA HANGS WITH BUDDY GUY
Joe Louis Walker Son Seals

PLUS: Megadeth Big Head Todd Testament Weezer

Clapton

OCTOBER The World's Greatest Rock Band is back, and Rolling Stones guitarist Keith Richards celebrates with candid reflections on his relationship with Ron Wood, his guitar playing and Bill Wyman's replacement.
COVER STORY BY GARY GRAFF; PHOTO BY JIM MARSHALL

NOVEMBER The man, the guitarist and the eccentric. An exclusive—and frustrating—encounter with the Artist Formerly Known as Prince.
COVER STORY BY ALAN DI PERNA; PHOTO BY NICOLE NODLAND

DECEMBER Eric Clapton revisits the highlights of his career, from his early blues-breaking days with John Mayall to his groundbreaking *Unplugged* performance.
COVER STORY BY DAVID MEAD; PHOTO BY SCOTT MCDOUGALL

1994 TOTAL ISSUES: 12

10 09 08 07 06 05 04 03 02 01 00 99 98 97 96 95 **94** 93 92 91 90 89 88 87 86 85 84 83 82 81 80

THE GOOD, THE RAD & THE UGLY

The erudite, engimatic Mr. Gibbons offers his comments on ten of the most bizarre items in his prodigious collection....

BY ALAN DiPERNA
PHOTOGRAPHS BY JAMES BLAND

MARCH 1994

VOL. 15 / NO. 3

Billy Gibbons

ZZ Top's frontman offers his comments on 10 of the most bizarre items in his prodigious collection.

1. Z Guitar "This guitar is seen here in the shape of a Z. However, it has a folding mechanism that turns it into the shape of a V. It was designed by Gibson guitar specialist Matthew Klein and manufactured at the Gibson plant."

2. Genesis Guitar "The Genesis guitar is a handy item because it's got a couple of holes cut in the body and it's easy to carry. It was manufactured by someone we don't know. But we didn't mind. We just dig those handy handles."

3. Fender Jaguar "Believe it or not, we still have a Jag lurking in our stable. This particular instrument is the second guitar I ever owned, and can be heard on 'PCH,' on *Antenna*. It features a single Seymour Duncan Pearly Gates pickup in the bridge position and a VU meter where the neck pickup probably would've existed. It also features a painting of a famous surfboard—a Rick surfboard. I don't know what that has to do with anything, but it's there."

4. Casio Guitar "A Casio guitar arrived on our doorstep one day, with the invitation to try it out. We never did, but it looks good. Can't afford the batteries."

5. Red Russian/Black Russian "These guitars were a gift from two Russian rockers. They were given to ZZ Top sometime between 1990 and '92, before the Berlin wall came down. They could probably be played, but we can't seem to find a cord that fits them. We suspect they use a DIN plug instead of a quarter-inch jack. Very weird. Very Russian-like.

6. Mummy Guitar "An Explorer in shape, covered in gauze and featuring the Sony Watchman, the Mummy guitars were also created by Matthew Klein at Gibson. They're used in the video for 'Sleeping Bag.' "

7. Twelve-String Mexican "This is a Mexican guitar with 12 strings called a *Bajo Sexto*. Difficult to play, according to some—we don't know how. We don't even know how to tune it, nor do we choose to. We enjoy border music: *conjunto* sounds. And for us, this is a reminder of what we enjoy. It was purchased in San Antonio, in a music/furniture store that has since closed."

8. One-String Guitar "This is kind of homemade. It was a gift from Willie the Workingman, the engineer at ZZ Top's Texas recording studio. It still works. But there again, we need batteries."

9. Viva Las Vegas "The Viva Las Vegas guitars were created down in Meridian, Mississippi, where you can throw dice or go by the Peavey specialty guitar shop and say, 'Hey, make me a Viva Las Vegas guitar!' They play quite well, by the way. The hardware was a gift from an actual slot machine."

10. La Warpa "A rather odd-looking guitar in the flavor of orange. The name La Warpa identifies its curved body. It's concave on one side and convex on the other. You can hear this one on 'My Head's in Mississippi.' "

Designing Woman Storms Off

When the *Guitar World* editors decided to team up Billy Gibbons with sexy long-legged model Tina for the cover of the March 1994 issue, everyone on the staff was excited about the concept—everyone except design director Susan Conley, that is. Conley objected to having a barely dressed model—especially one that was so blatantly fiddling with Gibbons' "instrument"—on a *Guitar World* cover "for no reason," and thus decided to remove her name from that issue's masthead. Good thing Susan didn't stick around long enough to witness the *Guitar World Buyer's Guide*!

PUBLISHER
Stanley R. Harris
EXECUTIVE PUBLISHER
Dennis S. Page
ASSOCIATE PUBLISHER/ADVERTISING
Greg Di Benedetto

EDITOR-IN-CHIEF
Brad Tolinski
DESIGN DIRECTOR

EXECUTIVE EDITOR
Harold Steinblatt
MANAGING EDITOR
Alan Paul

APRIL / VOL. 15 / NO. 4

GUITAR WORLD SURVIVAL GUIDE

A range of road warriors weigh in on essential items and touring rules.

Jerry Cantrell
Road Essentials
1) Get a great tech and don't spare any expense.
2) Don't spare any expense on your gear, either. Make sure you have a backup system—always.
3) Never wear your socks more than three days in a row.
4) Always take a dump before going onstage.
Rules of the Road
1) Take the phone off the hook when you go to sleep.
2) Always use a condom. Always.
3) If you meet Pantera or Slayer and they are drinking, run the other way, because you *will* have a hangover the next day.

Ted Nugent
Road Essentials
1) Attitude
2) Attitude
3) And of course, the Attitude of the Attitude
Rules of the Road
1) Be on your toes at all times.
2) Remain cocked, locked and ready to rock.
3) No drugs, no alcohol, no insubordination, no laziness, no irresponsibility.

4) The more guns on the deck the better. The more women below the deck, even better. And never the two shall meet—except on my deck!

Gene Simmons
Rules of the Road
1) Don't forget to wipe.
2) Don't call her back.
3) Try and play in tune.
4) Stay in a room close to the exit.

Gary Rossington
Road Essentials
1) A good wife.
2) An acoustic guitar to play on the bus and in the hotel room.
3) A great guitar tech. Never skimp in this area, because sooner or later he *will* save your ass.
Rules of the Road
1) Stay healthy
2) Don't overdo anything you like to do. Those are my old man rules. Here are the Lynyrd Skynyrd circa 1977 rules:
1) Do whatever you want.
2) Don't do anything you don't want.

Tom Morello
The Perfect Roadie
I have to be able to beat him at Sega's John Madden Football.

Guitar's Top 100 List

Our May 1994 issue was a cover-to-cover special dedicated to the 100 most important people in guitar. What made it even more special was that the list could only include living guitarists and inventors and current instrument manufacturers— in other words, an issue of *Guitar World* that contained no dead guys! A first, for sure.

Here, we see the top 10 and bottom 10 from the master list, as chosen by the editors.

1) Edward Van Halen
2) Eric Clapton
3) James Hetfield & Kirk Hammett
4) Neil Young
5) The Edge
6) Jim Marshall
7) Jimmy Page
8) Thurston Moore & Lee Ranaldo
9) Ace Frehley
10) Alan Douglas

90) John Nady
91) Roger Mayer
92) Bob Rock
93) Richard Thompson
94) John McLaughlin
95) David Gilmour
96) Steve Malkmus
97) Transperformance Tuning System
98) Stefan Grossman
99) Bruce Iglauer
100) Nigel Tufnel

"Warren is not replacing a legend. A legend was killed

JULY / VOL. 15 / NO. 7

DICKEY BETTS & WARREN HAYNES

Despite being in the Allman Brothers Band for five years, Warren Haynes can't escape constant comparisons to the late Duane Allman.

DICKEY BETTS Warren has his own style—though I don't think it's fully developed yet—so he's not pulled into sounding like me. And, more to the point, he's never been pulled into trying to sound like Duane. Still, he has been plagued with that comparison from day one—which isn't worth the change in my pocket. There's not a rock slide guitarist in the world who hasn't been influenced by Duane Allman, but Warren receives extreme scrutiny because of who he plays with.

GW Warren, has that "replacing a legend" thing been difficult for you to overcome?

WARREN HAYNES I'm constantly drawing the line of how much I should sound like Duane. The band has made it easier by leaving it up to me to decide how much of Duane's influence to insert. They've always said, "Play like you. That's what we hired you to do." For the music to be true to itself, I have to insert a certain amount of Duane's sound—especially in the older songs—and the more I play that way the more it sounds like the Allman Brothers Band. When it comes to slide playing, I naturally play with more of Duane's influence, because I'm influenced by hundreds and hundreds of guitar players, but only a handful of slide players. The situation definitely makes it harder to be myself on guitar, but the more comfortable I am within the band, the more I'm able to stretch out, and the more my own style comes to the fore.

BETTS And you have to understand something: Warren is not replacing a legend. A legend was killed over 20 years ago. And that was the end of that. Nobody's gonna replace Duane. We're not replacing anybody. We're just going on to the next day.

Guitar World Promises World Wide (Web) Domination

Although *Guitar World* wouldn't assert itself as a serious internet force until 2007, the magazine first made its online presence felt in the fall of 1994 with Guitar World Online. To access it, users needed a computer with a dial-up modem and a subscription to the CompuServe computer network. When the first announcement of it was made in the October 1994 issue, some lofty promises were made: "*Guitar World* will be offering a 24-hour bulletin board service (BBS) that will answer any guitar-related question you may have. But perhaps the most innovative section of the *GW* BBS will be our multi-media guitar lessons. Not only will you be able to download notes and tab, but our online service will also allow you to *hear* how the notes are played. Imagine Diamond Darrell's Riffer Madness column coming to life on your computer—complete with sound, photographs and even video!" In reality, none of this was really possible in 1994—but we give ourselves credit for providing a very accurate peek into the future of online guitar. Oh, and if you wished to contact editor Brad Tolinski back then, his address was 74431,3566.

FALL '94

GUITAR TITANS AND
LONGTIME PALS
BUDDY GUY AND CARLOS SANTANA
GET TOGETHER
AND DISCUSS
LIFE, LIBERTY AND THE BLUES

SHMOOZIN' THE
BLUES

K EYED UP LIKE A KID AT CHRISTMAS, CARLOS
SANTANA THROWS OPEN HIS FRONT DOOR.
"BUDDY!"
OUTSIDE, IT'S ANOTHER GLORIOUS,
SUN-DAPPLED LATE MORNING AT CARLOS' HOME
OVERLOOKING THE SAN FRANCISCO BAY.
HALFWAY UP A RED BRICK PATH ASCENDING A
GREEN SLOPE, BUDDY GUY PAUSES AND LOOKS
UP. A BROAD GRIN SPREADS ACROSS HIS
EXPRESSIVE FACE. TWO ARMS EXTEND FROM
HIS SUBSTANTIAL FRAME.
"HEY THERE, CARLOS."
THE TWO LEGENDARY GUITARISTS MEET MID-
WAY ON THE PATH. THEY SHAKE HANDS, THEN
EXCHANGE A BIG HUG.
"OH MAN, I'M SO GLAD YOU'RE HERE." CARLOS
SMILES.

BY ALAN DI PERNA

PHOTOGRAPH BY
MICHAEL SEXTON

DEC. 1994

VOL. 15 / NO. 12

Carlos Santana &
Buddy Guy

The guitar legends and longtime pals sit with writer Alan di Perna to swap war stories

GUITAR WORLD Carlos, can you recall the first time you ever heard Buddy Guy?

CARLOS SANTANA Yeah, it was in the mid Sixties. I went to this cat's house, a singer I knew, and he had *Hoodoo Man Blues* [*a Junior Wells album with Buddy Guy on guitar*]. I remember it because, even though I grew up in Tijuana, I'd never really hung around people who smoked pot before then. Because I was a kid, people would always do that away from me. But here at this guy's house, they were smoking pot and we were listening to the record. And it hit me so strong by being so soft. It was really beautifully recorded. And I said, "Man, who's that?" And someone answered, "Oh, that's Junior Wells' new album." After that I started buying all the Chicago blues I could find. I kept checking out the guitar players. And Buddy had a different kind of thing than B.B. King or the guitarist with Bobby Blue Bland [*Wayne Bennett*]. Buddy injected a different kind of passion into the mainstream of electric guitar. It reminds me of a bottle of Perrier that's been left in the car a long time, all shaken up. It's very effervescent. That was the first thing I heard. And it made me want to know more about that passion of Buddy's. And that effervescence. I heard it again later when I heard [*Jimi Hendrix's*] "Red House" for the first time. This guy says, "I know you love the blues, but wait till you hear this!" Boom, they put "Red House" on—the version from England, 'cause it didn't come out like that in America. And I said, "That's Buddy?" They go, "No, man, it's Jimi." "Jimi who?" "Jimi Hendrix." "Whoa." So Jimi gave birth to something that came from Buddy Guy. And I know that if Jimi were here, he'd be the first one to tell you that.

GW Well, didn't Hendrix often tape your gigs so he could learn your licks, Buddy?

BUDDY GUY Yeah. A couple of years ago, I actually got the tape he made of me the night of the death of Martin Luther King [*April 4, 1968*]. I'd like to know who sent me that tape.

My manager at the time was Dick Waterman, who was Bonnie Raitt's boyfriend and manager, and who stutters like John Lee Hooker. So we were at this club and he kept hollering "Dat-dat-dat's Hendrix!" And I say, "So what? Who the hell is that?" And everybody started looking and laughing. So Hendrix came up and he says, "Pay that no mind. Can I tape what you're playing?" And I said, "Yeah." Somebody had a tape machine on 'em and he got down on his knees and stayed there at the corner of the stage. And now I've got the tape from that club. But Jimi and I got a chance to jam a lot together, and I got to sit and talk with him—as much as he did talk, which wasn't much. And I really flipped out over the things he was doing. He reminds me so much of this guy here. [*Points to a video image of John Coltrane flickering silently on Carlos' TV screen.*] You know, Guitar Slim once said, "Every time you live one day, I live two." And I think Hendrix and Coltrane were just that creative. They was years and years ahead of their time, for what they was playing. Those kind of people come around once in a lifetime. I would love to see those two guys around today. Who knows what we would be listening to?

GW I know Carlos really feels the link between Coltrane and Hendrix.

SANTANA Yeah. It's just a tone that liberates. A long time ago, I realized that the blues is not just from the swamp, or the alley, or a certain walk of life. Miles Davis said, "I never had anything to do with the cotton, but I can play some blues." Miles came from really rich people in St. Louis. Miles breaks the stereotype, man. So blues, to me, comes from when a person can feel other people's pain and is able to articulate it. If you can feel the people's pain, like in Rwanda or on an Indian reservation, you can play some blues. 'Cause I've heard the blues from Japanese people, Italian people, all sorts of people. There's a different beauty, of course, in blues from Chicago and Texas vs. Tupelo, Mississippi. But the blues is still the blues. ✳

NINETEEN '95

Guitar World celebrates its 15th anniversary with an investigative piece on the legal battle for Jimi Hendrix's legacy, in-depth looks at the history of punk guitar, the thriving Minneapolis scene and the industrial music revolution, and rare interviews with Neil Young and Bruce Springsteen.

Dear *Guitar World*,

I have only received seven of the last 12 issues.
The ones I have received have been late and some
have been damaged. I demand my issues and some
sort of compensation for your ignorance.

And, by the way, if you guys don't set me
straight, it will cost you a hundred-fold what
it would cost just to pay your dues. I'm doing 25
years in Club Fed [*federal prison*], and I'll make
it my personal goal to f**k you guys up. I have
nothing better to do with my time anyway. I'll
just sit here and write letter after letter after
letter to every motherf**ker out there. Don't
even think about getting away with my money, you
f**ks.

—Calvin J. Coohey

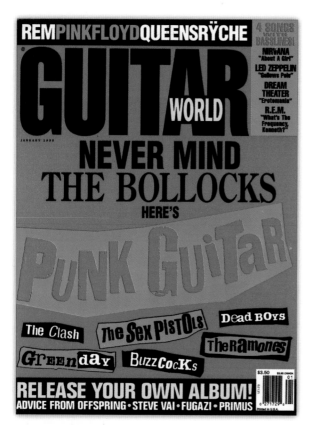

JANUARY *Guitar World* celebrates the punk-rock guitarists and bands that, in the late Seventies, changed the face of rock and roll into a hateful sneer. "It came and went, but it made a dent. Hey, that's a good line, that!" says Sex Pistols guitarist Steve Jones.

COVER STORIES BY ALAN DI PERNA, JIM TESTA AND DAVID GRAD

FEBRUARY Edward Van Halen discusses his alcoholism, the joys of parenting and, of course, Van Halen's new album, *Balance*. "God gives everyone a bottle when they're born, and they have to make it last a lifetime. Well, I drank mine too quickly, so I just can't drink anymore."

COVER STORY BY TOM BEAUJOUR; PHOTO BY MICHAEL SEXTON

MARCH A behind-the-scenes look at Nirvana's brilliant performance on MTV's *Unplugged*.
COVER STORY BY ALAN DI PERNA; PHOTO BY M. LINSSON

APRIL Pearl Jam guitarist Mike McCready comes clean on his battle with substance abuse, the price of fame and Mad Season, his new band with Alice in Chains' Layne Staley.
COVER STORY BY JEFF GILBERT; PHOTO BY LANCE MERCER

MAY *Guitar World* celebrates its 15th anniversary with an issue devoted to its greatest interviews, lists and lessons. In his Woodshed, editor-in-chief Brad Tolinski summed up the appeal of the magazine thusly: "In our own twisted way, we actually enjoy trying to please every last reader—even the psychopathic bastard who mailed us a paper mache replica of Dimebag Darrell's head last month."
COVER STORY BY VARIOUS; PHOTO COLLAGE BY MICHAEL SEXTON

1995 TOTAL ISSUES: 12

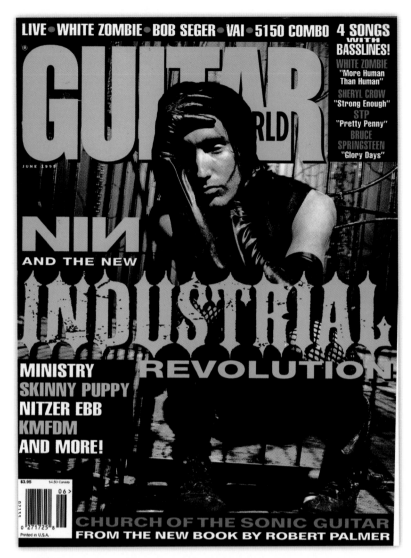

JUNE From the underground havoc of Throbbing Gristle to the multi-Platinum success of Nine Inch Nails, *Guitar World* takes an in-depth look at industrial music—the movement that gave a whole new meaning to the words "heavy metal." "The only thing I find interesting about rock music today is a sense of danger," says Nine Inch Nails frontman Trent Reznor. "Breaking rules, doing something that offends people, or at least smacks them in the face."

COVER STORY BY ALAN DI PERNA; PHOTO BY KEVIN WESTENBERG

JULY Al Hendrix is locked in a legal battle with his longtime lawyer. At stake is the recorded legacy of his son, Jimi Hendrix. *Guitar World* reports on this vicious family feud.

COVER STORY BY ALAN DI PERNA
PHOTO BY BARRIE WENTZELL / ILLUSTRATION BY TOM PITTS

AUGUST It took Soul Asylum 10 years of hard work to hit it big with 1992's *Grave Dancers Union*. The band's new album, *Let Your Dim Light Shine*, promises to be an even more glowing success.

COVER STORY BY TOM BEAUJOUR; PHOTO BY SILVIA OTTE

SEPTEMBER Neil Young discusses the making of his new album, *Mirror Ball*, the fruit of his collaboration with Pearl Jam.

COVER STORY BY GARY GRAFF; PHOTO BY ALBERT WATSON

OCTOBER Bruce Springsteen comments on his long career, the recent reunion of the E-Street Band and the state of rock music in the Nineties.

COVER STORY BY NEIL STRAUSS; PHOTO BY NIELS VAN IPEREN

NOVEMBER On *Ball Breaker*, AC/DC's Angus and Malcolm Young demonstrate yet again that they are randy as a pair of billy goats, out of their minds with lurid desires and obscenely concupiscent.

COVER STORY BY ALAN DI PERNA; PHOTO BY MICHAEL HALSBAND

DECEMBER In the grand tradition of the Beatles' White Album and Pink Floyd's *The Wall*, Smashing Pumpkins place their bid for rock greatness with *Mellon Collie and the Infinite Sadness*, a sprawling two-disc tour de force.

COVER STORY BY ALAN DI PERNA; PHOTO BY DANNY CLINCH

SAUCERFUL OF SECRETS

SINCE LAST JUNE, FANS OF PINK FLOYD, ROCK'S MOST MYSTERIOUS BAND, HAVE BEEN

Pink Floyd fans, take note! There's a treasure hunt going on, and *The Division Bell* is the map. In what could be the biggest mystery in the annals of rock, Floyd disciples around the world have been carefully following a trail of clues, left by a self-proclaimed messenger known only as Publius. The person who deciphers the enigma has been promised a special, secret reward.

Publius—who may or may not be a member of the band—first began leaving mysterious messages this past summer in the midst of a Pink Floyd discussion on the worldwide computer network known as the Internet. His rather cryptic clues have caused confusion and controversy among Pink Floyd stalwarts—and sent them racing back to listen to *The Division Bell* with new ears.

The mystery began last June 11 with an anonymous, generically titled note left in the alt.music.pink-floyd newsgroup, an electronic forum where Floyd fans from around the world "meet" on the Internet to discuss the band. It read:

My friends,
You have heard the message Pink Floyd has delivered but have you listened?
Perhaps I can be your guide, but I will not solve the enigma for you.
All of you must open your minds and communi-

cate with each other, as this is the only way the answers can be revealed.
I may help you, but only if obstacles arise.
Listen.
Read.
Think.
Communicate.
If I don't promise you the answers would you go.
– Publius

The message was immediately greeted with the nasty, often insulting responses known as "flames," which attempt to expose the messenger's phoniness. There was some speculation that Publius was out to mock Floyd fans for their penchant for seeking deep meanings in the band's music; others felt that the whole thing was a record company plot to drum up sales of *The Division Bell*. Less cynical fans suggested that Publius was David Gilmour himself. In any case, approximately every two weeks, Publius would offer more veiled clues and references to *The Division Bell*'s lyrics, such as this post from July 8:

AS SOME OF YOU HAVE SUSPECTED, "The Division Bell" is not like its predecessors. Although all great music is subject to multiple interpretations, in this case there is a central purpose and a designed solution. For the ingenious person (or group of persons) who recognizes this—and where this information points to—a

unique prize has been secreted.
How and Where?
The Division Bell
Listen again
Look again
As your thoughts will steer you
Leading the blind while I stared out the steel in your eyes.
Lyrics, artwork and music will take you there

With most net users remaining skeptical, Publius promised a demonstration of his legitimacy in the form of "flashing white lights" at the July 18th Pink Floyd concert in New Jersey's Meadowlands Arena. Sure enough, as the band performed *The Division Bell*'s "Keep Talking," the words "ENIGMA PUBLIUS" lit up the front of the stage. This occurred nowhere else on the tour—neither before the Giants Stadium show nor afterwards. To some, this special display was ample proof of Publius' validity, and readers eagerly

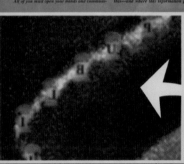
ART BY MICHAEL SEXTON

OF SECRETS

ENGAGED IN A BIZARRE TREASURE HUNT. PUBLICITY STUNT? BALD-FACED HOAX? YOU DECIDE.

scanned his previous messages for Floydian slips. Skeptics maintained that Publius was simply someone who knew the lighting staff at the stadium and had pulled a good scam.

While Publius' posts are cryptic and melodramatic—the classic signs of a net-crackpot—there's plenty of mysterious fodder surrounding *The Division Bell* to fuel his fire. Why is the artwork different for the CD and vinyl releases? What's going on in the audio collage that interrupts "Poles Apart"? Why does the boxing referee count out of order during "Lost For Words"? It certainly wouldn't be out of character for a band who put backwards messages and quirky audio tricks in many of their previous albums to plant a hidden puzzle within their latest release.

Proposed solutions to the mystery have involved a wide variety of people, places and things—among them physicist Stephen Hawking, Easter Island, the Federalist Papers and the geography of Cambridge, England. "My personal

favorite," says net user Allison Clark, "was when they were organizing an expedition to go dig up the grounds of Ely Cathedral [the structure pictured on the album cover], last August. I could just see the police picking up a bunch of teenagers chanting Pink Floyd lyrics as they excavated the grounds with their shovels, and the newspapers dutifully reporting that the youths would say only that Dave Gilmour had sent them there on a mission."

The band, meanwhile, will neither confirm nor deny any knowledge of or involvement with Publius. Whatever the outcome, most newsgroup readers agree that the experience hasn't been a complete waste of time—even if there isn't a hidden treasure buried somewhere, just waiting for some lucky Floyd fan. "It has been great to see people take heed of Pink Floyd's advice to 'keep talking,'" says Rudi Riet, a concertgoer who witnessed the ENIGMA PUBLIUS light show. "If anything, the Publius Enigma has widened channels of communication on alt.music.pink-floyd. And if

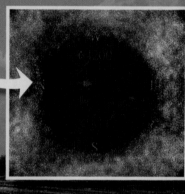

that was the ultimate goal, Publius—whoever he may be—has succeeded."

If you are interested in researching the Publius Enigma further, join and read the messages of the alt.music.pink-floyd newsgroup through a commerical online service, such as CompuServe, America Online or Delphi, or contact a local direct internet provider. Many colleges offer direct internet access to their students as part of their tuition. To subscribe to the Pink Floyd mailing lists, send Email to ECHOSERV@FAWNYA. TCS. COM, with ADD ECHOES (for general Pink Floyd discussion) or ADD PUBLIUS (for Publius-related messages only) as the message. Publius' previous posts are still readily available on the newsgroup and from many of its members. Watch the pages of Guitar World for more Publius information as it develops.

Special thanks to the members of alt.music.pink-floyd and the Echoes and Publius Concern mailing lists for their assistance with this story.

—DAN AMRICH

JAN.1995

VOL. 16 / NO. 1

Pink Floyd: The Publius Enigma

Guitar World's Dan Amrich reports on the mysterious Pink Floyd treasure hunt

Pink Floyd fans, take note:

There's a treasure hunt going on, and *The Division Bell* is the map. In what could be the biggest mystery in the annals of rock, Floyd disciples around the world have been carefully following a trail of clues left by a self-proclaimed messenger known only as Publius. The person who deciphers the enigma has been promised a special, secret reward.

Publius—who may or may not be a member of the band—first began leaving mysterious messages this past summer in the midst of a Pink Floyd discussion on the world wide computer network known as the internet. His rather cryptic clues have caused confusion and controversy among Pink Floyd stalwarts—and sent them racing back to listen to *The Division Bell* with new ears.

The mystery began on June 11, 1994, with an anonymous, generically titled note left in the alt.music.pink-floyd newsgroup, an electronic forum where Floyd fans from around the world "meet" on the internet and discuss the band. It read:

> *My friends,*
> *You have heard the message Pink Floyd has delivered, but have you listened?*
> *Perhaps I can be your guide, but I will not solve the enigma for you.*
> *All of you must open your minds and communicate with each other, as this is the only way the answers can be revealed.*
> *I may help you, but only if obstacles arise.*
> *Listen.*
> *Read.*
> *Think.*
> *Communicate.*
> *If I don't promise you the answers would you go.*
> *—Publius*

The message was immediately greeted with the nasty, often insulting responses known as "flames," which attempt to expose the messenger's phoniness. There was some speculation that Publius was out to mock Floyd fans for their penchant for seeking deep meanings in the band's music; others felt that the whole thing was a record company plot to drum up sales of *The Division Bell*. Less cynical fans suggested that Publius was David Gilmour himself. In any case, approximately every two weeks, Publius would offer more veiled clues and references to *The Division Bell*'s lyrics.

With most internet users remaining skeptical, Publius promised a demonstration of his legitimacy in the form of "flashing white lights" at the July 18, 1994, Pink Floyd concert at New Jersey's Giants Stadium. Sure enough, as the band performed *The Division Bell*'s "Keep Talking," the words "ENIGMA PUBLIUS" lit up the front of the stage. This occurred nowhere else on the tour. To some, this special display was ample proof of Publius' validity, and readers eagerly scanned his previous messages for Floydian slips. Skeptics maintained that Publius was simply someone who knew the lighting staff at the stadium and had pulled a good scam.

While Publius' posts are cryptic and melodramatic—the classic signs of a net.crackpot—there's plenty of mysterious fodder surrounding *The Division Bell* to fuel his fire. Why is the artwork different for the CD and vinyl releases? What's going on in the audio collage that interrupts "Poles Apart"? Why does the boxing referee count out of order during "Lost for Words"? It certainly wouldn't be out of character for a band who put backward messages and quirky audio tricks in many of their previous albums to plant a hidden puzzle within their latest release.

Proposed solutions to the mystery have involved a wide variety of people, places and things—among them physicist Stephen Hawking, Easter Island, the Federalist Papers and the geography of Cambridge, England. "My personal favorite," says net user Allison Clark, "was when they were organizing an expedition to go dig up the grounds of Ely Cathedral [*the structure pictured on the album cover*] last August. I could just see the police picking up a bunch of teenagers chanting Pink Floyd lyrics as they excavated the grounds with their shovels, and the newspapers dutifully reporting that the youths would say only that David Gilmour had sent them there on a mission."

The band, meanwhile, will neither confirm nor deny any knowledge of or involvement with Publius. Whatever the outcome, most newsgroup readers agree that the experience hasn't been a complete waste of time—even if there isn't a hidden treasure buried somewhere, just waiting for some lucky Floyd fan. "It has been great to see people take heed of Pink Floyd's advice to 'keep talking,'" says Rudi Riet, a concertgoer who witnesses the ENIGMA PUBLIUS light show. "If anything, the Publius Enigma has widened channels of communication on alt.music.pink-floyd. And if that was the ultimate goal, Publius—whoever he may be—has succeeded." ✳

In April 2005, Pink Floyd drummer Nick Mason revealed that the Publius Enigma was a plot hatched by the band's record label, EMI. "They had a man working for them who adored puzzles, and he suggested that a puzzle be created that could be followed on the web. The prize was never given out. To this day it remains unsolved."

Clapton reigns. Punk rocks.
Kurt is sorely missed.

Our opinions?
Nope. It's your word.

MOST VALUABLE PLAYER
1. ERIC CLAPTON
2. Jimmy Page
3. Kurt Cobain
4. Kurt Cobain
5. John Petrucci

BEST NEW TALENT
1. PETER KLETT (CANDLEBOX)
2. Billie Joe Armstrong (Green Day)
3. Noodles Wasserman and Dexter Holland (The Offspring)
4. Rivers Cuomo (Weezer)
5. Ed Roland, Dean Roland and Ross Childress (Collective Soul)

BEST ROCK GUITARIST
1. EDDIE VAN HALEN
2. Joe Perry
3. Slash
4. Jimmy Page
5. David Gilmour

BEST HEAVY METAL GUITARIST
1. DIMEBAG DARRELL
2. Kirk Hammett
3. John Petrucci
4. Marty Friedman
5. Zakk Wylde

BEST BLUES GUITARIST
1. ERIC CLAPTON
2. Buddy Guy
3. B.B. King
4. Chris Duarte

MARCH / VOL. 16 / NO. 3

1995 READERS POLL RESULTS

Our readers weigh in with their picks for the best and worst players and albums of the past year.

MOST VALUABLE PLAYER
1. Eric Clapton
2. Dimebag Darrell
3. Jimmy Page
4. Kurt Cobain
5. John Petrucci

BEST NEW TALENT
1. Peter Klett (Candlebox)
2. Billie Joe Armstrong (Green Day)
3. Noodles Wasserman & Dexter Holland (The Offspring)
4. Rivers Cuomo (Weezer)
5. Ed Roland, Dean Roland & Ross Childress (Collective Soul)

BEST LIVE BAND
1. Metallica
2. Pearl Jam
3. Pink Floyd
4. Pantera
5. The Rolling Stones

BEST SOLO
1. Dimebag Darrell—"Planet Caravan"
2. Kim Thayil—"Black Hole Sun"

3. Peter Klett—"Far Behind"
4. John Petrucci—"Lie"
5. Jerry Cantrell—"Whale and Wasp"

BEST HEAVY METAL ALBUM
1. Pantera—*Far Beyond Driven*
2. Megadeth—*Youthanasia*
3. Dream Theater—*Awake*
4. Slayer—*Divine Intervention*
5. Helmet—*Betty*

BEST ROCK ALBUM
1. Stone Temple Pilots—*Purple*
2. Pink Floyd—*The Division Bell*
3. The Rolling Stones—*Voodoo Lounge*
4. The Offspring—*Smash*
5. Candlebox—*Candlebox*

BEST ALTERNATIVE ALBUM
1. Nirvana—*MTV Unplugged in New York*
2. Soundgarden—*Superunknown*
3. Green Day—*Dookie*
4. Nine Inch Nails—*The Downward Spiral*
5. Hole—*Live Through This*

BIGGEST DISAPPOINTMENT
1. The death of Kurt Cobain
2. Queensrÿche—*Promised Land*
3. Jimmy Page and Robert Plant—*No Quarter*
4. Yngwie Malmsteen
5. Guns N' Roses—*The Spaghetti Incident?*

NOT TO MENTION...
"Daisy Fuentes won't return my calls."
"Jimi Hendrix is still dead."
"My kitty never came home."
"My girlfriend got knocked up."
"Anna Nicole Smith marrying that 90-year-old guy."
"I haven't gotten laid in five years."
"I wasn't chosen as a juror in the O.J. Simpson trial."

15 Years of Hot Guitar: A *Guitar World* Anniversary

MAY '95

The May 1995 issue marked a great milestone in *Guitar World*'s history: our 15th anniversary. For this special issue, the editors compiled some of the most scintillating interviews with the world's most respected artists (Keith Richards, Stevie Ray Vaughan, Frank Zappa, Randy Rhoads), transcribed rock's most famous riffs ("Crazy Train," "Back in Black," "Even Flow," "Master of Puppets"), celebrated 15 years of guitar gear and assembled lists of essential classic rock, hardcore, alternative, metal and blues albums. Even the Metal Detector was given the royal 15th anniversary treatment, despite the fact that it had only been in existence for four years. But who's counting.

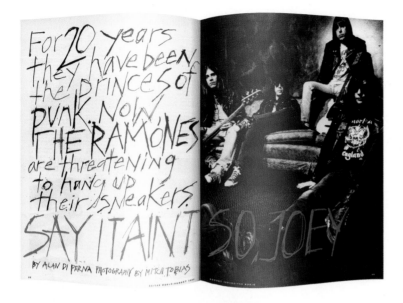

For 20 years they have been the princes of punk. Now THE RAMONES are threatening to hang up their sneakers. SAY IT AINT SO, JOEY

BY ALAN DI PERNA PHOTOGRAPHY BY MITRA TOBIAS

AUGUST / VOL. 16 / NO. 8

JOEY RAMONE

In this rare conversation, the punk rock icon conveys his thoughts on music and depression and rates his own abilities as a guitarist.

JOEY RAMONE With the death of Kurt Cobain, all these young kids have no one to look up to anymore. I mean, I thought Kurt was great too. He was real. But he bailed out. He couldn't handle it anymore. Everyone's got their demons, you know. Believe me, you wouldn't want my problems. I ride the roller coaster all the time, but I'm not one to bail. I'm an optimist. So maybe that song will inspire someone else who's feeling down. I know that whenever I was depressed I used to put on Lou Reed's *Berlin*. And that really picked me up. It's a real lift.

GUITAR WORLD When you're really depressed, sometimes really depressing music can be therapeutic.

RAMONE Yeah, Neil Young is great for that. I used to put on one of those Crazy Horse albums all the time. Music saves, you know? Music is salvation. Definitely. When I'm excited I'll put on the Stooges or the Who or Slade or T-Rex and it's definitely uplifting.

GW Do you write your songs on guitar?

RAMONE Well, I write all different ways. A lot of times I'll just write them in my head and work them out on the guitar later. And sometimes I write them right on the guitar. I think the day I wrote "Life's a Gas," I was sitting with the guitar and it just came. It's rare when you get that flood—that mental enema. But it's great when it comes your way.

GW How would you rate yourself as a guitar player?

RAMONE [*Holds his forefinger an inch away from his thumb*] I'd say I'm a little lower than Hendrix and a little above Page.

The Birth of
www.guitarworld.com

After barely a year living on the CompuServe computer network, *Guitar World* made the leap to the still-new world wide web in the early fall of 1995. While the www.guitarworld.com of '95 looked nothing like it does today, the basics were there: news, magazine content, a discussion forum, contests, etc. The visuals were crude, but what else would you expect from a web site that was meant to be viewed "using the NetScape 1.1n software with a 14,400 baud (or faster) modem and a dial-up internet connection."

Fresh Start

"Like Divine Brown, AC/DC are a guilty pleasure best enjoyed in the car."

—*Opening line of Alan di Perna's AC/DC cover story, November 1995*

NOV. '95

Bruce Springsteen reflects on his music, life with and without the E-Street Band, and the glory of rock & roll.

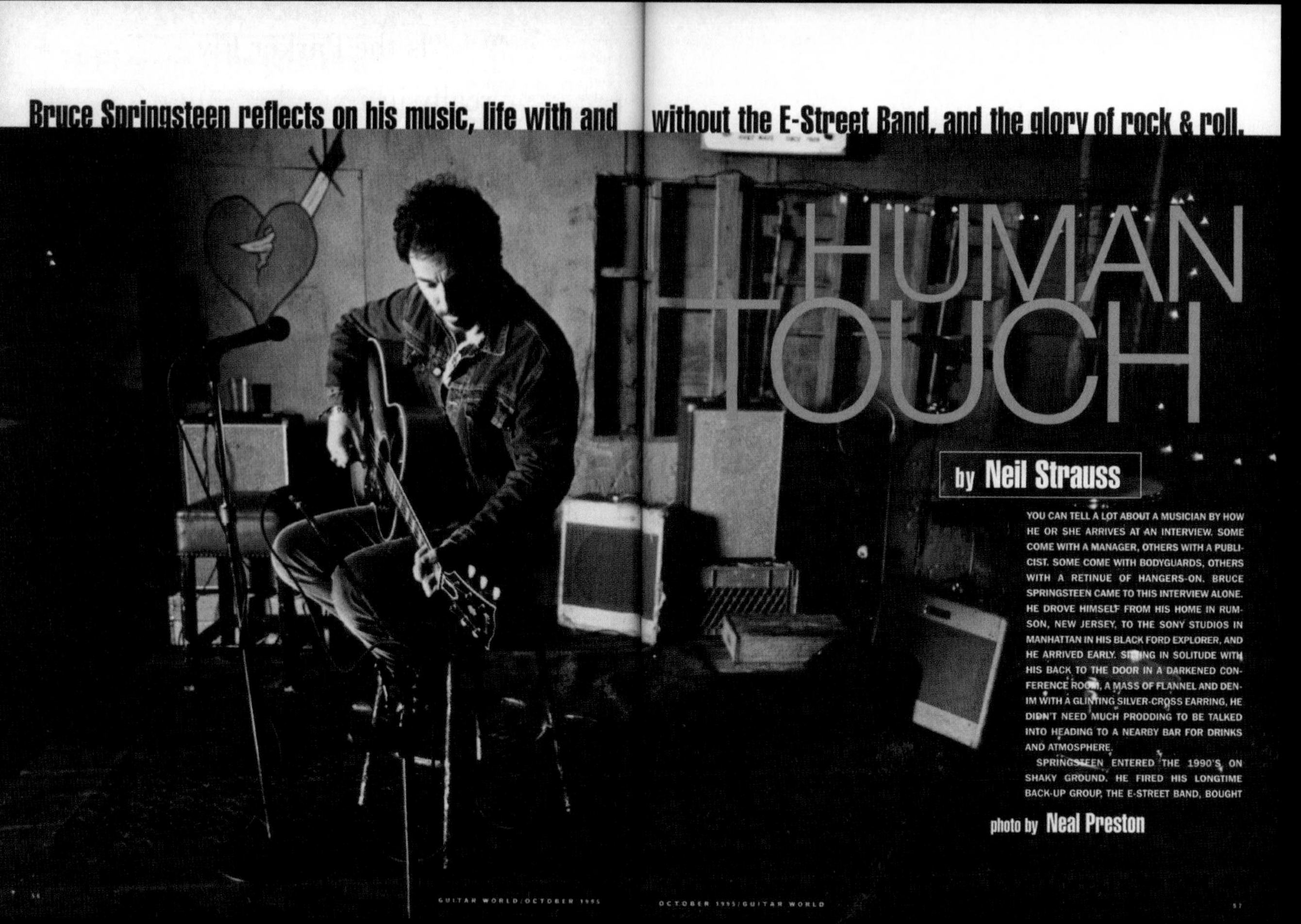

HUMAN TOUCH

by Neil Strauss

YOU CAN TELL A LOT ABOUT A MUSICIAN BY HOW HE OR SHE ARRIVES AT AN INTERVIEW. SOME COME WITH A MANAGER, OTHERS WITH A PUBLICIST. SOME COME WITH BODYGUARDS, OTHERS WITH A RETINUE OF HANGERS-ON. BRUCE SPRINGSTEEN CAME TO THIS INTERVIEW ALONE. HE DROVE HIMSELF FROM HIS HOME IN RUMSON, NEW JERSEY, TO THE SONY STUDIOS IN MANHATTAN IN HIS BLACK FORD EXPLORER, AND HE ARRIVED EARLY. SITTING IN SOLITUDE WITH HIS BACK TO THE DOOR IN A DARKENED CONFERENCE ROOM, A MASS OF FLANNEL AND DENIM WITH A GLINTING SILVER-CROSS EARRING, HE DIDN'T NEED MUCH PRODDING TO BE TALKED INTO HEADING TO A NEARBY BAR FOR DRINKS AND ATMOSPHERE.

SPRINGSTEEN ENTERED THE 1990'S ON SHAKY GROUND. HE FIRED HIS LONGTIME BACK-UP GROUP, THE E-STREET BAND, BOUGHT

photo by Neal Preston

GUITAR WORLD/OCTOBER 1995 OCTOBER 1995/GUITAR WORLD 57

OCT. 1995

VOL. 16 / NO. 10

Bruce Springsteen

In *Guitar World*'s one and only cover story interview with Bruce Springsteen, the Boss shares his views on the current state of alternative rock and where he'd like to see himself as a guitar player in the future.

GUITAR WORLD Before you ever started releasing records, you were known more as a guitarist than a songwriter. Do you ever think about stepping out as guitarist again?

BRUCE SPRINGSTEEN I was always the guitar player in the band. But I reached a point in the early Seventies where I said, "There are so many good guitarists, but there are not a lot of people who have their own songwriting voice." And I really focused on that. Then the label wanted a folk album, because I was really signed as a folk artist by John Hammond, who didn't know that I ever had a band.

Ultimately, my guitar playing came to be about fitting in with the ensemble. Then Clarence [*Clemmons*] came along with his saxophone. He's sort of a force of nature, so if I wanted to hear a solo, I let him do it. I put a lot of my guitar playing in the rear, but at this point I'd like to bring it back to the front. As a matter of fact, I played with the Blasters the other night, and it was really fun. I was back to being just a blues guitarist; I used to play the blues all the time.

One of these days I'd like to toy around with making a record that's centered around loud guitars and me playing more. At some point I sort of opted out of the jam thing and got more into the solo being in service of the song. I'd really like to play something where I've got to really play, you know. Now I feel like I'm at a place where I can do anything and I want to do it all.

GW You mentioned earlier that while "Thunder Road" wasn't a hit, or even a single, you included it on your *Greatest Hits* album because it seemed so central to your work. Why do you think that's so?

SPRINGSTEEN I'm not sure what that song has. We played it the other night at the Sony studio, when we were taping a European show, and it just felt all-inclusive. It may be something about trying to seize a particular moment in your life and realizing you have to make very fundamental and basic decisions that you know will alter your life and how you live it. It's a funny song because it simultaneously contains both dreaming and disillusionment.

GW That's similar to what Melissa Etheridge was saying when she introduced "Thunder Road" on MTV *Unplugged*. It was just before you came onstage and she said, "If anyone can make you dream, it's Bruce Springsteen."

SPRINGSTEEN You know, you write your music and you never know where the seeds that you sow are going to fall. Melissa Etheridge comes out of the Midwest, and she comes out of the gay bars, and I like that that's where some of my influence falls. I think that a big part of what my songs are about is being who you are, and trying to create the world that you want to live in. Generally, I think people use songs as a way to order their lives in a world that feels so out of order. It's a way of centering themselves and grounding themselves in a set of values, a sense of things they can go back and touch base with.

GW Today's alternative rock is almost a reaction against the experience of music you had growing up. These new bands don't want to carry the flame, they want to stamp it out.

SPRINGSTEEN Look at a band like Nirvana. They reset the rules of the game. They changed everything, they opened a vein of freedom that didn't exist previously. Kurt Cobain did something very similar to what Dylan did in the Sixties, which was to sound different and get on the radio. He proved that a guitarist could sound different and still be heard. So Cobain reset a lot of very fundamental rules, and that type of artist is very few and far between.

I think what people are feeling is other people's fingerprints on their minds. And that seems to be a real strong and vital subject currently running through a lot of alternative music. I feel it myself. And, hey, there needs to be a voice against that sort of co-option of your own thinking space. What are your memories? What are your ideas? Everything is pre-packaged and sold to you as desirable or seductive in some fashion. So how do you find out who you are, create your own world, find your own self? That's the business of rock music in the Nineties. ✳

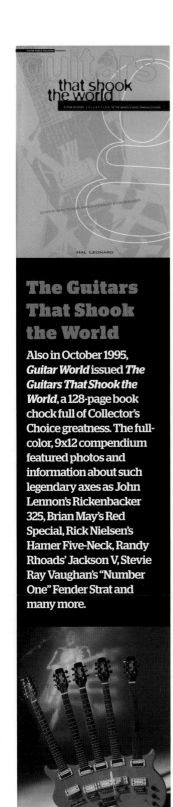

The Guitars That Shook the World

Also in October 1995, *Guitar World* issued *The Guitars That Shook the World*, a 128-page book chock full of Collector's Choice greatness. The full-color, 9x12 compendium featured photos and information about such legendary axes as John Lennon's Rickenbacker 325, Brian May's Red Special, Rick Nielsen's Hamer Five-Neck, Randy Rhoads' Jackson V, Stevie Ray Vaughan's "Number One" Fender Strat and many more.

NINETEEN

'96

A celebration of reunions (Kiss, Sex Pistols),
dynamic duos (Corgan/Van Halen, Rancid/Ramones)
and the Top 100 Albums of All Time.

Dear *Guitar World*,

What if Hendrix had played tuba? What if he had
been lactose intolerant? What if he had been
from Utah? What if he had gills? What if he had
been 60 feet tall and made from titanium steel
and had ray guns that shot out of his chest?
Or, what if he had spelled his name with a "y"?
Boy, would that be weird.

What if he came back from the grave to seek
revenge on the editor-in-chief of a sophomoric,
poorly written guitar magazine, who keeps
putting Jimi's name on the cover just to sell
magazines? Too bad wishing won't make it so.

—K.C. Smith, responding to *Guitar World*'s "What if
Jimi Hendrix had lived?" fantasy piece in the January
1996 issue.

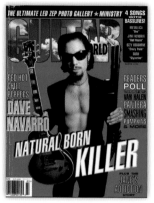

JANUARY Jerry Cantrell confronts his demons on *Alice in Chains*, the band's dark new album.
COVER STORY BY JEFF GILBERT
PHOTO BY MARTY TEMME

FEBRUARY On *Stripped*, Keith Richards and the Rolling Stones unplug their guitars and revisit some of their past triumphs.
COVER STORY BY GARY GRAFF
PHOTO BY MICHAEL PUTMAN

MARCH Dave Navarro exposes his personal demons and examines the pains and pleasures of being a Red Hot Chili Pepper.
COVER STORY BY ALAN DI PERNA
PHOTO BY MICHAEL SEXTON

APRIL Billy Corgan, alternative's boy wonder, interviews hard rock's guitar champion, Eddie Van Halen.
COVER STORY BY BILLY CORGAN
PHOTO BY LISA JOHNSON

MAY With their silly songs and bizarre guitars, the Presidents of the United States of America emerge as Seattle's latest frontrunners. "Kim Thayil says there are two different factions in Seattle," says guitarist Chris Ballew. "One thinks that we're an annoying joke, while the other thinks we're a good band...sort of."
COVER STORY BY ALAN DI PERNA; PHOTO BY LISA JOHNSON

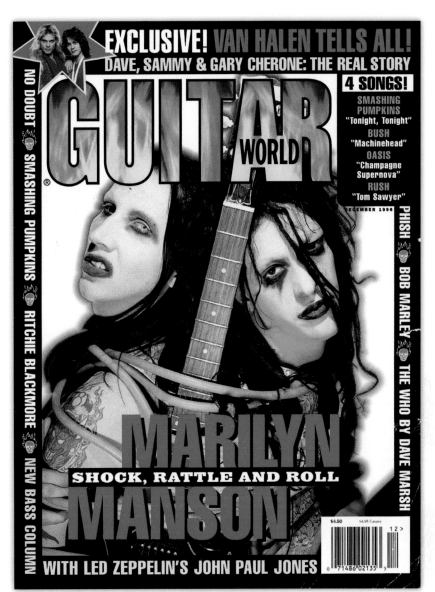

JUNE Dimebag Darrell and his Pantera brothers put the pedal to the metal on *The Great Southern Trendkill.*
COVER STORY BY NICK BOWCOTT; PHOTO BY JAMES BLAND

JULY After five long years, Metallica return with new haircuts, a startling new sound and a new album, *Load.*
COVER STORY BY TOM BEAUJOUR; PHOTO BY DANNY CLINCH

AUGUST After 20 years of long-distance bickering, the Sex Pistols have reunited for a summer tour and an upcoming album. Johnny Rotten and Steve Jones reveal what it's like to kiss and make up.
COVER STORY BY ALAN DI PERNA; PHOTO BY MITCH TOBIAS

SEPTEMBER Rock and roll, all over again: The triumphant return of the original Kiss, kings of bombast and theatrical excess.
COVER STORY BY JEFF KITTS; PHOTO BY MICHAEL SEXTON

OCTOBER A previously unpublished, no-holds-barred interview with Kurt Cobain, the late guru of grunge.
COVER STORY BY JON SAVAGE; PHOTO BY KIRK WEDDLE

NOVEMBER Guitarist Peter Buck takes us on an exclusive tour through the entire R.E.M. discography, from *Murmur* to their latest, *New Adventures in Hi-Fi.*
COVER STORY BY VIC GARBARINI; PHOTO BY ANTON CORBIJN

DECEMBER With *Antichrist Superstar*, Marilyn Manson takes shock rock into the mainstream. There goes the neighborhood... "I consider my life a concept, and this record is a soundtrack to that," says Manson. "It would probably be easier for a lot of the world to swallow the concepts that I deal with if they were to assume that I am merely a character. But it's very real to me."
COVER STORY BY ALAN DI PERNA; PHOTO BY JOSEPH CULTICE

1996 TOTAL ISSUES: 12

BRAVE foo WORLD

Ex-Nirvana drummer **Dave Grohl** picks up a
guitar and buries the past with **Foo Fighters**.

BY MARNIX PEETERS

n O ONE WOULD have found Dave Grohl wanting
in rock and roll spirit had he decided to take
a nice, long vacation. After all, Grohl and his
drum kit had survived three years of riding
the Nirvana roller coaster, a trip that ended
with the tragic death of Kurt Cobain.

Yet Grohl chose not to run away. Instead, he entered a studio and recorded more than a dozen of his own songs. He played drums—all the instruments, in fact. He labeled the project "Foo Fighters," and when Capitol decided to release the album, Grohl formed a band, also called Foo Fighters, to support his record. He was back from the abyss.

Not that it was so easy.

"After Kurt's death, I was about as confused as I've ever been," admits Grohl. "To continue almost seemed in vain. I

ILLUSTRATION BY MIKE O'DAY

FEB. 1996

VOL. 17 / NO. 2

Dave Grohl

**The 26-year-old former Nirvana drummer steps out from behind the kit, guitar in
hand, and launches his Foo Fighters project.**

GUITAR WORLD Was it difficult to make the transition from drums to the guitar?

DAVE GROHL Not really. I've been playing since I was about 10 years old. I started by taking some lessons after everyone got sick of hearing me play "Smoke on the Water." But I stopped because they weren't teaching me how to play music.

At about the same time, I was trying to figure out Beatles songs by myself. I was always really good at figuring out songs by ear. I think music is in my blood, because my mother was in singing groups as a teen and my father was an accomplished flautist.

GW Did you play guitar in any band settings?

GROHL Sure. After I discovered distortion at age 12, I joined a neighborhood cover band. We played stuff by the Who and the Stones. We actually performed "Time Is on My Side" at a nursing home. [*laughs*]

When I got into eighth grade, I got a drum kit and somehow already knew how to play it. My goal was to be Keith Moon, with the kick drum foot of John Bonham.

My next major shot at being a guitarist came in the summer of 1984. I met some guys at a Void show in Washington, D.C., who were in a band called Freak Baby that needed a guitar player. I offered my services and got an audition. I got in and my career as a punk rocker began. We played a few shows at a local high school and recorded a demo.

GW With Foo Fighters, is it difficult to get out from under the shadow of Nirvana?

GROHL Of course. If we were any other band, if I hadn't been in Nirvana, if there wasn't...the *legend* of Nirvana weighing on my shoulders, people wouldn't care. People would just be like, "Oh yeah, they're pretty good." But what will always hang over *my* head will be things like, "Yeah, they're a really good band, but they're not as good as Nirvana." When I read things like that, I go, "No shit." [*laughs*] I hate to compare the two. On the other hand, if we weren't under such a microscope, I wouldn't feel that need to prove something.

GW You can't get rid of your past that easily, obviously. Is that a scary thing?

GROHL I have so much respect for the past, for every person I've ever been in a band with. I have the ultimate respect for Kurt and Krist [*Novoselic, Nirvana bassist*]. But for me the most important thing is to move on. You have to feel like things keep going.

GW It must be difficult. For instance, there are those who search for Cobain references in your lyrics.

GROHL That's weird. Everybody wants more information. Everybody wants the answer—wants to know *why*. The thing is, I have just as many questions as most people.

As far as finding references, many of these lyrics were written over five fucking years ago. But people will read the lyrics, and every time I say, "he," they'll think I'm talking about Kurt. And every time I say "me," they'll think I'm talking about myself. It's not necessarily "me." It's *songwriting*. To me, the whole examination of the lyrics is nonsense.

GW Only one of your songs—"Marigold," the b-side of "Heart-Shaped Box"—was recorded by Nirvana. Didn't you feel tempted to write more with them?

GROHL Nirvana fooled around with some of my songs. But when you're in a band with someone like Kurt, who wrote really great songs, you have this feeling like, Man, I don't want to pollute this. I don't want this to change. And I don't want to be responsible for changing something that's so good. It's a restriction, but it's not a painful one. I felt like I was saving the band. [*laughs*]

GW Did you ever wonder where it would have ended if Kurt hadn't died?

GROHL Sometimes. I have different versions. I always had the feeling, as with anything, that you can only be so good for so long. I couldn't see myself being 45 years old, playing "Smells Like Teen Spirit." But in a lot of ways, nobody really knew what was gonna happen. And that's one of the reasons why it was so exciting, because even in the last year of the band, things were pretty unpredictable, in bad ways and in good. ✳

best
of
both
worlds

BILLY CORGAN, ALTERNATIVE ROCK'S CROWN
PRINCE, INTERVIEWS HARD ROCK'S
REIGNING KING, EDDIE VAN HALEN.

Make no mistake. Eddie Van Halen can still kick
your ass. The man who single-handedly changed
the face of rock is still mean, lean and sharp
as a tack. And if you dispute the
ownership of the crown, try to
imagine a world without him. I came to pay my
tribute, sneak a peak at that famous Marshall
and meet the man I most wanted to be at 17.

BY BILLY CORGAN
PHOTOGRAPHY BY LISA JOHNSON

MAY
'96

APRIL / VOL. 17 / NO. 4

BILLY CORGAN & EDDIE VAN HALEN

In this historic first-time meeting, alternative rock's
boy wonder interviews hard rock's guitar champion.

BILLY CORGAN So, after 20 years of recording, what makes you still want
to rock?

EDDIE VAN HALEN It's because I'm still 16 inside. I still have that passion,
and any true musician doesn't do it for any other reason than passion.
My motivation has never been financial. Music is what I do. It's the only
thing I know how to do.

CORGAN But don't you ever have to fight to keep your music exciting?

VAN HALEN Sure. I have my low points. For example, we recently finished a pretty grueling 11-month tour and I was beat to hell. I was depressed. I had the post-tour blues—whatever you want to call it. Usually,
I can shake it just by doing some work in my studio. Up until that time I
always thought of my studio as my sanctuary—a place to jam and clear
my head. But, for the first time, it didn't seem that way. I just didn't have
the desire to play at all. In fact, I was so fried I wondered whether I was
ever going to be able to write anything again. So, I just simply let go.
Then, boom, one day, all of a sudden the desire came back.

CORGAN You created the sound of Van Halen. After all these years, how
do you confront your own legacy? Do you ever worry about repeating
yourself?

VAN HALEN Not really. Change is a natural part of my evolution as a
player. It just happens, because everybody changes over a period of
time. It's a very unconscious thing. I think the unreleased acoustic piece
I just played you before the interview sounds different from anything
I've ever done, yet I didn't sit down and say, "I have to do something
different."

CORGAN I admire your attitude, because I feel like I'm always fighting
not to repeat myself.

VAN HALEN Every time I walk into the studio it seems like the first time.
It's like I've never written a song before. I am just as scared. I'm really
insecure that way.

Tony Iommi & Rob Halford: The Project That Wasn't

In our May 1996 issue, Chris
Gill reported on the possible
formation of a heavy metal
supergroup featuring Black
Sabbath guitarist Tony Iommi and former Judas Priest
singer Rob Halford. "Sab-
bath has stopped touring,"
said Iommi, although he refused to confirm the band's
demise. With Sabbath on the
verge of non-existence, Iommi met with Halford—who
was between solo projects
at the time—in Los Angeles
to discuss the new venture.
"I sat down with him and a
producer and it looks really,
really good," said Iommi.
"We're going to get together
to put a few ideas down and
see how it goes. I'm looking
forward to working with
Rob." For reasons unknown,
this union of metal gods never materialized—though we
get all gooey inside thinking
of what might have been.

———— "Music is what I do. It's the only thing I know how to do." *–Eddie Van Halen*

Five years have passed since Metallica released the epic "Black Album." During that time, the music world has radically changed—and so has Metallica.

born again

By Tom Beaujour
Photography by Danny Clinch

JULY / VOL. 17 / NO. 7

JAMES HETFIELD & KIRK HAMMETT

Metallica's guitar titans explain their shocking decision to perform at the mother of all alterna-rock festival tours, Lollapalooza.

GUITAR WORLD Were you asked to play Lollapalooza? Or did you do the asking?

JAMES HETFIELD They asked us. We thought about it and said, "All right, why the fuck not?" All it is is a European-style rock festival. We've done festivals all over the world.

KIRK HAMMETT The whole impetus behind Lollapalooza was to do something challenging. And I think that the bill with us on it is different and challenging—more recently, they were stuck in a rut where they had to have alternative bands and indie bands.

GW Is it true that you played an important role in selecting the bands for this year's lineup?

HAMMETT We did and we didn't. A lot of it had to do with availability. A lot of bands we wanted were touring on their own. I mean, I would have liked to have Al Green or the Cocteau Twins.

HETFIELD We're not picking Lollapalooza. We're not coming in to take it over. We're just gonna play. We really don't want to have anything to do with Lollapalooza except play it.

GW Are you looking forward to seeing any of the bands that will be on the bill with you?

HAMMETT I like the vibe of Lollapalooza. I've been to every single one; I've actually jammed at a few too. When Ministry was out I played with them a few times, and I did the same with Primus. I've fucking loved Soundgarden since 1985 or '86. And everyone loves the Ramones. I was talking to Johnny Ramone the other day and he was saying, "Goddamn it, Kirk, I'd already be retired and playing golf in L.A. if it weren't for you guys calling us up and asking us to do this summer tour." And I said, "Well, Johnny, there isn't any better way to go."

Mistakes R Us

We here at *Guitar World* are never ashamed to admit our blunders (right, former mangaging editor Alan Paul?). But the one error that baffles us even to this day is the unfathomable disaster on the cover of the June 1996 issue: yes, we spelled Led Zep's "Stairway to Heaven" wrong. On the cover. "Stairway to Heaven." The #1 rock song of all time. It was actually the first time the song was tabbed in the magazine (save for a reader-submitted transcription of the guitar solo in the early Eighties), and we screwed it up royally. "Stariway to Heaven" has become the benchmark for all mistakes—past, present and future—perpetrated by the magazine staff.

...lapton and Peter Green, [Ritchie] Black-more is one of the true gods of British rock guitar. The fierce vibrato, the sweet/biting Strat-through-Marshall tone, the sublimely savage blues-meets-classical licks are all trademarks of the much-copied Blackmore style (just ask Yngwie Malmsteen). All are much in evidence on *Stranger in Us All*, the latest offering from the man in black and his all-new, reconstituted Rainbow.

Though the faces are new—and against all reasonable expectations—the sound of the album is one hundred percent vintage Rainbow: melodic, majestic, metallic and positively medieval. But don't thank Ritchie for that, thank his latest titanium-lunged belter, Londoner Doogie White.

"Initially I wanted to do more of a blues thing," says Blackmore. "But Doogie doesn't really have a bluesy voice. He's into the old classic hard rock, and he *loves* Ronnie Dio *[Rainbow's original vocalist]*. So as soon as he puts his vocal stamp down, its naturally curved more toward a hard-rock sound. And I thought, 'Okay, I'll go with that. There's nothing wrong with that. That's great.' "

In truth, Blackmore didn't even want to call the new band (which came together shortly after his departure from Deep Purple last year) Rainbow. "I wanted to call it Moon, after my grandfather's surname," he says. "But the record company said, 'Oh no, no, no! It has to be called Ritchie Blackmore's Rainbow for sales.' And I said, 'C'mon! I've done all that.' I really wanted to call it something new. But

DEC. 1996

VOL. 17 / NO. 12

Ritchie Blackmore

The Deep Purple/Rainbow virtuoso looks back on some of his most famous recorded moments.

"Hush" (*Deep Purple*, 1968)

"**IT WAS MY IDEA** to do 'Hush,' a song by [*sessions guitarist/solo artist Joe South*]. I liked the guitar solo—especially the feedback. That was done with my Gibson ES-335, which I don't have anymore because my ex-wife stole it. I used that right up to the *In Rock* album, on 'Child in Time' and 'Flight of the Rat.' The reason I changed to a Stratocaster was because the sound had an edge to it that I really liked. But it was much harder to get used to. When you're playing a humbucking pickup, you've got that fat sound and it's quite forgiving. But when you play with Fender pickups, they're so thin and mean and edgy and hard. And every note counts; you can't fake a note."

"Child in Time" (*Deep Purple In Rock*, 1970)

"**THAT RECORD WAS SORT OF** a response to the one we did with the orchestra. I wanted to do a loud, hard rock record. And I was thinking, This record better make it, because I was afraid that if I didn't, we were going to be struck playing with orchestras for the rest of our lives.

" 'Child in Time' is a great song. Ian Gillan was probably the only guy who could sing that. It was done in three stages, sort of like an operatic thing. That's him at his best. Nobody else would have attempted that, going up in octaves.

"I think the guitar solo is relatively average. I did it in two or three takes. Back then, whenever it came to guitar solos, I was given about 15 minutes. In those days, that was enough for the guitar player. Paicey [*drummer Ian Paice*] would be there tapping his foot, looking at his watch going, 'How much longer?' And I'd be like, 'I've just got my sound together.' And he'd go, 'You going to be *much* longer?'

"Sometimes onstage I would play it much faster than the record. I'd like it real fast, and Paicey would like it really fast. Only problem was coming into that part at the end of the guitar solo that the band would do in unison. You can only play that so fast—unless you start tapping, which I don't do, out of principle. It's just an A minor arpeggio, but it's all downstrokes. *You* try and play that really fast after you've had 10 scotches! That's hard to do."

"Smoke on the Water" (*Machine Head*, 1972)

"**WE DID THAT TRACK IN** a different place than the rest of *Machine Head*, which was recorded in the Grand Hotel in Montreux. It was recorded in a big auditorium in Switzerland using the Rolling Stones' mobile studio, which was in a truck. For the backing track, we were going for a big echoey sound. The police started knocking on the door. We knew it was the police, and we knew that they were going to say, 'Stop recording!' because they'd had complaints about the noise. So we wouldn't open the door to the police. We asked Martin [*Birch, engineer*], 'Is that the one?' And he said, 'I don't know. I've got to hear the whole thing all the way through to know if it's the one.' The police, who had a fleet of cars outside, kept hammering at the door. We didn't want to open up until we knew we had gotten the right take. Finally, we got it: 'No mistakes. That'll do.' After that, the police said, 'You've got to stop. You've got to go somewhere else.' "

"Highway Star" (*Machine Head*)

"**I WORKED OUT THE SOLO** for that one before I actually recorded it, which I never used to do. I fancied putting a bit of Mozart over that chord progression, which itself is taken from Mozart."

"Lazy" (*Machine Head*)

"**THAT'S A WEIRD SOLO** because I did a particular part one day, and I did another part another day; you can hear the difference. I still criticize that solo. I think the song was great; the composition was good. But I could have done better. I was inspired to write that by Eric Clapton's 'Steppin' Out.' "

"Man on the Silver Mountain"
(*Ritchie Blackmore's Rainbow*, 1975)

"**THAT WAS ONE OF THE FIRST** tunes I put together with Ronnie James Dio. One night during our last tour in Europe, I went onstage to do an encore. I meant to play 'Smoke on the Water,' but I started playing 'Man on the Silver Mountain.' And it wasn't until I was a little bit into the riff that I realized, That is not 'Smoke on the Water' And I went, Fuck, what *is* the riff? And I couldn't remember the riff. So I'm looking at the audience, pretending I had meant to play that. And they're clapping, but they've got these puzzled expressions on their faces. So I look over at Greg [*Smith, Rainbow bassist*] and ask, 'How the hell does "Smoke on the Water" go? And he goes, 'Duh, duh, duh, da duh, da dah.' So I finally went into that." ✳

NINETEEN '97

In the post-Cobain era, rock's young guns try to figure out where they fit in while the legends wonder if they have what it takes to move with the times.

Dear *Guitar World*,

The day of judgment is dawning, and alternative shall be cast into the toilet bowl of fire. The strength and unity of metal shall be our salvation. Stand before the gates of hell and blow them down. The last great war will be fought not with weapons, but from the minds and roaring stacks of the faithful. Join us, and rule for all eternity!

—Rev. M. Frederick Smith

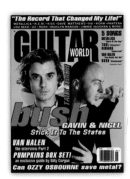

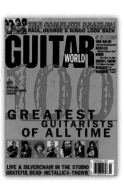

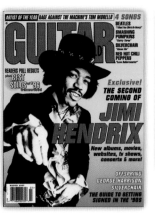

JANUARY Bush's Gavin Rossdale and Nigel Pulsford deny charges of grunge larceny while praising their own new album, *Razorblade Suitcase*.
COVER STORY BY ALAN DI PERNA
PHOTO BY ALASTAIR THAIN & NIL JOHNSON

FEBRUARY *Guitar World* offers up its very first list of all-time greats, from Blind Lemon to Yngwie; from Robert Johnson to Uli Jon Roth. A star-studded spectacular, with equipment lists and choice tracks peppering the pot and justifying our love.
COVER STORY BY VARIOUS

MARCH *Guitar World* celebrates the revitalization of Jimi Hendrix as the Hendrix family prepares to release a mother lode of newly remastered albums, previously unreleased songs, live concert tracks, films and television specials that will honor Jimi's legacy and carry his spirit forth to the dawn of a new age.
COVER STORY BY ALAN DI PERNA
PHOTO BY MICHAEL OCHS ARCHIVES

APRIL Aerosmith weather yet another band-battering storm and come up with *Nine Lives*, proving they can still squeeze plenty of blood out of their hard rock.
COVER STORY BY ALAN DI PERNA
PHOTO BY ALBERT WATSON

MAY Ace Frehley and Billy Gibbons help *Guitar World* celebrate the 100 rarest, weirdest and most expensive guitars on the planet.
COVER STORY BY CHRIS GILL & OTHERS; PHOTOS BY KEVIN KNIGHT & MICHAEL SEXTON

JUNE In this special report, *Guitar World* proudly brings you some of our patented behind-the-scenes looks at what you can expect in the upcoming "Summer of Loud" as a reunited Black Sabbath, Marilyn Manson, Pantera and Korn take to the road. The forecast? Sizzling temperatures. High humidity. And some *hard* rain.
COVER STORIES BY J.D. CONSIDINE, ALAN DI PERNA, JEFF GILBERT & NICK BOWCOTT; PHOTOS BY MICHAEL SEXTON

GUITAR WORLD

4 SONGS
WITH BASSLINES

NINE INCH NAILS
"Head Like A Hole"

FOO FIGHTERS
"Monkey Wrench"

U2
"Staring At The Sun"

JIMI HENDRIX
"Dolly Dagger"

JULY 1997

exclusive album preview!

311 kicks butt!

the phat, funky future of rock

NINE INCH NAILS
BLACK FLAG HISTORY
STYX ELO SKYNYRD
JOHN FOGERTY
ANI DIFRANCO

new column!
NO DOUBT
& KORN

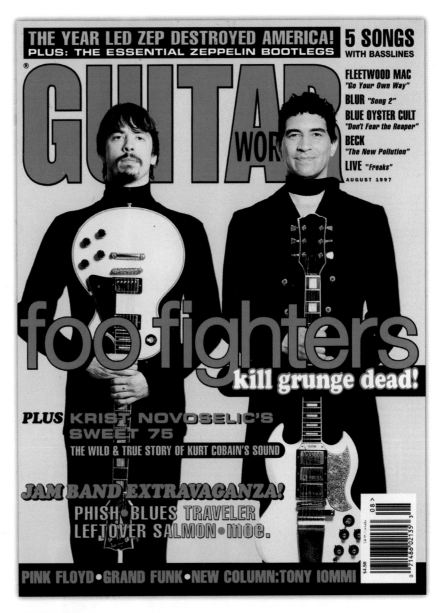

THE YEAR LED ZEP DESTROYED AMERICA!
PLUS: THE ESSENTIAL ZEPPELIN BOOTLEGS

5 SONGS
WITH BASSLINES

GUITAR WORLD

FLEETWOOD MAC
"Go Your Own Way"

BLUR "Song 2"

BLUE OYSTER CULT
"Don't Fear the Reaper"

BECK
"The New Pollution"

LIVE "Freaks"

AUGUST 1997

foo fighters
kill grunge dead!

PLUS KRIST NOVOSELIC'S
SWEET 75
THE WILD & TRUE STORY OF KURT COBAIN'S SOUND

JAM BAND EXTRAVAGANZA!
PHISH·BLUES TRAVELER
LEFTOVER SALMON·moe.

PINK FLOYD·GRAND FUNK·NEW COLUMN:TONY IOMMI

JULY 311's Nick Hexum and Tim Mahoney, two of the dopest brovas ever to represent Omaha, Nebraska, drop da bomb on their new album, *Transistor*. "A lot of this album is about production and space," says Hexum. "It's psychedelic, definitely, and dub, as well. We're trying to be as creative as possible but still be rocking."

COVER STORY BY JIM DEROGATIS; PHOTO BY ROGER ERICKSON

AUGUST Foo Fighters Dave Grohl and Pat Smear go deep on fashion, Nirvana and their new album, *The Colour and the Shape*. "The last thing I want to do is go onstage in a Dolce and Gabana suit and ruin it by jumping around and sweating it up. I'll stick with a T-shirt, thank you very much."
COVER STORY BY ALAN DI PERNA; PHOTO BY MICHAEL LAVINE

SEPTEMBER The Edge, U2's great innovator, thoughtfully examines his groundbreaking approach to the guitar, and provides a behind-the-scenes look at the band's bombastic PopMart tour.
COVER STORY BY GARY GRAFF; PHOTO BY ANTON CORBIJN

OCTOBER Keith Richards gives an intimate glimpse into a life spent rolling and stumbling with the Stones.
COVER STORY BY ALAN DI PERNA; PHOTO BY MAX VADUKUL

NOVEMBER Jane's Addiction guitarist Dave Navarro and Red Hot Chili Peppers bassist Flea rap about the good old days and their bad old ways.
COVER STORY BY ALAN DI PERNA; PHOTO BY JOHN EDER

DECEMBER Metallica, once and future kings of metal, take aim at their detractors and shoot their *Re-Load*.
COVER STORY BY JON WIEDERHORN; PHOTO BY DANNY CLINCH

1997 TOTAL ISSUES: 12

FOUNDING FATHERS

CHET ATKINS

"Merle Travis and I taught this country to play fingerstyle guitar, and I want credit for that sometime."

—Chet Atkins

CHET ATKINS is a guitarist and, as he might say, a "music man" whose influence extends far beyond questions of genre to the way the instrument is made and played, and beyond that the way the music business works.

Atkins's distinct style of picking developed as an "upgrade" of the Merle Travis approach, involving the same sort of alternating finger-and-thumb picking but generally with three or four fingers in action rather than one or two. Atkins took an almost classical approach to his fingerpicking, carefully defining both the overall polyphonic texture and the counterpoint of individual lines.

The guitarist was an ubiquitous session player who signed with RCA in 1947 as a recording artist in his own right. In the mid Fifties, pulling double duty as an A&R man, the guitarist played an active role in RCA's signing of Elvis Presley, working as a rhythm guitarist and bandleader on such records as "Heartbreak Hotel." Atkins also played the acoustic "power chords" on Everly Brothers recordings, fashioning riffs that were later adapted to the electric guitar by Keith Richards, among others. His style of playing, both on electric and the nylon string acoustics he often favors, has influenced legendary players across the musical spectrum, from rockabilly Scotty Moore to Beatle George Harrison to jazzman Lenny Breau to just about every guitarist in country music.

EQUIPMENT: Gretsch Country Gentleman, Gibson Chet Atkins CEC; Fender Deluxe Reverb Standel amplifier; Echoplex
SIGNATURE SONG: "Chinatown, My Chinatown" from The RCA Years (RCA, 1992)
CLASSIC ALBUM: Galloppin' Guitar (Bear Family, 1993)

CHUCK BERRY

"If you wanted to play rock and roll you would end up playing like Chuck, or what you learned from Chuck, because there isn't any other choice. He's really laid the law down."

—Eric Clapton

CHUCK BERRY INVENTED rock and roll guitar, but his playing was not without its influences and precursors. By far the most evident influences in Berry's playing, and the ones Berry himself always mentions, are T-Bone Walker and Carl Hogan, the tasteful, rhythmically incisive guitarist for Louis Jordan's Tympany Five, the most popular r&b group of the Forties. Walker, of course, strongly affected most of the guitarists of Berry's generation. It can be startling to hear fully formed Berry riffs, especially those ringing, hammered intros, showing up in T-Bone's recordings from the Forties and early Fifties, but they do.

However, none of the musicians who were Berry's inspirations really played rock and roll; Chuck did. He achieved a seamless integration of blues, country-and-western and pop. And of course, he wrote the songs that defined the first rock and roll generation: "Roll Over Beethoven," "School Day," "Rock and Roll Music" and others.

Berry put even his most blatantly "borrowed" bits into a strikingly fresh format, however. His pumping shuffle-rhythms on the guitar might be reminiscent of T-Bone's, but Berry's pianists had a much freer hand in embroidering around the rhythm, and on most of his classic records, the guitar shuffles are undergirded not by a rhythm-section shuffle but by bass and drums playing swing time—straight, walking 4/4. It's the tension between guitar shuffle and rhythm section-swing that give Berry's Chess recordings much of their get-up-and-go.

EQUIPMENT: Gibson ES-350T, Gibson ES-355; Fender Dual Showman
SIGNATURE SONG: "Johnny B. Goode," from The Great Twenty-Eight (Chess, 1982)
CLASSIC ALBUM: Chuck Berry: The Chess Box (Chess, 1988)

EXPERIMENTS · AND · ORIGINATES

ORIGIN

Illustration by Anastasia Vasilakis

Photos: Michael Ochs Archives
● Merle Travis ● Andres Segovia
● Les Paul ● Dick Dale
● Charlie Christian ● Chuck Berry
● Chet Atkins ● Bo Diddley
● Django Reinhardt

Right: Michael Ochs Archives

Icons by Kalynn Campbell

BIG BILL BROONZY

"A good blues man don't play so much when he singing, because when you're moving them fingers too devilish fast, it takes away from your voice... The feeling all goes into your fingers."

—Big Bill Broonzy

AN EARLY BRIDGE between country blues and its urban cousin, Big Bill Broonzy also played a personal role in the development of British blues-based rock. Arriving in Chicago from his native Mississippi in 1920, he introduced a crisp, relatively intricate finger-picking style that differed markedly from the work of most Delta-bred artists, reflecting pre-blues influences as well as a cosmopolitan familiarity with the many blue styles of the South and Southeast.

Broonzy was equally exceptional playing bouncy ragtime in C ("Skoodle Do Do"), straightforward blues in E ("Keys to the Highway"), and flatpicking in open G ("How You Want It Done"). Blessed with an exceptional memory, he seems to have known a hundred songs, ranging from "folk blues" with authentic pedigree to pop, ragtime and vaudeville-style "hokum."

Ever adaptable, Broonzy rapidly became the pre-war Blues King of Chicago, gracing literally hundreds of recordings on his own or backing other artists. But perhaps his most significant pioneering effort was yet to come. In the Fifties, having returned at least part-time to performing solo in order to cash in on the folk music revival, Broonzy made several visits to England. There he influenced the first wave of young British bluesmen, and he paved the way for Muddy Waters's first English tour in 1958. In August of that year, Broonzy died in Chicago; Muddy recorded one of his most impressive later albums in tribute.

EQUIPMENT: Martin 00-28, Gibson Style O
SIGNATURE SONG: "See See Rider"
CLASSIC ALBUM: The Young Bill Broonzy (Yazoo, 1991)

CHARLIE CHRISTIAN

"Charlie Christian sounds old and brand-new at the same time. His solo on 'I Found a New Baby' is simple and complicated. It's as hip as any bop I've ever heard."

—Jim Hall

CHARLIE CHRISTIAN was the first musician to realize the electric guitar's potential as a solo instrument in jazz. He improvised solos with the fluidity and power of a horn player, liberating the guitar from its traditional, exclusive role as a rhythm instrument and paving the way for the transition from swing to bop (not coincidentally, "Swing to Bop" was the title of one of his most famous recordings). Christian may well have heard the pioneering electric guitar solos of a fellow Texan, Eddie Durham, and he certainly listened to Lonnie Johnson and Django Reinhardt, both of whom played blazing

Big Bill Broonzy

FEB. 1997

VOL. 18 / NO. 2

The 100 Greatest Guitarists of All Time

A categorical breakdown of the best, most influential and original axmen since the beginning of

Founding Fathers

Chet Atkins
Chuck Berry
Big Bill Broonzy
Charlie Christian
Dick Dale
Bo Diddley
Robert Johnson
Les Paul
Django Reinhardt
Andres Segovia
Merle Travis

Fallen Heroes

Duane Allman
Kurt Cobain
Jimi Hendrix
Randy Rhoads
Stevie Ray Vaughan

British Giants

Jeff Beck
Eric Clapton
George Harrison
& John Lennon
Jimmy Page
Keith Richards
Pete Townshend
Nigel Tufnel

Rockabilly

James Burton
Scotty Moore
Cliff Gallup
Brian Setzer

Virtuosos

Ritchie Blackmore
Al Di Meola
Danny Gatton
Allan Holdsworth
Eric Johnson
Yngwie Malmsteen
John McLaughlin
Steve Morse
Uli Jon Roth
Steve Vai
Joe Satriani
Edward Van Halen

They Might Be Giants

Trey Anastasio
Jerry Cantrell
Dimebag Darrell
Billy Corgan
Charlie Hunter

Lords of Hard Rock

Ace Frehley
James Hetfield
& Kirk Hammett
Tony Iommi
Joe Perry
& Brad Whitford
Slash
Angus & Malcolm Young

Jazzmen

Lenny Breau
Freddie Green
Jim Hall
Pat Metheny
Wes Montgomery
Johnny Smith

Progressive Rockers

Robert Fripp
David Gilmour
Steve Howe
Alex Lifeson
Brian May

Traditionalists

Dickey Betts
Peter Buck
John Fogerty
Roger McGuinn
Richard Thompson
Neil Young

Bluesmen

Reverend Gary Davis
Buddy Guy
John Lee Hooker
Blind Lemon Jefferson
Albert King
B.B. King
Freddie King
Hubert Sumlin
T-Bone Walker
Muddy Waters

Country Gentlemen

Jimmy Bryant
Albert Lee
Brent Mason
Clarence White

Space Cadets

Syd Barrett
Jerry Garcia
Robby Krieger
Carlos Santana

Free Radicals

The Edge
Thurston Moore
& Lee Ranaldo
Bob Mould
Lou Reed

Visionaries & Madmen

Billy Gibbons
Sonny Sharrock
Link Wray
Frank Zappa

Punk & Disorderly

Ron Asheton
Steve Jones
Johnny Ramone
Johnny Thunders

Unplugged Heroes

Michael Hedges
Leo Kottke
Joni Mitchell
John Renbourn
Doc Watson

Three Funkateers

Steve Cropper
Eddie Hazel
Jimmy Nolen

Think we forgot anyone? Our 1997 readers certainly did, and they weren't afraid to let us know. The following is just a sample of "how could you leave out?!" names sent in by the *GW* faithful: Peter Green, Joe Walsh, Wayne Kramer, Tommy Bolin, Vernon Reid, Prince, El Hefe, Larry Lalonde, Hank Sherman/Michael Denner, Gary Moore, Roy Buchanan, Mark Knopfler, Ted Nugent, John Petrucci, Carl Perkins, Phil Keaggy, Andy Summers, Tom Petty, Stone Gossard... ✱

APRIL / VOL. 18 / NO. 4

WHERE ARE THEY NOW?

As grunge took over the rock universe, Eighties hair metallers were shoved into the bargain bins of obscurity. *Guitar World*'s Alan Paul caught up with some of yesterday's guitar heroes to get their views on various aspects of their topsy-turvy careers.

Tracii Guns

Career Low Point: Riding the crest of success with *Cocked and Loaded.* "When the album got popular due to one song that was completely uncharacteristic of us, I knew that it was locking me into something I just couldn't be comfortable with. That was the hardest time in my life—we played in front of a lot of people, but I was the loneliest guy in the world."

Why He Shaved His Head in 1989: "I opened up *Circus* magazine one day and every guy on every page had the same hairstyle. I realized right then that the whole thing was bullshit."

C.C. DeVille

Career High Point: "Being rich and famous for doing something you love is a blessing and a miracle. I got to walk out onstage and play a 10-minute guitar solo in front of 20,000 people every night. That was a marvelous, magical thing."

Career Low Point: Failing to realize just how good he had it. "I had everything and just didn't see it. I was like a little baby."

Interesting Fact: DeVille was a member of Stryper before they "started doing the whole religious thing. They were called Roxx Regime."

Lita Ford

What Really Pisses Her Off: The speed with which MTV abandoned metal bands. "They switched over in a second—they aced out all the straight-ahead rock bands who had anything to do with the Eighties."

Financial Status: "I'm okay. I didn't put all my money up my nose—just some of it."

Blackie Lawless

Career Low Point: Lawless calls 1987's *Electric Circus* "the biggest pile of shit ever made by anyone in the recording industry. It was a tired record made by a tired band."

His Views on Marilyn Manson, His Shock-Rock Child: "He is as intelligent, if not more so, than anyone who's ever come down the pike. The kid is good. He's real good. His Hitler-esque rap is top-notch. Although I've never met him, I know this kid. I know what he's thinking before he does."

AUG. '97

What the Halen?

In response to Van Halen's revolving door of late-Nineties vocalists—David Lee Roth, Sammy Hagar, Gary Cherone—*Guitar World* asks its readers for new frontman suggestions and a new band name to go with it.

VH + Ronnie James Dio = Mini Van

VH + Phil Anselmo = Vantera

VH + Johnny Rotten = Vanarchy in the U.K.

VH + David Duke = Klan Halen

VH + Meatloaf = Van Needs New Shocks

VH + Robin Zander = Cheap Van

VH + John Wayne Bobbit = Vansectomy

VH + George Hamilton = Tan Halen

VH + The Chipmunks = Al Van

VH + Trey Anastasio = Van Halibut

VH + Shaquille O'Neal = Slam Halen

VH + Olivia Newton-John = Vanadu

VH + Ho Chi Minh = Nam Halen

VH + Jimmy Hoffa – Van-Ished

"I didn't put all my money up my nose—just some of it."—*Lita Ford*

THE *WIZARD OF OZ–DARK SIDE OF THE MOON* CONNECTION

Imagine, if you will: The cosmic synchronicities between the legendary Pink Floyd album and the classic film. A *Guitar World* "Trends" report.

HERE'S HOW IT WORKS: Start playing the album at the exact moment Tanner, the MGM lion, finishes its third and final roar. It's a good idea to have the CD on pause at 00.00 so there isn't an extra gap as the record loads up when you press play.

Now, sit back and watch. Here is a partial list of the cosmic connections between *Dark Side of the Moon* and *The Wizard of Oz.*

* The Wicked Witch, in human form, first appears on her bicycle at the same moment a burst of alarm bells sound on the album.
* During "Time," Dorothy breaks into a trot to the line: "No one told you when to run."
* Dorothy leaves the fortune teller to return to her farm at the same moment the words, "home, home again" are sung in "Breathe."
* Glinda, the Good Witch of the North, appears in the bubble just as the band sings, "Don't give me that do goody goody bullshit," in the song "Money."
* A few minutes later, the Good Witch confronts the Wicked Witch during "Us and Them" as the band sings, "and who knows which is which." (Or is that "witch is witch?")
* The song "Brain Damage" starts around the same time as the Scarecrow launches into "If I only had a brain."
* Floyd sings "the lunatic is on the grass," from "Brain Damage," just as the Scarecrow begins his floppy jig near a green lawn. The line "got to keep the loonies on the path" from the same song comes just before Dorothy and the Scarecrow start traipsing down the Yellow Brick Road.
* It takes two and a half spins of the entire album to get through the entire movie, and the synchronicities just keep coming. The "home, home again" line plays again just as Dorothy opens her eyes at the end of the movie to see her worried aunt and uncle hovering by her Kansas bedside.
* The real clincher, though, comes at the end of the first playing of the album, which tails off with the insistent sound of a beating heart. On screen, Dorothy has her ear to the Tin Man's chest, listening for a heartbeat.

As rap-rock continues to assert itself as a valid musical force, *Guitar World* lists the 10 hip-hop/rock crossover landmarks that shook the world.

1. Run-D.M.C. "Rockbox" (1984)
2. Run-D.M.C. "Walk This Way" (1986)
3. Beastie Boys "Rhymin & Stealin" (1986)
4. Beastie Boys "(You Gotta) Fight for Your Right (To Party!)" (1986)
5. Public Enemy "Sophisticated Bitch" (1987)
6. Sir Mix-a-Lot with Metal Church "Iron Man" (1988)
7. Tone-Loc "Wild Thing" (1988)
8. Schoolly D "Signifying Rapper" (1988)
9. Anthrax with Public Enemy "Bring the Noise" (1991)
10. *Judgment Night: Music from the Motion Picture* (1993)

NOV. '97

Billie Joe Armstrong sounds a little uncertain about the answer when he confides, "I feel like we are the last successful rock and roll band on the planet. We are a dying breed. It's a little scary because nobody else is doing that rock purist thing these days."

The Green Day guitarist, vocalist and principal songwriter has other reasons to be concerned about the band's future. Not only has his brand of pop punk—which the band's major label debut, *Dookie* (Reprise, 1994), propelled into the mainstream—been swept off the cutting edge by a wave of electronica, ska and shock rock bands, but Green Day has just embarked on the biggest gamble of their career. At a time when conventional wisdom would dictate that the Berkeley, California-based three-chord wonders just stay the course to preserve their die-hard fan base, they have reinvented themselves—so much so that much of *Nimrod,* their new album, is sure to confound the fresh-faced adolescents who once embraced Green Day as punk's second coming.

From the rockabilly resonance of "Hitchin' a Ride" to the strings on "Good Riddance" to the classic rock dynamics of "Haushinka," *Nimrod* is a virtual tour through pop history. The wide range of genres on the album might lead cynics to believe that Green Day is desperately searching for a new voice. But Armstrong is ready to take some flak for his stance and even sends a few warning shots of his own at

DEC. 1997

VOL. 18 / NO. 12

Green Day

Billie Joe Armstrong and Mike Dirnt talk to *Guitar World* about their rise to prominence and how their new album, *Nimrod*—with "Good Riddance" leading the charge—marks a bold statement for the pop-punk rockers.

GUITAR WORLD How do you explain your early success?

BILLIE JOE ARMSTRONG We were at the right place at the right time. We happened to strike a nerve. The whole early Nineties was about that introverted grunge sound, and people were getting tired of it. They were looking for a little bit of a performance, and we happened to do it. That's one thing we have always been capable of—taking advantage of an opportunity. All I did was be honest and sing about myself, and people identify with it. Kids don't sugar coat anything and that was what they saw in us—something that was fast and hard and got the point across.

GW Also, for a punk band you weren't all that threatening...

ARMSTRONG We aren't Neurosis, but I don't think they are particularly threatening either. We are a pop band. Maybe it's not packaged the same way as Duran Duran—it's definitely more aggressive—but if you strip it down, it's a hook, a melody and has good lyrics—that's all.

MIKE DIRNT We write classic pop songs. The way you can tell that is just by taking away the production on any one of our songs. They can still be played on an acoustic guitar, and they are still great tunes. You can't say that about techno.

GW Do you like the new wave of electronica?

DIRNT Let me put it this way: the Prodigy is really innovative because they took techno and applied it to a song format. I think that's really great because now, instead of listening to six minutes of crap, I have to listen to only three.

GW Are there things that you like that might surprise your fans?

DIRNT I don't know. I was heavily into jazz for a while, and that's where "Longview" came from. I've been into a blues phase recently. I've liked slower grooves like Stevie Wonder and old Motown. I'm never influenced by players. I'm influenced by tunes—anything that has its own motor or its own pocket.

ARMSTRONG I like early Van Halen—David Lee Roth is a great performer. And I am a sucker for a good song no matter how you package it. I like the Pretenders; I really liked the last Wallflowers record. I like some stuff on the last Counting Crows record, and I think Oasis is pretty good.

GW In an earlier *Guitar World* interview [*August 1996*], you said that Green Day needed to redefine itself. Have you succeeded in doing so on *Nimrod*?

ARMSTRONG From my point of view, it would have been wrong to put out the same kind of record because that would have been boring. But maybe you took me a little too literally when I said "redefine" the band—it wasn't about turning into Radiohead or something; that was the last thing I wanted to do. I wanted to stick to what we had done together as a band but also branch out and test our boundaries a little bit. I think we were successful at doing that, and that's why there are so many songs on this album. We didn't want to break away completely from our past or what we do best—which is write two-and-a-half-minute pop/punk songs—but at the same time, I think we were successful at going outside of that and not looking pretentious or anything.

GW Was that a difficult process for you? Is that why you spent four and a half months in the studio recording *Nimrod*?

DIRNT No. We came to this record with a ridiculous approach: record everything. We went into the studio with 40 songs and recorded 30. Eighteen made the record. We wanted to write good old rock and roll tunes. In the past, we always knew what songs were going to be on the record. This time we decided to let the songs themselves tell us what to include.

GW There are several surprises on *Nimrod*. "Good Riddance," which features an acoustic guitar and strings, is a fairly drastic departure from the past.

ARMSTRONG Yeah, we never had strings before, and I never played a song solo with an acoustic guitar. We've always wanted to do that, but we had to approach it slowly, without abandoning anything. The great thing was that it came so naturally. It was something we knew we could do. That song was written just after *Dookie* came out, and I wanted to save it and wait for the right opportunity.

GW Aren't you concerned that your punk fans are going to hate the band's current direction?

ARMSTRONG There was pressure to take a big step forward. We needed to do it. If people can adapt to it, that's fine, but if they can't...I can understand that. When I was 17 I didn't like it when bands changed in a dramatic way. ✳

NINETEEN '98

Soundgarden bites the dust as grunge shifts to the bargain bins, James Hetfield meets up with his favorite band, Gov't Mule, and *Guitar World* readers submit their votes for the 100 Greatest Solos of All Time.

Dear *Guitar World*,

I am a computer systems analyst. I'm in a union with 500 other computer hackers on a national and international level. Our union is seven-million strong, worldwide. If an apology is not given to Yngwie J. Malmsteen regarding your review of *Facing the Animal*, we will launch a worldwide computer attack on your fail safe systems, starting with your electricity. You have until April 5, 1998, to do this, or face our all-out war against your magazine and company.

—Christopher L. Osborne

P.S. Vengeance will be ours.

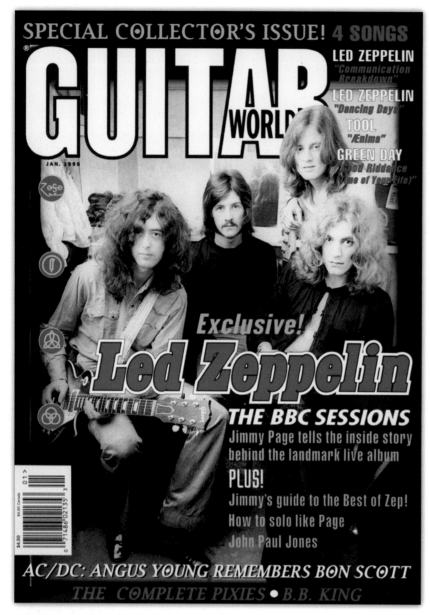

JANUARY In this Led Zeppelin extravaganza, Jimmy Page expounds on the new *BBC Sessions*, his group's first authorized release of live material in more than two decades. "The BBC sessions show in graphic detail just how organic the group was. Led Zeppelin was really moving the music all the time."

COVER STORIES BY BRAD TOLINSKI; PHOTO BY CHRIS WALTERS

FEBRUARY Van Halen, Metallica, Smashing Pumpkins, Marilyn Manson, Kiss, Jeff Beck, Joe Satriani and others give *GW* the inside skinny on their plans for the coming year.
COVER STORIES BY VARIOUS; PHOTOS BY VARIOUS

MARCH It's been three years since the last Van Halen album, and much has changed. Eddie talks about *Van Halen III* and the band's third frontman, Gary Cherone.
COVER STORY BY VIC GARBARINI; PHOTO BY NATHANIEL WELCH

APRIL The 1998 Readers Poll results are in, and *Guitar World* celebrates by catching up with Radiohead (Best Alternative Album), Eddie Van Halen (#4 Best Hard Rock/Metal Guitarist), Dimebag Darrell (Best Hard Rock/Metal Guitarist), Days of the New (Best New Talent), Pearl Jam (#5 Worst Band) and others.
COVER STORIES BY VARIOUS; PHOTOS BY VARIOUS

MAY An exclusive interview with Eric Clapton about his latest masterpiece, *Pilgrim*.
COVER STORY BY BRAD TOLINSKI AND HAROLD STEINBLATT PHOTO BY ALBERT WATSON

JUNE An open discussion with Jimmy Page detailing his latest collaboration with Robert Plant, *Walking into Clarksdale*.
COVER STORY BY ALAN DI PERNA; PHOTO BY ROSS HALFIN

JULY With alternative dead and buried, Billy Corgan smashes into the future with the Smashing Pumpkins' latest effort, *Adore*.
COVER STORY BY BRAD TOLINSKI; PHOTO BY PAUL ELLEDGE

1998 TOTAL ISSUES: 12

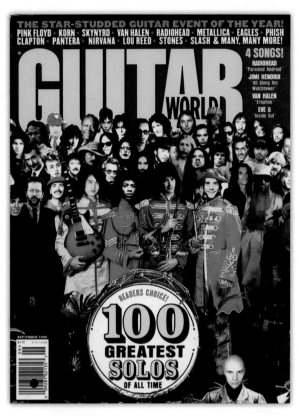

AUGUST The complete story behind Ozzy Osbourne, rock's foremost madman. "The whole hippie thing was still happening around that time, and for us, that was bullshit. We lived in a dreary, polluted, dismal town in Birmingham, England, and we were angry about it—and that was reflected in our music."

COVER STORY BY JEFF KITTS; PHOTO BY MICHAEL SEXTON

SEPTEMBER We asked and our beloved readers responded: Presenting the 100 greatest guitar solos ever, and the stories behind them. The top five: "Stairway to Heaven," "Eruption," "Free Bird," "Comfortably Numb" and Hendrix's "All Along the Watchtower."

COVER STORY BY VARIOUS; PHOTO BY VARIOUS

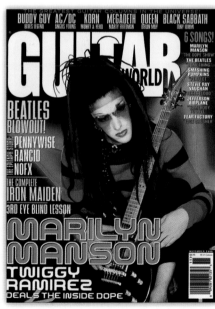

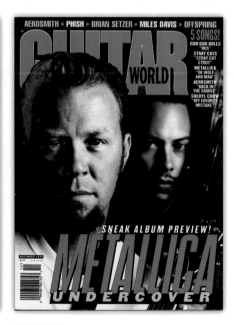

OCTOBER With their first recording together in more than 18 years, a reunited Kiss prepare to unleash *Psycho Circus* upon a waiting world.

COVER STORY BY ALAN DI PERNA; PHOTOS BY MICHAEL SEXTON

NOVEMBER Marilyn Manson's right-hand man deals the inside dope on the recording of *Mechanical Animals*.

COVER STORY BY ALAN DI PERNA; PHOTO BY ALBERT SANCHEZ

DECEMBER James Hetfield and Kirk Hammett give *Guitar World* a sneak preview of their upcoming album of covers.

COVER STORY BY JEFF KITTS; PHOTO BY MICHAEL SEXTON

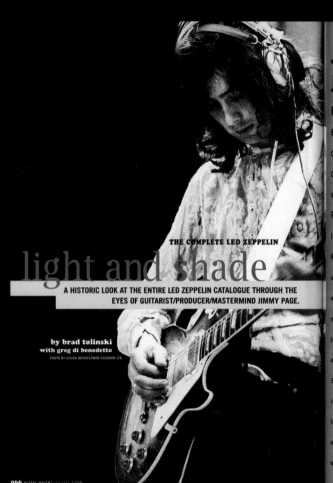

THE COMPLETE LED ZEPPELIN

light and shade

A HISTORIC LOOK AT THE ENTIRE LED ZEPPELIN CATALOGUE THROUGH THE
EYES OF GUITARIST/PRODUCER/MASTERMIND JIMMY PAGE.

by brad tolinski
with greg di benedetto
PHOTO BY CHUCK BOYD/FLOWER CHILDREN LTD.

Jimmy Page, Robert Plant, John Paul Jones and John Bonham

did not invent hard rock. They did, however, elevate it to an art form. ✳ Unlike many of their lead-footed contemporaries who painted in sludgy, monochromatic fuzztones, Led Zeppelin created sweeping aural vistas. Every song in the band's catalog packs the wallop of a full-blown, three-dimensional, four-star rock and roll movie. With guitarist Page in the director's chair, Zeppelin performed brilliantly in bluesy, X-rated features like the orgasmic "Whole Lotta Love," Disney-esque fantasies like the whimsical "The Song Remains the Same" and exotic 70mm epics like "Kashmir" and "Stairway to Heaven." ✳ No one in rock before or since has equaled Led Zeppelin's flair for musical drama. Page has claimed that the band was designed so its sound would have "shadow and light." Screw that—they lived, breathed and performed in nothing less than Technicolor. ✳ In the early 1990's *Guitar World* was granted two rare opportunities to discuss the band's incredible output with Jimmy Page, who produced, composed and played guitar on Zeppelin's eight ground-breaking studio albums. Now, with the release of *Led Zeppelin: The BBC Sessions*, we thought it would be a perfect time to revisit these remarkably candid and in-depth interviews for the diamond-hard perspective they offer. ✳ Below, in an interview first presented in *GW* in December of 1993, Jimmy Page offers a frank, often eloquent assessment of Zeppelin's entire catalogue. He was equally forthcoming in a January '91 interview (see sidebar, page 70) when he gave *GW* his take on some of the band's greatest individual tracks.

JAN. 1998

VOL. 19 / NO. 1

Jimmy Page

As Led Zeppelin celebrates the release of its *BBC Sessions* collection, founder Jimmy Page discusses his Yardbirds days and how serving as Zeppelin's producer ensured studio harmony.

GUITAR WORLD Led Zeppelin was one of the first bands to break away from the more casual hippie look of the Sixties and adopt a more glamorous personae. Did playing bigger venues and arenas demand a more stylized presentation?

JIMMY PAGE I considered myself quite a dandy in those days, so what I wore onstage was simply an extension of what I was wearing off stage. It wasn't anything like, "Oh, we're playing an arena so we must go out and buy ourselves nice new suits."

GW Before you joined Led Zeppelin you were the lead guitarist in the Yardbirds, and before that you were one of England's leading session guitarists. What impact did those experiences have on your work with Zeppelin?

PAGE They were very valuable. I learned an incredible amount of discipline. When I was initially brought in to play sessions, I was just a rock musician who couldn't even really read music, but because I was one of the only guitarists on the scene, they started giving me all kinds of work. Eventually, I learned how to read charts and started playing on things you'd never expect, like film scores and jingles. I even played some jazz, which was never my forte. But having to vamp behind people like Tubby Hayes, who was a big jazz saxophonist in England, or play on several of Burt Bacharach's pop sessions gave me a fantastic vision and insight into chords.

Being a session player, however, wasn't really me—it wasn't rock and roll. Eventually, it became very confining, and I was looking to get out. In 1966, I got this offer to join the Yardbirds. Jeff Beck and I were friends, and he always wanted me to be part of the group. We talked about it and thought we could do some interesting things with two guitars. After I joined, I retired from session work overnight.

Once I got on the guitar with Jeff, I started really expressing myself. Then, after Jeff left, I stayed with the band and just kept stretching and stretching. The Yardbirds had several songs that called for lengthy improvisations, like "I'm a Man" and "Smokestack Lightning," and I took full advantage of them to develop a bunch of new ideas.

After the Yardbirds fell apart and it came time to create Zeppelin, I had all those ideas as a textbook to work from. And as it was stuff I developed on my own while I was in the band, it was fair game for me to use.

So both things—the studio work and the experience in the Yardbirds—were really important. They both set the scene for Zeppelin. The studio gave me discipline and an incredible working knowledge of many kinds of music, and the Yardbirds gave me time to develop my ideas.

GW What was your original concept for Zeppelin?

PAGE Ultimately, I wanted Zeppelin to be a marriage of blues, hard rock and acoustic music topped with heavy choruses—a combination that had never been done before. Lots of light and shade.

GW Right from the beginning you were able to translate the extreme dynamism of Led Zeppelin's live act into a dynamic studio recording: What was your secret?

PAGE That *is* interesting, isn't it? One usually thinks of a dynamic album being translated into a dynamic live performance, but in the early days, it was the other way around for us.

I think part of the key was ambient miking. I remember playing on some rock sessions, and you'd find that the drummer would be put into this little box-like area with a low ceiling, where he'd thrash away. And nothing would be coming out of the drums. It would sound like he was hitting packing boxes because all the ambience and all the tuning was lost. From observing enough of those sessions, I knew straight away that drums should be miked like a proper acoustic instrument in a good acoustic environment.

When I started producing the first Zeppelin album, I knew the drums had to sound good because they were going to be the backbone of the band. So I worked hard on microphone placement. But then again, you see, when you have someone who is as powerful as John Bonham going for you, the battle is all but sold!

GW How did the four members of Zeppelin interact on a personal level? Was everything as smooth internally as it appeared to be?

PAGE I think the atmosphere in Led Zeppelin was always an encouraging one. We all wanted to see the music get better. And part of the reason things ran smoothly is that I had the last decision on everything. I was the producer, so there weren't going to be any fights.

The atmosphere was always very professional. I was meticulous with my studio notes, and everybody knew that they would get proper credit, so everything was fine.

Another key: we all lived in different parts of the country, so when we came off the road we didn't really see each other. I think that helped. We really only socialized when we were on the road. We all really came to value our family lives, especially after being on the road so much, which is how it should be. It helped create a balance in our lives. Our families helped keep us sane. ✱

KIM THAYIL

The Soundgarden guitarist comments on what finally caused the once-great Seattle rock outfit to call it quits after 12 long years.

GUITAR WORLD Who was the first member of Soundgarden to suggest breaking up?

KIM THAYIL It wouldn't have mattered who brought it up. It was pretty obvious from everybody's general attitude over the course of the previous half year that there was some dissatisfaction.

GW Where did that dissatisfaction come from?

THAYIL From everywhere dissatisfaction arises in a relationship or working situation. We were together 12 years. That's a long time.

GW Were the differences primarily personal or creative?

THAYIL It's not that clear cut. There were so many factors. Everyone in the band had their homes, their families, friends, girlfriends and pets to deal with...

GW It's been said that with the breakup of Soundgarden came the death of grunge. Which do you feel more guilty about—starting it, or ending it?

THAYIL Grunge died way before we broke up. I don't know when grunge came to be born. As a convenient reference point, grunge might have existed in terms of marketing. It was convenient for retail record stores so that they'd know where to file things. Grunge was a way to sell magazines, not a way to sell music. And I'm not simply saying this to criticize *Guitar World*—I'm saying this to criticize *all* publications. To answer your question, I don't feel guilt, I feel shame for having to be associated with someone else's starting of grunge, and having to share that label.

GW Would you say Soundgarden went out with a whimper instead of a bang?

THAYIL I felt we went out at the point of the band's bang, but the way we went out may have been a quiet whimper. There really isn't a good story behind our breakup. It was a common-sense thing. See, rock and roll is not comprised of company men, or religious zealots or genuflecting parishioners...

GW That could be argued.

60 Minutes with Joan Jett

One of *Guitar World*'s most popular departments through the late Nineties and 2000s was 60 Minutes, where we asked famous rockers to compile a list of the tracks they would pick if they were compiling a 60-minute mix tape. Subjects ranged from Lou Reed, Paul McCartney and Jeff Beck to Dimebag Darrell and Triumph the Insult Comic Dog. In this segment from February 1998, Joan Jett lists the hour of music that rocks her world:

Black Sabbath "Iron Man"
T.Rex "Jeepster"
The Sweet "Ballroom Blitz"
The Clash "I'm So Bored with the U.S.A."
Gary Glitter "Do You Wanna Touch Me (Oh Yeah!)"

David Bowie "Suffragette City"
Sex Pistols "Anarchy in the U.K."
The Ramones "I Wanna Be Sedated"
The Rolling Stones "Midnight Rambler"
Bikini Kill "Rebel Girl"/"New Radio"
L7 "Pretend We're Dead"

FEB. '98

APRIL / VOL. 19 / NO. 4

JAMES HETFIELD MEETS GOV'T MULE

Warren Haynes and Allen Woody come face to face with their biggest fan, Metallica's James Hetfield.

JAMES HETFIELD I really like your lyrics a lot. There's a lot of sarcasm, and a lot of rich-versus-poor imagery.

WARREN HAYNES Well, I like to think of it more as "us and them," us being people who want to help each other and them being people who only want to help themselves. Maybe when I was a kid I had it out for all rich people, but now I know that there are as many good rich people out as there are bad poor people.

HETFIELD But there's a definite underdog vibe to your lyrics that I really dig.

HAYNES There is, and there's a lot of social commentary, but it's all tongue-in-cheek. None of it's meant to be taken too seriously.

GW Metallica has also always championed the underdog.

HETFIELD Yeah, but it's all so vague that it could mean anything to anyone. I know what it means to me, but it changes all the time, so I'd rather not put ideas in people's heads. I'd rather people figure it out for themselves.

HAYNES Right, I've found it's better for people to decide for themselves because they'll come up with grandiose visions that relate to their own lives, and which you could never match.

You guys have been spreading the writing credits around a bit. I notice Jason [*Newsted*] had one on *ReLoad*.

HETFIELD Yeah, Jason finally got in there. When we put a song together, everyone contributes, but that's not really writing to us. Now we're letting everyone play the way they play, instead of dictating everything. I guess that's especially true of Jason.

ALLEN WOODY Man, he's a slamming bass player.

HETFIELD Yeah, and he's gotten so much better on this record. I was just blown away.

Crack Addicts

JUN. '98

When we printed this magnificent Storm Thorgerson Pink Floyd creation in our February 1998 issue, readers responded in droves, asking where they could get their hands on a poster of the breathtaking photo. We answered those prayers in the June issue, which contained a special fold-out poster of the image known as "Back Catalogue" (originally used as a U.K. promotion for the band's 1995 box set, *Box 1975–1988*). The flip-side, on the other hand, was the epitome of rock and roll ugliness: corpse-like Marilyn Manson and Twiggy Ramirez wrapped in tourniquet tubing.

MARILYN MANSON

1 "STAIRWAY TO HEAVEN"
SOLOIST: JIMMY PAGE
LED ZEPPELIN *Led Zeppelin IV* (Atlantic, 1971)

IF JIMMY PAGE IS THE GEORGE LUCAS OF GUITARISTS, THEN "Stairway" is his *Star Wars*. Driven by a solid, uplifting theme — man's quest for salvation — the epic starts slowly, gains unstoppable momentum and finally rushes headlong to a shattering conclusion. The grand finale in this case is the song's thrill-a-second guitar solo.

Page remembers: "I'd been fooling around with the acoustic guitar and came up with several different sections which flowed together nicely. I soon realized that it could be the perfect vehicle for something I'd been wanting to do for a while: to compose something that would start quietly and then build to a huge crescendo. I also knew that I wanted the piece to speed up, which is something musicians aren't supposed to do.

"So I had all the structure of it, and ran it by [bassist] John Paul Jones so he could get the idea — [drummer] John Bonham and [singer] Robert Plant had gone out for the night — and then on the following day we got into it with Bonham. You have to realize that, at first, there was a hell of a lot for everyone to remember on this one. But as we were sort of routining it, Robert started writing the lyrics, and much to his surprise, he wrote a huge percentage of it right there and then."

Plant recalls the experience: "I was sitting next to Page in front of a fire at our studio in Headley Grange. He had written this chord sequence and was playing it for me. I was holding a pencil and paper, when, suddenly, my hand was writing out the words: 'There's a lady who's sure all that glitters is gold and she's buying a stairway to heaven.' I just sat there and looked at the words and almost leaped out of my seat. Looking back, I suppose I sat down at the right moment."

While the spontaneous nature of Plant's anthemic lyrics came as a pleasant surprise, the best was yet to come. The beautifully con-

THE 100 GREATEST SOLOS OF ALL TIME

SEPT. 1998

VOL. 19 / NO. 9

The 100 Greatest Solos of All Time

From "Stairway to Heaven" (#1) to "Wanted Dead or Alive" (#100): *Guitar World* **readers vote for the greatest leads in rock history.**

To the rock guitarist, the solo is many things—the electric orgasm, the essence of all existence, the best way to impress sleek women. Not only do we love to play solos, we love to hear 'em. And the best solos thrill us beyond measure.

With that in mind, *Guitar World* asked its readers to compile a list of their five favorite guitar solos on a postcard and mail it in to our offices. The idea was that we would tabulate the responses and come up with a master list of the 100 greatest solos. Nice idea, huh? Well, you don't know the half of it. The cards came. And they kept coming. They came until we had to pack up and find offices big enough to accommodate the flood of cards bearing your well-reasoned votes for the greatest solos of all time. We counted until our arms ached, until we put together the list of solos, with some very cool commentary, presented over the following pages.

So, how did you vote? Ultimately, only one pattern emerged: The guitar heroes of yesterday remain the guitar heroes of today. And the great solos of rock's heyday in the Seventies are loved by the fans who heard them when they were new, and loved by the fans of today.

All this is as it should be, for we asked for the *greatest* solos. Greatness can be truly applied only to things that have withstood the test of time. As you'll soon see, *GW*'s readers intuitively understood this essential provision when they voted. This random sampling from the top 100 screams for itself.

1) "Stairway to Heaven"
Soloist: Jimmy Page
Album: Led Zeppelin—*Led Zeppelin IV* (1971)

2) "Eruption"
Soloist: Edward Van Halen
Album: Van Halen—*Van Halen* (1978)

3) "Free Bird"
Soloists: Allen Collins, Gary Rossington
Album: Lynyrd Skynyrd—*pronounced leh-nerd skin-nerd* (1973)

4) "Comfortably Numb"
Soloist: David Gilmour
Album: Pink Floyd—*The Wall* (1979)

5) "All Along the Watchtower"
Soloist: Jimi Hendrix
Album: The Jimi Hendrix Experience—*Electric Ladyland* (1968)

6) "November Rain" Slash
9) "Crazy Train" Randy Rhoads
12) "Johnny B. Goode" Chuck Berry
14) "Layla" Eric Clapton & Duane Allman
19) "Floods" Dimebag Darrell
22) "Sultans of Swing" Mark Knopfler
24) "Fade to Black" Kirk Hammett
29) "For the Love of God" Steve Vai
33) "The Thrill Is Gone" B.B. King
36) "Black Star" Yngwie Malmsteen
38) "Whole Lotta Love" Jimmy Page

41) "Brighton Rock" Brian May
44) "Alive" Mike McCready
45) "Light My Fire" Robby Kieger
48) "Sympathy for the Devil" Keith Richards
50) "Shock Me" Ace Frehley
53) "Too Rolling Stoned" Robin Trower
56) "War Pigs" Tony Iommi
60) "Zoot Allures" Frank Zappa
63) "Scar Tissue" John Frusciante
68) "Starship Trooper" Steve Howe

76) "Cinnamon Girl" Neil Young
78) "Truckin'" Jerry Garcia
83) "Scuttle Buttin'" Stevie Ray Vaughan
88) "Kid Charlemagne" Larry Carlton
94) "Mr. Scary" George Lynch
97) "Beyond the Realms of Death" Glenn Tipton
99) "Cause We've Ended As Lovers" Jeff Beck
100) "Wanted Dead or Alive" Richie Sambora

NINETEEN '99

Guitar World parties with Kurt and Courtney, Kid Rock and the Chili Peppers, goes 3D with Limp Bizkit and pays tribute to John Lennon and Stevie Ray Vaughan.

Dear *Guitar World*,

You guys have really done it now. It's bad enough that I had to *live* through the Nineties—but having to remember it because of your March issue is a horrible thing. This has been the worst decade in music history. Not only did self-absorbed morons like Kurt Cobain ruin rock music with their non-solos and depressing lyrics but they paved the way for such post-punk crap as Bush and Smashing Pumpkins. As I flipped through your Decade in Review section, I practically cried as I saw it go from Ozzy, George Lynch and Joe Satriani to Korn, Radiohead and the Pumpkins. I know it's not the Eighties anymore, but classic metal bands like Ozzy, Dio, Iron Maiden, Black Sabbath, Rush and even Yngwie Malmsteen are still active and relevant and should be recognized. As far as I'm concerned, the Nineties bands killed musicianship and quality.

—Alex Ponder

80 81 82 83 84 85 86 87 88 89 90 91 92 93 94 95 96 97 98 99 00 01 02 03 04 05 06 07 08 09 10

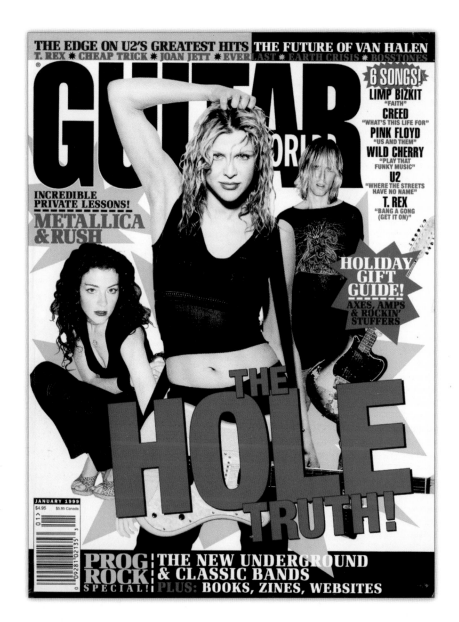

JANUARY After a four-year absence from the rock world, Courtney Love and company return with a vengeance and bare their *Celebrity Skin.* "I think I walk in Madonna's shadow sometimes. People see that she's a blonde and I'm a blonde, and she's super-famous and I'm super-famous, and I feed the fuel that makes a person super-famous, for whatever retarded reason."
COVER STORY BY ALAN DI PERNA; BY PHOTO BY ROSS HALFIN

FEBRUARY Yoko Ono and some of John Lennon's closest collaborators examine the solo career of the man who taught the world to imagine.
COVER STORY BY ALAN DI PERNA; PHOTO BY BOB GRUEN

MARCH The stunning rise and fall of Kurt Cobain, Seattle's reluctant King of Grunge and *Guitar World*'s Artist of the Decade.
COVER STORY BY ALAN DI PERNA; PHOTO BY YOURI LENQUETTE

APRIL The explosive history of Stevie Ray Vaughan, the man who saved the blues and then himself, only to die a tragic death. As told by Stevie Ray and his closest friends and associates.
COVER STORY BY ALAN PAUL PHOTO BY ROBERT KNIGHT

MAY Normal, everyday guys Dexter Holland and Noodles Wasserman of the Offspring are just like you and me, except that their latest album, *Americana,* is the biggest thing in rock.
COVER STORY BY TOM BEAUJOUR; PHOTO BY ANTHONY SAINT JAMES

JUNE *Guitar World* celebrates 1969, the greatest year in rock, with the stories behind such landmark albums and events as *Led Zeppelin,* Cream's *Goodbye,* Woodstock, the Who's *Tommy,* the Rolling Stones' *Let It Bleed,* the birth of Blind Faith and much more.
COVER STORY BY VARIOUS

JULY The California funk-rock kings look back at a turbulent career and ahead to a more stable future.
COVER STORY BY J.D. CONSIDINE; PHOTO BY ANTHONY SAINT JAMES

1999 TOTAL ISSUES: 12

AUGUST *Guitar World* goes 3D as Limp Bizkit, with their ferocious new album, *Significant Other*, stake their claim as the new kings of metallic rap.
COVER STORY BY J.D. CONSIDINE
PHOTO BY CLAY PATRICK MCBRIDE

SEPTEMBER Mötley Crüe bassist Nikki Sixx reflects on a decade of decadence and looks back at the classic albums that made his band the most notorious in hard rock.
COVER STORY BY TOM BEAUJOUR
PHOTO BY NEIL ZLOZOWER

OCTOBER *Guitar World* celebrates the millennium a few months early with exclusive interviews with some of the all-time guitar greats: Jimmy Page, Jeff Beck, Eddie Van Halen, James Hetfield and Kirk Hammett.
COVER STORIES BY BRAD TOLINSKI, ALAN PAUL AND VIC GARBARINI; PHOTO BY ROSS HALFIN

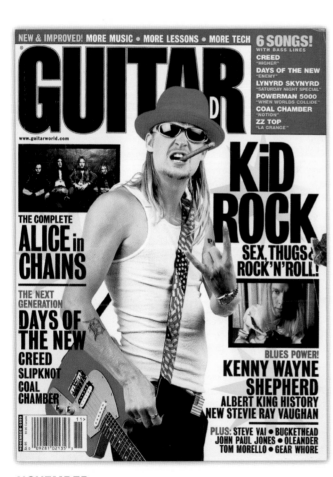

NOVEMBER Kid Rock is white trash with black pride, learned to play heavy metal via turntables and cites Fleetwood Mac, Hank Williams and Public Enemy as influences. *Guitar World* hails the new King of Rock.

COVER STORY BY J.D. CONSIDINE; PHOTO BY CLAY PATRICK MCBRIDE

DECEMBER On *The Battle of Los Angeles*, Rage Against the Machine's Tom Morello defies guitar convention and shows why he is rock's preeminent experimenter.

COVER STORY BY J.D. CONSIDINE; PHOTO BY CLAY PATRICK MCBRIDE

MAXIMUM BOB

In little over a year, he's won a Grammy, survived a dangerous illness, hobnobbed with religious royalty and toured endlessly. He's Bob Dylan, forever young prince of rock and roll. **by Murray Engleheart**

BOB DYLAN, WHO FOR MUCH OF HIS FABLED career has been the hippest, has now spent more than a year being the hottest as well. He's the man on everyone's A-list, from Eddie Vedder, an avowed fan, to Pope John Paul II, for whom Dylan performed three songs in Bologna, Italy. Dylan even impressed the online retailer amazon.com, which recently voted *Bob Dylan Live 1966: The "Royal Albert Hall" Concert* the best album of 1998. As remarkable as it seems, one of the most vital post-grunge artists in rock is 58-year-old Bob Dylan. After a rather lean decade, the Sixties folk-rock icon has, against all odds, revitalized his career by polishing off the Nineties with two albums that rank among his very best.

Along with the highly acclaimed *"Albert Hall"* reissue, Dylan's 1997 Grammy-winning release, *Time Out of Mind*, produced by Daniel Lanois, has put the singer back in rock's vanguard.

Perhaps even more remarkable than Dylan's albums have been his brilliant live shows, showcasing his feisty lead guitar playing and a crack band. After bouncing back from a life-threatening heart infection in mid-'97, Dylan has played well over 200 shows, performing fierce, jam-oriented reinterpretations of his best songs, at times recalling the tightly wound, three-guitar army of Lynyrd Skynyrd's "Free Bird." It's all been a far cry from the disappointingly ramshackle shows that became his stock-in-trade in the Eighties and early Nineties.

When Bob Dylan talks—which is rarely—people listen. Especially these days. We recently had the opportunity for a brief chat with the enigmatic legend, who finally took a break from what has come to be known as his "Never Ending Tour." Dylan seemed relaxed, and was kind enough to reflect on the turbulent events of his recent career, and to speculate on his future.

GUITAR WORLD Bruce Springsteen once said that without you there'd be no Beatles' *Sgt. Pepper's*, no Beach Boys' *Pet Sounds*, no Sex Pistols' "God Save the Queen."

BOB DYLAN Well...you know, you can influence all kinds of people, but

"WE SEEM TO BE ATTRACTING A NEW AUDIENCE, NOT JUST THOSE WHO KNOW ME AS SOME KIND OF **FiGuReHeaD** FROM ANOTHER AGE."

sometimes it gets in the way—especially if somebody is accusing you of influencing somebody that you had no interest in influencing in the first place. I've never given it any mind at all, really. I don't really care to influence anybody at this time, and if I have influenced anybody, what can I say?

GW Certain albums of yours—*Blood on the Tracks, Infidels, Highway 61 Revisited*—inspired great critical plaudits in their day, and have stood the test of time. In your view, do those records live up to their reputation?

DYLAN Well, those records were made a long time ago, and you know, truthfully, records that were made in that day and age all were good. They all had some magic to them because the technology didn't go beyond what the artist was doing. It was a lot easier to get excellence back in those days on a record than it is now. I made records back then just like a lot of other people who were my age, and we all made good records. Those records seem to cast a long shadow. But how much of it is the technology and how much of it is the talent and influence, I really don't know.

I know you can't make records that sound that way any more. The high priority is technology now. It's not the artist or the art. It's the technology that is coming through. That's what makes *Time Out of Mind*...it doesn't take itself seriously, but then again, the sound is very significant to that record. If that record was made more haphazardly, it wouldn't have sounded that way. It wouldn't have had the impact that it did. The guys that helped me make it went out of their way to make a record that sounds like a record played on a record player. There wasn't any wasted effort on *Time Out of Mind*, and I don't think there will be on any more of my records.

GW A writer once noted that Delta bluesman Skip James' records always sound best at night. The same could be said about *Time Out of Mind*.

DYLAN You think it sounds like Skip James?

GW In a sense. *Time Out of Mind* sounds best late at night.

DYLAN That would be a tremendous compliment to me, to hear that it was even in any kind of...that it would be in the same realm as Skip James.

GW In terms of mood and ambience, it's almost like there's ghosts running through it. Are those ghosts of, or for, any- **continued on page 112**

MARCH 1999

VOL. 20 / NO. 3

Bob Dylan

The folk-rock legend finally takes a break from his "Never Ending Tour" and gives *Guitar World* **a rare interview.**

GUITAR WORLD Bruce Springsteen once said that without you there'd be no Beatles' *Sgt. Pepper's*, no Beach Boys' *Pet Sounds*, no Sex Pistols' "God Save the Queen," etc.

BOB DYLAN Well...I mean, you know, you just have to go on. We can influence all kinds of people, but sometimes it gets in the way—especially if somebody is accusing you of influencing somebody that you had no interest in influencing in the first place. I've never given it any mind at all, really. I don't really care to influence anybody at this time, and if I have influenced anybody, what can I say?

GW There's always talk about the peaks in people's work. With you, the talk centers on *Blonde on Blonde, Blood on the Tracks, Infidels*, etc. Do you sense that too? Have you got a good sense of your own magic?

DYLAN Well, those records were made a long time ago, and you know, truthfully, records that were made in that day and age all were good. They all had some magic to them because the technology didn't go beyond what the artist was doing. It was a lot easier to get excellence back in those days on a record than it is now. I made records back then just like a lot of other people who were my age, and we all made good records. Those records seem to cast a long shadow. But how much of it is the technology and how much of it is the talent and influence, I really don't know.

GW There seems to be a renewed interest in your music, particularly among young people. Have you noticed a shift in your audience?

DYLAN Ah, no, I haven't found any shift but I've found a different audience. I'm not good at reading how old people are, but my audience seems to be livelier than they were 10 years ago. They react immediately to what I do, and they don't come with a lot of preconceived ideas about who they would like me to be, or who they think I am. Whereas a few years ago they couldn't react quickly. They had to get through too much, er...

GW Baggage?

DYLAN Mental, yeah, mental psychic stuff, so [*sighs*] I was still kind of bogged down with a certain crowd of people. It has taken a long time to bust through that crowd. Even the last time I toured with Tom Petty, we were kind of facing that same old crowd.

But that's changed. We seem to be attracting a new audience. Not the people who might know me as some kind of figurehead from another age or a symbol or a generational thing. I don't really have to deal with that any more, if I ever did.

GW Do you find that choosing songs for your live performances gets harder or easier as the years go on?

DYLAN I have so many songs that finding them is the least of my problems. I've got songs that I've never even sung live. I've got 500, 600, 700 songs. I don't have a problem with the backlog of songs. Some fade away and diminish in time, but others take their place.

GW Have you fully recovered from your heart attack?

DYLAN Well, let me say first of all, it was not a heart attack. It was an infection that went into my heart area. It was something called Histoplasmosis that came from just accidentally inhaling a bunch of stuff that was out on one of the rivers by where I live. Maybe one month, or one or two days out of the year, the banks around the river get all mucky, and then the wind blows and a bunch of swirling mess is in the air. I happened to inhale a bunch of that. That's what made me sick. It went into the heart area. But it wasn't anything really attacking my heart.

GW You were pretty seriously ill, though?

DYLAN Oh, I was real seriously ill, yeah.

GW Did that make you pause and rethink things?

DYLAN I really didn't, you know, because it wasn't something that I brought on myself. It's not like I even needed the time to slow down and re-examine my life. It was just one of those things. I was down for about six weeks, but I don't remember particularly having any kind of great illuminations at that time.

GW The performance for the Pope at the World Eucharistic Congress in Bologna must have been tremendously moving for you.

DYLAN Well, it's all surreal, you know? But yeah, it was moving. I mean, he's the Pope. [*laughs*] You know what I mean? There's only one Pope, right?

GW Did the irony of playing "Knocking on Heaven's Door" strike you at the time?

DYLAN No, because that's the song they wanted to hear. It seemed to be a good correspondent to the situation. ✱

JUNE / VOL. 20 / NO. 6

1969

It began with the release of the first Led Zeppelin album and concluded with Jimi Hendrix's legendary Fillmore East performances—and in between were three albums by CCR, the Woodstock festival and classic albums by the Who, the Doors, the Beatles, the Stones and others. *Guitar World* celebrates the albums and events that made 1969 the greatest year in rock.

Led Zeppelin—*Led Zeppelin*
Cream—*Goodbye*
Creedence Clearwater Revival—*Bayou Country*
MC5—*Kick Out the Jams*
The birth of Blind Faith
The Allman Brothers Band—*The Allman Brothers Band*
The Velvet Underground—*The Velvet Underground*
Sly and the Family Stone—*Stand!*
The Who—*Tommy*
Jethro Tull—*Stand Up*
Crosby, Stills & Nash—*Crosby, Stills & Nash*

Frank Zappa—*Uncle Meat*
The Jeff Beck Group—*Beck-Ola*
The Doors—*The Soft Parade*
Grand Funk Railroad—*On Time*
James Brown—*Say It Loud I'm Black and I'm Proud*
Creedence Clearwater Revival—*Green River*
Woodstock Music and Art Fair
Santana—*Santana*
The Stooges—*The Stooges*
The Beatles—*Abbey Road*
The Band—*The Band*
The Kinks—*Arthur (Or the Decline and Fall of the British Empire)*

Johnny Winter—*Second Winter*
King Crimson—*In the Court of the Crimson King*
Creedence Clearwater Revival—*Willy and the Poor Boys*
Led Zeppelin—*Led Zeppelin II*
The Grateful Dead—*Live/Dead*
The Jefferson Airplane—*Volunteers*
Captain Beefheart & His Magic Band—*Trout Mask Replica*
The Rolling Stones—*Let It Bleed*
Jimi Hendrix performs at the Fillmore East

AUG. '99

Guitar World Goes 3D

Eleven years before *Avatar* brought 3D to the masses, *Guitar World* took a bold step toward the future by producing its August 1999 issue in three dimensions. Sandwiched between pages 50 and 51 were a pair of 3D glasses that could be used to view all the interior images—including the Limp Bizkit cover story, a photo gallery of guitar heroes, various advertisements and the Metallica/Limp Bizkit two-sided poster in the middle—in eye-popping 3D. As editor-in-chief Brad Tolinski wrote in his Woodshed, "A few months ago I woke up feeling flat. The pancakes I was eating were flat. The CD I was playing was flat. The women on the street—flat. It was like Christopher Columbus had never been born! That day, I vowed that I would do everything in my power to fight all that was two-dimensional."

——————— "I knew I wanted a song about a runaway train, where things are

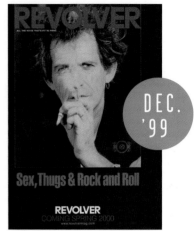

SEPTEMBER / VOL. 20 / NO. 9

IAN ANDERSON

Jethro Tull's wild-eyed frontman talks about the inspiration behind *Aqualung* and how one of that album's most beloved tracks, "Locomotive Breath," came to be.

"*AQUALUNG* MARKS THE POINT at which I had the confidence as a songwriter and as a guitar player to actually pick up and play the guitar and be at the forefront of the band. It's also the album on which I began to address religious issues in my music, and I think that happened simply because the time was right for it. Addressing religious issues in simplistic pop-rock terms was permissible then. I'd have to disguise some of those sentiments to make it pass muster today.

"*Aqualung* wasn't a concept album, although a lot of people thought so. The idea came about from a photograph my wife at the time took of a tramp in London. I had feelings of guilt about the homeless, as well as fear and insecurity with people like that who seem a little scary. And I suppose all of that was combined with a slightly romanticized picture of the person who is homeless but yet a free spirit, who either won't or can't join in society's prescribed formats.

"So from that photograph and those sentiments, I began writing the words to 'Aqualung.' I can remember sitting in a hotel room in L.A., working out the chord structure for the verses. It's quite a tortured tangle of chords, but it was meant to really drag you here and there and then set you down into the more gentle acoustic section of the song.

"With 'Locomotive Breath,' I knew I wanted a song about a runaway train, where things are going out of control and you can't get off the train. It's safe to say that kind of situation mirrored an aspect of the band's life at the time, what with all the touring we were doing. We actually had to record *Aqualung* in a rather short time between tours, so it was done very quickly. Island Studios had just opened up, and it was a shakedown period for the studio; there were a lot of technical problems. Adding to them, the band was having problems recording 'Locomotive Breath.' We just couldn't get the feeling, and I was failing to convey to the band what the song was about and how it should work. So I went out and played high-hat and bass drum for four minutes to lay down a rhythm track; this was in the days before drum machines and sequencers. Then I played an acoustic guitar part and some electric guitar parts, and then we tacked on John Evans' piano intro at the front of it, and the others overdubbed their parts onto mine. So nobody actually played on that track at the same time, but it's not a bad performance whatsoever. That was the only time we ever did anything like that back then."

The Birth of *Revolver* Magazine

Those who like their music hard and heavy are no doubt well familiar with *Revolver* magazine—but how many know that *Revolver* was actually conceived as *Guitar World*'s genre-blending sister publication in 1999? This advertisement announcing the new magazine's existence appeared in the December issue of *GW*, a few months before the mag's official debut in the spring of 2000. When it hit newsstands, *Revolver*'s premiere issue contained a unique mix of content, including an oral history of the Doors, a behind-the-scenes look at the Japanese pop scene and members of Slipknot wearing fashionable men's suits. But perhaps the world wasn't quite ready for such an eclectic combo. After only a few issues, *Revolver* was retooled and relaunched into the magazine metal fans know and love today.

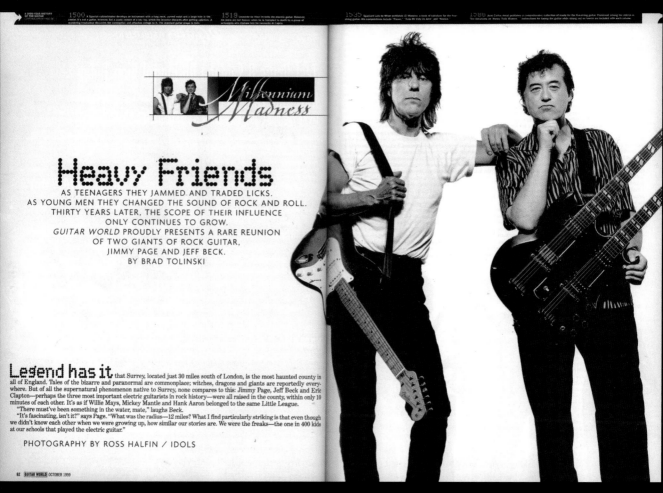

A 3000-YEAR HISTORY OF THE GUITAR

1500 A Spanish cabinetmaker develops an instrument with a long neck, curved waist and a large hole in the center. It's not a guitar, however, but a crude version of a key toy, which the bassist discards after getting splinters. A wandering troubadour discovers the contraption and attaches strings to it. The standard guitar shape is born.

1519 Leonardo da Vinci invents the electric guitar. However, his ideas are not known to be transposed to death in a group of archeologists who mistake him for Leonardo di Caprio.

1535 Spaniard Luis de Milan publishes El Maestro, a book of tablature for the four-string guitar. His compositions include "Pavan," "Toda Mi Vida Os Ame" and "Nadine."

1586 Juan Carlos Amat publishes a comprehensive collection of music for the five-string guitar. Prominent among the entries is "Ten Variations on Honky Tonk Women"—instructions for tuning the guitar while strung, and no bands are included with each column.

Millennium Madness

Heavy Friends

AS TEENAGERS THEY JAMMED. AND TRADED LICKS.
AS YOUNG MEN THEY CHANGED THE SOUND OF ROCK AND ROLL.
THIRTY YEARS LATER, THE SCOPE OF THEIR INFLUENCE
ONLY CONTINUES TO GROW.
GUITAR WORLD PROUDLY PRESENTS A RARE REUNION
OF TWO GIANTS OF ROCK GUITAR,
JIMMY PAGE AND JEFF BECK.
BY BRAD TOLINSKI

Legend has it that Surrey, located just 30 miles south of London, is the most haunted county in all of England. Tales of the bizarre and paranormal are commonplace; witches, dragons and giants are reportedly everywhere. But of all the supernatural phenomenon native to Surrey, none compares to this: Jimmy Page, Jeff Beck and Eric Clapton—perhaps the three most important electric guitarists in rock history—were all raised in the county, within only 10 minutes of each other. It's as if Willie Mays, Mickey Mantle and Hank Aaron belonged to the same Little League.

"There must've been something in the water, mate," laughs Beck.

"It's fascinating, isn't it?" says Page. "What was the radius—12 miles? What I find particularly striking is that even though we didn't know each other when we were growing up, how similar our stories are. We were the freaks—the one in 400 kids at our schools that played the electric guitar."

PHOTOGRAPHY BY ROSS HALFIN / IDOLS

OCT. 1999

VOL. 20 / NO. 10

Jimmy Page & Jeff Beck

As teenagers they jammed and traded licks. As young men they changed the sound of rock and roll.
Guitar World **proudly presents a rare reunion of two giants of rock guitar.**

GUITAR WORLD Both of you started playing the electric guitar when it was still a relatively exotic and unusual instrument. What inspired you to pick it up?

JEFF BECK I was galvanized by the rock and roll movies of the day, particularly *The Girl Can't Help It*, which featured performances by Eddie Cochran, Little Richard and Gene Vincent and the Blue Caps. That movie completely did me in, particularly seeing the Blue Caps, who looked really dangerous. It started me wanting my own guitar.

The guitar was initially presented more as just a fashion accessory, but somehow a small group of us suddenly became more discriminating about who was actually playing and who was just hanging onto it. It was like, "I know who played lead on Elvis' records—it's Scotty Smith!" And somebody else would say, "No, it ain't, it's Scotty Moore." But it was all part of the detective work, trying to find out who these guys were that were making us so happy.

JIMMY PAGE And then sitting down and really studying all of those records. All of us—Eric [*Clapton*], Jeff and all of our contemporaries—went through the same process. Those early rock records grabbed us hard...

BECK ...and threw us on to the floor. [*laughs*]

GW Why do you think you both progressed so fast? Was it because you were pushing each other?

BECK Yeah, I used to be very thrilled that Jimmy was living so near. You need a pal to bounce ideas off. But my sister was also a very important part of my progress, because she used to bring the records home. She was four years older, so she had some money and could swing abroad and buy the new rockabilly records. And you had to have the albums to learn from, because you would never actually hear rock and roll on British radio.

PAGE What saved the day was that there were other people that just really loved rock, blues and R&B, and they also began collecting these obscure records. Soon, a whole network formed of people who would swap and trade music. None of us really had any money to buy all of these rare imported albums, but it all built up. It was a very, very important period.

GW Do you remember any of the specific licks that you'd show each other when you were hanging out?

BECK We would play Ricky Nelson songs like "My Babe" and "It's Late" because his guitarist, James Burton, was so great. And just a lot of jamming. I remember Jim had a two-track tape recorder, which was a dream. He used to stick the mic, which came with the tape recorder, under a cushion on the couch. I used to bash it, and it would make the best bass drum sound you ever heard. [*laughs*]

GW Does the guitar have any place to go? Or has it reached the stage where it's only a matter of refinement?

BECK I've been trying to show you folks! [*laughs*]

PAGE Yeah, let's be fair. Look at Jeff's journey on the guitar. It's fantastic, and his new album really pushes the envelope. But what it comes down to is that it's Jeff's character coming through—that's his persona on six strings.

People always think the guitar is reaching its limits. They thought guitar music was stagnating in the late Seventies, and then Eddie Van Halen comes in and changes everything. But who knows? It's just a matter of somebody's imagination.

BECK I don't think you need to worry yourself about the millennium being any drastic or significant cutoff point for the guitar. I mean, my mom thought the guitar was going to fizzle out in two weeks—that it was just a fad—and that was in 1958!

The thing I've noticed is the astonishing standard that has been attained by so many young kids. But the problem is that the framework that it sits on is not...it doesn't have a strong undercarriage. So you see the most devastating techniques emerging, but the question will be whether the music is worthy. The guitar playing is good right now, but it ain't wrapped in the right package, you know?

GW Jimmy, what's your favorite Jeff Beck performance?

PAGE I still remember the time Jeff came over my house when he was in the Yardbirds and played me "Shapes of Things." It was just so good—so out there and ahead of its time. And I seem to have that same reaction whenever I hear anything he does.

GW Jeff, what is your favorite Jimmy Page performance?

BECK Golly, what can I say? The sense of inner pride...when I see people waxing so lyrical about Led Zeppelin and to know where the origin of that was. There's a much bigger picture there, bigger than selecting something he's done. I'm partial to "Kashmir," but whenever I hear Jimmy on the radio I immediately think of all the great times we've had and the music we've played. ✳

TWO THOUSAND

'00

Guitar World enters the Millennium with reigning rock superstars Korn, Smashing Pumpkins, Limp Bizkit and Green Day, plus tributes to Hendrix and Stevie Ray and lessons with AC/DC and Kirk Hammett.

Dear *Guitar World*,

God bless *Guitar World* for informing us about
Jason Becker's struggle with ALS. When I read
about how such a gifted guitarist could no
longer play his ax, I decided to never again
take for granted that I could play a D chord.
I call on all guitarists reading this to donate
what they pay for a set of strings to Jason
and Chuck Schuldiner's funds—a small price
to pay for something so much more important
than a fresh tone. Hats off to Jason for still
writing music, and I can't wait to pick up his
new release. Ditto for Chuck—when his new band,
Control Denied, comes to Chicago, I'll be there
to cheer him on.

—Mwealan

JANUARY Korn guitarists Munky and Head and singer Jonathan Davis discuss the making of *Issues*, their aggressively psychotic new album.
COVER STORY BY JOHN PECORELLI; PHOTO BY CLAY PATRICK MCBRIDE

FEBRUARY The complete 30-year history of Carlos Santana, from his 1969 appearance at Woodstock to his current reign as chart-topping guitar hero.
COVER STORY BY ALAN DI PERNA; PHOTO BY JAY BLAKESBERG

MARCH To commemorate the 20th anniversary of *The Wall*, *Guitar World* takes an in-depth look at the making of the legendary Pink Floyd album.
COVER STORY BY ALAN DI PERNA

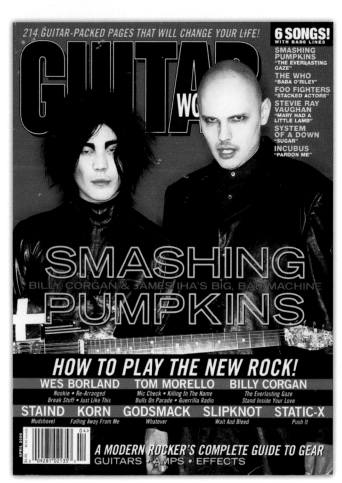

APRIL With their latest album, *MACHINA/the machines of god*, Smashing Pumpkins guitarists Billy Corgan and James Iha make a bold return to the hard rock of their early days. "We were completely bored with the guitar; there was absolutely nothing we could do that we found exciting," says Corgan. "So we decided that, whether the guitars sound shitty or great, they just had to sound unique. And that became our method."
COVER STORY BY CHRISTOPHER SCAPELLITI; PHOTO BY ROSS HALFIN

MAY To celebrate the release of Pantera's first studio album in four years, *Guitar World* heads down to Texas and talks with guitarist Dimebag Darrell. "It's been bam-bam-bam—nonstop. Most bands don't make it past two albums and tours, if that. We pulled it off, but we got to the point where we knew it was time to take a break."
COVER STORY BY CHRIS GILL; PHOTO BY CLAY PATRICK MCBRIDE

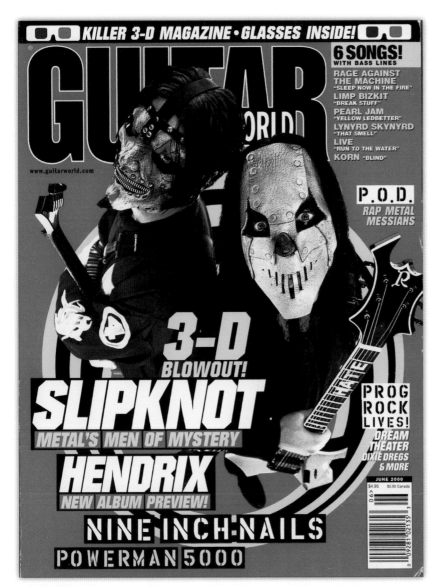

JUNE In a special 3D feature, *Guitar World* explores the dark and brutal world of Slipknot, where concerts are a war zone, guitar riffs can kill and only the strong survive. "The most important thing is that we connect with our audience," says guitarist Mick Thomson. "The bands that can't connect with their audience are the bands that you eventually see on *Where Are They Now?*"

COVER STORY BY BRIAN STILLMAN; BY PHOTO BY CLAY PATRICK MCBRIDE

2000 TOTAL ISSUES: 12

JULY The story of how Jimmy Page and the Black Crowes got together to record *Live at the Greek*, their revolutionary new internet-only live album of Zeppelin classics.
COVER STORY BY ALAN DI PERNA; PHOTO BY ROSS HALFIN

AUGUST Ten years after the death of Stevie Ray Vaughan, *Guitar World* pays homage to the great Texas bluesman with an extensive look at his album catalog, a reprint of the first interview ever conducted with the young SRV and three rare and revealing backstage conversations.
COVER STORY BY ANDY ALEDORT; PHOTO BY ROBERT KNIGHT

SEPTEMBER As *Mission: Impossible 2* rules the box office, Metallica's Kirk Hammett sits with *Guitar World* for a private lesson on how to play "I Disappear," the pounding single from the movie soundtrack.
COVER STORY BY NICK BOWCOTT; PHOTO BY MICK HUTSON

OCTOBER As Limp Bizkit gets set to release its anxiously awaited new album, *Chocolate Starfish and the Hot Dog Flavored Water*, guitarist Wes Borland gives *GW* a private tour of his bizarre inner world.
COVER STORY BY ALAN DI PERNA; PHOTO BY CLAY PATRICK MCBRIDE

NOVEMBER Thirty years after the death of Jimi Hendrix, *Guitar World* honors the master with a remarkable collection of interviews and new information, including a soup-to-nuts overview of Jimi's life and musical career, an extensive look at Jimi's complete catalog of recorded music, an exclusive interview with Experience drummer Mitch Mitchell and more.
COVER STORY BY ALAN DI PERNA; PHOTO BY KARL FERRIS

DECEMBER Billie Joe Armstrong, Mike Dirnt and Tre Cool gather 'round to talk about the current state of punk rock and how the new Green Day album, *Warning*, does or does not fit into it.
COVER STORY BY ALAN DI PERNA; PHOTO BY CLAY PATRICK MCBRIDE

Over the course of history, only a handful of guitarists have become mainstream icons. The names Jimi Hendrix, Eric Clapton, Jeff Beck and Jimmy Page are known far and wide. And although Johnny Winter has earned his place alongside these fellow rock gods, history has not afforded him the same stature.

And yet, back in the late Sixties, Winter turned the world of rock on its head when he blasted out of Texas, armed with a truly original sound exemplified by blazing speed, a razor-sharp attack, fiery vocals and an inspired improvisational flair. Johnny Winter held his own alongside the greatest players rock guitar had to offer, and no less worthy a constituent than Jimi Hendrix sought out any opportunity to get together with him and jam.

"People always ask me about playing with Hendrix, but we didn't really play together that much," says Winter. "When I first came up to New York, we played together a bunch of times at my manager's club [The Scene, in Greenwich Village, owned by rock entrepreneur Steve Paul], and we had kind of a mutual admiration thing going. But Jimi wasn't really all that interested in being friends—with him, it was music, music, music. He really just wanted to pick up a few things from my slide playing."

On the strength of his first two releases, Johnny Winter and Second Winter, both released in 1969, Winter was rapidly hailed as a guitar deity, right alongside his contemporaries Hendrix, Clapton, Beck and Page. Johnny Winter And...Live, released in 1971, served to fan the flames, with his incendiary versions of the Rolling Stones' "Jumping Jack Flash" and Chuck Berry's "Johnny B. Goode" receiving generous airplay. In 1973, when Johnny launched his tour to support the certified classic Still Alive and Well, he had attained the highest level of rock guitar heroism imaginable, filling major stadiums the world over on the strength of his name.

But that high point also signaled the beginning of the next, less successful phase of Winter's career. Though his recorded output remained consistent throughout the Seventies, his position at the cutting edge of rock began to slip. By the late Seventies, he had refocused his attention on bluesier material (his role as producer of four Muddy Waters records signifies a high-water mark of this era), and by the mid Eighties he was recording for the small, independent Alligator label.

After a brief stint with MCA, during which he released Winter of '88, Johnny signed with the Virgin subsidiary Pointblank/Charisma, for whom he still records (his latest release is Live in NYC '97). While he may be relegated to the club circuit—and although he may not garner the acclaim of his early days—his faithful legion of fans still turn out in droves. But, as Johnny likes to say, "I just enjoy playing, as long as there's people out there listening. I feel real lucky, because I'm enjoying it more now than I ever have before."

One of the interviews that was conducted for this story took place at SIR Studios in New York, where Johnny has held regular weekly rehearsals for many years. When it came time to play, the bass player had yet to arrive. The next thing I knew, I was handed a bass and found myself laying down the low end while Johnny tore through the Freddie King classics "Hideaway" and "Sen-Sa-Shun," as well as "She Likes to Boogie Real Low," "Sick and Tired," "Going Down," "Blackjack" and "Johnny Guitar." Winter then wrapped up the proceedings with an extended workout on Muddy Waters' "Got My Mojo Workin'." After we finished, Johnny ambled over to me. "Hey, you sound real good," he said. Believe me, the pleasure was all mine.

GUITAR WORLD Despite your status as one of rock guitar's living legends, the guitar was not your first instrument.

JOHNNY WINTER No. I started on the clarinet when I was about four years old. Both of my parents were musicians; my mother played the piano, mostly just for fun, and my father played saxophone and the banjo, and played gigs on the weekends. His real job was as a contractor, building houses. I can remember my daddy teaching me how to play chords on the banjo and when I was very young. He'd show me some of the old standards, like "Bye Bye Blackbird" and "Ain't She Sweet," things like that.

GW How old were you when you first picked up the guitar?

WINTER Eleven. I had to stop playing the clarinet because I wore braces, and playing it was making my overbite worse. That's when I moved over to the ukulele. After playing the uke for a while, I switched over to the guitar because that was just the natural progression. My father encouraged me to move onto the guitar, too, because he said the only famous people he knew of that played the ukulele were Arthur Godfrey and Ukulele Ike! He thought I had better chances for success with the guitar.

GW Were there any particular guitar players that piqued your interest in the instrument?

WINTER Yeah, Merle Travis and Chet Atkins. Right around the time I picked up guitar, I met a guy named Luther Nally, who began to teach me how to play. Luther was into the Chet Atkins style, and he got me into using the thumb pick, which is what you need to play fingerstyle. A lot of the blues guys, like Muddy Waters and Jimmy Reed, used one too. Later on, I kind of wished I hadn't stuck with the thumb pick, because it probably slowed me down a little. I really wish I'd learned to play without it, but when I tried to play with just my fingers, it didn't sound as good to me as I would have liked. So, I'm stuck with the thumb pick and it's too late to change.

GW As a youngster, were you fanatical about practicing?

WINTER Oh yeah. I really loved to play, and I played every chance I got. And my parents were very encouraging; they were used to me being musically inclined. I also sang in the church choir, which helped me develop my voice.

GW One of your first releases was "Ice Cube,"

> "I BOUGHT LITERALLY *EVERY* BLUES RECORD I COULD LAY MY HANDS ON. ALL I DID WAS LISTEN TO RECORDS AND LEARN LICKS EVERY CHANCE I HAD. BLUES WAS SOMETHING I COULD NEVER GET ENOUGH OF."
> —JOHNNY WINTER

MARCH 2000

VOL. 21 / NO. 3

Johnny Winter

Twenty years after serving as *Guitar World*'s premiere issue cover artist, the blues legend sits with Andy Aledort to discuss his formative years, the development of his technique and the recording of his first two classic albums, *Johnny Winter* and *Second Winter*.

GUITAR WORLD Despite your status as one of rock guitar's living legends, the guitar was not your first instrument.

JOHNNY WINTER No. I started on the clarinet when I was about four years old. Both of my parents were musicians; my mother played the piano, mostly just for fun, and my father played saxophone and the banjo, and played gigs on the weekends. His real job was as a contractor, building houses. I can remember my daddy teaching me how to play chords on the banjo and the ukulele when I was very young. He'd show me some of the old standards, like "Bye Bye Blackbird" and "Ain't She Sweet," things like that.

GW How old were you when you first picked up the guitar?

WINTER Eleven. I had to stop playing the clarinet because I wore braces, and playing it was making my overbite worse. That's when I moved over to the ukulele. After playing the uke for a while, I switched over to the guitar, because that was just the natural progression. My father encouraged me to move onto the guitar, too, because he said the only famous people he knew of that played the ukulele were Arthur Godfrey and Ukulele Ike! He thought I had better chances for success with the guitar.

GW Were there any particular guitar players that piqued your interest in the instrument?

WINTER Yeah, Merle Travis and Chet Atkins. Right around the time I picked up guitar, I met a guy named Luther Nally, who began to teach me how to play. Luther was into the Chet Atkins style, and he got me into using the thumb pick, which is what you need to play fingerstyle. A lot of the blues guys, like Muddy Waters and Jimmy Reed, used one, too. Later on, I kind of wished I hadn't stuck with the thumb pick, because it probably slowed me down a little. I really wish I'd learned to play without it, but when I tried to play with just my fingers, it didn't sound as good to me as I would have liked. So, I'm stuck with the thumb pick and it's too late to change.

GW As a youngster, were you fanatical about practicing?

WINTER Oh yeah. I really loved to play, and I played every chance I got. And my parents were very encouraging; they were used to me being musically inclined. I also sang in the church choir, which helped me to develop my voice.

GW One of your first releases was "Ice Cube," which you cut in 1959 at the age of 15. Although you'd been playing guitar for only four years, many elements of your style—your speed and the precision, for example—were already firmly in place.

WINTER I had a good idea of what I wanted to sound like when I started to play, so it was just a matter of doing it. It didn't seem difficult; it came very naturally. Playing was something that I loved to do, and I just kept doing it because there was always more that I wanted to learn.

Clarence Garlow was a disc jockey on KJET, a radio station in Beaumont, Texas, where I grew up. We became friends, and he taught me a lot about music. For instance, when I first started to play, the only strings you could get were Gibson Sonomatics, which came with a wound G string. I couldn't figure out how Chuck Berry did all of those great string-bending licks, because I just couldn't get that sound with the wound G. Then Clarence turned me onto the unwound G string, and it was like a revelation!

GW What kind of guitar were you playing back then?

WINTER It was a Gibson Les Paul Custom, a black one. It was supposed to have three pickups, but I ordered it with just two because the middle pickup got in the way of my picking.

GW Your first two CBS records, *Johnny Winter* and *Second Winter*, were both recorded in Nashville. Why did you record there?

WINTER If you were signed to CBS in those days, you had to use their studios, and I felt the studios in New York and Los Angeles were a little too sterile. The Nashville studio was better, even though I thought the engineers at that time didn't really know how to capture the sound I was looking for. I ended up producing both of those albums because I just didn't trust anybody else. In retrospect, I wish I had had someone there to help me, because I think the records might have sounded better. I didn't really know what I was doing. On the first record, I was miking everything real close, and I wouldn't have done that if I'd known what to do. But, overall, I was pretty happy with the results.

GW *Second Winter* was the first—and only—three-sided record ever released.

WINTER The explanation that's printed on the record is accurate: What we had recorded amounted to three sides' worth of material. We didn't want to cut anything out, and we didn't have any extra material. The funny thing is, the length of those three sides is about the same as the length of the average CD today. ✱

APRIL / VOL. 21 / NO. 4

CHUCK SCHULDINER

Guitar World lends a hand as the founding
father of death metal fights for his life.

WHEN CHUCK SCHULDINER, founder of the seminal Florida death metal band Death, woke up on the morning of his thirty-second birthday, he had planned for a rip-roarin' day of celebration with friends and family. But instead of the usual cake and ice cream, he was given the worst news of his life—that he may not live to see 33. For on that day, Schuldiner was jolted by the diagnosis that he had a cancerous tumor lodged at the base of his brain.

"It all started when we were recording the album for my latest project, Control Denied," says Schuldiner. "My neck was beginning to hurt, then my arms started to feel weird. When we finished recording the album, I went for some massage therapy, then I saw an acupuncturist. But nothing was helping. Then someone suggested I go for an MRI. I did, and that's when they discovered the tumor."

For the next few months, Schuldiner flew around the country meeting with the nation's top specialists and underwent periods of intense chemotherapy. Ultimately it was decided that Schuldiner needed an operation in order to get rid of the tumor, otherwise he would surely die. As an uninsured musician, the guitarist began to panic. However, friends and family were able to assemble a team of five surgeons, who volunteered to perform the operation free of charge. Unfortunately, there was one last hurdle. New York University Medical Center's Tisch Hospital was still demanding somewhere between $70,000 and $100,000 from the Schuldiner family to host the operation.

Despite Schuldiner's grave situation, the hospital remained steadfast in their unwillingness to open up an operating room for the procedure. With the clock ticking, a desperate Beth Schuldiner, Chuck's sister, called *Guitar World*—a longtime supporter of the guitarist's efforts—to see if there was anything the magazine could do to help.

We contacted noted rock publicist Ana Adame, who then informed key members of the New York media—including MTV News' Kurt Loder, ABC Rock Wire and news crews from both ABC and CBS television—that the hospital was turning away the musician because he could not meet their financial demands. The media rallied behind Schuldiner's cause, generating so much publicity that the hospital—responding to the negative press they were getting—was ultimately forced to allow the surgery to take place.

The operation lasted only four hours—much less than the doctors had anticipated—and was a great success. Schuldiner still needs some additional radiation therapy to get rid of the tumor completely before he can go back to playing with Control Denied. But while he'll live to see many more birthdays, the death metal pioneer still owes a mountain of money. The Schuldiner family is accepting donations via the Chuck Schuldiner Medical fund in Altamonte Springs, Florida.

JUN. '00

Guitar World 3D, Pt. 2

Guitar World's August 1999 issue—the magazine's first foray into the eye-popping world of 3D—was such a runaway success that we decided to have another go at it. The June 2000 issue also came with a pair of 3D glasses and featured photos of Slipknot, Jimi Hendrix, Nine Inch Nails and Powerman 5000—as well as advertisements from Boss and Marshall—in three-dimensional glory. "After all," said editor-in-chief Brad Tolinski in his Woodshed, "any magazine that brings you features on Slipknot, Steve Morse, Albert Collins and Nine Inch Nails in the same issue needs at least one more dimension to fit it all in."

BIRDS
OF A
FEATHER

JIMMY PAGE,
THE LEGENDARY LEADER OF
THE HIGH-FLYING LED ZEPPELIN
TEAMS UP WITH
THE BLACK CROWES
FOR THE INTERNET EVENT OF THE YEAR
AND THE CONCERT TOUR OF A LIFETIME.

JULY / VOL. 21 / NO. 7

JIMMY PAGE & THE BLACK CROWES

The Led Zeppelin guitarist and the Robinson brothers explain how they selected and rehearsed songs for their historic 2000 tour and internet-only album, *Live at the Greek*.

"**W**E WANTED TO DO SOME** songs, like 'Ten Years Gone,' that Jimmy and Robert Plant haven't played that much on the last couple of tours they did together," says Black Crowes singer Chris Robinson. "Also, we chose songs where the Black Crowes could add something of their own."

As before, the Crowes did some rehearsing on their own before getting together with Page. "They sent me some soundcheck tapes—versions of the songs," Jimmy Page recalls. "And I thought, Wow, these are sounding good. I wasn't even playing on them at this point and they were really good anyway. I thought, When we get together, I'll probably have to top and tail a few things. But they'd done their homework so well that there was hardly anything where I had to say, 'Actually, it goes like this, as opposed to that.'"

"There were a few songs," Chris admits, "that we played by ourselves, before Jimmy got there, where we said, 'We're not really killin' this one. Let's drop it.' Like 'Houses of the Holy.' I just didn't think we had the funk."

Much credit is due to the Crowes and Page for taking on difficult Zeppelin material like "Nobody's Fault but Mine" and "Ten Years Gone."

"I was afraid we were gonna spend the whole rehearsal time learning 'Nobody's Fault but Mine,'" guitarist Rich Robinson says with a laugh.

"I think we all were," Page counters.

"We put on the record to get the arrangement down," says Chris. "And Jimmy's writing out a chart for himself, 'cause Zeppelin only did it that one time in the studio. So Jimmy's writing this chart out, and at one point he just looks up and scratches his head, like, *What* were we doing? I said, 'I don't know, man. This shit is *hard*!'"

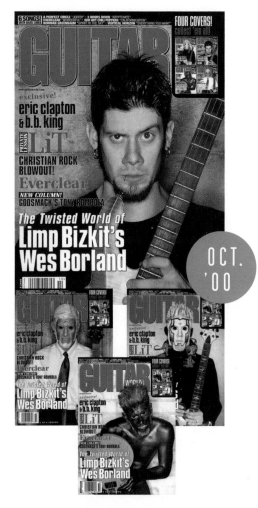

OCT. '00

Wes Is More

At the dawn of the Millennium, Limp Bizkit guitarist Wes Borland was among the biggest names on the six-string circuit—and whether he was dressed in a bunny suit, covered from head to toe in greasy black paint or slathered with white corpsepaint, Borland wasn't afraid to make a visual statement anytime he and his rap-rock cohorts took the stage. With that in mind, *Guitar World* decided Borland was the perfect subject to have four different covers in a single issue. The October 2000 issue featured the guitarist in various states of dress and paint, and could be ordered as a complete set for a cool $19.99.

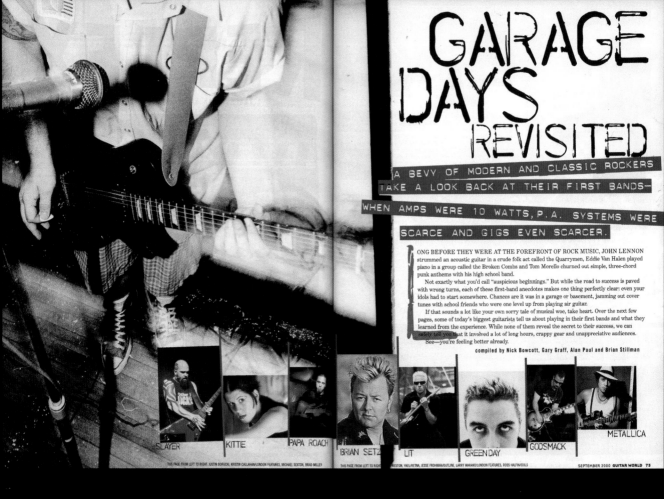

GARAGE DAYS REVISITED

A BEVY OF MODERN AND CLASSIC ROCKERS TAKE A LOOK BACK AT THEIR FIRST BANDS— WHEN AMPS WERE 10 WATTS, P.A. SYSTEMS WERE SCARCE AND GIGS EVEN SCARCER.

ONG BEFORE THEY WERE AT THE FOREFRONT OF ROCK MUSIC, JOHN LENNON strummed an acoustic guitar in a crude folk act called the Quarrymen, Eddie Van Halen played piano in a group called the Broken Combs and Tom Morello churned out simple, three-chord punk anthems with his high school band.

Not exactly what you'd call "auspicious beginnings." But while the road to success is paved with wrong turns, each of these first-band anecdotes makes one thing perfectly clear: even your idols had to start somewhere. Chances are it was in a garage or basement, jamming out cover tunes with school friends who were one level up from playing air guitar.

If that sounds a lot like your own sorry tale of musical woe, take heart. Over the next few pages, some of today's biggest guitarists tell us about playing in their first bands and what they learned from the experience. While none of them reveal the secret to their success, we can safely tell you that it involved a lot of long hours, crappy gear and unappreciative audiences.

See—you're feeling better already.

compiled by Nick Bowcott, Gary Graff, Alan Paul and Brian Stillman

SLAYER   KITTIE   PAPA ROACH   BRIAN SETZ   LIT   GREEN DAY   GODSMACK   METALLICA

THIS PAGE FROM LEFT TO RIGHT: JUSTIN BORUCKI, KRISTIN CALLAHAN/LONDON FEATURES, MICHAEL SEXTON, BRAD MILLER   THIS PAGE FROM LEFT TO RIGHT: ...RESTON, YAEL/RETNA, JESSE FROHMAN/OUTLINE, LARRY MARANO/LONDON FEATURES, ROSS HALFIN/IDOLS   SEPTEMBER 2000 GUITAR WORLD 73

SEPT. 2000

VOL. 21 / NO. 9

My First Band

An assortment of modern and classic rockers recall the formation of their first bands.

Zakk Wylde

"My first band was called Stonehenge and it was beyond fucking stupid. We used to do covers of Sabbath, Ozzy, Hendrix, Queen and Rush. I had a 50-watt Marshall combo and a Gibson SG, so I was the coolest kid in town. We played our first gig when I was in eighth grade. It was a keg party at Bobbie Bush's house. I swear to God, that was her real name! She said, 'I don't know how much money I could pay you, but there'll be beer there.' We said, 'Hell yeah.' I think we ended up getting paid 50 bucks, because they passed a hat around while we were playing."

Billie Joe Armstrong

"Mike Dirnt [*Green Day bassist*] and I lived about a mile from each other when we were growing up in Rodeo, California. We put together our first band, Truant, when we were 11. We played hard rock songs like 'Runnin' with the Devil,' 'Back in Black' and 'High 'n' Dry.' "

Kirk Hammett

"I started playing in a group pretty much as soon as I got my first guitar, which was the cheapest piece of shit, Montgomery Ward thing you could get. After I'd been playing it for all of about two weeks, I figured it was time to get in a band, which I did with some friends of mine. We called ourselves Stormbringer."

Peter Frampton

"I put together my first band for one show when I was at Bromley Technical High School. My father was head of the art department, and David Bowie was in his class. My dad was in charge of a concert held at the end of the school year, and because I played guitar, I was asked to accompany a lot of the acts. In return I was given my own performance spot. Since I didn't have a band, I put one together with a friend who played piano. We called ourselves the Little Ravens."

Ted Nugent

"I formed my first band, the Royal Highboys, on the not-so-mean streets of Detroit around 1959. It was just me and a drummer, and I can't even remember the young man's name. How sad is that? We only played at sock hops, community center dances and a malt shop until I changed the name of the band to the Lourds about a year later."

Dan Donegan

"I grew up in Alsip, Illinois, in the south of Chicago. I didn't have many friends that played instruments, so it was kind of hard for me to find a band. When I was about 16, I ran into a local guy named Steve Massari, who's now in a band called Flathead Phillips. We met in the park one day while watching a fight between a couple of guys from our school bus. After the fight he told me he played drums, and so we started hooking up after school. We were just writing our own stuff; it was actually kind of heavier than what I'm doing now in Disturbed. I think we might have called ourselves Vengeance, or something stupid like that."

Warren Haynes

"I got into my first band when I was 12 and living in Asheville, North Carolina. We were called Royal Flush. I had just started playing guitar, and none of us could play. We just found people who were all equally shitty and formed a band. We played a lot of Grand Funk, Black Sabbath, some Uriah Heep. Eventually we started playing some Allman Brothers tunes. I don't think we ever did a gig. We would just get about 10 people listening to us rehearse, or we might play a couple of little parties."

Neal Schon

"My first band was called Old Davis, and we played in the San Francisco Bay area, down the peninsula in San Bruno–San Mateo. All the guys were much older than I was—I was only 14—and we played a country/rock/soul thing: Junior Walker–style tunes and some Jerry Lee Lewis. We had another guitar player who was sort of a country picker. We sounded sort of like the Band."

Brian Setzer

"My first band was called Meringue, as in 'lemon meringue.' How's that for a stupid name? I was like 13, 14 years old. We played dances at the local recreation center, playing stuff by Chuck Berry, the Allman Brothers, Creedence Clearwater Revival and Fifties stuff too. We rehearsed on Long Island in people's living rooms and basements. The parents would take turns letting us practice, so if there were four guys in the band, we'd be in one place for a couple of nights, then we'd move it to another kid's house. It was typical suburban rock band stuff."

Kerry King

"My first band was called Quits, and it was pretty lame. But it was actually my guitar teacher's band, and it was really cool for a kid of 16 to be asked to be in his teacher's band. We played covers: stuff by Van Halen and Montrose and other songs I'd been working on in my lessons. I realized later that my teacher probably taught me the stuff so he could use me in his band." ✳

TWO THOUSAND

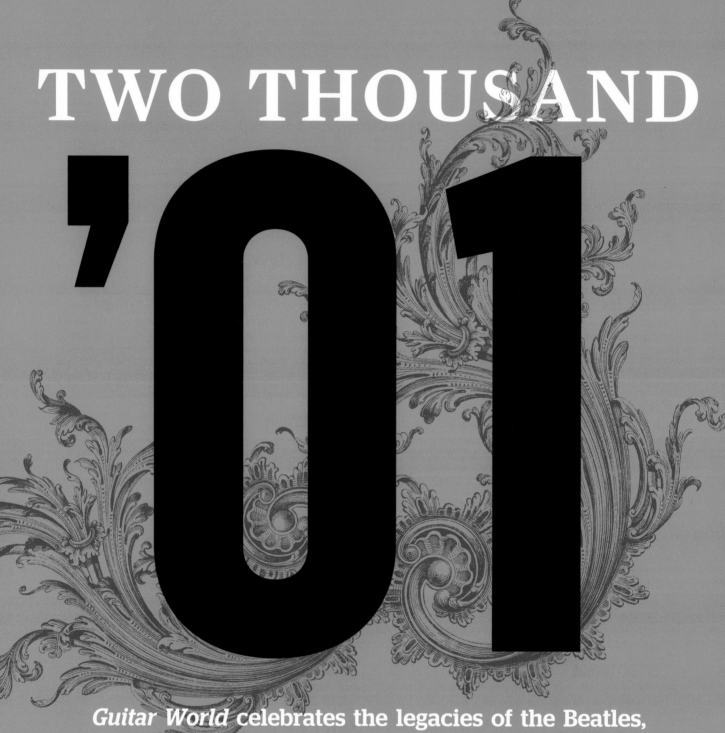

'01

Guitar World celebrates the legacies of the Beatles, Nirvana, Black Sabbath, Pink Floyd and more while recognizing Staind, Papa Roach, Tool, Slipknot and the Offspring as the new kings of rock.

Dear *Guitar World*,

Please tell me if your article about Jimi Hendrix still being alive today [*November 2000*] is true or not. The pictures sure look like Jimi, if he were a 58-year-old man. The whole article was mind-numbing. If it is true that Jimi is alive and well and living in Hawaii, I will have a very large phone bill on my hands next month after I call everyone I know and tell them. Please don't let this be a publicity stunt, because Jimi's death was tragic to a lot of us.

—Don L. Carver

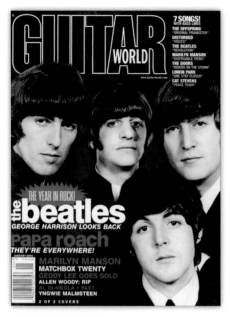

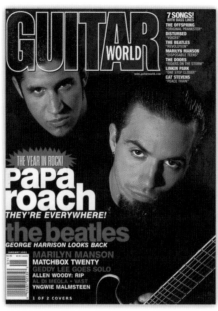

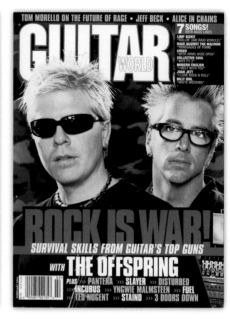

JANUARY *Guitar World* kicks off 2001 with a dual-cover extravaganza featuring Papa Roach on one cover and the Beatles on the other.

COVER STORIES BY DAN EPSTEIN & VIC GARBARINI; PHOTOS BY GREG WATERMANN & BOB WHITAKER

FEBRUARY Who's afraid of the big, bad Internet? Not the Offspring, who are determined to make the world wide web their punk rock bitch.

COVER STORY BY ALAN DI PERNA; PHOTO BY CLAY PATRICK MCBRIDE

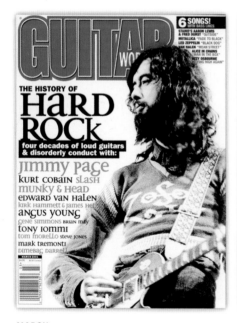

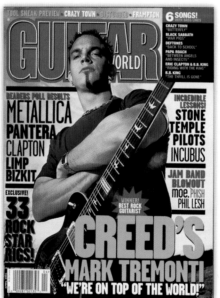

MARCH The stories behind the most important albums in hard rock history, from Black Sabbath's *Paranoid* and Queen's *A Night at the Opera* to AC/DC's *Back in Black* and Metallica's *Ride the Lightning* to Soundgarden's *Badmotorfinger* and albums from the new generation of hard rock heroes, including Korn, Creed and Slipknot.

COVER STORY BY ALAN DI PERNA, GARY GRAFF, CHARLES R. CROSS AND JOHN PECORELLI; PHOTO BY MICHAEL PUTLAND

APRIL Creed have been knocked by critics and goaded into fights by their alterna-rock brethren. Guitarist Mark Tremonti talks about his band's uphill battle. "People accuse us of being middle of the road, but that's exactly what we are. We're average kind of guys that play in a band that's written a lot of songs that people like."

COVER STORY BY ANDY LANGER; PHOTO BY MICHAEL SEXTON

MAY Aerosmith's Joe Perry, Steven Tyler and Brad Whitford explain how the self-produced *Just Push Play* came to be a homegrown affair. "Historically, when you have a producer you immediately create this insulated process, this wall," says Whitford. "So the only way to remove that wall is to produce the album yourself."

COVER STORY BY ALAN DI PERNA; PHOTO BY EXUM

WES BORLAND'S FAVORITE MUSIC SLAYER IN THE STUDIO TANTRIC

7 SONGS! WITH BASS LINES

STAIND "IT'S BEEN AWHILE"
THE EAGLES "TAKE IT EASY"
FEAR FACTORY "LINCHPIN"
COLD "NO ONE"
OLEANDER "ARE YOU THERE?"
VAN HALEN "DANCE THE NIGHT AWAY"
KORN "A.D.I.D.A.S."

GUITAR WORLD

tool returns!
ROCK'S MYSTERY MEN REINVENT THE STEEL

blues power!
THE DOUBLE TROUBLE ALL-STAR JAM

WITH ERIC JOHNSON JIMMIE VAUGHAN KENNY WAYNE & MORE!
NEW! BUDDY GUY GARY MOORE ROBERT CRAY JOHN MAYALL

metal mayhem!
STAIND • FEAR FACTORY • MEGADETH

JUNE 2001 $4.95 $5.95 Canada

JULY After more than 30 years of demonic riffing and hard living, the Black Sabbath juggernaut still reigns supreme. *Guitar World* presents the complete history of metal's indestructible monarchs.
COVER STORY BY DAN EPSTEIN
PHOTO BY ROSS HALFIN

AUGUST The masters of metallic mayhem get set to unleash *Iowa*, their hotly anticipated new album.
COVER STORY BY RICHARD BIENSTOCK; PHOTO BY CLAY PATRICK MCBRIDE

SEPTEMBER As *Break the Cycle* continues to sell in astonishing numbers, Staind guitarist Mike Mushok talks about being on top of the nu-metal world.
COVER STORY BY ALAN DI PERNA
PHOTO BY MICHAEL SEXTON

2001 TOTAL ISSUES: 12

JUNE Missing in action for the past four years, Tool make a triumphant return with *Lateralus*, their hotly anticipated new album. "What we do is magical," says guitarist Adam Jones. "And I wouldn't trade it for anything."
COVER STORY BY BRIAN STILLMAN; PHOTO BY JEFF NOVAK

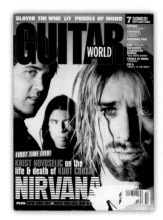

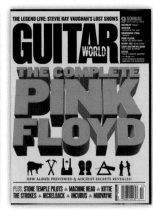

OCTOBER *Guitar World* celebrates the 10th anniversary of the release of *Nevermind* with a shocking look at the life and death of Kurt Cobain.
COVER STORY BY CHARLES R. CROSS
PHOTO BY FRANK W. OCKENFELS

NOVEMBER The godfather of metal welcomes guitarist Zakk Wylde back into the fold for *Down to Earth*, Ozzy's crushing new album.
COVER STORY BY DAN EPSTEIN; PHOTO BY ROSS HALFIN

DECEMBER To celebrate the release of the new Pink Floyd box set, *Guitar World* recounts the long and storied history of the great British rock group.
COVER STORY BY ALAN DI PERNA; COVER ICONS BY KEVIN DRESSER

After the great psychedelic lovefest of the late Sixties, there was an explosion of rock subgenres. The early Seventies saw the birth of glam, progressive rock, fusion, southern boogie, mellow country rock and, of course, heavy metal. Rock critics of the day—not to mention devotees of glam, prog, fusion, etc.—tended to regard metal as Neanderthal and moronic. But it has proven to be the most enduring of all the styles of rock that came into being at that time.

The roots of Seventies metal lay in late-Sixties power trios such as Cream, the Jimi Hendrix Experience and Blue Cheer. The actual name for the genre most likely came from a phrase—"heavy metal thunder"—in Steppenwolf's 1967 hit, "Born to be Wild," although Iron Butterfly named their '67 debut album *Heavy*, making perhaps the first explicit connection between the word and a specific rock sound.

By the time the Seventies got underway, there was an avalanche of bands that took a heavy approach to playing rock, including Led Zeppelin, Deep Purple, Black Sabbath, Uriah Heep, Humble Pie, Bad Company, Aerosmith, Mountain, Grand Funk Railroad, Blue Oyster Cult, Judas Priest and the Scorpions, to name just a few. Emphasis was on high-pitched vocals, "unison" riffing—with guitar and bass running the same pentatonic scales in different octaves—and plenty of six-string histrionics.

By mid-decade, there was a rich and varied hard rock scene. Old vets like the Who were not only hanging in there but doing some of their most exciting work. Alice Cooper and Kiss had introduced makeup to metal. Heart had pioneered chick metal. Ted Nugent, formerly of the Amboy Dukes, had emerged as a solo act. Motörhead, AC/DC and Van Halen were on the horizon.

But the mid Seventies also gave birth to a style of rock that was, in many ways, the antithesis of metal. Punk rock shared the loud guitar aggression of metal. (So did its more sociable cousin, power pop.) But the tempo was much brisker. Blues riffs and showy guitar solos were frowned upon. There was a completely different look and lyrical sensibility.

By the end of the Seventies, punk and metal had become rival claimants to rock's loud legacy. It has been that way ever since. Even today's rock charts are split between the "kid punk" of Blink-182, Green Day and the Offspring and the mutant metal of Korn, Limp Bizkit and Slipknot.

The Seventies

BY ALAN DI PERNA

WITH BLACK SABBATH, LED ZEPPELIN, QUEEN AND KISS AT THE HEIGHT OF THEIR POWERS, IT'S NO WONDER THEY REFER TO THIS AS THE "CLASSIC" ROCK ERA.

LED ZEPPELIN 1972

MARCH 2001

VOL. 22 / NO. 3

The History of Hard Rock

The stories behind the most important hard rock albums of the past four decades.

The History of Hard Rock cover feature in our March 2001 issue traced hard rock's lineage back through grunge, hair metal, punk, classic rock and heavy metal, while it examined key albums from each of the previous decades. For anyone who arrived late to the party, it was indispensable reading. Here, for your review, is a brief encapsulation.

The Seventies

THE ROOTS OF SEVENTIES metal lay in late-Sixties power trios such as Cream, the Jimi Hendrix Experience and Blue Cheer. The genre's name most likely came from the phrase "heavy metal thunder" in Steppenwolf's 1967 hit, "Born to be Wild," although Iron Butterfly named their '67 debut album *Heavy*, making perhaps the first explicit connection between the word and a specific rock sound.

Much of what everyone loves, and hates, about heavy metal can be traced directly to Black Sabbath. Guitarist Tony Iommi was the first to tune his guitar down to E♭, D and even C♯, creating the ominously dark and sludgy sound that became Sabbath's aural signature and later empowered the grunge and rap metal revolutions of the Nineties. Singer Ozzy Osbourne was the first to write lyrics on satanic themes, and while this later became a cause for concern among Bible-thumping alarmists and other right-wing conservatives, it wasn't much more than a healthy working-class contempt for the hippie utopianism that had dominated late-Sixties rock.

"If you think back to the late Sixties and early Seventies, it was all fuckin' flower power and how wonderful the world is," Ozzy says. "That just didn't seem true to us. The world was fucked."

Led Zeppelin, too, played a huge role in ushering in the hard-rock era at the dawn of the Seventies. Their first two albums went a long way toward establishing their mastery of riff-heavy, blues-inflected rock music before they took a surprising acoustic turn on their third album. These different strains came together on the standout track of their fourth album, the epic "Stairway to Heaven." "That number gave us the musical respectability we deserved all along," Jimmy Page later noted.

By mid-decade, there was a rich and varied hard rock scene. Alice Cooper and Kiss had introduced makeup to metal, and in the decade's latter years, punk arrived from England, where it was regarded as a menace to home, family, government, the crown and every other sacred institution of British society. The Sex Pistols personified that threat. Their gigs were banned in many English towns, and singer Johnny Lydon and drummer Paul Cook were attacked at knifepoint by thugs who took exception to singles like "Anarchy in the U.K." and "God Save the Queen."

The Eighties

THE EIGHTIES BROUGHT FORTH a new rock and roll generation: the offspring of the Woodstock Nation, if you will. Rock was no longer dangerous; it was the music kids grew up listening to. That phenomenon helped vault hard rock into Top 40 radio and multi-Platinum sales. In the process, it made superstars out of Eighties acts like Def Leppard, Mötley Crüe, Poison, the Scorpions, Metallica, Bon Jovi and Guns N' Roses. The advent of music videos only bolstered the size of that audience.

But the Eighties were not all about looks. There was plenty of innovation as well from guitarists such as Randy Rhoads, Steve Vai and Joe Satriani, who followed Edward Van Halen's virtuoso lead and stretched the instrument into the sonic netherworld. Likewise, Metallica, Megadeth and Slayer brought their fury into thrash metal, while Mötley Crüe and Guns N' Roses knitted together the realms of glam and punk with more classic conventions for their own instantly copied sounds.

The Nineties

IN THIS DECADE, it was impossible to distinguish between what was punk and what was hard rock. Bands were louder and played harder than ever been before. Although the long, wanky guitar solo went by the wayside, it was a decade when guitar rock, and the guitar, dominated both the charts and airwaves.

The first great hard rock album of the Nineties arrived in the summer of 1990: Pantera's *Cowboys from Hell*. "We look at our music as ball-busting, gut-wrenching heavy, whatever," guitarist Dimebag Darrell Abbott told *Guitar World* at the time of the album's release. "After listening to *Cowboys from Hell*, you'll view the world with a bigger pair of balls."

As if to demonstrate the diversity of hard rock, the autumn of 1991 saw grunge launch into the mainstream with the release of Nirvana's *Nevermind*. That same fall brought Pearl Jam's *Ten* and Soundgarden's *Badmotorfinger*, two of the genre's biggest hits. By then, the alt-rock revolution had been launched, and Warrant and every other hair metal band of the era were out of a job.

The Millennium

AS THE NINETIES GAVE WAY to a new century, musically inclined headbangers were drawing influence from 30 years of hard rock and calling it "nu-metal." Acts like Korn culled inspiration from old-school death metal and West Coast hip-hop, while Limp Bizkit lifted from Korn and East Coast hip-hop. Bands like Papa Roach and System of a Down cite hardcore punk as an influence, while Slipknot and the Deftones retain elements of grindcore and even straight-up alternative rock. For all of its historical reference points, nu-metal would prove to be a distinct chapter in rock history, albeit a short one. ✱

MOST VALUABLE PLAYER Kirk Hammett
2. Wes Borland   4. Tom Morello
3. Mark Tremonti   5. Dimebag Darrell

Kirk is captain. B.B. is still the blues king. And Limp Bizkit is either the shit or just plain shit. Our opinions? Nope—it's your two cents.

APRIL / VOL. 22 / NO. 4

2001 READERS POLL RESULTS

Guitar World readers let their voices be heard as they vote for the best—and worst—of the year in our annual Readers Poll.

MOST VALUABLE PLAYER
1. Kirk Hammett
2. Wes Borland
3. Mark Tremonti
4. Tom Morello
5. Dimebag Darrell

BEST NEW TALENT
1. Tony Rombola (Godsmack)
2. Jerry Horton (Papa Roach)
3. Dan Donegan (Disturbed)
4. Marcos Curiel (P.O.D.)
5. Mike Einziger (Incubus)

BEST METAL GUITARIST
1. Dimebag Darrell
2. Kirk Hammett
3. Wes Borland
4. Tony Rombola
5. Jim Root & Mick Thomson (Slipknot)

BEST ROCK GUITARIST
1. Mark Tremonti
2. Jimmy Page
3. Billie Joe Armstrong
4. Carlos Santana
5. Trey Anastasio

BEST METAL ALBUM
1. Pantera—*Reinventing the Steel*
2. Godsmack—*Awake*
3. Deftones—*White Pony*
4. Limp Bizkit—*Chocolate Starfish and the Hot Dog Flavored Water*
5. Disturbed—*The Sickness*

BEST ROCK ALBUM
1. Orgy—*Vapor Transmission*
2. 3 Doors Down—*The Better Life*
3. Green Day—*Warning*
4. Joe Satriani—*Engines of Creation*
5. A Perfect Circle—*Mer de Noms*

BEST BLUES ALBUM
1. Eric Clapton and B.B. King—*Riding with the King*
2. *The Jimi Hendrix Experience* box set
3. Eric Johnson—*Live and Beyond*
4. Stevie Ray Vaughan—*Blues at Sunrise*
5. Gov't Mule—*Life Before Insanity*

BEST BLUES GUITARIST
1. B.B. King
2. Kenny Wayne Shepherd
3. Eric Clapton
4. Stevie Ray Vaughan
5. Warren Haynes

WORST BAND
1. Limp Bizkit
2. 'N Sync
3. Korn
4. Blink-182
5. Backstreet Boys

BIGGEST DISAPPOINTMENT
1. Zack de la Rocha leaving Rage Against the Machine
2. Smashing Pumpkins breaking up
3. Metallica Vs. Napster
4. No new Van Halen album
5. Limp Bizkit's success

Water Boy

In our May 2001 issue, Red Hot Chili Peppers guitarist John Frusciante sits for a private lesson and chat with *Guitar World*'s Andy Aledort, and provides the following explanation when asked about the bizarre title of his new solo album, *To Record Only Water for Ten Days*:

"The correlation is that drinking water for 10 days is an act of purification for the body, but I knew I could not do that at that time. But I could record only water for 10 days: I could record a river, a sink, a bathtub—there are a million ways to record the sound of water. When you listen to a recording of water, the sound actually creates positive ions in the air, which has a very good effect on the vibe of a room. This is a proven fact. People who grow marijuana hydroponically will sometimes have a waterfall in the room, solely for the effect the sound of the water has on the potency of the weed. I know it works, because the strongest weed I ever smoked was grown this way."

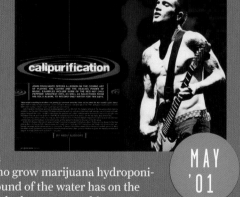

MAY '01

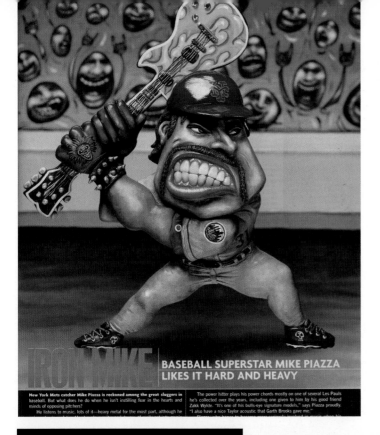

IRON MIKE — BASEBALL SUPERSTAR MIKE PIAZZA LIKES IT HARD AND HEAVY

New York Mets catcher Mike Piazza is reckoned among the great sluggers in baseball. But what does he do when he isn't instilling fear in the hearts and minds of opposing pitchers?

He listens to music, lots of it—heavy metal for the most part, although he

The power hitter plays his power chords mostly on one of several Les Pauls he's collected over the years, including one given to him by his good friend Zakk Wylde. "It's one of his bulls-eye signature models," says Piazza proudly. "I also have a nice Taylor acoustic that Garth Brooks gave me."

JUNE / VOL. 22 / NO. 6

MIKE PIAZZA

Guitar World swings for the fences with the New York Mets power hitter and confirmed metalhead.

H E PLAYS CATCHER FOR the New York Mets and is reckoned among the great sluggers in baseball. But what does Mike Piazza, Big Hitter, do when he isn't instilling fear in the hearts and minds of opposing pitchers?

He listens to music, lots of it—heavy metal for the most part, although he enjoys classic rock too. He also plays guitar and drums. "I really got into music in the Eighties," says the 32-year old Piazza, "which is why I love all that commercial rock and metal. Iron Maiden, AC/DC, UFO, Accept—those types of bands. And listening to that stuff got me into playing guitar."

Piazza, who downplays his instrumental skills—"catching fastballs isn't exactly conducive to manual dexterity"—taught himself guitar by playing along with his favorite records. "I was such a jock in school, I never had time to learn about music," he says regretfully. "Now that I've established myself in baseball, it's good to go back and learn new things."

The power hitter plays his power chords mostly on one of several Les Pauls he's collected over the years, including one given to him by his good friend, Zakk Wylde. "It's one of his signature models—with EMG pickups and the bulls-eye paint scheme," says Piazza proudly. "I also have a nice Taylor acoustic that Garth Brooks gave me."

Piazza, who hopes to become more seriously involved in music when his baseball days are over—"maybe as a producer"—says hitting a ball and playing guitar have many things in common. "Both require that you have a certain sort of groove—you can't be mechanical about either."

But the future Hall of Famer says the two great loves of his life are also similar in ways that touch his soul.

"I've been at shows, maybe watching Slayer breaking into 'Angel of Death' or something, and this adrenaline just *hits* me. It's like hitting a 450-foot home run."

"JUST CALL ME

SEPT. '01

The Gas, Man

On September 11, 1970, seven days before Jimi Hendrix's death, writer Keith Altham sat down with the rock guitarist in a hotel room at London's Cumberland Hotel to discuss his future plans. The following is a brief section from what would be Jimi's last interview, which was printed in its entirety in the September 2001 issue of *Guitar World*:

KEITH ALTHAM Are the days of Jimi Hendrix as "The Wild Man of Rock" over?

JIMI HENDRIX I was beginning to feel that too many people were coming to see "the freak" and not enough to listen to the music. I lost the rings one by one, cut my hair, got rid of the baubles and bangles and changed my clothes because I felt too loud visually. People wanted to turn me into something heavier than what I was. I have this saying, "Just call me helium—the latest gas known to man." My writing is just a mash between fantasy and reality. You have to give people something to dream on. I'm working on a kind of interspace symphony. Anything you write that is worthwhile comes from deep inside. Sometimes I get so deep I feel I am walking around on the bottom of the sea watching the sunset.

NEVERMIND
10TH ANNIVERSARY TRIBUTE

REQUIEM FOR A DREAM

IN A WORLD EXCLUSIVE INTERVIEW, **NIRVANA BASSIST KRIST NOVOSELIC** REFLECTS AT LENGTH ON HIS BRILLIANT AND TROUBLED BANDMATE, THE LATE KURT COBAIN.

BY CHARLES R. CROSS

OCT. 2001

VOL. 22 / NO. 10

Krist Novoselic

The Nirvana bassist sits with Charles R. Cross to discuss Novoselic's brilliant and

GUITAR WORLD You and Kurt met in high school through mutual friends. What led to your friendship?

KRIST NOVOSELIC I wasn't paying a lot of attention when Kurt first started coming around. I was hanging out with Buzz Osborne [*of the Melvins*]. I was only two years older, but that's a big difference when you're that age. I didn't want anything to do with the people Kurt was hanging around with. I don't want to mention any names. But then I met Kurt, and he had a Peavey amp, and he seemed like a cool guy. He lent me the amp for a while. We decided to start a band because we were watching the Melvins.

It came together because we wanted to play, and it just dawned on us: "Hey, let's start a band." We could barely get together enough equipment. I borrowed a bass amp and a bass guitar and we started playing. But Kurt was ready. He already had riffs going.

GW What were your first impressions of Kurt's music?

NOVOSELIC He was artistic, and he had this aesthetic that was pretty wild, particularly in his artwork. The songs he was writing were always intriguing to me.

GW What are your memories of the first time Kurt brought "Smells Like Teen Spirit" into rehearsal?

NOVOSELIC I wish I had a tape of what Kurt was playing. We were playing just the chorus, "When the light's out, and it's dangerous, here we are now," over and over again. I said, "Wait a minute. Why don't we just kind of slow this down a bit?" So I started playing the verse part. And Dave [*Grohl*] starting playing a drum beat.

Kurt said, "What do you think of these lyrics?" And I checked them out and said, "I think they're pretty cool." But then he seemed disappointed that I wasn't just raving about them. But the thing was that I just didn't get it the first time I read them. And then I started listening to it in the song format, and *then* I had an idea of what he was talking about. He was talking about kids, commercials, Generation X, the youth bandwagon and how he's really disappointed in it, and how he doesn't want anything to do with it.

GW Looking back, why do you think *Nevermind* had the impact it did?

NOVOSELIC A lot of it was because we were in the right place at the right time. There were bands that opened doors for us, like Jane's Addiction and Faith No More. And then there were bands like Sonic Youth and Dinosaur Jr. that made beautiful records. But for mainstream impact, Kurt's knack for melody and that whole sensibility is something that humans really responded to on a big level.

When we were touring around the country and making *Nevermind*, we had no expectations that we were going to do anything. Being on the radio, and making hit records—that wasn't an option. The only reason we did music was that we were out for kicks basically. We thought society really sucked and mainstream people were really stupid. We were part of a world, the underground world, where there were bands and people we respected. We just wanted to be part of that scene and have people respect our stuff the way we respected their stuff. And as far as the mainstream coming to us, that was really shocking. We felt that we lived in a plastic world. A lot of that feeling had to do with Desert Storm, and a lot of it had to do with going to the Tacoma Mall and seeing all the stores and merchandise. So right after *Nevermind* came Nirvana entered a time of crisis that we never busted out of. Kurt finally killed himself, because that guy was happy being in his little shitty crackerbox apartment in Olympia. He should have just stayed there. He didn't need all this attention and he never wanted it. He just wanted to express himself.

GW In some ways when I look at Kurt's life in terms of the circumstances he came from—and that he was able to create art out of pain—I see his life, however short, as a victory of sorts. Do you agree?

NOVOSELIC He had that drive in him to do that. That's the most important thing about Kurt; not his death. The details of his death are just lurid. There was the dysfunction, the drug abuse, the disconnection. But it's not uncommon what happened with Kurt—the same story happens all over this country every day. It's a combination of drug abuse and a lack of coping skills. And Kurt had access to resources and he could afford to be on drugs. It's nothing; it's pretty classic.

But Kurt was expressive. The music was this dark, angry, beautiful, rage-filled thing. It had beauty, but there was something not quite right about it. It was kind of disturbed. That's what separated him from all the other people of the era—he was an artist and they weren't. His heart was his receiver and his transmitter. ✳

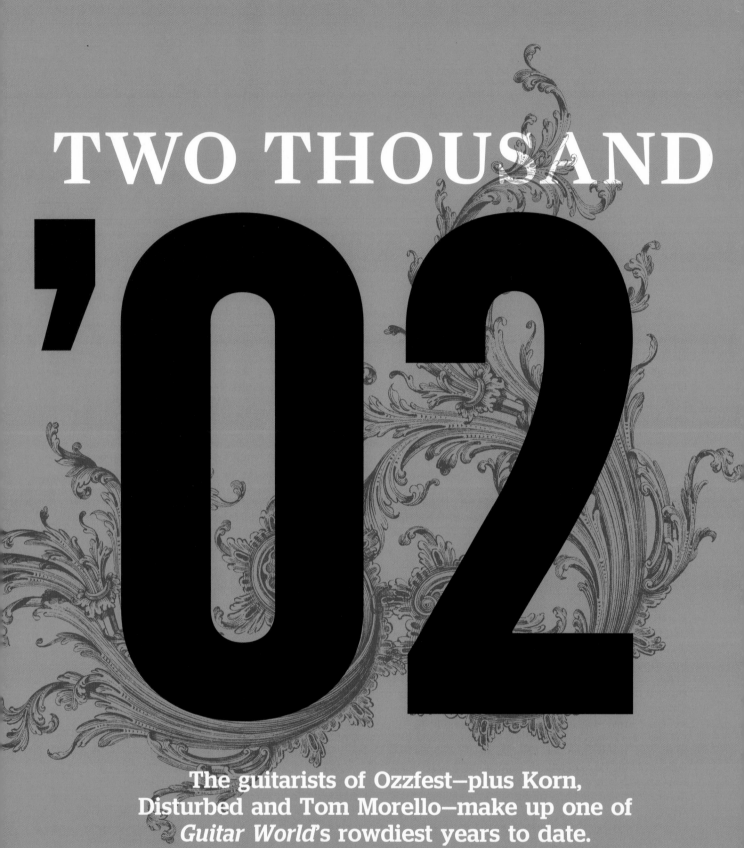

TWO THOUSAND '02

The guitarists of Ozzfest—plus Korn, Disturbed and Tom Morello—make up one of *Guitar World*'s rowdiest years to date.

Dear *Guitar World*,

I'm trying to get back in touch
with Jerry Cantrell. You see, I am
the original lead singer of Alice
in Chains, and I would like to ask
Jerry to give me another shot. My
state of mind is much better now. I
also apologize to anyone I may have
offended in the past. I miss making
music with Jerry and would like to get
back in touch with him. Hopefully,
I'll be out of jail by then.

—Wes Armstrong

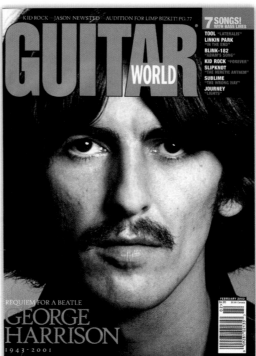

JANUARY In celebration of the 30th anniversary of *Led Zeppelin IV*, *Guitar World* travels to England for a chat with Jimmy Page, who reveals the secrets behind the making of the most classic of classic-rock albums. "The album cover was designed as a response to the music critics who maintained that the success of our first three albums was driven by hype, and not talent," says Jimmy Page.
COVER STORY BY BRAD TOLINSKI
PHOTO BY ROSS HALFIN

FEBRUARY He was the soft-spoken lead guitarist for the Beatles, but his playing shook up the world and ushered in the modern era of rock and roll. *Guitar World* pays tribute to the great George Harrison.
COVER STORY BY CHRISTOPHER SCAPELLITI
PHOTO BY JOHN KELLY

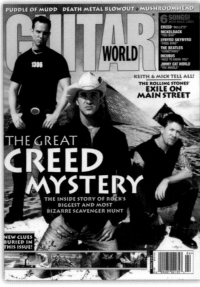

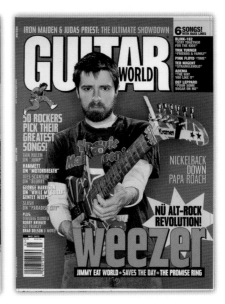

MARCH Kirk Hammett, the first inductee into the *Guitar World* Hall of Fame, reflects on the past, present and future of his band, Metallica. "I lost a lot of sleep over the guitar solos on *…And Justice for All*."

COVER STORY BY DAN EPSTEIN; PHOTO BY MICHAEL SEXTON

APRIL *Guitar World* sifts through the map coordinates, cryptic messages and bizarre online postings in an attempt to unravel Creed's massive brain-bending internet mystery. "For a lot of our diehard fans," says guitarist Mark Tremonti, "half of their social life is spent on the computer reading our bulletin board sites. It's a freak community in there."

COVER STORY BY J.D. CONSIDINE; COVER IMAGE BY DAN TREMONTI

MAY A revealing conversation with Weezer frontman Rivers Cuomo, who speaks freely about his well-documented idiosyncratic behavior, his frustration with Weezer fans and his secret heavy metal tendencies. "Fans are annoying. They're all little bitches, so I avoid them at all costs."

COVER STORY BY TOM BEAUJOUR; PHOTO BY CLAY PATRICK MCBRIDE

2002 TOTAL ISSUES: 12

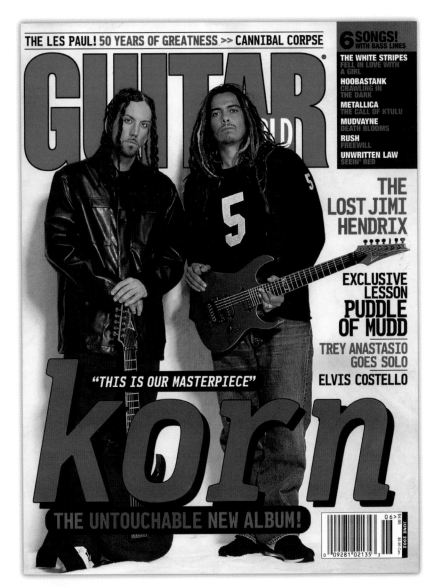

THE LES PAUL! 50 YEARS OF GREATNESS >> CANNIBAL CORPSE

GUITAR WORLD

6 SONGS! WITH BASS LINES

THE WHITE STRIPES
FELL IN LOVE WITH A GIRL

HOOBASTANK
CRAWLING IN THE DARK

METALLICA
THE CALL OF KTULU

MUDVAYNE
DEATH BLOOMS

RUSH
FREEWILL

UNWRITTEN LAW
SEEIN' RED

THE LOST JIMI HENDRIX

EXCLUSIVE LESSON
PUDDLE OF MUDD

TREY ANASTASIO GOES SOLO

ELVIS COSTELLO

"THIS IS OUR MASTERPIECE"

korn

THE UNTOUCHABLE NEW ALBUM!

JUNE 2002

JUNE Guitarists Munky and Head and singer Jonathan Davis take *Guitar World* on a behind-the-scenes look at the making of Korn's upcoming CD, *Untouchables*. "I think this is our masterpiece," says Davis. "It's the best thing we've ever done."
COVER STORY BY ALAN DI PERNA; PHOTO BY STEPHEN STICKLER

JULY On the eve of Ozzfest 2002, Ozzy Osbourne, Zakk Wylde, P.O.D.'s Marcos Curiel and System of a Down's Daron Malakian get together to discuss their heroes and favorite live performances.
COVER STORY BY VARIOUS; PHOTO BY ROSS HALFIN

AUGUST On the 35th anniversary of *Sgt. Pepper's Lonely Hearts Club Band*, *Guitar World* tells the story behind the psychedelic souvenir from the Summer of Love.
COVER STORY BY CHRISTOPHER SCAPELLITI
PHOTO BY CLAY PATRICK MCBRIDE

SEPTEMBER Author Charles R. Cross chronicles the astounding rags-to-riches story of Jimi Hendrix and the creation of *Are You Experienced*, rock's greatest debut album.
COVER STORY BY CHARLES R. CROSS; PHOTO BY GERED MANKOWITZ

OCTOBER In an exclusive and unprecedented *Guitar World* interview, Rolling Stones guitarist Keith Richards looks back at 40 years of revolutionary music making.
COVER STORY BY ALAN DI PERNA; PHOTO BY MICHAEL LAVINE

NOVEMBER According to singer David Draiman and guitarist Dan Donegan, Disturbed are putting the "old" back in nu-metal with their latest album, *Believe*.
COVER STORY BY RICHARD BIENSTOCK; PHOTO BY CLAY PATRICK MCBRIDE

DECEMBER Rising from the ashes of Rage Against the Machine, Tom Morello joins with former Soundgarden vocalist Chris Cornell to form Audioslave, a supergroup for the new millennium.
COVER STORY BY ALAN DI PERNA; PHOTO BY ROSS HALFIN

He was the soft-spoken lead guitarist for the Beatles, the world's greatest rock group. But **George Harrison**'s playing shook up the world and ushered in the modern era of rock and roll.

THE QUIET STORM

To the millions who grew up on his music, he was the Quiet Beatle. To the Hamburg teens that in the early Sixties witnessed the Beatles' evolution from crude protopunks to polished professional rock stars, he was the Beautiful One.

But as far as George Harrison was concerned, he could be best described by the name he chose for his record label in the mid Seventies: the Dark Horse—the straggler who vaults from behind to win the race.

The choice of title was ironic for Harrison, the Beatles' former lead guitarist, who died of cancer on November 29, 2001. Of the group's four members, he was the one most disinterested in the spoils of stardom, the loner less concerned with winning the race than running it on his own terms. For those who watched as he abandoned the spotlight for a more domestic lifestyle in the Eighties and Nineties, it was hard to know what to make of Harrison; normality, after all,

was not what we'd come to expect from a member of the Fab Four, the group that rose out of Liverpool, England, to conquer our senses. Beatles were supposed to be larger than life, yet iconic enough to be describable within a space the size of a postage stamp: guitarist John Lennon was the outspoken radical, bassist Paul McCartney the eager-to-please prodigy and drummer Ringo Starr the happy-go-lucky luminary. Harrison, on the other hand, defied easy definition.

As he noted in 1989, long after his career had passed its zenith, "I don't have to prove anything. I don't want to be in the business full-time, because I'm a gardener: I plant flowers and watch them grow."

He was a lead guitarist first, of

course, an ace practitioner of r&b and rockabilly riffs who became the architect of his own singularly fluid guitar tone. In this alone he was essential to the Fab Four's success, since neither Lennon nor McCartney possessed his talent on the instrument. More consequential, Harrison's skills as a lead guitarist are what elevated the Beatles from a rhythm-based pop act to a guitar rock group, and it was in this form that they changed popular music forever: Before the Beatles, no group wrote and performed its own material. After them, no self-respecting band would not.

It was easy to overlook his significance, for he made no show of it. The youngest of the Beatles, Harrison was in

BY CHRISTOPHER SCAPELLITI

FEB. 2002

VOL. 23 / NO. 2

George Harrison

Guitar World **mourns the loss of the Quiet Beatle**

On the morning of November 30, 2001, the day after sending our February 2002 issue to the printer, we awoke to the awful news that George Harrison had succumbed to brain cancer. Our sense of tragedy's proportions had only recently undergone a seismic shift—at the time, Ground Zero was still smoldering some two miles south of our New York City offices. Harrison's death, though incomparable to 9/11's losses, fit the new dimensions with numbing precision. Another icon of 20th century idealism had been toppled, and a refrain once sung as a comfort came back as a caution: *all* things must pass. Arriving at the office, we tore a section out of the issue we'd just completed, ripped up the cover and started over. Executive editor Christopher Scapelliti went home and spent the next 24 hours turning out a feature-length requiem for the Beatle they'd called the Quiet One, from which the following excerpt is taken.

To the millions who grew up on his music, he was the Quiet Beatle. To the Hamburg teens that in the early Sixties witnessed the Beatles' evolution from crude protopunks to polished professional rock stars, he was the Beautiful One.

But as far as George Harrison was concerned, he could be best described by the name he chose for his record label in the late Seventies: the Dark Horse—the straggler who vaults from behind to win the race.

The choice of title was ironic for Harrison, the Beatles' former lead guitarist, who died of cancer on November 29, 2001. Of the group's four members, he was the one most disinterested in the spoils of stardom, the loner less concerned with winning the race than running it on his own terms. For those who watched as he abandoned the spotlight for a more domestic lifestyle in the Eighties and Nineties, it was hard to know what to make of Harrison; normality, after all, was not what we'd come to expect from a member of the Fab Four, the group that rose out of Liverpool, England, to conquer our senses. Beatles were supposed to be larger than life, yet iconic enough to be describable within a space the size of a postage stamp: guitarist John Lennon was the outspoken radical, bassist Paul McCartney the eager-to-please prodigy and drummer Ringo Starr the happy-go-lucky luminary. Harrison, on the other hand, defied easy definition.

As he noted in 1989, long after his career had passed its zenith, "I don't have to prove anything. I don't want to be in the business full-time, because I'm a gardener: I plant flowers and watch them grow."

He was a lead guitarist first, of course, an ace practitioner of R&B and rockabilly riffs who became the master of his own singularly fluid guitar tone. In this alone he was essential to the Fab Four's success, since neither Lennon nor McCartney possessed his talent on the instrument. More consequential, Harrison's skills as a lead guitarist are what elevated the Beatles from a rhythm-based pop act to a guitar rock group, and it was in this form that they changed popular music permanently: Before the Beatles,

no group wrote and performed its own material. After them, no self-respecting band would not.

It was easy to overlook his significance, for he made no show of it. The youngest of the Beatles, he was in the group's early days its most humble member, a young man unguardedly insecure of his talents, who would greet reporters' questions with self-mockery and a large dose of laconic Liverpudlian charisma. When in 1964 he and his shaggy bandmates were asked at their first U.S. press conference when they planned to get haircuts, it was Harrison who impishly replied, "I had one yesterday."

Some six years later, when the Beatles broke up, how those charms seemed to fade. As ex-Fabs go, Harrison seemed the loneliest, a hermit lodged in his mock-Gothic English mansion and hiding behind a mane of hair and squire's beard. No longer required to beguile and amuse, Harrison seemed eager to be taken seriously, and he gave the world good reason to do so. As a solo artist he released what many regard as the best solo Beatles album, 1970's *All Things Must Pass*, and launched a benefit show the following year to help war-ravaged Bangladesh, thus laying the foundation for Live Aid, Farm Aid, Concert for New York City and every other music-oriented charity event since.

In more recent years, when Harrison's albums came more slowly and his life appeared more monkish, it was hard to remember he was there at all. Having renounced the fame that bloomed from his diligence and talent, Harrison followed a path of solitude few celebrated artists dare to tread. No wonder he remained an enigma to so many, not least his former bandmate John Lennon, who once remarked, "George himself is no mystery. But the mystery of George inside is immense."

To George Harrison, however, those who questioned the complexity of his choices were simply missing the point. "It's good to boogie once in a while," he remarked a few years into his post-Beatles career. "But when you boogie all your life away, it's just a waste of a life and of what we've been given." ✳

IAN MACKAYE

Guitar World's Jeff Perlah scores a rare interview with the Fugazi frontman, who comments on his band's beginnings, Fugazi's place in the current scene...and Hendrix.

GUITAR WORLD You rehearsed and toured for a year before you recorded the first Fugazi album. Why is that?

IAN MacKAYE I don't know if we would have lasted as a band if we hadn't toured, because touring really bakes you into something whole. We spent a lot of time together before the first record, so by the time the album [*1988's* Fugazi *EP*] came out, we were a solid unit; we had baked. We could take the critiques, the comparisons and all that stuff, because we understood who we were.

GW You didn't really need to tour, though. It would've been easy for Fugazi to present themselves as a punk supergroup.

MacKAYE Right. We mandated that "ex–Minor Threat, ex–Rites of Spring" couldn't be put on the flyers. We just went out and earned our bones.

GW Rites of Spring and Fugazi are considered to be the fathers of emocore. Do you feel comfortable with that notion?

MacKAYE To be honest with you, it's not a term we use. I actually know its roots. It was originally derogatory—it was used as a straight-up insult. The "emo" tag was short for "emotional hardcore," but somehow it evolved into a legitimate form of music. I mean, the word "punk" was an insult, too, but eventually people started using it because it made sense to them. "Emo" didn't make any sense to us, but later on, bands identified with it.

GW What music have you been listening to lately?

MacKAYE I listen to a lot of stuff—Queen, Black Flag, Nina Simone, Fela Kuti, Parliament and of course Jimi Hendrix. Hendrix is definitely my favorite guitarist. Period.

GW Why?

MacKAYE Because he didn't play the guitar, he played music. I never get tired of hearing him, and I've never stopped looking for more live tapes. I'm very interested in hearing all his different phases. He was constantly reinterpreting and improvising. During the last year of his life, particularly in the summer of 1970, he really set sail. Check out "Villanova Junction Blues" on the *Jimi Hendrix: Live at Woodstock* video or DVD. It's just celestial.

In Remembrance of Me

In our May 2002 issue we posed the same question to a wide range of rockers: "Which song would you most want to be remembered by?" The following is a sample of the printed responses.

Eddie Van Halen "Jump"
Stone Gossard "Nothingman"
Kirk Hammett "Motorbreath"
Slash "Paradise City"
Zakk Wylde "No More Tears"
John Paul Jones "D'yer Maker"
Jerry Cantrell "Rain When I Die"
Steve Vai "Love Secrets"

Robby Krieger "Light My Fire"
Kerry King "Payback"
Gary Rossington "Simple Man"
Ace Frehley "Shock Me"
Michael Schenker "Lipstick Traces"
Johnny Winter "Be Careful with a Fool"
Dickey Betts "In Memory of Elizabeth Reed"
Dave Mustaine "Holy Wars...The Punishment Due"

MAY '02

odd-er than hell

He used to look just like Buddy Holly, but these days alternative-music icon Rivers Cuomo prefers to be compared to Ace Frehley and Van Halen. In an exclusive interview, Weezer's rugged individualist explains his need to shed his sensitive-guy image and rock like a hurricane.

by Tom Beaujour
photography by Clay Patrick McBride

MAY / VOL. 23 / NO. 5

RIVERS CUOMO

The Weezer frontman and *Guitar World*'s Tom Beaujour enjoy a nice friendly chat—and the shockwave rips across the Weezer fan community with devastating effect.

GUITAR WORLD It's always seemed to me that the level of chops you keep in reserve is much higher than what you display in your leads. Is this true?

RIVERS CUOMO I don't dumb it down, but my point in playing lead is not to show the extremes of my technique, it's to try to say something melodically. But if you put a gun to my head and said, "Shred!" I could blow some motherfuckers away. It would probably be shocking. [*laughs*]

GW If you were growing up now, would you be into Weezer or would you be into nu-metal?

CUOMO I would think Weezer were a bunch of fags. [*laughs*] I know I'd be into System of a Down, or whoever had the oddest time signatures and the most notes per second.

GW Even though you have a million fans, they're a million fans who feel for you in an intense way usually reserved for underground bands.

CUOMO Yeah. We have a lot of fans but we're not really in the mainstream. We're not in all the magazines. We're not on MTV or radio stations. I think that they can tell we're not faking anything. We're experimenting, trying to come up with the best music we possibly can, so our motivation is pure. We're not just trying to cash in. So I think people are willing to check out every album just to see what's going on.

GW I think some of your fans expect you to be distraught 24/7.

CUOMO Emotionally extreme. Yeah, I think most of them would be shocked if they met me, because I'm pretty bland.

GW Sometimes, when you meet the fans, do you feel that they're disappointed because you're even-keeled?

CUOMO I never meet fans.

GW You never meet them?

CUOMO Never. I like talking to them over the internet, but that's it.

GW Weezer don't do in-store record signings or after-show meet-and-greets?

CUOMO Hell no! Fans are annoying. They all want something.

GW Whether it be asking you to sign something or expecting you to act a certain way...

CUOMO Yeah, or asking me to play a certain song. They're all little bitches, so I avoid them at all costs.

"Fans are annoying. They all want something." —*Rivers Cuomo*

TUNE UPS

MAR. '02

Hero of the Day

When Metallica lead guitarist Kirk Hammett learned he'd been voted the first *Guitar World* Hall of Fame inductee in our March 2002 issue Readers Poll, his response was to graciously thank the magazine and its readers. Then he asked if he would receive a trophy or plaque—forcing the *Guitar World* staff to spring into action. We called world-famous jeweler Tiffany & Co. and had the company create the fabulous, solid-crystal plaque pictured here. And before you could say "ride the lightning," Kirk had the first-ever *Guitar World* Hall of Fame award in his hot little hands.

CLOSE ENCOUNTERS

Sammy Hagar comes clean on touring with David Lee Roth, a possible Van Halen reunion and his visitors from outer space.

"**I've gotta tell you straight up,**" says Sammy Hagar, "**at my age, it is definitely physically exhausting** to tour. I used to be able to do five shows in a row with no problem. But now, after three in a row, my body's hurtin'!"

Aches and pains notwithstanding, the 55-year-old Red Rocker still rips it up onstage. Maybe it's down to the sheer amount of tequila he's ingested—or the healing rays he soaks up in his adopted home of Cabo San Lucas, Mexico—but Sammy rocks as hard today as he did back in 1973, when he sang lead on the first Montrose album. "I'll still be doin' this when I'm 70," Sammy declares. "It's music, it's what I do, and I've been doin' it my whole life. Fuck, nobody asked Muddy Waters or John Lee Hooker when they were gonna hang it up!"

Not 4 Sale (Cabo Wabo Music), the new album by Sammy Hagar and the Waboritas, certainly doesn't sound like the work of an old codger on his last legs. Easily the strongest, most focused record he's released since his not-so-amicable departure from Van Halen in 1996, *Not 4 Sale* crackles with the joy of a man doing exactly what he wants. The cosmic musings of "Karma Wheel," the proudly independent title track, the rafter-shaking anthems "Stand Up" and "Hallelujah," the gleefully boneheaded Led Zeppelin tribute of "Whole Lotta Zep"—it's all pure, unfiltered Sammy.

Best known in his pre-Halen years for such rabble-rousers as "Three Lock Box," "There's Only One Way to Rock" and the immortal "I Can't Drive 55," Sammy seems poised for a massive solo resurgence, thanks to his recent high-profile tour with David Lee Roth. But the man himself has too much on his plate right now—finishing his startling autobiography (in which his recounts his numerous close encounters with extraterrestrials), running his Cabo Wabo nightclub and tequila company, playing with his two young

story dan epstein
+
photography ellen stagg

DEC. 2002

VOL. 23 / NO. 12

Sammy Hagar

The Red Rocker and *Guitar World*'s Dan Epstein talk about touring with David Lee Roth, Hagar's exit from Van Halen and his visitors from outer space.

GUITAR WORLD What's the story behind "I Can't Drive 55"?

SAMMY HAGAR Now there's a reflective, straight, honest experience song. I got a fuckin' ticket at two in the morning on a four-lane highway doing 62 miles an hour, and I'm goin', "What the hell's wrong with these people?" I said to my wife, "I can't drive 55!" And then it was, like, "Oooh!" The light went on, I went and wrote the song. Back then people would say, "Oh, this is a commercial gimmick song," and it was like, "You motherfuckers, you don't know me!" [*laughs*]

GW Is "Not 4 Sale," the title track of your new album, a pretty accurate description of a day in the life of Sammy Hagar?

HAGAR All but the computer part. I don't go online! [*laughs*] I have my wife do it—she checks all my emails and all that stuff for me—because the second I get in front of a computer, I know I'm there for two or three hours. But it is an accurate description, and I know the song seems so light-hearted, but the message in there is so honest. You could offer me a hundred thousand dollars—half a million dollars—to do something, and the first thing I think of is, Wait a minute, do I really want to do that? Money isn't gonna make the difference. You can't believe how much money I've turned down in my life. I pursue happiness, not fame and fortune.

GW There's a line in the song about a friend of yours who's a millionaire but is still unhappy. A reference to Eddie Van Halen, perhaps?

HAGAR [*laughs*] Well, honest to God, it really is, a little bit. It's so funny, but his was the first face that popped into my head on that line. It ain't specifically about him, but he *is* one of those people that's just miserable all the time.

GW There's also a line in there about "UFOs in my backyard." Any extraterrestrial visitations we should know about?

HAGAR Absolutely. It's been a long, long time, but back in about '68, in Fontana, California, I had this unbelievable experience that would take this whole interview to even go into. But I'm a firm believer—have seen, have felt, have been contacted three or four different times. I have received information that has been valuable in my life from these people, and they have used me. I'm gonna sound like a complete nut here, but they have used me in an experimental fashion. The easiest way to put it is that they downloaded my brain information. When I was about 19 or 20 they downloaded everything that was in my head.

And I caught 'em doin' it! I woke up in the middle of the night, thinkin', What's goin' on? They were like, Oh my god, he's waking up! But this was all telepathy; there were no words being spoken. And as soon as I woke up—it was probably three o'clock in the morning—my whole room was so bright that I could hardly keep my eyes open. I was wide-awake, I could not move, eyes open, white room, they were still disconnecting—and when they did, it just went *bang!* Everything went back to normal, back to black. I was shaking, I almost passed out, I was sick to my stomach and almost had to throw up, it was so scary...

GW Did you ever ask yourself, "Why me? Why did they want to download information from *my* brain?"

HAGAR Yeah, sure. I think it was just random—I don't think I'm anything special. But I think it enlightened my brain; it opened it up. Just like some people take acid, some people take mushrooms, peyote, whatever; they get this kind of experience, and it just kind of opens their eyes up a little bit. And that's what it's done for me—I've been led to situations that have led to other situations that were very obvious.

GW Now that it's over, what are your lasting impressions from your tour with David Lee Roth?

HAGAR I think it was pretty good, but it could have been a heck of a lot better. Dave's an unreasonable guy; he's not a cool guy, he's not a fun guy. He's got this persona, this image like he's Mr. Party—but the guy's Mr. Fuckin' Uptight! [*laughs*] I mean, you can't even imagine.

The whole tour threw me back into where I had to compete with a guy that I shouldn't have been competing with. Dave doesn't belong with me; Dave belongs on those Poison/Ratt tours, which are fine, but you know what you're gettin'—you're going for this Eighties trip. And that's where Dave belongs. When you start puttin' on a platinum wig, wearing spandex bell-bottoms and singing all Van Halen shit, doing the classic leap off the drum riser—I mean, he was pretending he was *in* Van Halen. And I'm going, "Oh boy, look what I've let my manager and my agent talk me into!" [*laughs*]

GW In retrospect, was your exit from Van Halen all for the best?

HAGAR Oh, yeah. There's no question about it. Because if we'd gone on, we'd have been miserable; we wouldn't have loved each other at all by now. We'd have probably killed each other. ✳

TWO THOUSAND '03

It's the height of nu-metal mania as *Guitar World* celebrates such chart-topping heavies as Mudvayne, Linkin Park, Staind, Deftones and Korn.

Dear *Guitar World*,

We are three recovering alcoholics/drug addicts from Texas. The time we used to spend injecting various chemicals into our bodies we now spend honing our guitar skills and reading *Guitar World*. Your story on the 100 Essential Guitar Albums [*April 2003*] nearly made us relapse. Where was Eric Johnson's *Ah Via Musicom* and My Bloody Valentine's *Loveless*? The Garage category was a cool idea, but where were Pavement's *Slanted and Enchanted* or any albums from the early Guided by Voices catalog? As for the Jam Band category, how could there be no moe. or String Cheese Incident? The fact that we approved of your blues choices and the inclusion of Sleater-Kinney's brilliant *Dig Me Out* is the only reason the three of us are not huddled in a gutter fighting over a crack pipe right now.

—Mike D., John D. and Lee H.

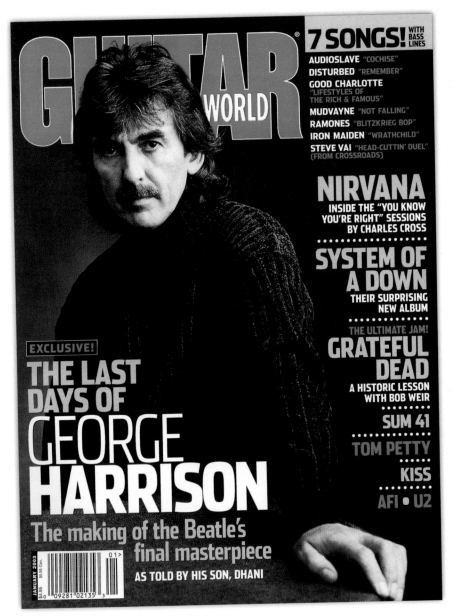

JANUARY George Harrison's son, Dhani, talks candidly about his father and how he and Jeff Lynne accepted the task of completing Harrison's final masterpiece, *Brainwashsed*. "We were very careful to tread lightly," says Dhani. "I only ever dared do anything with this album that I knew my dad would like."

COVER STORY BY CHRISTOPHER SCAPELLITI; PHOTO BY MARK SELIGER

FEBRUARY The return of nu-metal's freakiest quartet, complete with a new out-of-this-world look and a killer CD, *The End of All Things to Come*.

COVER STORY BY DAN EPSTEIN; PHOTO BY DALE MAY

MARCH Zakk Wylde and Dimebag Darrell go ballistic as they address the state of metal and their dreams of yanking Eddie Van Halen out of retirement.

COVER STORY BY DAN EPSTEIN; PHOTO BY MATTHEW SALACUSE

APRIL *Guitar World* celebrates 100 Essential Guitar Albums—in the fields of classic rock, classic metal, modern metal, virtuoso, garage, alternative, screamo, punk, blues and jam—complete with inspirational licks, fashion tips and tools of the trade.

COVER STORY AND PHOTOS BY VARIOUS

MAY Guitarist Brad Delson and rapper/Pro Tools expert Mike Shinoda explain how taking care of business and working overtime helped Linkin Park craft *Meteora*, their ambitious new album.

COVER STORY BY ALAN DI PERNA; PHOTO BY DALE MAY

JUNE Staind's Mike Mushok and Aaron Lewis aren't rock stars, just two regular guys who want nothing more than to quit smoking, go fishing and write some really great songs.

COVER STORY BY BRIAN STILLMAN; PHOTO BY NICHOLAS BURNHAM

JULY In his most comprehensive interview ever, guitarist Jimmy Page talks about the magic, the myth and the music of Led Zeppelin, the best live band in rock history.

COVER STORY BY BRAD TOLINSKI; PHOTO BY NEAL PRESTON

2003 TOTAL ISSUES: 12

AUGUST After infighting, alcoholism and creative stagnation threatened to bring the big Metallica machine to a screeching halt, James Hetfield and Co. decided it was time to make some major repairs. "I had to learn to explain to the band what I need and not do it forcefully and not just roll over like I used to do," says Hetfield.

COVER STORY BY MICHAEL ANSALDO; PHOTO BY JILL GREENBERG

SEPTEMBER When it comes to metal, the Deftones will tell you it's not about looks. It's not about race. It's about being true...and maybe just a little high. "It's so funny that we're considered nu-metal," says guitarist Stephen Carpenter. "I was just trying to be fucking metal. I don't know where the nu-metal part came from."

COVER STORY BY JIM DEROGATIS; PHOTO BY CLAY PATRICK MCBRIDE

OCTOBER To celebrate the 10th anniversary of *In Utero*, *Guitar World* goes deep inside the making of Nirvana's often misinterpreted and arguably finest recording.
COVER STORIES BY JIM DEROGATIS AND CHARLES R. CROSS; PHOTO BY GIE KNAEPS

NOVEMBER The explosive story of how ex-Guns N' Roses members Slash, Duff McKagan and Matt Sorum replaced their broken Axl with STP's Scott Weiland and created Velvet Revolver.
COVER STORY BY DAN EPSTEIN PHOTO BY STEPHEN STICKLER

DECEMBER Head, Munky and singer Jonathan Davis reflect on the making of Korn's ferocious new album, *Take a Look in the Mirror*.
COVER STORY BY RICHARD BIENSTOCK PHOTO BY ROSS HALFIN

Conquering heroes
Dimebag Darrell (left)
and Zakk Wylde

STRAIGHT SHOOTERS

MVP ZAKK WYLDE AND
BEST METAL GUITARIST
DIMEBAG DARRELL GO
BALLISTIC AS THEY
ADDRESS THE STATE OF
METAL, THE DISSOLUTION
OF PANTERA AND THEIR
DREAMS OF YANKING
HALL OF FAMER EDWARD
VAN HALEN OUT OF
RETIREMENT. BY DAN EPSTEIN
PHOTOGRAPHS BY MATTHEW SALACUSE

"Okay, Zakk, it's time!"
   As the morning sun begins to break over
the Texas hills, Dimebag Darrell thrusts the
keys to a waiting sport utility vehicle into
Zakk Wylde's enormous hand. All through
the night, over countless shots of Blacktooth
Grin—the particularly potent and tasty mixture of Crown Royal and Coca-Cola that
flows like water at Dime's Arlington-area
compound—the Pantera guitarist has been
psyching up Ozzy Osbourne's right-hand
man for this very moment. Zakk once nearly
destroyed a large metallic Christmas tree
placed on Dime's decked-out lawn, and now
that the holidays are here again, Dime just
won't be satisfied until Zakk finishes the job.
   While Zakk loudly and repeatedly plows
the hulking vehicle into the tree, a bespecta-
cled gent in tie and khakis looks on with
resigned amusement. A driver for the local
limo service, he's been summoned to take
Zakk to the airport in time for the first flight
of the day back to Los Angeles. Unfortunately,
Zakk is in no hurry to leave. He's too busy
shredding the bottom of the driver's SUV on
the tree's twisted metallic corpse.

MARCH 2003

VOL. 24 / NO. 3

Zakk Wylde
& Dimebag Darrell

Guitar World's Dan Epstein moseys on down to Dimebag Darrell's Arlington, Texas-area compound for a round of booze, some healthy gunplay and a little talk about the state of guitar with the Pantera axman and his trusted compatriot, Zakk Wylde.

GUITAR WORLD When Van Halen first came out with "Eruption," every town had some kid who knew how to play the whole thing in its entirety. Nowadays, none of the newer acts seem to be coming up with the sort of solos that inspire kids in the same way.

ZAKK WYLDE Put it this way: I love Ozzfest, because Ozzy and Sharon started the whole thing to promote metal. But two summers ago, I was actually laughing. I was telling Freddy McTaggart, who does my guitars, "I think Dime and I are the only motherfuckers on this whole tour that actually can get up from low E to high E and back, safely!" [*laughs*] We were sitting out there, watching fucking Pantera just blow the fucking stage up, and Dime just shredding all sick and fucking insane. I was watching the other bands, and no one else was playing solos! And it's just like, why wouldn't you want to get better? I don't understand that.

DIMEBAG DARRELL I'm into the whole song-as-a-piece-of-music thing: if it literally doesn't call for it, if it already has enough stuff going on, then it's okay not to play a solo. I've tried to force a solo before, but sometimes it's like, "That fuckin' thing don't really fuckin' *fit*, man!" You know, you end up on a groove part that's powerful, I understand that. But let's have some fuckin' *action* out there! There's more to it than two or three strings on the low-end side, you know? I mean, I could see how some people might hear some of the shit Zakk does and say, "I'm not ever gonna catch up, so why even try?" And that's the wrong way to look at it, if you ask me, man. You ain't gonna catch him, but why not do your own thing?

WYLDE When you listen to Randy Rhoads do a solo, or Eddie, or Jimi Hendrix or Jimmy Page, it brings the song to another spot. It's not like he's just going, "I'm the guitar player—I've gotta put a solo here."

GW This past year, a number of popular guitar bands like the Hives, the White Stripes and the Vines seemed to take pride in playing few, if any, solos at all.

WYLDE The only thing I think is really cool about that stuff is that it's guitar based. They're not doing solos, but thank fuck it's not, like, tons of Pro Tools. The band's actually performing live, and the shit's actually kind of a little out of tune, but that's how it is—that's how a fuckin' rock and roll band *sounds*, you know? It shouldn't be perfect. At least the Hives have two guys plugging their guitars right into the fuckin' amp, and the bass player's got a P-Bass or whatever, and they're just grinding it out. It's just meat and potatoes shit, like the Kinks on steroids. But at least they're a band, and they're writin' their own shit, as opposed to songwriters writing their music for 'em. The whole joy of being a real musician is writing your own music, you know what I mean? Backstreet Boys, 'N Sync, all those bands—in Black Label, we call 'em skin puppets, man, because that's what they are. They ain't fucking real musicians.

DARRELL But that's for somebody else, man. It ain't something for real music lovers, at all. It's just a form of entertainment for some kids, you know what I mean?

WYLDE I agree. But you look at Jimi Hendrix, Jeff Beck, Jimmy Page... I mean, Jimmy Page wasn't exactly fucking Al Di Meola, but at the same time, you can't take his songwriting away from him. Like "The Rain Song"—you can't take the fucking "Rain Song" away from Jimmy Page! He *wrote* that! Or Randy Rhoads playing "Over the Mountain," Eddie Van Halen playing "Eruption" or "Hear About It Later"—not only did he perform it, he wrote it and played it! That's a real fucking musician. Bach, Mozart and all those other motherfuckers, they wrote their own shit, man. All the greats always write their own fucking shit, I don't care what anybody fucking says. ✳

A PREPARED STATEMENT TO GUITAR WORLD READERS FROM DIMEBAG DARRELL

A Statement from Dimebag

At the time of our March 2003 issue, Pantera seemed to be in a state of disarray, and fans were clamoring for a status report on their favorite band. Dimebag was happy to oblige by writing this statement:

"What's up with Pantera? I'd like to know myself. I thought Pantera would be the Rolling Stones of heavy metal, but Phil [*Anselmo, vocalist*] and Rex [*Brown, bassist*] seem content with doin' their own stuff. It's really weird, but this is the clear-headed, honest truth: they've up and left us hangin' and won't let us know their intentions or future plans. For the last 20 years, my brother Vinnie and I have put our heart and soul into Pantera and we never thought this situation would ever happen to us... By now I thought for sure we would've done another record, but they don't seem to care how it affects Vinnie and I, or the road crew or, most of all, all the Pantera fans that have been so fuckin' awesomely great to us for so long. We've made several attempts to talk to those guys and they keep putting us off. This is *not* a situation we've created, it's a situation we've been forced into.

"Bottom line, for Vinnie and me it's all about the music, kickin' ass, and havin' a good time. So we've got together with some of our close buds and formed a new band called New Found Power. The record is almost done and will be out soon. We've put 110 percent into it, just like we always do, so I guarantee, you won't be let down."

JACK WHITE

The White Stripes frontman chooses the Top 10 bands and artists who have influenced his band's sound.

The Sonics
"Probably the epitome of Sixties punk. 'Psycho,' 'Cinderella,' 'The Witch'—animalistic screams signifying the base thoughts of mid-Sixties bored teens."

Robert Johnson
"Of all the blues artists that we love, our favorites would probably be Son House, Blind Willie McTell and Skip James—but it's Robert Johnson who inspired and influenced us most. He was a full-ranged, truly beautiful singer; good and evil are equally present in his songs."

Captain Beefheart and His Magic Band
"Captain Beefheart brought the feeling of Howlin' Wolf into white rock and roll. The album *Trout Mask Replica* is his masterpiece and is probably one of the most unique records in music history."

Loretta Lynn
"The greatest female singer-song-writer of the 20th century. She broke down numerous barriers for women, wrote her own songs at a time when nobody—let alone women—did, and tackled subject matter that everyone else was afraid to touch."

The Monks
"The Monks were American soldiers stationed in Germany who became 'anti-Beatles.' They had a banjo with a microphone in it to make it electric, a fuzz bass (this was in '66) and an amazing singer, not to mention a drummer and organist who were out of this galaxy."

The Rats
"They only released one 45, and its B-side, 'Rat's Revenge Part 2 (Black Cat),' is my favorite garage rock record. No other record is a better example of being in a group of teenage boys working on something together."

Bob Dylan
"Important: do not trust people who call themselves musicians or record collectors who say that they don't like Bob Dylan or the Beatles. They do not love music if those words come out of their mouths. They love record sleeves and getting attention for their hobby, but they don't love music."

The Gories
"The best garage band in America since the Sixties—very primitive, very good and not very good."

The Stooges
"Their second album, *Fun House*, is the greatest rock and roll record ever made."

The Gun Club
"The songwriting of Kid Congo Powers and Jeffrey Lee Pierce has the freshest white take on the blues of its time. 'Sex Beat,' 'She's Like Heroin to Me' and 'For the Love of Ivy'...why are these songs not taught in schools?"

A Fire at the Station: The Great White Tragedy

The fire that tore through the Station nightclub in West Warwick, Rhode Island, on February 20, 2003, minutes after Great White took the stage, may very well go down as the most horrific incident in rock history. 100 people lost their lives that night, including 31-year-old Great White guitarist Ty Longley. Mark Kendall, the band's longtime guitarist, spoke with *Guitar World*'s Joe Lalaina the morning after the incident. The complete article appeared in the May issue.

"Less than a minute after we launched into 'Desert Moon,' the first song of our set, I felt this strange heat on my back," says Kendall. "When I turned around, the back wall of the venue was on fire. I didn't see any fire extinguishers around, so I stopped playing. I walked down the steps on the left side of the stage and there was a door that led me outside. When I got outside I looked at the building and these huge flames were shooting off the side of it, and there was billowing black smoke everywhere. People in the parking lot were screaming hysterically, with fear in their eyes—some of them had flames burning off their clothes. But the reality of what transpired didn't hit me until I saw my soundman outside the building a few seconds later—he was bleeding from his eyes and his mouth and his skin was torched. I knew right then and there that this was real."

MAY '03

"I'M LUCKY I SURVIVED"
In his only interview following the Rhode Island nightclub inferno, Great White guitarist Mark Kendall mourns the dead—and counts his blessings.

THE ROADKILL Q&A

Select guitarists from the summer of 2003's Lollapalooza and Warped tours weigh in with answers to various questions.

Lollapalooza

Dave Navarro
(Jane's Addiction)

What was your worst gig?
"I remember a gig in Texas in the late Eighties, though I don't remember exactly where. I had experimented with chemicals that evening, and it led to a really horrific show for me. I hid behind my amplifier for a lot of it. To be honest, I smoked a lot of crack before that show. Horrible. Not recommended."

What was the best live show you've ever seen?
"Van Halen on the *Fair Warning* tour."

Tom Morello (Audioslave)

Who are you looking forward to seeing this summer?
"Probably Jane's Addiction. They've always been one of my favorite bands and they're a really phenomenal live band, too, so I can't wait to see them rock it every day on Lollapalooza."

Josh Homme (Queens of the Stone Age)

Do you remember your first gig?
"Um...the Champagne Room at the Lambada Whore House and Tequilaria in Canstoppa, Mexico. It was tits."

What is your current favorite song to play live?
"Track five on album number five...whatever it's called."

Who are you looking forward to seeing this summer?
"Everybody, except me...and you."

Warped

Zacky Vengeance (Avenged Sevenfold)

What is your current favorite song to play live?
"A new song called 'Unholy Confessions.' "

What was the best live show you've ever seen?
"Seeing the Murder City Devils playing on their final tour was amazing."

Who are you looking forward to seeing this summer?
"AFI, Thrice, the Used and Killswitch Engage."

54 LOLLAPALOOZA
Jane's Addiction, Audioslave, Incubus, the Donnas and more!

60 OZZFEST
Korn, Zakk Wylde, Chevelle, Disturbed and many more!

68 WARPED
Poison the Well, Sum 41, the Ataris, Thrice, Taking Back Sunday and many, many more!

Jeff Stinco (Simple Plan)

Do you remember your first gig?
"My first gig was at one of my high school's talent shows. I was competing against a band that featured our drummer, Chuck Comeau, and our singer, Pierre Bouvier. Everyone lost to some guitar shredder. I played a Simon and Garfunkel song and forgot some of the chord changes in the bridge. It was quite embarrassing."

What was the best live show you've ever seen?
"When we toured with Green Day and Blink-182, we got to see both bands play every night, and it was amazing. Green Day would completely blow me away. Every song was great, and Billie Joe Armstrong would have the coolest and meanest guitar tone ever and would play like it was the last show of his life."

Who are you looking forward to seeing this summer?
"I can't wait to see AFI, since I am really hooked on their new album. I'm also looking forward to seeing Rancid, the Ataris, Glassjaw and the Used."

Guitar World Launches *Bass Guitar* Magazine

The bass-playing community has never been afraid to tell us that they wish *Guitar World* featured more interviews with bassists and more gear reviews of the four- and five-string variety. It may have taken 23 years, but we finally decided to do something about the constant clamoring for bass content by launching *Bass Guitar* magazine, with James Volpe Rotondi at the editorial helm, in the summer of 2003. The premiere issue featured new Metallica bassist Robert Trujillo on its cover, instructional columns by John Paul Jones, Shavo Odadjian from System of a Down and Korn's Fieldy, plus transcriptions to Metallica "Orion," Green Day's "Longview" and the Red Hot Chili Peppers' "Pea." *Bass Guitar* enjoyed a small but loyal audience in its four years of publication and eventually came to a close with its Pete Wentz–fronted June 2007 issue.

Street Survivors

Death. Disaster. Heart attacks. Southern rock icons **LYNYRD SKYNYRD** have weathered 30 years of bad luck while making incredible music, proving the age-old adage that you can't keep a good band down.

by Alan Paul

PHOTOGRAPH BY *Matthew Salacuse*

* * *

THE ROSTER OF MUSICAL artists inducted into the Rock and Roll Hall of Fame is riddled with glaring omissions. Yet few are more curious than the exclusion of Lynyrd Skynyrd. This is, after all, the band that single-handedly established the southern rock genre's artistic and aesthetic foundations, and composed such Seventies classic rock cornerstones as "Free Bird," "Gimme Three Steps" and "Sweet Home Alabama," songs that endure today as FM radio anthems. Is it any wonder the legendary Florida rockers are upset and stung by what they perceive as an industry snub?

"Lynyrd Skynyrd are terribly underrated," says Rickey Medlocke, who with Gary Rossington

SEPT. 2003

VOL. 24 / NO. 9

Lynyrd Skynyrd

Gary Rossington, Rickey Medlocke and Hughie Thomasson express their views on what it means to carry on the Skynyrd name after 30 years of incredible music and a little bad luck.

GUITAR WORLD What do you think is Lynyrd Skynyrd's legacy?

GARY ROSSINGTON That's not really for me to say, but I'm really grateful and humbled by our success. We're still out there bringing music to the people, and they still come out and support us. I see people singing along and crying and bringing their kids. We have generations together enjoying the music, and it's all overwhelming and real heavy. It just shows that Ronnie [*Van Zant, singer*] and the [*former band members*] really created something memorable. Ronnie was a great lyricist and storyteller. He wrote about things that were going on, things we saw every day, and people related to it. And they still do.

RICKEY MEDLOCKE Nobody really knew it at the time, but Ronnie was a freaking genius. He had the ability, which a few magic songwriters do, to paint a picture that you can vividly see in your head as the song is being sung. These songs he wrote will be Lynyrd Skynyrd's legacy until time stops.

GW In light of your popularity, do you think all those years of flying the Confederate flag hurt the band's reputation?

HUGHIE THOMASSON That's a tough question. Last year we actually took the Stars and Bars [*Confederate*] flag and combined it with the American flag, and made it into one. We are the *United* States of America, and it just so happens that Lynyrd Skynyrd is from the South. If anyone takes offense to it, I'm terribly sorry, but this is a free country.

ROSSINGTON I think it's all one country now. In fact, it's really one world now connected by satellites and the world wide web, and we all have to live in it together. In the Sixties and Seventies bands were identified by where they came from—you were a California band or a southern band—but today you hear a band like Train and you don't know where they're from. And no one cares. Overall, I don't think being from the South means as much today as it did when we were

kids. Where we were brought up—Ronnie especially—the southern heritage was a big deal. And race was a huge issue, whether you were black or white. It was just in your face.

Because of all that, people used to cut down the South, and that got our backs up. It was like having long hair back then—a strike against you in many places—and we just always stood up to it. But we never felt like we were standing for specific political positions or made any claim to having a lot of knowledge about this stuff, and we still don't. With a song like "Red, White and Blue," we're just writing about things we see around us, same as we ever have.

GW Do you think Lynyrd Skynyrd would be in the Rock and Roll Hall of Fame today if you'd never reformed after the plane crash?

MEDLOCKE Of course. Isn't it funny how the demise of people makes things bigger? I hate that. It blows my mind. Why should Gary or Billy [*Powell, keyboards*] be kept out of the Rock and Roll Hall of Fame because they love this music and they have kept the group going—not with strangers but with the original singer's brother and myself, who was in the band for three years before we ever recorded, and Hughie, who is an old, old friend who played with the original group many times? They didn't take the easy road and collect royalty checks. We're out there our whole lives busting our asses and playing music for the fans, and we love it. We've tried to keep the whole legacy going with pride, and some people scoff and say, "That's not the real Skynyrd." Tell that to the 20,000 people coming out to cheer and have a great time at our shows. We're playing for them, anyhow.

ROSSINGTON We talk about the original members all the time, and I really do feel like their spirits are with us. I feel like there are a lot more people onstage than you can actually see. ✱

TWO THOUSAND
'04

Guitar World cranks it up to 13 issues a year and adds a CD-ROM laden with multimedia content to every issue.

Dear *Guitar World*,

I agree with the rest of the *Guitar World* readers
that there is a definite lack of "new" guitar
heroes in the musical landscape of the 21st
century. But is this because of lack of exposure?
I have a very strong opinion that, because of the
internet, there is absolutely no excuse for not
finding new and better music—because it *does* exist.
After listening to the fresh, jazz-influenced
hard rock and psychedelia of bands like the Mars
Volta and Dredge, I can't help but smile, because
the guitar playing is so fresh and inventive
that it continually brings me back for more. And
what about the fact that Tom Morello's greatest
influence to innovation was the DJ? Guitarists need
to start exploring outside themselves and begin
to understand that the reason people like Morello
are so great is because they have the ability to
blend ideas and concepts from outside of the guitar
universe and fuse them into a new vision.

—Mr. E.

JULY Zakk Wylde shows you how to be all you can be with his 100 percent brewtal guitar boot camp. "You either strive for greatness or you go home, 'cause you've gotta give all or nothing."
COVER STORY BY NICK BOWCOTT; PHOTO BY JIMMY HUBBARD

JANUARY Blink-182 turn in their whoopee cushions and assume their role as pop-punk elder statesmen on their surprisingly "all growed-up" new album.
COVER STORY BY ALAN DI PERNA
PHOTO BY STACY KRANITZ

FEBRUARY Dave Grohl gets metal thrashing mad with his brutal new project, Probot.
COVER STORY BY DAN EPSTEIN
PHOTO BY RANKIN

MARCH Dimebag Darrell tells the whole truth and nothin' but the truth about the untimely demise of Pantera and the rise of Damageplan.
COVER STORY BY NICK BOWCOTT
PHOTO BY CLAY PATRICK MCBRIDE

APRIL The guitar titans of Led Zeppelin and Aerosmith discuss the sacred power of the blues.
COVER STORY BY BRAD TOLINSKI
PHOTO BY ROSS HALFIN

MAY Jack White explains why he's a force to be reckoned with—both on and off the charts.
COVER STORY BY CHRISTOPHER SCAPELLITI
PHOTO BY CLAY PATRICK MCBRIDE

JUNE *Guitar World* goes behind the scenes of Metallica's forthcoming, critically acclaimed new movie, *Some Kind of Monster*.
COVER STORY BY RICHARD BIENSTOCK
PHOTO BY JAMES MINCHIN

AUGUST In his first major interview in five years, Edward Van Halen talks about his battle with cancer and the triumphant return of his band. "There is nothing that can keep me down. Whatever stands before me I will deal with."
COVER STORY BY BRAD TOLINSKI
PHOTO BY ROSS HALFIN

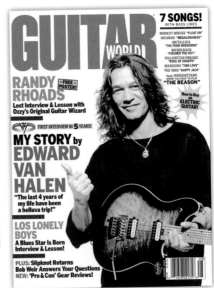

2004 TOTAL ISSUES: 13

SEPTEMBER *Guitar World* celebrates Ozzfest 2004 with cover stories on metal legends Black Sabbath and Judas Priest. "Playing the big summer show is a great career move," says Priest guitarist K.K. Downing, "and we plan to shine every night."

COVER STORIES BY DAN EPSTEIN (SABBATH) AND JOE BOSSO (PRIEST); PHOTOS BY ROSS HALFIN

OCTOBER Phish guitarist Trey Anastasio explains why he had to put an end to rock's biggest jam band. "The guys were and have been so understanding. There's still this very deep love. It's weird."
COVER STORY BY ANTHONY DECURTIS
PHOTO BY NICHOLAS BURNHAM

NOVEMBER Guitarists Nic Cester and Cameron Muncey tell why Jet is Australia's hottest export since AC/DC. "To me, it's more about attitude than actual musical knowledge," says Cester. "I think musical knowledge can be more of a hindrance to rock and roll."
COVER STORY BY JOE BOSSO
PHOTO BY CLAY PATRICK McBRIDE

DECEMBER After two decades of kissing ass, *Guitar World* tips over a few sacred cows in a definitive guide to guitar parts that blow.
COVER STORY BY RICHARD BIENSTOCK, JOE BOSSO, DAN EPSTEIN, CHRIS GILL, ALAN PAUL AND JON WIEDERHORN

HOLIDAY With *American Idiot*, Green Day's Billie Joe Armstrong declares war on the government, religion and whatever else he can find. "I finally felt like the media had crossed that line between journalism and reality TV."
COVER STORY BY ALAN DI PERNA
PHOTO BY ROSS HALFIN

Foo Fighter **DAVE GROHL** says goodbye to rock and roll and hello to heavy metal with his smashing new project, **PROBOT**.

By Dan Epstein

Man of Steel

"Hey! I need a roll of tape for my boobs!"

It's a quiet Sunday afternoon in Hollywood, but inside this Sunset Boulevard soundstage, where a music video shoot is underway, it looks like a red-blooded rocker's version of the ultimate Saturday night. Strategically positioned around the room are several dözen attractive young women from the SuicideGirls.com web site, each attired to varying degrees in leather and fishnets, and sporting tattoos and piercings. One girl is strapped to a torture table, another is cuffed to a gallows

and one hangs from a circular cage in the center of the room. The one who just called out for the roll of tape laughs while a production assistant "reluctantly" applies enough adhesive to keep her ample breasts from spilling out under her too-short T-shirt.

Standing on a circular stage at the center of this Dionysian scene are three musicians. On bass, there's Lemmy Kilmister from Motörhead, the white-booted, cowboy-hatted embodiment of badass rock and roll. On guitar, his face temporarily hidden behind a long curtain of hair, is Wino, the legendary leader of the

FEB. 2004

VOL. 25 / NO. 2

Dave Grohl

The Foo Fighters' main man has a knack for writing bigtime commercial rock hits, but he's never forgotten his true-metal roots. In this conversation with Dan Epstein, Grohl details the inspiration behind his scorching new Probot project.

GUITAR WORLD There have been Probot rumors floating around for several years now. When and how did the whole project actually get underway?

DAVE GROHL Well, the whole thing started in February of 2000. The Foo Fighters had made our third album, *There's Nothing Left to Lose*, in 1999, which was a pretty mellow record for us. It was about exploring low-level dynamics and melody, and simple arrangements and acoustic guitars—it was more about those things than about hitting the Turbo Rat and turning it up to 10.

So we went out and played a lot of those songs live, and they were pretty mellow. I would find myself listening to Sepultura's *Chaos A.D.* before going onstage, and then singing a song like "Learn to Fly." Which I thought was kind of funny—like, What am I doing with my life, man? [*laughs*] When I was young, my favorite bands were fucking Bad Brains, Void, Minor Threat, MDC, D.R.I., Corrosion of Conformity, Slayer, Trouble, Voivod, Venom, the Obsessed and Mercyful Fate, and here I am playing music that sounds like the fucking Eagles or something! I love Foo Fighters' music, and I love that album, but at the same time I never lost that love of heavy music.

So I went into my home studio after being on tour, and I'm like, Man, I've gotta fucking record some *riffs*. I've gotta get in there and do something heavy. As much as I love this acoustic guitar shit, I've just gotta feel it in my bones again.

GW How did all the metal singers get involved?

GROHL Well, we started coming up with the idea of the wish list: "God, could you imagine if Cronos from Venom sang on that song? Fuck! It would be amazing!" Or like, "What if we could get King Diamond? What if we got his number and just asked if he'd do it?" So I made up a really specific list of my 11 favorite vocalists from that time, and that's where the whole idea of this project started. Personally, I didn't think it would work; I couldn't imagine any of these people wanting to make an album with the guy from the Foo Fighters. [*laughs*] But I had a buddy of mine, Matt Sweeney, make the calls, because I had to go right back out on tour. He started getting in touch with these people, and I'd get calls from him saying, "Dude, I talked to King Diamond today!" "No fucking way! What's

he like?" "Great, super-nice guy. He's totally into it. He wants to hear the track."

GW Was anyone reluctant to participate, or was everyone pretty much onboard from the beginning?

GROHL I think everyone was pretty much onboard from the beginning. It was mostly a matter of letting them hear the track. Because I think some of them were sort of suspicious, as I'd imagined they would be: "Hmm, Dave Grohl? Underground metal? I'd better hear this first." Then, when they heard the track and understood that it was the real deal, and that I truly had a love and passion for the music...

GW And that this wasn't some sort of parody thing...

GROHL Well, see, that's something that we've been very sensitive to throughout the whole project. Rock music has become kind of in vogue, and rock cliché has become kind of in vogue, and the *irony* of rock has become kind of chic, you know? You start seeing supermodels in Motörhead T-shirts, or pop stars wearing fucking MC5 shirts. But to me, rock and roll has never been a fashion thing, and metal has never been ironic. Of course, there are great examples of metal that is completely laughable. I've never really been a Manowar fan, but I've got a couple of their home videos that I'd probably take over Spinal Tap any day, you know?

See, when you mention metal, there's usually a negative connotation that comes with a lot of the bands that died out in the late Eighties, bands that were paying way too much attention to their hair and makeup and not enough to their music. But to me, there was never anything funny about Venom.

GW Is part of Probot's mission to turn Foo Fighters fans on to guys like Lemmy, Wino and Cronos?

GROHL Well, all of these musicians deserve incredible amounts of credit. I mean, these people have been so influential to hundreds of thousands of people all over the world. By asking all of these people to be on the album, I'm saying, "Hey, man, I've worshipped your band for 20 years, and it's an honor for me to be the backing band for you for this one moment." That's something that's so special to me. But of course, if I can have a hand in helping people realize the true talent or genius behind these vocalists, then I'm even happier. ✳

...rzealous fan ships ...rself to Cheap Trick

the band members to sing a seductive chorus of "If You Want My Love." "The thing smelled kind of rank, to tell you the truth," says Nielsen. "She had some food and sandwiches and water in there, but

APR. '04

Guitar World's True Stories from the Road: Cheap Trick's Rick Nielsen recalls the time his band received a living, breathing package.

Cheap Trick's fans, particularly those of the female persuasion, thought frontman Robin Zander meant it when he crooned "I Want You to Want Me." In the Platinum wake of *At Budokan* and *Dream Police*, they wanted Cheap Trick—badly. And some were willing to do anything to get them.

And so it was that one fan from the Minnesota area actually shipped herself to Cheap Trick at a late-Seventies show somewhere in central Texas.

"There was this huge box for the band that came through some overnight shipment company, and there was a girl inside it," recalls guitarist Rick Nielsen. "She had mailed herself to us." Neither he nor his band mates remember specific details, such as the city they were in or the fan's name. But, he says, "Apparently she had tried everything to meet us, and this was the only way she could figure out to do it. It was pretty ingenious—and probably pretty expensive."

And it certainly didn't inspire the band members to sing a seductive chorus of "If You Want My Love." "The thing smelled kind of rank, to tell you the truth," says Nielsen. "She had some food and sandwiches and water in there, but she wasn't in great shape." The band hustled the fan to the backstage showers ("Of course we all looked," says Nielsen), then signed autographs, took pictures "and told her not to do that again."

Fights! Camera! Action! What started as a simple documentary about Metallica nearly became an account of the group's destruction. *Guitar World* goes behind the scenes of Metallica's forthcoming, critically acclaimed new movie, *Some Kind of Monster*, for a scorching blow-by-blow report.

By Richard Bienstock

JUNE / VOL. 25 / NO. 6

MONSTER MOVIE

In the June 1994 issue, *Guitar World*'s Richard Bienstock got the inside scoop on *Some Kind of Monster*, the rockumentary that nearly ripped Metallica apart.

THROUGHOUT THE two-hour-and-twenty-minute film, the actions of Metallica's core members—James Hetfield, Lars Ulrich and Kirk Hammett—are sometimes petty, sometimes reprehensible and occasionally downright embarrassing. And that's exactly what makes the documentary such a riveting piece of work. Equally impressive is the fact that Metallica, who have been practicing rigorous damage control on their image for nearly a decade, wholeheartedly endorsed being shown in such a revealing and often negative light.

"Our attitude from the beginning was 'warts and all,' " says Hammett. "We said to the filmmakers, 'Show us good, show us bad. Just show us.' And you know, sometimes we look like assholes and sometimes we look like spoiled rock stars—but we also look like human beings. I think presenting the full picture offers more insight into who we are as people."

Added Hetfield, "There's still a little part of me that fears this film will come out and people will actually go to see it. But then there's another part of me that thinks, Hell yeah, people are going to see your struggles, they're going to see your high points and your low points and they're going to get to know you better. And that's exciting."

Even filmmaker Bruce Sinofsky was ultimately surprised at the band members' level of candor. "If I were Lars, James or Kirk, there are certainly moments in the film that *I* would've demanded to have deleted. That art auction scene? Lars was pressured to take it out by many people in the band's inner circle—from wives to managers to lawyers—who all told him that it's no good for his image. And to Lars' credit, he was like, 'Fuck it! This is who I am.' And you have to have respect for that."

Guitar World Announces Guitar Design Contest

Tony Iommi, **Joe Perry** and **Tom Morello** *judge your designs. Fender builds the winning entry.*

EVERY GUITARIST DREAMS of designing his own guitar. But unless you're blessed with fame, talent or money, there isn't an axmaker on earth that will consider your whacked-out ideas of cutting-edge luthiery.

Well, take heart: *Guitar World* and Fender Musical Instrument Corporation are offering you, dear reader, the chance to design your own guitar and

have it judged by three hard rock icons—Tony Iommi, Joe Perry and Tom Morello. From the entries, one winning design will be built to spec by the Fender Custom Shop.

Best of all, you don't even have to be able to draw. Scrawl your design on a cocktail napkin or map it out on graph paper via CAD engineering—but send it to us by August 1, 2004!

We'll present some of the entries in our forthcoming issues and announce the winner in the October 2004 issue. The winning entry will be shown in our January 2005 issue.

Send your entry to: Guitar Design Contest, c/o *Guitar World*, 149 Fifth Avenue, 9th Floor, New York, NY 10010. Entries will not be returned. •

JULY   **HOLIDAY**

JULY / VOL. 25 / NO. 7

Guitar World and Fender Team Up for the Design Your Dream Guitar Contest

IN THE JULY 2004 ISSUE *Guitar World* announced what would ultimately prove to be the most successful contest in the magazine's history: The Design Your Dream Guitar contest. Readers were asked to submit a drawing of their dream guitar, with the winning design to be built by the Fender Custom Shop. We knew we'd get at least a few pro-level renderings (as well as some angry prisoner art, crayon sketches and grade-school illustrations), but what we didn't expect was the sheer number of entries. By the time our New York City mail carrier delivered the last envelope to our doorstep, thousands of submissions had been received. The winning design, which was announced in the Holiday 2004 issue, was by reader Jimmy Stout, whose "Splat-O-Caster" featured a Strat-shaped aluminum body with clear, fluid-filled cavities. It took Fender Custom Shop veteran Scott Buehl nearly two years to build the one-of-a-kind ax for Stout, who commented to *Guitar World*, "I'm totally ecstatic about winning, man. I wouldn't sell it for a million dollars." Make it more like $30,000...some four months after taking possession of the Splat-O-Caster, Stout—who had come under a mountain of debt—attempted to sell the guitar on eBay for 30 grand. "I will hate myself five years from now, I know, but at this point, it's my only way out of this situation," said Stout in 2007. We're not sure of whatever became of the Splat-O-Caster, but one thing is certain: the Design Your Dream Guitar contest still reigns as the mother of all *GW* contests.

Practice Tips from the Stars

Dimebag Darrell "Whenever I feel my chops are slacking, I'll play some wide-stretch trilling exercises and take them up and down the neck as well as across it. I'll start off with a two-fret stretch trill between my index and middle fingers and do that until I feel a burn. Then I'll do the same thing with a three-fret trill between my index and ring fingers, and then a four-fret one between my index and pinkie."

Joe Satriani "Don't spend more than an hour on any one thing. The brain can only hold so much new information before it says 'enough.' Scientists have studied the changes that occur to the brain when a person learns something new. They've found it takes a while for the brain to recover before it can process new information. So limit yourself to one hour a day on anything that is new or especially challenging."

John Petrucci "Record yourself. After you've practiced for an hour or so, turn down the lights and record yourself playing. Improvise and go nuts, then play back what you've recorded and listen for your strengths and weaknesses. We record Dream Theater shows and I'll sit on the bus and listen to my playing—what worked, what didn't. A lot of times it's embarrassing and humbling, but that's what you have to do to get better."

Jon Donais (Shadows Fall) "Jam with other guitarists' music. I do this all the time, especially with DVDs, because you can see what they're doing. Even if you mess up a lot, jamming like this will often unearth new playing ideas that you would never have come up with otherwise."

Practice Tips From:
Damageplan's Dimebag Darrell

1) Play trills. Whenever I feel my chops are slacking, I'll play some wide-stretch trilling exercises and take them up and down the neck as well as across it. I'll start off with a two-fret stretch trill between my index and middle fingers and do that until I feel a burn. Then I'll do the same thing with a three-fret trill between my index and ring fingers, and then a four-fret one between my index and pinkie.

2) Run through scales. Play the pentatonic blues scale, just for fret- and pick-hand dexterity and to mesh them both together.

3) Practice to records. Learn licks and songs from records.

4) Play with yourself. Set up a four-track or a jambox, lay down a rhythm track off the top of your head and then jam a solo over the playback.

5) Play from the heart. Even though I'll do finger warm-ups that go up and down the neck to build up my chops and dexterity, I never, ever sit around and practice the actual licks I'm gonna play live. If you do then you'll be all worried about the complexity of getting the fingering right and everything else

about it, as opposed to the feel...and to me the feel overrides everything.

Recommended Book: *Riffer Madness* by Dimebag Darrell (Warner Bros. Books). I don't use books or videos, so the only one I can really recommend is my own book, not because I'm just bullish[...]

JUL. '04

THE HAND OF DOOM

THE GRAND WIZARD OF HEAVY METAL, TONY IOMMI, REFLECTS ON THE VERY WICKED WORLD OF BLACK SABBATH.

BY DAN EPSTEIN
PHOTOGRAPHS BY ROSS HALFIN

THERE'S SOMETHING vaguely sinister about Tony Iommi. Perhaps it's the Mephistophelean beard, or the fact that he seems barely to have aged in the 35 years since he and his Black Sabbath mates first sold their souls for rock and roll. Maybe it's the contrast between the dark intensity of his work—he has penned some of music's most evil-sounding riffs—and the unflappably calm demeanor he displays in person. Whatever it is, one gets the impression that, were Beelzebub himself to appear suddenly in the room, Iommi would think nothing of it. † Not that he's on a first-name basis with any demons. The wizardry Iommi's practiced for the past four decades has been strictly musical, even if the diabolical power of Sabbath's heaviest moments has convinced many to believe otherwise. That much is evident in Warner Bros./Rhino's new eight-CD+DVD box set, *Black Box: The Complete Original Black Sabbath (1970–1978)*. The collection contains every studio track released by the group's original lineup of Iommi, Geezer Butler, Bill Ward and Ozzy Osbourne, from its groundbreaking self-titled 1970 debut to the last gasp of its ironically titled 1978 release, *Never Say Die!* It's one hell of an impressive legacy, a veritable Rosetta stone of hard rock and heavy metal. † *Black Box* is by no means inclusive of every great Black Sabbath moment; today

GUITAR WORLD **63**

SEPT. 2004

VOL. 25 / NO. 9

Tony Iommi

The Godfather of Metal reveals some of the writing and recording techniques employed by Black Sabbath in the band's early days.

GUITAR WORLD People typically point to the song "Black Sabbath" as the template for the Sabbath sound, but the main riff of "N.I.B." seems to be a direct precursor to later Sabbath classics like "Sweet Leaf," "Supernaut" and "Sabbath Bloody Sabbath." Was your sliding, slurring style the result of not being able to feel the frets and strings with your fingertips?

TONY IOMMI I've never really thought about it. It's just how I feel I should play the parts. People will often ask me how I play a song, and I have to say I don't really know: I just play it; it just comes naturally. But it probably *is* down to what I'd done with me fingers. That's certainly been a big part of how I play. There's only one style I can play, and there are certain things I can't do—certain chords I've never been able to play—because the finger caps are so big.

GW Were you guys all playing in the same room when you recorded "N.I.B."?

IOMMI Oh, yeah. We played everything together. It was all done as a band, and I loved it that way. The first couple of albums we did quickly. We did the first album in a day: we'd play the whole lot just as it was, and then I'd do an overdub, Ozzy'd do a vocal overdub, and that was it. Later on, we started taking more time in the studio, but we still played the songs live in the studio; it was never drums, then guitar, or anything like that. With Sabbath, I think it was very important to play the songs live. I don't think it would have sounded right if we'd ever tried it any other way. For instance, if we tried to put drums down first, it would be all over the place, because Bill [*Ward, drums*] is not the sort to play along with a metronome, and probably the end of the song is faster than the beginning of it. And I think if we lost that, if we tried to make it perfect tempo, it would be awful.

GW "N.I.B." also has a double-tracked solo where the two guitar parts are similar but not exactly the same. It's a technique you returned to again and again. Where did that idea come from?

IOMMI I just thought it was a good idea, that it would be something different to have two solos instead of one, and just have them crossing over each other.

GW Would you plot out the solos before tracking them?

IOMMI Oh no, never. Never! I can't do that—I can't work solos out. I'm really awful at that. I have to play them off the cuff. Even after playing these songs for many years, if you asked me to play the solo, I'd have to start thinking about it. I just play it as it comes, and that's it.

GW Is that a wah-wah pedal you're using on "Electric Funeral," from the *Paranoid* album?

IOMMI Yes. It was one of the only effects I had. [*laughs*] It might have actually been a Vox, though I did eventually go to Tychobrahe pedals, and I still have about four of them. They did one for Hendrix, and they did one for me. Those pedals were great, but in the early days it was very difficult for me to use any kind of pedal. Back then, putting a guitar through any device would cut down the volume level and the sustain, and cause a horrendous racket, especially with my Gibson—I had the single-pole pickups, which picked up everything! [*laughs*] I tried to get designers to make pedal boards that would work for my guitar, but the technology just wasn't working successfully for me. So plugging straight into the amp was always the best thing.

GW The intro riff of "After Forever," from *Master of Reality*, sounds kind of like a backward version of the Beatles' "Paperback Writer." Were you conscious of that at the time?

IOMMI [*laughs*] No, I never thought of that. It just came out of my head. A lot of Sabbath's writing was just off the cuff, and that's how the riffs came out. I can't sit down and work a riff out; it's just the way I am. Brian May, for instance: he'll sit down and work out a riff, and he'll come up with all the harmonies—all the clever-dick. But I can't do that; it has to come there and then. When we got into rehearsal, it was always expected that I would walk in and come up with the riffs right away, and everybody would play them. And that usually happened. If it didn't, they'd all sit down and wait until I came up with something.

GW And then the song would develop out of whatever new riff you came up with?

IOMMI Yeah. Once we got the initial riff of the song, we'd go along until we felt like it wanted to change to something else, then I'd start experimenting with another riff. And then we'd play them over and over again so we could bloody remember them, because we didn't have a cassette player in those days. We'd get there the next day and go, "How did that go, now?" [*laughs*] Once we could afford a reel-to-reel tape recorder, we taped everything. ✳

TWO THOUSAND

'05

Guitar World celebrates its 25th year in publication,
looks back at the making of such legendary
records as Zeppelin's *Physical Graffiti* and Nirvana's
Nevermind, and pays heartfelt tribute
to our friend and brother, Dimebag Darrell.

Dear *Guitar World*,

I'm sitting in jail, and what's this I
see? Dimebag is dead! No, no, this can't
be! He was an icon. A legend with skill.
A rock-solid heart, with an iron will!
Strong was this man. Determined was he. A
merciless musician, who will forever be!

—Chad Gomez

JANUARY *Guitar World*'s Breakthrough Artist of the Year, Los Lonely Boys' Strat-wielding superstar Henry Garza, pays tribute to his heroes, including Stevie Ray Vaughan, B.B. King and Carlos Santana. "Carlos' music was always a part of our Thanksgiving, our Christmas, our Easter, because he represents our people."
COVER STORY BY ANDY ALEDORT
PHOTO BY CLAY PATRICK MCBRIDE

25TH ANNIVERSARY SPECIAL ISSUE!

HOW TO PLAY **10 RIFFS** THAT **CHANGED THE UNIVERSE**
GUITAR WORLD'S **STUPIDEST MISTAKES**
THE 25th ANNIVERSARY **READER'S POLL WINNERS**
JIMMY PAGE ANSWERS YOUR QUESTIONS
SYSTEM OF A DOWN'S NEW ALBUM
THE **BUYER'S GUIDE BABES REVISITED**
ULI JON ROTH SHOWS YOU "SAILS OF CHARON"
ZAKK WYLDE'S NEW ALBUM
RANDY RHOADS LIVES!
JOE PERRY ROCKS THIS WAY
+ MUCH, MUCH MORE!

AND FEATURING
A SPECIAL SALUTE TO
KURT COBAIN
METALLICA
EDDIE VAN HALEN
JIMI HENDRIX
STEVIE RAY VAUGHAN
STEVE VAI
LED ZEPPELIN
AND THE ZILLION OTHER GUITARISTS THAT MADE US THE WORLD'S BEST-SELLING GUITAR MAGAZINE!

FEBRUARY *Guitar World* turns 25 and looks back at its greatest triumphs, most shocking stories and a few idiotic mistakes.
COVER STORY BY VARIOUS; PHOTO BY ROSS HALFIN

MARCH *Guitar World* recounts the life and times of Dimebag Darrell, the original cowboy from hell, whose explosive style and live-wire personality forever changed the face of heavy metal guitar.
COVER STORY BY CHRIS GILL
PHOTO BY CLAY PATRICK MCBRIDE

APRIL Three demons of shred—Steve Vai, Zakk Wylde and Alexi Laiho—converge on one *Guitar World* cover for some rifferiffic good times.
COVER STORIES BY ALAN PAUL AND BRIAN STILLMAN
PHOTO BY ROSS HALFIN

MAY Jimmy Page and *Guitar World* celebrate 30 years of *Physical Graffiti*.
COVER STORY BY MARK BLAK
PHOTO BY MICHAEL PUTLAND

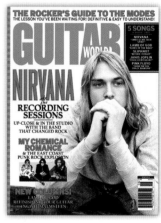

JUNE *Guitar World* delves deep into the Nirvana recording sessions with pieces on the making of *Bleach* and an inside look at the groundbreaking *Nevermind* sessions.
COVER STORIES BY CHARLES R. CROSS AND ROB JOVANOVIC; PHOTO BY STEVE DOUBLE

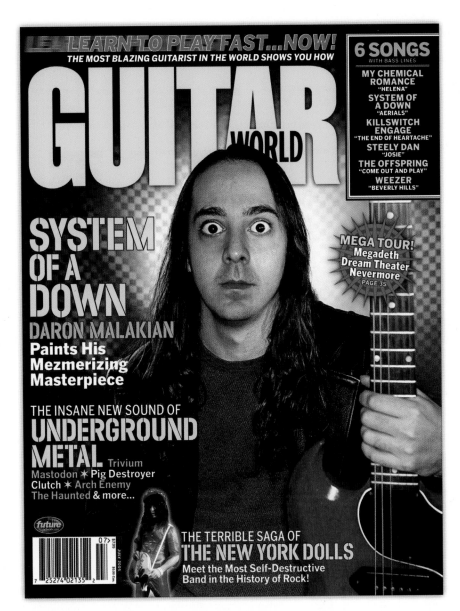

JULY System of a Down's Daron Malakian has so many sides that it took two new albums to contain them. *Guitar World* goes deep inside the making of *Mezmerize/Hyponotize*. "Songwriting to me is just as mysterious as serial killing."

COVER STORY BY ALAN DI PERNA; PHOTO BY ZACH CORDNER

2005 TOTAL ISSUES: 13

AUGUST Tom Morello, rock's exacting mad scientist of the guitar, rages against his own machine and brews up spontaneous six-string combustion on Audioslave's new *Out of Exile*.
COVER STORY BY ALAN DI PERNA; PHOTO BY ROSS HALFIN

SEPTEMBER U2's innovative guitarist, The Edge, reflects on his 25 years with rock's most musically adventurous band.
COVER STORY BY JOE BOSSO; PHOTO BY RAYON RICHARDS

OCTOBER For the first time in 36 years, Jimi Hendrix's rhythm section of Mitch Mitchell and Billy Cox get together to discuss Jimi's legendary performance at Woodstock.
COVER STORY BY ANDY ALEDORT; PHOTO BY ALLAN KOSS

NOVEMBER After drugs and illness nearly destroyed the world's greatest rock and roll band, Keith Richards tells how he and the Rolling Stones survived and got back to their roots for their new album, *A Bigger Bang*.
COVER STORY BY ALAN DI PERNA; PHOTO BY KEVIN MAZUR

DECEMBER In his first interview since his brother's murder one year ago, drummer Vinnie Paul pays heartfelt tribute to Dimebag Darrell and reveals his plans to keep Dime's memory alive.
COVER STORY BY NICK BOWCOTT; PHOTO BY NEIL ZLOZOWER

HOLIDAY A who's-who of guitar notables—from Keith Richards, Ace Frehley and Joe Perry to members of Lamb of God, Mastodon and Killswitch Engage—weigh in on the record that had the most profound impact on their musical upbringing.
COVER STORY BY VARIOUS; PHOTOS BY ROSS HALFIN AND JIMMY HUBBARD

The 25th Anniversary Readers Poll

Jimi Hendrix rules. "Stairway" is still heavenly. And Alexi Laiho is a legend in the making. Our opinions? Nope—it's your party.

GREATEST CLASSIC ROCK GUITARIST
- Jimi Hendrix 47%
- Jimmy Page 30%
- Tony Iommi 12%
- David Gilmour 8%
- Keith Richards 3%

GREATEST CLASSIC ROCK ALBUM
- Led Zeppelin—*Led Zeppelin IV* 38%
- Pink Floyd—*The Dark Side of the Moon* 24%
- Black Sabbath—*Paranoid* 21%
- Jimi Hendrix Experience—*Are You Experienced* 15%
- Rolling Stones—*Exile on Main Street* 2%

GREATEST CLASSIC SOLO
- "Stairway to Heaven" (Jimmy Page) 38%
- "Voodoo Chile (Slight Return)" (Jimi Hendrix) 20%
- "Comfortably Numb" (David Gilmour) 15%
- "Hotel California" (Joe Walsh & Don Felder) 14%
- "Free Bird" (Allen Collins & Gary Rossington) 13%

GREATEST GUITARIST OF THE PAST 25 YEARS
- Eddie Van Halen 35%
- Randy Rhoads 23%
- Slash 18%
- Kirk Hammett 15%
- Angus Young 9%

GREATEST CLASSIC RIFF
- "Smoke on the Water" 33%
- "Iron Man" 24%
- "Purple Haze" 17%
- "Black Dog" 14%
- "Layla" 12%

GREATEST GUITAR ALBUM OF THE PAST 25 YEARS
- Guns N' Roses—*Appetite for Destruction* 28%
- Metallica—*Metallica* 23%
- AC/DC—*Back in Black* 19%
- Van Halen—*1984* 19%
- Nirvana—*Nevermind* 11%

GREATEST GUITAR SOLO OF THE LAST 25 YEARS
- "Crazy Train" (Randy Rhoads) 26%
- "Sweet Child O' Mine" (Slash) 25%
- "One" (Kirk Hammett) 24%
- "Hot for Teacher" (Eddie Van Halen) 16%
- "Cemetary Gates" (Dimebag Darrell) 9%

GREATEST RIFF OF THE PAST 25 YEARS
- "Crazy Train" 30%
- "Sweet Child O' Mine" 20%
- "Enter Sandman" 20%
- "Back in Black" 17%
- "Smells Like Teen Spirit" 13%

CLASSIC METAL ICON
- James Hetfield & Kirk Hammett 31%
- Randy Rhoads 23%
- Tony Iommi 21%
- Dave Mustaine 21%
- Kerry King & Jeff Hanneman 4%

CONTEMPORARY METAL ICON
- Zakk Wylde 60%
- Dimebag Darrell 21%
- Adam Jones 8%
- Daron Malakian 6%
- Munky & Head 5%

HAIR METAL ICON
- George Lynch 32%
- Mick Mars 23%
- C.C. DeVille 20%
- Nuno Bettencourt 19%
- Reb Beach 6%

PUNK ICON
- Johnny Ramone 55%
- Joe Strummer 18%
- Billie Joe Armstrong 18%
- Tim Armstrong 5%
- Greg Ginn 4%

GRUNGE ICON
- Kurt Cobain 61%
- Jerry Cantrell 21%
- Billy Corgan 9%
- Kim Thayil 5%
- Mike McCready 4%

JAM ICON
- Carlos Santana 51%
- Jerry Garcia 21%
- Trey Anastasio 11%
- Warren Haynes 11%
- Dickey Betts 6%

BLUES ICON
- Stevie Ray Vaughan 42%
- B.B. King 26%
- Eric Clapton 23%
- Robert Johnson 7%
- Duane Allman 2%

ALTERNATIVE ICON
- Tom Morello 31%
- Jorn Frusciante 28%
- The Edge 20%
- Jack White 11%
- Robert Smith 10%

EXTREME METAL ICON
- Chuck Schuldiner (Death) 33%
- Hagström & Thordendal (Meshuggah) 21%
- Trey Azagthoth (Morbid Angel) 18%
- Mantas (Venom) 16%
- Donais & Bachand (Shadows Fall) 12%

VIRTUOSO ICON
- Steve Vai 25%
- Yngwie Malmsteen 24%
- Joe Satriani 22%
- Buckethead 16%
- John Petrucci 13%

WHO WOULD YOU MOST LIKE TO GET A LESSON FROM?
- Steve Vai 40%
- Eric Clapton 25%
- Joe Satriani 24%
- Tom Morello 9%
- Warren Haynes 4%

SNAPPIEST DRESSER
- Jimi Hendrix 38%
- Jimmy Page 22%
- Angus Young 21%
- Ace Frehley 13%
- Jack White 6%

LEGENDARY GUITAR
- Randy Rhoads' Flying V 28%
- Van Halen's "Frankenstein" 27%
- Page's double-neck 23%
- B.B. King's "Lucille" 13%
- SRV's "Number One" 9%

BEST EFFECT
- Wha-wha 45%
- Overdrive 31%
- Delay 12%
- Phase 7%
- Fuzz 5%

FUTURE LEGEND
- Alexi Laiho (Children of Bodom) 29%
- Ómar Rodríguez-López (Mars Volta) 25%
- Derek Trucks (Allman Brothers Band) 23%
- Henry Garza (Los Lonely Boys) 14%
- Mark Morton & Willie Adler (Lamb of God) 9%

WHO WOULD YOU MOST LIKE TO GET A DRINK WITH?
- Angus Young 33%
- Zakk Wylde 24%
- Keith Richards 21%
- Dimebag Darrell 15%
- Billy Gibbons 7%

MOST UNDERRATED
- Malcolm Young 31%
- Prince 29%
- George Harrison 27%
- Bradley Nowell 7%
- Robby Krieger 6%

82

83

FEB. 2005

VOL. 26 / NO. 2

25th Anniversary Readers Poll Results

As *Guitar World* celebrates its 25th year in publication, readers cast their votes in the most extensive of our many Readers Polls.

Greatest Classic Rock Guitarist
- **Jimmy Page**
- Jimi Hendrix
- Tony Iommi
- David Gilmour
- Keith Richards

Greatest Classic Rock Album
- **Led Zeppelin**—*Led Zeppelin IV*
- Pink Floyd—*The Dark Side of the Moon*
- Black Sabbath—*Paranoid*
- Jimi Hendrix Experience—*Are You Experienced?*
- Rolling Stones—*Exile on Main Street*

Greatest Classic Solo
- **"Stairway to Heaven" (Jimmy Page)**
- "Voodoo Chile (Slight Return)" (Jimi Hendrix)
- "Comfortably Numb" (David Gilmour)
- "Hotel California" (Joe Walsh & Don Felder)
- "Free Bird" (Allen Collins & Gary Rossington)

Greatest Classic Riff
- **"Smoke on the Water"**
- "Iron Man"
- "Purple Haze"
- "Black Dog"
- "Layla"

Greatest Guitarist of the Last 25 Years
- **Eddie Van Halen**
- Randy Rhoads
- Slash
- Kirk Hammett
- Angus Young

Greatest Guitar Album of the Last 25 Years
- **Guns N' Roses—** *Appetite for Destruction*
- Metallica—*Metallica*
- AC/DC—*Back in Black*
- Van Halen—*1984*
- Nirvana—*Nevermind*

Greatest Guitar Solo of the Last 25 Years
- **"Crazy Train" (Randy Rhoads)**
- "Sweet Child O' Mine" (Slash)
- "One" (Kirk Hammett)
- "Hot for Teacher" (Eddie Van Halen)
- "Cemetery Gates" (Dimebag Darrell)

Greatest Riff of the Last 25 Years
- **"Crazy Train"**
- "Sweet Child O' Mine"
- "Enter Sandman"
- "Back in Black"
- "Smells Like Teen Spirit"

Classic Metal Icon
- **James Hetfield & Kirk Hammett**
- Randy Rhoads
- Tony Iommi
- Dave Mustaine
- Kerry King & Jeff Hanneman

Contemporary Metal Icon
- **Zakk Wylde**
- Dimebag Darrell
- Adam Jones
- Daron Malakian
- Munky & Head

Hair Metal Icon
- **George Lynch**
- Mick Mars
- C.C. DeVille
- Nuno Bettencourt
- Reb Beach

Punk Icon
- **Johnny Ramone**
- Joe Strummer
- Billie Joe Armstrong
- Tim Armstrong
- Greg Ginn

Grunge Icon
- **Kurt Cobain**
- Jerry Cantrell
- Billy Corgan
- Kim Thayil
- Mike McCready

Jam Icon
- **Carlos Santana**
- Jerry Garcia
- Trey Anastasio
- Warren Haynes
- Dickey Betts

Blues Icon
- **Stevie Ray Vaughan**
- B.B. King
- Eric Clapton
- Robert Johnson
- Duane Allman

Alternative Icon
- **Tom Morello**
- John Frusciante
- The Edge
- Jack White
- Robert Smith

Extreme Metal Icon
- **Chuck Schuldiner (Death)**
- Marten Hagström & Fredrik Thordendal (Meshuggah)
- Trey Azagthoth (Morbid Angel)
- Mantas (Venom)
- Jon Donais & Matt Bachand (Shadows Fall)

Virtuoso Icon
- **Steve Vai**
- Yngwie Malmsteen
- Joe Satriani
- Buckethead
- John Petrucci

Who Would You Most Like to Get a Lesson From?
- **Steve Vai**
- Eric Clapton
- Kirk Hammett
- Tom Morello
- Warren Haynes

Who Would You Most Like to Get a Drink With?
- **Zakk Wylde**
- Angus Young
- Keith Richards
- Dimebag Darrell
- Billy Gibbons

Most Underrated
- **Prince**
- George Harrison
- Malcolm Young
- Bradley Nowell
- Robby Krieger

Snappiest Dresser
- **Jimi Hendrix**
- Jimmy Page
- Angus Young
- Ace Frehley
- Jack White

Legendary Guitar
- **Randy Rhoads' Flying V**
- Van Halen's "Frankenstein"
- Page's doubleneck
- B.B. King's "Lucille"
- SRV's "Number One"

Best Effect
- **wha-wha**
- overdrive
- delay
- phase
- fuzz

Future Legend
- **Alexi Laiho (Children of Bodom)**
- Omar Rodriguez-Lopez (Mars Volta)
- Derek Trucks (Allman Brothers Band)
- Henry Garza (Los Lonely Boys)
- Mark Morton & Willie Adler (Lamb of God) ✱

THE DIMEBAG DARRELL MEMORIAL SERVICE

Guitar World senior editor Nick Bowcott reports from the star-studded Dimebag Darrell memorial service one week after the hard-partying guitarist was killed onstage.

FUNERAL FOR A FRIEND

Guitar World senior editor Nick Bowcott reports from the Dimebag Darrell memorial service, where the hard-rock elite turned out to pay final respects to their fallen brother.

By Nick Bowcott

THE PROFOUND IMPACT OF Dimebag's phenomenal talent and his positive, larger-than-life persona was never more apparent than on Tuesday, December 14, 2004, the day of his private funeral and public memorial service in his hometown of Arlington, Texas. Although his rowdy but harmless late-night antics had made the local police frequent visitors to his house, Dime was much loved by Arlington's finest, as illustrated by the almost presidential escort they gave his procession. Traffic was stopped at every junction to ensure the journey taken by Dime's family and closest friends was uninterrupted.

A plethora of well-known rockers attended the service to pay their respects to the popular man with the purple goatee. Among them were his "blood brother" Zakk Wylde, Eddie Van Halen and Rob Zombie, as well as members of Anthrax, Shadows Fall, Slipknot,

Nick Bowcott speaking at Dimebag's memorial service on Dec. 14, 2004

Afterward, rock guitar legend Edward Van Halen stepped up to the podium and played a recent cell phone message from Dime. Only a few weeks earlier, Darrell and his brother, drummer Vinnie Paul, had finally met their Van Halen counterparts, Eddie and Alex, an occasion Dime described to me as inspirational, uplifting and almost religious. Darrell had asked Van Halen if there was any way he could jump the queue and buy one of the limited-edition black- and yellow-striped Charvel guitars. Ed replied that he would tape the thing up himself, in Dime's presence. As this was no longer possible, Edward explained, he wanted to give Dime the original black-and-yellow ax, the guitar depicted on the back of *Van Halen II.* It is this guitar Dime was holding when he was laid to rest. "Darrell was full of life," Van Halen told the crowd. "He lived and breathed rock and roll.

THE PROFOUND IMPACT of Dimebag's phenomenal talent and his positive, larger-than-life persona was never more apparent than on December 14, 2004, the day of his private funeral and public memorial service in his hometown of Arlington, Texas. Although his rowdy but harmless late-night antics had made the local police frequent visitors to his house, Dime was much loved by Arlington's finest, as illustrated by the almost presidential escort they gave his procession.

A plethora of well-known rockers attended the service to pay their respects to the popular man with the purple goatee. Among them were his "blood brother" Zakk Wylde, Eddie Van Halen and Rob Zombie, as well as members of Anthrax, Shadows Fall, Slipknot, Disturbed, Prong, Type O Negative, Static-X, Soil, Kittie and Skid Row, among others.

Dime was laid to rest in an official Kiss Kasket, wearing his beloved Black Label Society leather vest, shorts and flip-flops, and holding a very special guitar. His coffin also contained personal essentials, including his signed Judas Priest *Metalogy* boxset, an MXR EVH Phase 90 pedal and, of course, the ingredients for his legendary Black Tooth Grin: a bottle of Crown Royal and a can or two of Coke.

An emotional Zakk Wylde made the mourners roar with laughter with a typically irreverent Dime story about how, after downing several bottles of Crown following an Ozzfest show, they woke up together in Zakk's tour bus bunk, "spooning." Jerry Cantrell, along with bassist Mike Inez, Damageplan vocalist Pat Lachman and Dime's good friend Shawn Mathews, performed a pair of emotionally charged acoustic Alice in Chains songs before Anthrax drummer Charlie Benante continued the celebration of Dime's life with an eloquent and entertaining eulogy.

Afterward, rock guitar legend Edward Van Halen stepped up to the podium and played a recent cell phone message from Dime. Only a few weeks earlier, Darrell and his brother, drummer Vinnie Paul, had finally met their Van Halen counterparts, Eddie and Alex, an occasion Dime described to me as inspirational, uplifting and almost religious. Darrell had asked Van Halen if there was anyway he could jump the queue and buy one of the limited-edition black- and yellow-striped Charvel guitars. Ed replied that he would tape the thing up himself, in Dime's presence. As this was no longer possible, Edward explained, he wanted to give Dime the original black-and-yellow ax, the guitar depicted on the back of *Van Halen II*. It is this guitar Dime was holding when he was laid to rest. "Darrell was full of life," Van Halen told the crowd. "He lived and breathed rock and roll. I'm here for the same reason as everyone else: to give some of the love back."

ve Black Label Society, Vinnie Paul
mber Dimebag Darrell and
Guitar World's 25th anniversary.

tragically gunned down this past December. In the audience were Dime's longtime girlfriend, Rita, and his brother, Vinnie Paul, both of whom were clearly moved by Bowcott's gritty performance and the audience's fist-pumping response.

The main event of the party, which was cosponsored by EV and GHS Strings, was a generous two-hour performance by Black Label

Zakk Wylde with Jon Donais and Chris Jericho (top right) and Vinnie Paul (bottom right)

Society that had every ax slinger in the house shaking his head in awe. After the show, Wylde noted, "It was a great night for the guitar. Dime was my best friend and *Guitar World* has been a great supporter of my music. It was fucking great to celebrate both in one amazing night."

Guitar World celebrates its 25th anniversary with a rockin' House of Blues bash.

MAY '05

It was a righteous evening filled with high spirits, tear-jerking emotion, hot babes and kick-ass rock and roll. And for many, *Guitar World's* 25th Anniversary party will be a night they'll never forget. Held at the Anaheim House of Blues in California this past January, the party celebrated two profound events: *Guitar World's* quarter-century mark and the first public performance of songs from *Mafia*, the latest release from Zakk Wylde's Black Label Society. Guests included top dogs and bigwigs from almost every musical instrument manufacturer on the planet, not to mention a gaggle of genuine rock stars, including members of Shadows Fall, Jerry Cantrell and Alexi Laiho, who came to hear Wylde shred up a storm.

THE REAL DEAL

HE MAY LOOK LIKE THE CRYPTKEEPER AND SUFFER FROM A DEGENERATIVE DISEASE, BUT MAKE NO MISTAKE: **MICK MARS** IS THE BACKBONE OF THE MIGHTY **MÖTLEY CRÜE**

By Joe Bosso

MAY / VOL. 26 / NO. 5

MICK MARS

As Mötley Crüe prepare for a grueling reunion tour, the band's mysterious guitarist details the circumstances surrounding his battle with a debilitating arthritic condition.

GUITAR WORLD Let's talk about your medical condition. How are you feeling these days?

MICK MARS I'm fine. The press likes to blow these things out of proportion.

GW So you feel up for the tour? Any problems with stamina?

MARS I'm going to be fine. We've got over two hours of songs to pick from. It's going to be an evening with Mötley. I'll pace myself. No worries.

GW Even so, your disease doesn't sound like a walk in the park. Pardon the pun.

MARS It's no walk in the park. In fact, it's why I kind of walk like Frankenstein. [*laughs*] The thing about ankylosing spondylitis is it's caused by a gene. You start noticing pain in your hips, usually when you're in your teens. What it does is it slowly fuses your bones together—your spine, your ribs... With most people, it stops in their thirties, when the disease is still in their lower back. I have a rare form of the disease that hasn't stopped, so it's all the way up my whole back and into my brain stem. It's literally squeezing my rib cage together, so I've lost some height. And now that it's up in my brain stem, it's hard for me to move my head in any direction, be it up and down or sideways. So I can't drive. I can't do any of that kind of stuff. This isn't a boohoo. It's just the facts.

I'm going to get an operation at some point. There's no cure, but the doctors say they might—*might*—be able to chip away some of the bone growth at the brain stem. It'll grow back, but I'll take any improvement. If I could just move my head a little and stand up straight, I'd be a happy man.

GW This hasn't affected your hands or fingers?

MARS Nope. It's not in my hands or finger joints. I can be thankful for that. We really, really, *really* have to get going on stem cell research. It can help so many people: people in wheelchairs, with spinal injuries or osteoporosis. There are so many diseases and conditions we could stop in their tracks if we just got serious.

JUL. '05

What's Your Most Spinal Tap Moment?

In our July 2005 issue, we asked an array of rockers to give us their best horror stories from the road. Here, ZZ Top's Billy Gibbons recalls the night the critters took over. "Somehow I got it into my head that it would be a good idea to get a huge stage set and 'take Texas to the people.' We had a stage in the shape of the state of Texas, and a number of rattlesnakes, vultures and even a couple of buffalo onstage. It was authentic! It was disastrous. At first, everything went well: the rattlers behaved, the birds seemed to stand the noise and the buffalo grazed quietly— until one night one buffalo decided he'd had enough. He rammed two glass cages containing the snakes. Suddenly we had a dozen rattlers crawling around onstage. Our drummer suggested we play 'something quiet, to soothe them'—a stupid idea, 'cause most snakes are deaf. We didn't even attempt it. We just fled and left the roadies to minimize the damage."

RECORD THAT CHANGED MY LIFE

ASK ANY MUSICIAN WHEN he knew that he wanted to play an instrument, and most likely he'll tell you about a song or album that stirred something inside him for the first time. That epiphanic experience is so universal that musicians of every genre, age group and nationality can rightfully claim it as the moment at which their lives were forever changed—the instant at which music set them on a path to spiritual

awakening, financial gain, megastardom or existential ruin. In that respect, the record that changed a musician's life can tell you a lot about not only the artist's music but also the choices he's made for his life and career.

With that in mind, *Guitar World* asked some of your favorite guitarists to name the record that changed their life. Their responses were diverse and, in many instances, surprising. You're certain to find several albums among their selections that have made a difference in your life. But hopefully, you'll also discover something new that will send you racing to your nearest record store and, perhaps, down your own path to sonic salvation.

RAY TORO
(My Chemical Romance)
OZZY OSBOURNE
Blizzard of Ozz (1980)

"My brother introduced me to Ozzy's music when I was 14, and right away Randy Rhoads became my biggest influence. I loved the fact that he wrote such incredibly heavy stuff as well as 'Dee'—a short classical piece for his mother—and 'Goodbye to Romance,' which is so different from any other song on the record. It just shows his remarkable range. After I heard that record, I was inspired by his mix of classical music and metal and started modeling a lot of my playing after his. I got interested in tapping, because he used little bits of that in certain sections of his solos just to move up the scale or move up the fretboard. I also started playing classical scales. I think you can most directly hear his influence on my playing in the song 'Thank You for the Venom' [*from* Three Cheers for Sweet Revenge]. Toward the end of the solo, there's a really fast triplet run down the scale that's totally reminiscent of him."

GERARD WAY
(My Chemical Romance)
THE MISFITS
Walk Among Us (1982)

"This record changed everything for me. I was in middle school at the time and was a big Iron Maiden fan. I was playing Dungeons & Dragons and had yet to learn about punk rock. When I heard some of *Walk Among Us* from a friend, I knew I had to have it. Thanks to the PMRC [Parents Music Resource Center, the group responsible for getting parental warning labels placed on music CD, tapes and records], I had to be sneaky about how I got the record, because they made it difficult for kids to buy records. My mom wouldn't buy it for me because it has a song called 'Devil's Whorehouse,' so I got my grandfather to buy it for me. I put it on and immediately I felt more liberated, free and pissed off than I'd ever been. It hit me all at once. This album made me realize that there is no right way to do anything—there are no rules. That's the beauty of punk rock: if you believe in it, you can accomplish it. I was an outcast, and that record really got me through some bad times."

FRANK IERO
(My Chemical Romance)
NIRVANA
In Utero (1993)

"When I was really young I listened to a lot of classic blues that I discovered through my dad. When I was older and heard *In Utero*, it was so eye opening. Through it, I found out about bands like Big Black [whose frontman, Steve Albini, produced In Utero] and other guitar players like [Black Flag's] Greg Ginn and [Sonic Youth's] Thurston Moore. Basically, it helped me discover the underground hardcore and punk scenes. I also think Kurt Cobain's distortion sounds great, and I love how you can hear every pick scrape and finger slide. *In Utero* changed the way I thought about playing guitar. It made me realize that you don't have to play like Van Halen; you just have to play from the heart and put your personality and emotion into it."

Photograph by JIMMY FISHBEIN

HOLIDAY 2005

VOL. 26 / NO. 13

The Record That Changed My Life

A host of six-string luminaries cast their vote for the record that had the most profound impact on

Claudio Sanchez (Coheed and Cambria)

Jimi Hendrix—*Axis: Bold As Love* (1967)

"Probably Hendrix's prettiest- and softest-sounding record; it's not as violent as *Are You Experienced*. It has a sound that really spoke to me and pushed me to start a band of my own."

Joe Perry

The Yardbirds—*Having a Rave Up* (1965)

"That album was incredibly important to me as a young, budding guitarist, because it was set in a blues genre that I really gravitated toward—the raunchy, basic sound of the electric blues. It was the first album I heard on which the guitar solos were as important as the lead vocals or the songs themselves. Up until then, a lot of guitar solos would just be there to take up a little space between a chorus and a verse; they were really organized and premeditated. But when you heard the guitar solos on the Yardbirds stuff you felt that Jeff Beck didn't know what he was going to play until he played it. There was freedom to jam."

Kirk Hammett

UFO—*Force It* (1975)

"I really learned a lot about solo structure, phrasing and melody, as well as playing for the song from this record. I was amazed how UFO could be so heavy and so melodic in the course of one song. I think the band I was in at the time added two UFO songs to our set later on that week."

Yngwie Malmsteen

Deep Purple—*Fireball* (1971)

"My sister gave me *Fireball* for my eighth birthday, June 30, 1971, and that day my life forever changed. I knew immediately that I was going

to be a guitarist for life and there would be no turning back. It's like one minute I was a kid playing with cap guns, and then someone handed me a fuckin' nuclear bomb!"

Michael Schenker

Jeff Beck—*Truth* (1968)

"I heard this album at a friend's house when I was around 14 or 15 years old, and it completely transformed me. I walked home that night humming improvised solos. I knew I was on my way—I was unstoppable. When I arrived home, I took my guitar and practiced at a totally new level."

Mark Morton (Lamb of God)

Megadeth—*Peace Sells...But Who's Buying?* (1986)

"*Peace Sells* made me realize that I could take all my adolescent rebelliousness and negative energy and craft it into something that was both sophisticated *and* dangerous. Basically, it made me want to be a metal guitar player."

Zacky Vengeance (Avenged Sevenfold)

Pantera—*Far Beyond Driven* (1994)

"When I first heard *Far Beyond Driven*, I was in eighth grade and heavily into punk music. Some scary-looking girl let me listen to it on her headset, and it nearly knocked me on my ass. After that, I really wanted to play music that would make me feel the way I did when I first heard that album."

Dave Mustaine

AC/DC—*Let There Be Rock* (1977)

"I was 16 or 17 when I got this album. I remember taking it home, putting it on my cheap turntable and dropping the

needle down on the vinyl. The first couple of notes of 'Overdose' just blew my mind. The sound of the guitar was so untamed, and it lit a fire inside me to approach the guitar like a weapon.

"To this day, I listen to *Let There Be Rock* and it motivates me. That album marked the defining moment in my life when I made my mind up that I was gonna do this, no matter what."

Mikael Akerfeldt (Opeth)

Camel—*Moon Madness* (1976)

"I was already in my twenties when I first heard it. I was working at a record store in Stockholm at the time, and one of my co-workers, who was in his early forties, suggested I check out Camel. I bought a couple of their albums on second-hand vinyl, including *Moon Madness* and *The Snowgoose*, and took them home on a lunch break. I was floored by *Moon Madness*, and especially by Andy Latimer's guitar playing. It was so heartfelt and emotional, and every note felt like it served a purpose."

Brent Hinds (Mastodon)

Neurosis—*Enemy of the Sun* (1994)

"My experience with *Enemy of the Sun* still affects the way I think about music today. I go back to that situation and think about what it did to my psyche and my approach to guitar playing and writing music. Songwriting is like making a nice meal, and when I'm writing music with Mastodon, I'll always try to give it a Neurosis flavor."

Slash

Aerosmith—*Rocks* (1976)

"I first heard *Rocks* when I was 13 or 14. There was this girl, Laurie, and I'd been trying to get into her pants

for what seemed like forever. She was the hottest chick in school and just exuded—no, *excreted*—sex appeal. One day I rode my BMX bike over to her place. We smoked a bunch of pot, and she started playing me records.

"From the moment she put it on and 'Back in the Saddle' started playing, I was glued to the album. After I digested the album six or seven times, I just got up, grabbed my smokes, jumped on my bike and went home. I never did get laid. But not too long after, I picked up a guitar, and I've been doing this ever since."

Trey Anastasio

Jimi Hendrix—*Band of Gypsys* (1970)

"As the years go by, I find it more and more amazing that everything came together for Jimi while he was playing with a new band on New Year's Eve, and that it was captured on an album. Thirty-five years later, there's still nothing that comes close. I can't fathom how any guitar player would not consider this the greatest example of electric guitar playing ever recorded."

Stephen Carpenter (Deftones)

Meshuggah—*Chaosphere* (1998)

"The greatest metal record of all time. *Chaosphere* gave me a whole new perspective on playing with its unusual time signatures. Their tuning alone influenced me: I've used seven-string guitars on the last two Deftones records. It's kind of hard to find the parts in Deftones songs that sound like Meshuggah unless you're looking for them, but they're there—little shifts in the music that you might not pay attention to that give the songs their flavor." ✱

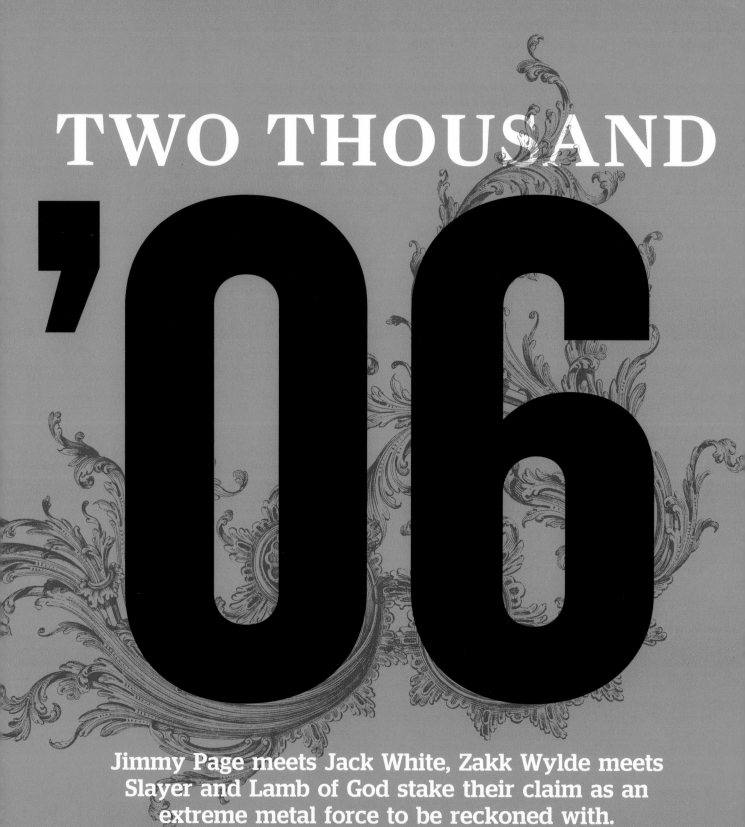

TWO THOUSAND '06

Jimmy Page meets Jack White, Zakk Wylde meets Slayer and Lamb of God stake their claim as an extreme metal force to be reckoned with.

Dear *Guitar World*,

In the first paragraph of the article on
harmony guitar soloing [*Holiday 2005*], you
make mention of "poopular music." What
exactly is poopular music?

—Kevin Tipman

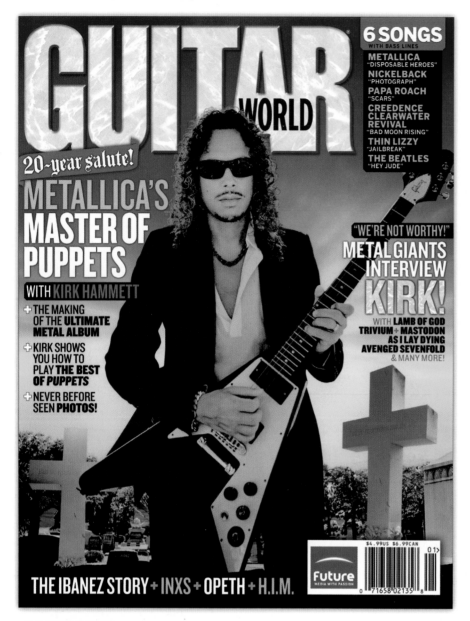

FEBRUARY In this historic meeting between two guitar masters, Led Zeppelin legend Jimmy Page and garage rock icon Jack White talk about their development as players and explain why the blues is good for your soul.
COVER STORY BY BRAD TOLINSKI; PHOTO BY ROSS HALFIN

MARCH A tribute to the late, great Randy Rhoads in which Ozzy and Sharon Osbourne, as well as various former bandmates, reflect on the superstar shredder. Plus, an insider's look at the making of two landmark guitar recordings: Ozzy's *Blizzard of Ozz* and *Diary of a Madman*.
COVER STORY BY JAMES MCNAIR; PHOTO BY ROSS HALFIN

APRIL When it comes to fretboard speed, few can match the fleet-fingered prowess of Joe Satriani. In this detailed lesson, the chrome-domed master of shred discusses the art and science of playing rock lead guitar.
COVER STORY BY ANDY ALEDORT; PHOTO BY PAMELA LITTKY

MAY Pink Floyd guitarist David Gilmour details the making of his 2006 album *On an Island*, the headline-making reunion with his former Floyd bandmates at Live 8 and what the future may hold for the legendary prog-rock band.
COVER STORY BY ALAN DI PERNA; PHOTO BY ROSS HALFIN

JUNE After a five-year absence, Tool return with a transformed sound on *10,000 Days*. In this exclusive interview, Adam Jones tries to explain the methods and madness behind metal's most mysterious and unpredictable band.
COVER STORY BY CHRIS GILL; PHOTO BY JEFF NOVAK

JULY Red Hot Chili Peppers guitarist John Frusciante tells how Jimi Hendrix, meditation and a few friendly spirits shaped his band's 2006 double-length album, *Stadium Arcadium*.
COVER STORY BY ALAN DI PERNA; PHOTO BY ROSS HALFIN

JANUARY Kirk Hammett and *Guitar World* take an in-depth look at the making of Metallica's 1986 thrashterpiece, *Master of Puppets*. "It's still my favorite Metallica album," said Hammett. "It was just an amazing time for us."
COVER STORY BY MICK WALL; PHOTO BY ROSS HALFIN

2006 TOTAL ISSUES: 13

AUGUST Former Blink-182 guitarist Tom DeLonge launches his Angels & Airwaves project while AFI guitarist Jade Puget talk about his band's acceptance as a prog-punk force.
COVER STORIES BY ALAN DI PERNA
PHOTO BY ZACH CORDNER

SEPTEMBER The masters of metal—Slayer's Kerry King and Jeff Hanneman and Ozzy Osbourne/Black Label Society axman Zakk Wylde—join forces for a true headbanger's ball.
COVER STORIES BY RICHARD BIENSTOCK AND DAN EPSTEIN; PHOTO BY TRAVIS SHINN

OCTOBER In a massive online poll, *Guitar World* readers voted for the greatest guitar albums of all time—and this issue celebrates each and every record that made up the top hundred, from *Led Zeppelin IV* (#1) to the Doors' self-titled debut (#50) to the Black Crowes' 1992 smash, *The Southern Harmony and Musical Companion* (#100).
COVER STORY BY TOM BEAUJOUR, RICHARD BIENSTOCK, JOE BOSSO, ALAN DI PERNA, TED DROZDOWSKI, DAN EPSTEIN, CHRIS GILL, JOE LALAINA, ALAN PAUL, MAC RANDALL, BRAD TOLINSKI AND JON WIEDERHORN
PHOTO BY JUSTIN BORUCKI

NOVEMBER *Guitar World* celebrates the 25 most important new voices in guitar, including DragonForce, Avenged Sevenfold, Mars Volta, Mastodon and Lamb of God.
COVER STORY BY RICHARD BIENSTOCK
PHOTO BY DARAGH MCDONAGH

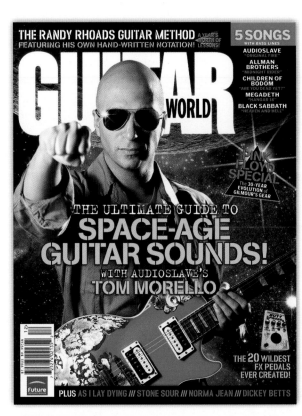

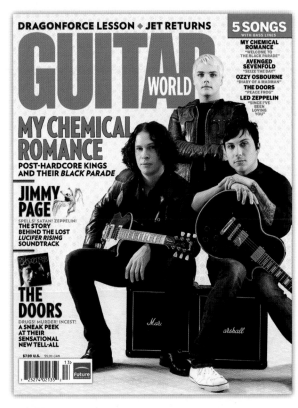

DECEMBER Rage Against the Machine/Audioslave guitarist Tom Morello talks about freaky tones, fractious band mates and Audioslave's funked-up 2006 album, *Revelations*. "The guitar is capable of so many different sounds," says the guitarist. "I don't think I've scratched the surface of what it can do."
COVER STORY BY JOE BOSSO; PHOTO BY JUSTIN BORUCKI

HOLIDAY Once pegged as emo darlings and goth-punk flavors of the week, My Chemical Romance raise the stakes and make their bid for rock immortality with their elaborate 2006 album, *The Black Parade*. "The goal was to make a classic album," says singer Gerard Way. "Something that would really stand the test of time."
COVER STORY BY ALAN DI PERNA; PHOTO BY JUSTIN BORUCKI

HERO OF THE DAY

IN THIS SPECIAL EDITION OF **DEAR GUITAR HERO,** **KIRK HAMMETT** GETS QUIZZED BY OUR **READERS** AND A HOST OF **METAL LUMINARIES,** INCLUDING MASTODON, LAMB OF GOD, EXODUS, EVERY TIME I DIE AND AVENGED SEVENFOLD.

Is it true that you broke your high E string when recording the solo in "Master of Puppets" when you hit that crazy high note toward the end?
—John Mulder

I didn't break the E string; I accidentally pulled the string down and off the fretboard. I actually fretted the string on my bridge pickup, creating a 27th or 32nd fret or whatever it is. It was just one of those happy accidents that was too cool to get rid of, and I've not been able to recreate it since.

How much time did you spend fine tuning your sound before you started recording Master of Puppets?
—Marcus Siepen
(Blind Guardian)

Three days of utter hell. [laughs] Three days of twisting knobs, placing mics and going through different amps. At the end of the first day, I was pretty bummed 'cause I hadn't gotten anything. At the end of the second day, the engineer, Flemming Larsen, and James [Hetfield] were getting on my case. By the third day, I managed to find a sound I was happy with, and everything else just flowed really quickly after that.

✛✛✛✛

When Master of Puppets was finished, did the band realize it had created such an important piece of heavy metal history?
—Mark Morton
(Lamb of God)

Master of Puppets wasn't written with that intention; we just wanted to make the best album we could. For us, it was just another Metallica album. We had put out Kill 'Em All, and it was a great album. We put out Ride the Lightning, and it seemed to have all the elements of Kill 'Em All and then some. Then we put out Master, and we were very proud of it. It was like having another feather in our cap.

At that point, we were firing on all cylinders and the songs just kept coming, so we really seized the moment. After we finished the album, we went straight out on tour. We were very intent on getting the music out to the people and touring as much as humanly possible. But Cliff's death changed all of that.

None of us had any idea Master of Puppets would still sound fresh after 20 years. I mean, I put it on the other day and the album's sound, songs and concepts are just as relevant today as they were back then.

✛✛✛✛

Can you pinpoint a time when you feel Metallica was at its creative peak, or do you feel that time has yet to come?
—Doc Coyle (God Forbid)

That's hard to answer. Maybe if you ask me that question in 20 years, I can give you a better answer. At this point in time, I can see many different creative peaks in our career. Master of Puppets and the Black Album were definitely peaks. The symphony album [S&M] was a different kind of peak, while St. Anger was yet another completely different peak. We've peaked in so many different ways. Some people would also say we have had a lot of valleys, too...which is a fair statement. [laughs]

I think Metallica have a lot more to say. We're the type of band that likes to experiment. We don't like to stay in one spot for too long; all the albums after the Black Album prove that. We're not afraid to take artistic risks, even at the cost of pissing off our audience and our friends.

✛✛✛✛

How did you feel about having the band's inner workings and conflicts exposed to the world in Some Kind of Monster?
—Julio Navarre

I've learned through my recording experience that weird magic can happen in tracking. Often my favorite songs in the writing process become my least favorite, and tunes that I'd barely paid attention to become my favorites. When Master of Puppets was completed, what surprised you the most about it?
—Mark Morton (Lamb of God)

I love Lamb of God! As for surprises, Mark, I'd have to say "The Thing That Should Not Be" shocked me the most. It was the second-to-last song written for the album; we wrote it fairly quickly and recorded it a week later. It was like jumping into a nice shiny sports car that you've never driven and being told to race it; you're just going to try to drive it as fast and as well as possible.

That was pretty much the case with "The Thing That Should Not Be." The guitar solo was done in half an hour because I had to catch a flight to New York. Even then, the song wasn't really finished; there were still a lot of guitar layers that needed to be added. When I finally got back to it and heard the rough mixes, I was like, "Wow, this sounds a lot better than I expected!"

I'm a very private person who enjoys his solitude, so I have my issues with the movie in that regard. At the same time, I think its great, 'cause it sheds light on what we went through. It also sheds light on the benefits of psychotherapy. If watching the movie can help people see the light they need to see, then I think that's a beautiful thing. I don't care if my solitude and privacy are sacrificed if ultimately it helps people.

I've discovered that people tend to see us as we were in the movie, but the film doesn't truly represent us. It was filmed several years ago, and we've moved on. We've grown as people and changed since then.

✛✛✛✛

In Some Kind of Monster we get to see Metallica's writing process from an interesting vantage point. Do you think the way you went about writing St. Anger had a negative impact on the final product?
—Andy Williams
(Every Time I Die)

I like Every Time I Die. You know, Andy, I actually forgot about the cameras most of the time. They just became nonentities after a while, because we had no idea that the footage would be turned into a movie that would be seen by fans all over the world. We thought it was just going to be a low-key documentary.

If anything impacted the writing process, it was just the inconvenience of having more bodies around. Cameramen would be standing over my pedal board when I needed to get to it, or sometimes there wouldn't be a chair to sit in 'cause there'd be a camera guy sitting there. Stupid stuff like that.

✛✛✛✛

Do you ever listen back to solos and cringe? If you could change any of your solos which one would it be?
—John Kempainen
(The Black Dahlia Murder)

JAN. 2006

VOL. 27 / NO. 1

Kirk Hammett

As *Guitar World* celebrates the 20th anniversary of *Master of Puppets*, **Kirk Hammett** gets quizzed by a host of metal luminaries.

Master of Puppets is considered one of the greatest metal albums, a classic album in a classic style that inspired generations of musicians. Do you think that style of epic, blistering, solo-filled metal will ever become popular again?

—Matt Heafy (Trivium)

HAMMETT In retrospect, *Master of Puppets* is my favorite Metallica album, and I would like to see other people make more albums like it. While a lot of metal bands have taken the basic elements we established on *Master* and expanded on them, no one has yet to make an album as good. At least I haven't heard it yet. But then again, I'm biased. [*laughs*]

I'm not saying that *Master* was the peak of metal or anything; there have been a lot of great metal albums since we recorded it. All I'm saying is that, from song to song, *Master of Puppets* is very consistent. It stays within the niche it carved for itself. And that niche is either very big, because of its range of influence, or very narrow, because I haven't really heard any album like it since.

When Master of Puppets was finished, did the band realize it had created such an important piece of heavy metal history?

—Mark Morton (Lamb of God)

HAMMETT *Master of Puppets* wasn't written with that intention; we just wanted to make the best album we could. For us, it was just another Metallica album. We had put out *Kill 'Em All*, and it was a great album. We put out *Ride the Lightning*, and it seemed to have all the elements of *Kill 'Em All* and then some. Then we put out *Master*, and we were very proud of it. It was like having another feather in our cap.

At that point, we were firing on all cylinders and the songs just kept coming, so we really seized the moment. After we finished the album, we went straight out on tour. We were very intent on getting the music out to the people and touring as much as humanly possible. But Cliff's death changed all of that.

None of us had any idea *Master of Puppets* would still sound fresh after 20 years. I mean, I put it on the other day and the album's sound, songs and concepts are just as relevant today as they were back then.

I fucking loved St. Anger. It seemed like you went back to your roots, said "Fuck you!" and did something totally different. And though I can see that dropping the solos was part of that attitude, I do miss them. When you record your next album, are you gonna throw some solos back on it?

—Zacky Vengeance (Avenged Sevenfold)

HAMMETT To be quite honest, I think the band misses solos just as much as the fans do. I mean, I play guitar solos every day! We've all expressed the fact that we think guitar solos are fun. They're dynamic, expressive and another distinct aspect of Metallica's music. And we miss that aspect.

Do you ever listen back to solos and cringe? If you could change any of your solos which one would it be?

—John Kempainen (The Black Dahlia Murder)

HAMMETT Yeah, there are a few solos I listen to and think, What the *hell* was I trying to do there? [*laughs*] There were a couple of solos on *Kill 'Em All* that were rushed, and I wish I could redo the solo on "The Frayed Ends of Sanity" from *...And Justice for All*. I recorded that solo at four in the morning. I was exhausted, but we needed to finish because the next day we were leaving for the Monsters of Rock tour with Van Halen. I really wish I had time to go back and redo that one. But the funny thing is, I've run into people who say it's their favorite solo on that album.

Have you taken lessons from anyone since you studied with Joe Satriani? Do you feel like you have learned anything from younger artists or players since Metallica became huge?

—Benjamin Weinman (Dillinger Escape Plan)

HAMMETT Oh, I love Dillinger! When I hear you all, I think, Oh my God, I was so *bad* at algebra. [*laughs*]

I'm the kind of guy who believes there's something to learn from every guitar player, because every player approaches his instrument differently. I think the guy in Muse [*Matthew Bellamy*] is an amazing guitarist, but I think Omar Rodriguez from the Mars Volta is the guitarist of the new generation who stands above everyone else. The things he can do with his instrument are just so amazing and exotic. I love the risks he takes and how he'll surprise you. He's not afraid to play out or come up with a crazy little song right in the middle of a passage. I also like how he paints colors with his playing and use of effects. I can say that Omar is a pretty good friend of mine, and playing with him is always a pleasure. I'm just so blown away by his unique approach. His overall vision is tremendous.

Do you still collect monster memorabilia? How big is your collection at this point?

—Brent Hinds (Mastodon)

HAMMETT Do I still collect? Is there *ever* an end? [*laughs*] My collection defines part of who I am. It's really important to me, because it's outside of the realm of music and Metallica. And, "How big is it?" Well, after all these years, let's just say my collection is *enormous*. Why? You got anything good, Brent? [*laughs*]

FEBRUARY / VOL. 27 / NO. 2

JIMMY PAGE & JACK WHITE

The Led Zeppelin legend and the garage rock icon explain how the blues plays a vital role in their distinct crafts.

GUITAR WORLD Jimmy, in Zeppelin you started with the blues and built outward.

JIMMY PAGE I wanted Zeppelin to have a lot of different elements to it. I wanted it to be a marriage of blues, hard rock and acoustic music, with lots of light and shade. It was also important for me to build unexpected melodies and harmonies within that framework. But I will say this: blues is the most challenging thing to play because it is so hard to say something original.

GW Jack, you've used primitive elements of the blues to rebel against what you perceive as an excessive and overly processed and technological culture.

JACK WHITE That's the main thing to rebel against in America right now—overproduction, too much technology, overthinking. It's a spoiled mentality; everything is too easy. If you want to record a song, you can buy Pro Tools and record 400 guitar tracks. That leads to overthinking, which kills any spontaneity and the humanity of the performance. What was interesting about Led Zeppelin was how well they were able to update and capture the essence of the scary part of the blues. A great Zeppelin track is every bit as intense as a Blind Willie Johnson recording.

GW Led Zeppelin's version of Bukka White's "Shake 'Em on Down" on Led *Zeppelin III* [*entitled "Hats Off to (Roy) Harper"*] is a great example of a track that captures the terrifying essence of the country blues without copying them.

PAGE The key is you don't want to copy the blues; you want to capture the mood. On *III*, we knew we wanted to allude to the country blues, but, in the tradition of the style, we felt it had to be spontaneous and immediate. I had this old Vox amp, and one day Robert [*Plant*] plugged his mic into the amp's tremolo channel, and I started playing and he started singing. And what you hear on the album is essentially an edit of our first two takes. The band had an incredible empathy that allowed us to do things like that.

Roger—Over & Out

MAY '06

Granting *Guitar World* his first interview in 10 years, David Gilmour spoke in the May 2006 issue about his *On an Island* album and Pink Floyd's historic reunion with bassist Roger Waters at the Live 8 benefit in 2005. The same issue featured an interview with Waters, who after years of battling with his erstwhile band mates expressed his eagerness to bury the hatchet and hit the road. It was, alas, too late for Gilmour, who told us, "I have moved on."

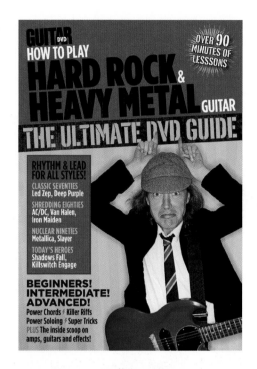

ADAM JONES

The Tool guitarist talks about his band's weird-and-wild composition methods and their first album in five years, *10,000 Days*.

GUITAR WORLD The songs on *10,000 Days* are structured more like classical music: they start in one place, go somewhere else and end in a completely different place altogether. It's as if the songs are telling a story in a linear fashion.

ADAM JONES Thanks. That's the thinking. This is going to sound really pretentious, but it's more emotional. For us, writing music is very therapeutic. You get to these different states, and it's almost like you're entertaining yourself. You're leading someone by the hand, but the hand you're leading is your own. I don't get choked up when I hear other people's music, except in a few rare instances. But if we write something I really like, I get teary eyed. I'm the kind of guy who can cry really easily.

GW You have an extensive background in the visual arts. Do you tend to visualize things when you're writing songs?

JONES I like soundtracks and I like film. I try to think in those terms, but it's more emotional. How can you describe something without telling the person what it is? If you wanted to explain the yellow color of that Kodak [*film*] box without showing the person yellow, how would you do that? You might be able to do it by saying, "You know when you feel like this or when this has happened or you're sitting under a tree?..."

GW How did you prepare for this record?

JONES There's always the influence of music, film, art and the other things that drive me. I'm usually inspired by my environment and whatever is making me happy or mad. By the time we decide to get together again and start jamming, Justin [*Chancellor, bass*] and I have a huge amount of material. We bring it in and everybody rips it apart like wolves. We explore every avenue and path of it and then choose the paths that work best with one another.

Guitar World Brings Metal to the DVD Masses

In 2005 *GW* launched a product line that would ultimately prove to be one of the most successful endeavors in the magazine's history: instructional DVDs. *How to Play Hard Rock & Heavy Metal: The Ultimate DVD Guide*, released in the summer of 2006, contained more than 90 minutes of instructional content, including how to riff like Tony Iommi and Angus Young, how to shred like Kirk Hammett and Zakk Wylde and strategies for drop tunings and harmonized lead lines...everything a player needs to be the heavy metal star of their dreams.

"If we write something I really like, I get teary eyed."—*Adam Jones*

OCT. 2006

VOL. 27 / NO. 10

The 100 Greatest
Guitar Albums
of All Time

GUITAR WORLD IS NO STRANGER TO LISTS. Over the years, we've devoted issues to such weighty matters as the 100 Greatest Solos of All Time, the 100 Greatest Guitarists of All Time and, though many would prefer to forget it, the 100 Worst Solos of All Time.

In 2006, for the first time in our 25-year history, we asked our readers to do the picking for us. The subject: nothing less than the 100 Greatest Guitar Albums of All Time. Here they are, in all their six-stringed glory.

1) Led Zeppelin—*Led Zeppelin IV*
2) Guns N' Roses—*Appetite for Destruction*
3) The Jimi Hendrix Experience—*Are You Experienced*
4) Metallica—*Master of Puppets*
5) Pink Floyd—*Dark Side of the Moon*
6) Black Sabbath—*Paranoid*
7) Van Halen—*Van Halen*
8) Nirvana—*Nevermind*
9) Led Zeppelin—*Physical Graffiti*
10) The Beatles—*Revolver*
11) Pantera—*Cowboys from Hell*
12) Metallica—*...And Justice for All*
13) Ozzy Osbourne—*Blizzard of Ozz*
14) Tool—*Aenima*
15) Pearl Jam—*Ten*
16) Stevie Ray Vaughan and Double Trouble—*The Essential Stevie Ray Vaughan and Double Trouble*
17) Iron Maiden—*The Number of the Beast*
18) The Red Hot Chili Peppers—*Blood Sugar Sex Magik*
19) The Rolling Stones—*Exile on Main St.*
20) Joe Satriani—*Surfing with the Alien*
21) Rage Against the Machine—*Rage Against the Machine*
22) Pink Floyd—*Wish You Were Here*
23) The Who—*Who's Next*
24) Yngwie J. Malmsteen—*Rising Force*
25) Megadeth—*Peace Sells...But Who's Buying?*
26) Kiss—*Alive!*
27) Rush—*Moving Pictures*
28) Radiohead—*OK Computer*
29) Slayer—*Reign in Blood*
30) Judas Priest—*British Steel*
31) Steve Vai—*Passion and Warfare*
32) Black Label Society—*Mafia*
33) System of a Down—*Toxicity*

34) U2—*The Joshua Tree*
35) Van Halen—*1984*
36) Pantera—*Vulgar Display of Power*
37) The White Stripes—*Elephant*
38) Smashing Pumpkins—*Mellon Collie and the Infinite Sadness*
39) Cream—*Disraeli Gears*
40) The Jimi Hendrix Experience—*Electric Ladyland*
41) Bob Dylan—*Highway 61 Revisted*
42) Korn—*Follow the Leader*
43) Lynyrd Skynyrd—*pronounced leh-nerd skin-nerd*
44) Children of Bodom—*Hate Crew Deathroll*
45) Soundgarden—*Badmotorfinger*
46) Metallica—*Metallica*
47) Queen—*A Night at the Opera*
48) Boston—*Boston*
49) Lamb of God—*Ashes of the Wake*
50) The Doors—*The Doors*
51) Deep Purple—*Machine Head*
52) Trivium—*Ascendency*
53) King Crimson—*Red*
54) Opeth—*Ghost Reveries*
55) The Mars Volta—*De-Loused in the Comatorium*
56) Aerosmith—*Toys in the Attic*
57) Ozzy Osbourne—*Diary of a Madman*
58) The Allman Brothers Band—*At Fillmore East*
59) Slipknot—*Slipknot*
60) Kiss—*Destroyer*
61) Alice in Chains—*Dirt*
62) Derek and the Dominos—*Layla and Other Assorted Love Songs*
63) Avenged Sevenfold—*City of Evil*
64) Frank Zappa—*Strictly Commercial: The Best of Frank Zappa*
65) Pink Floyd—*The Wall*
66) Blind-182—*Enema of the State*
67) Yes—*Close to the Edge*

68) AC/DC—*Highway to Hell*
69) Coheed and Cambria—*Good Apollo I'm Burning Star IV, Volume 1: From Fear Through the Eyes of Madness*
70) The Clash—*London Calling*
71) Neil Young & Crazy Horse—*Rust Never Sleeps*
72) Santana—*Abraxas*
73) Stone Temple Pilots—*Purple*
74) Green Day—*American Idiot*
75) Sonic Youth—*Goo*
76) Weezer—*Pinkerton*
77) AFI—*Sing the Sorrow*
78) Meshuggah—*Chaosphere*
79) Eric Johnson—*Ah Via Musicom*
80) In Flames—*Clayman*
81) Mötley Crüe—*Shout at the Devil*
82) Death—*Human*
83) Led Zeppelin—*Led Zeppelin II*
84) Robert Johnson—*The Complete Recordings*
85) Ted Nugent—*Cat Scratch Fever*
86) Shadows Fall—*The War Within*
87) Jeff Beck—*Blow by Blow*
88) Nevermore—*This Godless Endeavor*
89) ZZ Top—*Eliminator*
90) John Mayall—*Blues Breakers with Eric Clapton*
91) Tool—*10,000 Days*
92) Extreme—*Extreme II: Pornograffitti*
93) Venom—*Black Metal*
94) At the Drive-In—*Relationship of Command*
95) Dream Theater—*Scenes from a Memory*
96) Robin Trower—*Bridge of Sighs*
97) Scorpions—*Love at First Sting*
98) Ozzy Osbourne—*No More Tears*
99) Jimi Hendrix—*Band of Gypsys*
100) The Black Crowes—*The Southern Harmony and Musical Companion*

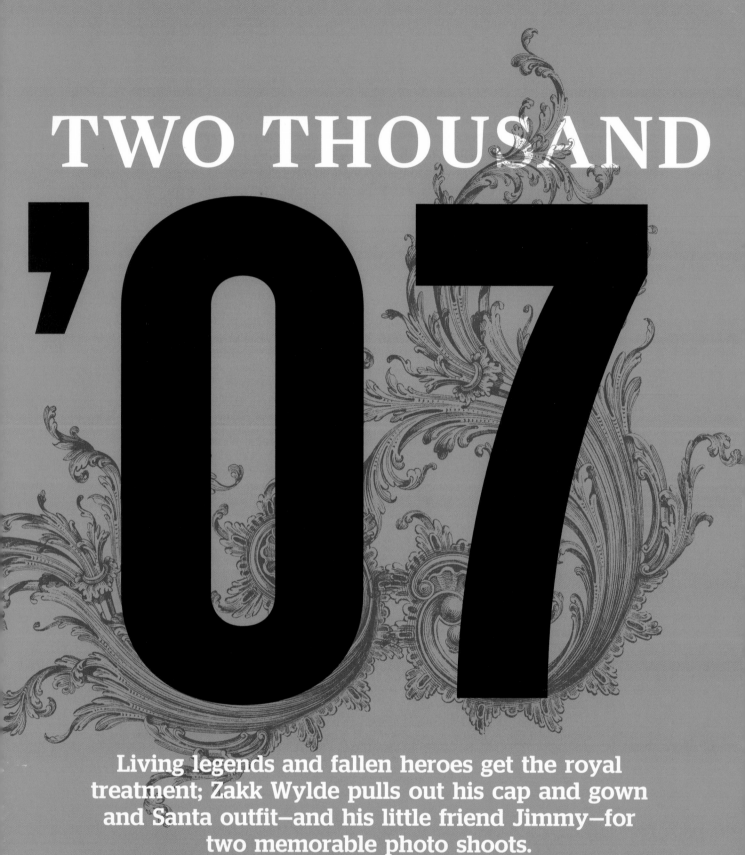

TWO THOUSAND
'07

Living legends and fallen heroes get the royal
treatment; Zakk Wylde pulls out his cap and gown
and Santa outfit—and his little friend Jimmy—for
two memorable photo shoots.

Dear *Guitar World*,

I know most girls can't play an instrument—we were only created to be enjoyed by the male form. Then once we get knocked up and used up, they move on to the next younger girl. Thank you for throwing women back in time with your Girls of *Guitar World* online gallery. I appreciate it. We don't deserve to keep our clothes on. I'm glad none of your models know how to play guitar, because if we were capable of playing, that just would not make sense. Don't mind people who come to your web site to look up a tab and are then bombarded by images of girls who have no idea how to play guitar, let alone hold one. They are just as ignorant as the imbeciles who decided that putting chicks with guitars in a magazine might help something. Congratulations, you've lost a reader.

—Jeanie Moore

JANUARY *Guitar World* presents a first-hand guide to shredding the modern metal way, with tips and techniques from members of Lamb of God, Megadeth, Arch Enemy and Trivium. "I think the secret to accurate picking is slowly speeding up," says Dave Mustaine. "Learn your rhythm parts slow, then gradually bring them up to speed."

COVER STORY BY NICK BOWCOTT; PHOTO BY DALE MAY

FEBRUARY 2007 Readers Poll MVP Zakk Wylde answers reader questions in a special double-length edition of Dear Guitar Hero. "If I can inspire 14-year-old kids to pick up the guitar the same way Eddie Van Halen and Randy Rhoads did to me, then I'm all for it."

PHOTO BY NEIL ZLOZOWER

MARCH Eddie Van Halen reveals the secrets behind his homemade Frankenstein guitar and the other gear that helped him create his famous "brown" sound.

COVER STORY BY CHRIS GILL
PHOTO BY ROSS HALFIN

APRIL *Guitar World* pays tribute to three fallen legends: Dimebag Darrell, Randy Rhoads and Duane Allman. In addition, we celebrate Chuck Schuldiner, death metal's pioneer and spiritual guide, on the fifth anniversary of his passing.

COVER STORIES BY NICK BOWCOTT, ALAN DI PERNA AND ANDY ALEDORT
COVER PAINTING BY TIM O'BRIEN

MAY Black Sabbath's historic reunion with Ronnie James Dio, the making of AC/DC's classic *Highway to Hell* album and Led Zeppelin's celebrated touring escapades make up this tribute to three living legends.

COVER STORIES BY GEORGE CASE, RICHARD BIENSTOCK AND MURRAY ENGLEHEART; COVER PAINTING BY TIM O'BRIEN

JUNE On the 40th anniversary of the Beatles' *Sgt. Pepper's Lonely Hearts Club Band*, engineer Geoff Emerick reveals the secrets behind rock and roll's most cataclysmic event.

COVER STORY BY CHRISTOPHER SCAPELLITI
PHOTO BY EVERETT COLLECTION

2007 TOTAL ISSUES: 13

AUGUST Jack White unleashes his demons on *Icky Thump*, the strangest, scariest, most intense White Stripes album ever. "Rock and roll is not really known for its great examples of human decency."
COVER STORY BY ALAN DI PERNA
PHOTO BY ROSS HALFIN

SEPTEMBER In his first post-rehab interview, Eddie Van Halen details the making of his new EVH 5150 III amp. "This amp is the cleanest and dirtiest and all things in between of anything I've ever played through."
COVER STORY BY CHRIS GILL
PHOTO BY OLAF HEINE

OCTOBER Joe Satriani and Steve Vai, the long-reigning kings of shred, trace their progression from teenage pals to masters of the fretboard universe.
COVER STORY BY ALAN DI PERNA
PHOTO BY TRAVIS SHINN

JULY On Velvet Revolver's new album, *Libertad*, former Guns N' Roses guitarist Slash sounds better and badder than ever. "When it came time to record, it really felt like everyone had put their stamp on each song."
COVER STORY BY RICHARD BIENSTOCK; PHOTO BY TRAVIS SHINN

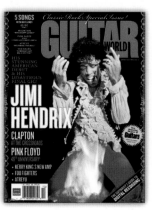

NOVEMBER *Guitar World* presents the ultimate guitar IQ challenge featuring 666 brain-bending questions about gear, musical theory, bands, albums and more.
COVER PHOTO BY PAMELA LITTKY

DECEMBER *Guitar World* delves deep into Jimi Hendrix's incendiary U.S. debut at the Monterey Pop festival in 1967 and takes a close look at the last gig the guitarist ever played, the disastrous Love + Peace festival.
COVER STORY BY ALAN DI PERNA; PHOTO BY ED CARAEFF

HOLIDAY Avenged Sevenfold guitarists Zacky Vengeance and Synyster Gates give *Guitar World* a sneak peak into the making of their spunky new self-titled album.
COVER STORY BY RICHARD BIENSTOCK; PHOTO BY DALE MAY

PAUL STANLEY
OF KISS

He plays in one of rock's most successful acts and has just released his first solo album in almost 30 years. But what Guitar World readers really want to know is...

What prompted you to record a new solo album, *Live to Win*, now when you hadn't recorded one for 28 years?
—Tom McAllister

You answered the question yourself. [*laughs*] For a long time I felt like I was the gatekeeper to Kiss. There were times, during lineup shifts or when people went off to try other projects, when I thought Kiss was in jeopardy. If I felt somebody had to be there to either mind the store or bail water, and I felt that somebody had to be me. But everybody reaches a point where they feel they have to satisfy their own creative challenges and aspirations, and this was really just the right time for me.

Are all the songs on the album new compositions, or did you cull from things you had lying around over time?
—Brandon Murphy

Everything's totally new. I'm not somebody who believes in saving or recycling songs. I've always believed that if a song was good enough when I wrote it, it would've been recorded. I also like the idea that when you buy something that I've had a hand in, it's today's news; it's not something that's been lying around. It's a reflection of where things are at for me right now.

For the album, did you work with session guys or players you were friends with?
—Steve Tanner

It wasn't a matter of going out and getting the hired guns. Most of the players were recommended to me by other players. I was really fortunate that I quickly wound up with a bunch of

players who were very in tune with what I was doing and who could give me what I wanted. All the players are top-notch guys, but I didn't want perfection in the studio; I wanted creativity and great feel.

How different was it making a record when you didn't have to have Gene Simmons' input for 50 percent of the time? Is it better to be the boss, or do you find yourself second guessing your decisions?
—Arthur Grabil

Actually, it was much more liberating not to write with a fixed group of people in mind. Making *Live to Win* was like being a film's director *and* casting agent: for each song, I knew exactly what I was looking for, so I was able to cast whomever I wanted to play it. With Kiss, it's more like knowing who's in the film and then writing the parts for them.

If you could play only one guitar for the rest of your life, what would it be?
—B.C. Bones

Wow. That's a tough one. My roots are in vintage guitars, and at this point I want a guitar that has a vintage feel but also feels like it's always been mine. Actually, Washburn and I are currently finishing the prototype for a really great guitar that embodies all the classic features of the guitars I grew up playing. I've always thought that guitar players, at least rock players, are pretty much divided between the Fender and the Gibson schools. In that sense, I've always been a Gibson man, but my guitar doesn't have to be a Gibson, as long as it embodies the

Do you ever feel competitive with other guitar players or feel you have something to prove?
—Don Crutchfield

Do I feel competitive? Oh gosh, no. I've spent the better part of 40 years playing guitar, really honing what I do. Are there people who play faster? Sure. Are there people who know more chords? Sure, but that's never been what I've been about. My goal is to be a guitar player who can pretty much handle anything—someone who can hold down the fort. To me, that's a guitar player's most important role. There are some really flashy lead guys around who couldn't play a solid rhythm with a gun to their head. [*laughs*] But no, I never feel competitive. I'd feel totally comfortable getting up and playing with anybody.

same features. Whew! That was a long answer to a short question.

You have stated in the past that the Kiss guitar sound is basically two guitars that sound like one big one. Can you expand on that?
—Jim

I remember going to see Humble Pie and loving how the guitar work of Steve Marriott and Peter Frampton, and later, Clem Clempson, melded into one big guitar sound. It doesn't mean playing in unison or playing the same chord formation; it's more like having two different voicings playing against one another and creating a chord that couldn't be produced by one guitarist alone.

I've heard that the long-term plan for Kiss is to get to a point where even you and Gene don't have to be onstage anymore. Is there any truth to that, and can Kiss exist without any of the four original members?
—John Estep

Well, the only part I take exception to in your question is the idea that we wouldn't *have* to be onstage. I think it's more that we might not *belong* onstage. We may reach a point where Kiss may be better off, and the fans may be better served, without us. The goal, as time goes on, is to be able to separate ourselves from what we created and still have it live on. Practically speaking, eventually our choice will be to do that or call it quits. I think that Kiss, loved or hated, has been a source of inspiration or irritation for as long as I can remember. And I'm proud of it.

Are you planning to record a new album with the current members of Kiss?
—Paul

I don't know. It's something that certainly comes up from time to time, but I have concerns. One concern is that the songs on which we've based our career have grown larger than life. They've become more than music: they're snapshots of people's lives, of what was going on when these people first heard a song or came to a concert. There's no way we can compete with that. I can write a song like "Psycho Circus," which I would put up against a lot of my earlier songs, and know that people will listen to it and say, "Oh, that's good. Now play 'Love Gun.'" And I understand that sentiment, because what is attached to those early songs is huge. So the idea of going into the studio to do a Kiss album, knowing that writing anything short of Beethoven or "Hey Jude" is not gonna cut it...it's the kind of reality check that may stop a person from giving it his all.

But having said that, under the right conditions, I would probably do it. With *Live to Win*, I've made an album that sounds exactly the way I think an album should sound. I can't imagine going backward from there, so if everyone was agreeable with the idea of me producing the album [*laughs*], then there would be something to talk about. But the idea of going in and having too many "cooks" is just not appealing to me.

What are your thoughts on Peter Criss' ex-wife, Lydia, writing a tell-all book [*Sealed with a Kiss; lydiacriss.com*] about the early days of Kiss? Have you spoken to Peter about it?
—Seth Myers

No, I haven't, and I really couldn't care less. When people write tell-all books, they write them from their perspective. It's like people looking at a car accident: things look very different depending on where you're standing. Also, we tend to make ourselves much more important in the story than we actually were. You know, the paper is probably too hard to use for toilet paper, but... [*laughs*] No, I'm not a fan of any of *those* types of books, whether they're memoirs or autobiographies or whatever. I think it was George Orwell who said it best, [*that*] the autobiography is the most outrageous form of fiction.

You've written so many classic songs. Can you pick one that you felt never lived up to the rest of the record and explain why?
—Dave Streud

I never felt that at the time I wrote a song. But in hindsight, there are some songs that I listen to and think, This is

not great. There have definitely been periods where Kiss' music has lost some of its direction or focus. Some of our songs from the Eighties don't hold up. An album like *Carnival of Souls*, to me, is a mistake of at least the magnitude of [*Music From*] *The Elder*. That's because *Carnival of Souls* was—not of my design, mind you—an attempt to be current or competitive with a style of music that we weren't a part of. It fell flat for that reason. That's not to say that it wasn't a good album, just that it had nothing to do with Kiss. Some of our songs from the Eighties were shallow. They just don't have the depth or the foundation of our other songs.

Have you watched *Gene Simmons Family Jewels*? You're much more private than Gene. Could you see cameras in your house following you around?
—Chad Smithfield

No, I haven't watched it. It has no appeal to me, whatsoever. Any attempt to film a reality program—whether it's a pseudo-reality show or an actual reality show—is going to make the situation itself unreal, just by nature of having cameras present. And no, I couldn't imagine it for myself. I'd rather have bamboo slivers put under my nails. To me, your sanity comes from your privacy. It's something sacred and all your own.

In the early days of Kiss, before you hit it big, what tactics helped you get through the rough spots?
—Steve Lott

Believing that I was right. You have to believe in yourself, because if you don't, who else will? And you always gotta meet the opposition with twice the force that they meet you. ❋

"Love Gun" intro!

Tune down one half step (low to high: Eb Ab Db Gb Bb Eb).

JAN.2007

Do you ever feel competitive with other guitar players or feel you have something to prove?

—Don Crutchfield

DO I FEEL COMPETITIVE? Oh gosh, no. I've spent the better part of 40 years playing guitar, really honing what I do. Are there people who play faster? Sure. Are there people who know more chords? Sure, but that's never been what I've been about. My goal is to be a guitar player who can pretty much handle anything—someone who can hold down the fort. To me, that's a guitar player's most important role. There are some really flashy lead guys around who couldn't play a solid rhythm with a gun to their head. [*laughs*] But no, I never feel competitive. I'd feel totally comfortable getting up and playing with anybody.

If you could play only one guitar for the rest of your life, what would it be? *—B.C. Bones*

WOW. THAT'S A TOUGH ONE. My roots are in vintage guitars, and at this point I want a guitar that has a vintage feel but also feels like it's always been mine. Actually, Washburn and I are currently finishing the prototype for a really great guitar that embodies all the classic features of the guitars I grew up playing. I've always thought that guitar players, at least rock players, are pretty much divided between the Fender and the Gibson schools. In that sense, I've always been a Gibson man, but my guitar doesn't have to be a Gibson, as long as it embodies the same features. Whew! That was a long answer to a short question.

You have stated in the past that the Kiss guitar sound is basically two guitars that sound like one big one. Can you expand on that? *—Jim*

I REMEMBER GOING TO SEE Humble Pie and loving how the guitar work of Steve Marriott and Peter Frampton, and later, Clem Clempson, melded into one big guitar sound. It doesn't mean playing in unison or playing the same chord formation; it's more like having two different voicings playing against one another and creating a chord that couldn't be produced by one guitarist alone.

You've written so many classic songs. Can you pick one that you felt never lived up to the rest of the record and explain why? *—Dave Streud*

I NEVER FELT THAT at the time I wrote a song. But in hindsight, there are some songs that I listen to and think, This is not great. There have definitely been periods where Kiss' music has lost some of its direction or focus. Some of our songs from the Eighties don't hold up. An album like *Carnival of Souls*, to me, is a mistake of at least the magnitude of *The Elder*. That's because *Carnival of Souls* was—not of my design, mind you—an attempt to be current or competitive with a style of music that we weren't a part of. It fell flat for that reason. That's not to

say that it wasn't a good album, just that it had nothing to do with Kiss. Some of our songs from the Eighties were shallow. They just don't have the depth or the foundation of our other songs.

Have you watched *Gene Simmons Family Jewels*? You're much more private than Gene. Could you ever see cameras in your house following you around?

—Chad Smithfield

NO, I HAVEN'T WATCHED IT. It has no appeal to me, whatsoever. Any attempt to film a reality program—whether it's a pseudo-reality or an actual reality show—is going to make the situation itself unreal, just by nature of having cameras present. And no, I couldn't imagine it for myself. I'd rather have bamboo slivers put under my nails. To me, your sanity comes from your privacy. It's something sacred and all your own.

What other rock vocalists do you admire?

—Roddy Currin

YOU CAN'T TALK ABOUT rock vocalists without talking about Robert Plant, Steve Marriott, Paul Rodgers and Paul McCartney. Those guys are the backbone of pretty much everything that's done, I don't care who's doing it. If you're not steeped in the work of one of those guys, you're most certainly steeped in the work of someone who was. It's amazing that those few guys—the founders, the role models—created the template for so many people.

My band is playing "Detroit Rock City" and I have the hardest time finding your tone. Please help! *—Jeff*

I TRY TO KEEP THINGS SIMPLE. Most of my main sound will come from my Randall head. Interestingly enough, it's one of the solid-state models that I was using during the *Psycho Circus* tour. Before that, I would never deviate from the classic British valve amps, but the fact is that this amp sounds every bit as good. We were once in the studio checking out amps, playing different heads, when Tommy [*Thayer*] famously said, "That's the best Marshall we have." And I said, "Well, that Marshall is a Randall." [*laughs*] I think it's always about the combination of your guitar, pickups and amp. And when it comes to a guitar's electronics, I'm not a big fan of overdistorted pickups. I prefer the sound of vintage PAF [*Patent Applied For*] pickups. To me, that's how a guitar should sound.

In the early days of Kiss, before you hit it big, what tactics helped you get through the rough spots?

—Steve Lott

BELIEVING THAT I was right. You have to believe in yourself, because if you don't, who else will? And you always gotta meet the opposition with twice the force that they meet you.

JUNE / VOL. 28 / NO. 6

"A DAY IN THE LIFE"

"A DAY IN THE LIFE"

TRACK 13 OF ALL THE TRACKS ON *SGT. PEPPER'S*, "A DAY in the Life" was the most difficult to record. The basic recording of instruments and vocals were on one four-track tape, while the orchestral overdubs that appear midway through the song and again at the end were on a second reel. To mix the song, two four-track machines had to be locked together, and even then, one of the machines would inevitably begin to run out of synchronization.

Despite—perhaps because of—the headaches that it caused, "A Day in the Life" is a special track to Emerick. "It's one of my favorites, right up there with 'Tomorrow Never Knows,'" he says. "Even from when John first started singing it, the shivers just went down our backs. I can still see that first session now: we used to turn the lights off in the control room and just work that way, from the glow of the tubes in the equipment."

Even 40 years on, he can find something new in its plaintive sounds. "Now that we're talking about it, I'm thinking for the first time that that was the romantic side of John trying to come out. Everyone says that the magic combination of Paul and John is that Paul was the romantic and John was the aggressive one, and it was that combination that made these tracks. But now thinking about it, I think that was John's romantic side coming out in his vocals. There's so much feeling in those vocals. There's a lot of meaning, and it just came out. It wasn't contrived."

For all the power of Lennon's vocal, the orchestral climaxes that punctuate the song are among its most exciting

Guitar World's Christopher Scapelliti, along with *Sgt. Pepper's Lonely Hearts Club Band* engineer Geoff Emerick, detail the making of the great Beatles track.

OF ALL THE TRACKS ON *Sgt. Pepper's*, "A Day in the Life" was the most difficult to record. The basic recording of instruments and vocals were on one four-track tape, while the orchestral overdubs that appear midway through the song and again at the end were on a second reel. To mix the song, two four-track machines had to be locked together, and even then, one of the machines would inevitably begin to run out of synchronization.

Despite—perhaps because of—the headaches that it caused, "A Day in the Life" is a special track to Emerick. "It's one of my favorites, right up there with 'Tomorrow Never Knows,'" he says. "Even from when John [*Lennon*] first started singing it, the shivers just went down our backs. I can still see that first session now: we used to turn the lights off in the control room and just work that way, from the glow of the tubes in the equipment."

For all the power of Lennon's vocal, the orchestral climaxes that punctuate the song are among its most exciting moments. To create them, a 40-piece orchestra was hired to play a crescendo over 24 measures, starting quietly on the lowest note of their instruments and moving up in pitch to their highest E. Furthermore, the performers were instructed to climb the scales at their own pace and not to follow what their neighbor was playing. To classically trained musicians, accustomed to working from a prepared score and playing as a unit, this was simply unacceptable, and several of them adamantly refused to play.

"Oh, they were pretty stuffy," says Emerick. "It's unbelievable that, for musicians of that caliber, such a score would cause such confusion and discussion." It didn't help that the Beatles had decided to turn the recording of the event into a party—a "happening," as they were called in the day—complete with balloons, costumes, red rubber noses and bear paws.

Completed in late February, "A Day in the Life" was a major event in the making of *Sgt. Pepper's*, one that influenced the Beatles' sense of what they were achieving. "Once we recorded that," says Emerick, "they became more positive and more confident in the tracks we made—because it was like the best thing you've ever heard in your life."

THE G SPOT / THE ANNUAL G3 SHREDFEST IS THE HOTTEST PLACE FOR DAZZLING DISPLAYS OF GUITAR VIRTUOSITY. THIS YEAR'S TOUR MATES—JOE SATRIANI, JOHN PETRUCCI AND PAUL GILBERT—SIT DOWN TO RAP ABOUT LICKS, TECHNIQUE AND THE ELUSIVE VIRTUE KNOWN AS "STYLE." BY ALAN DI PERNA

G3 tour mates Joe Satriani, John Petrucci and Paul Gilbert sound off on guitar clichés.

JUL. '07

JOE SATRIANI I think that if you play rock music, the top cliché is that Albert King jumping-off point and returning point.
GUITAR WORLD You mean the lick that Clapton appropriated in "Strange Brew"?
SATRIANI All of that. Just the whole minor pentatonic box. We're all guilty. If we share anything, it's that little Albert King thing that everyone has agreed to steal and never talk about.
PAUL GILBERT I think one of the worst clichés is not stopping. If you're a rock guitar player, you tend to have a lot of distortion. And if you stop, bad things start happening. The amp starts hissing and buzzing. But if you continue to play, the notes are louder than the noise. So guitar players tend to be the opposite of singers or horn players, who have to breathe.
JOHN PETRUCCI I don't have the ability to stop. [*laughs*] No idea at all. I play with way too much gain.
GW Alright, now John has to contribute a cliché to the list.
PETRUCCI A cliché that always finds its way into a jam at least once is that Chuck Berry riff. You can't have a jam without it.

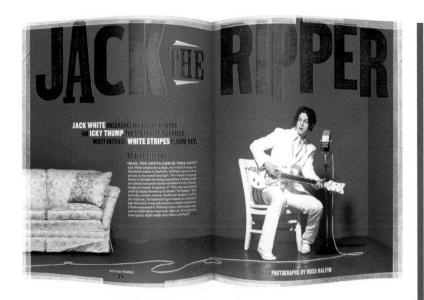

AUGUST / VOL. 28 / NO. 8

JACK WHITE

The White Stripes frontman explains the haunting themes and mystical motifs found in "300 M.P.H." and other songs from *Icky Thump*.

GUITAR WORLD "300 M.P.H." is one of several songs on *Icky Thump* where this figure of the red-headed woman appears—the scarlet woman, the temptress. What's with that motif?

JACK WHITE I guess that's always been there in my songs. There's this Mexican folktale of La Llorona, the crying woman, who is sometimes a redhead as well. There's these figureheads when you're writing songs, and you can base things off them. On *Get Behind Me Satan*, the redhead was [*Forties actress*] Rita Hayworth. I think redheads are most compelling to me when I'm writing, because they're so different and some cultures find them evil or are scared of them. Some cultures make fun of redheads when they're kids. They just seem a little bit left of center and a lot more interesting to talk about.

GW Plus red is part of the White Stripes color motif.

WHITE Yeah...luckily.

GW It's a death-haunted song, too, "300 M.P.H."

WHITE In a lot of these songs, the characters are at some kind of turning point in their lives, one of those moments when they're taking a deep breath and saying, "Hey, I don't have much time on this earth. Maybe I should think about some of this stuff." There are all these fundamental questions: Why do you bother getting up in the morning? How much should you care about other people and how much should you care about yourself? How considerate should you be? And how much should you just look out for your own self. These characters are trying to find some kind of purpose for what they do on a daily basis. You know, it's sometimes hard to get a perspective on this when you're surrounded by people in the music business and on tour all the time. Rock and roll is not really known for its great examples of human decency.

Immortal

Norway's black metal legends reflect on the murder that rocked their scene to its core.

GUITAR WORLD Do you remember your reaction when you first heard about [*Burzum founder*] Varg Vikernes murdering [*Mayhem guitarist*] Euronymous?

DEMONAZ It was a shock to us all. Basically, it was a conflict between him and Varg. Up until that time we were very much in contact with Euronymous. I had known him from a long time before, and he was always really into Immortal's stuff.

ABBATH Euronymous was very supportive of Immortal and we really liked and appreciated that. He meant a lot for Immortal in our early stage. And that he got killed...I just wished...it was just so *extra* bad that Varg was involved in that murder, because Varg was also a friend of ours. It was a *fucking tragedy*. There's just no other way to say it.

THE ULTIMATE GUITAR I.Q. CHALLENGE

THINK YOU KNOW EVERYTHING ABOUT MUSIC, GUITARISTS AND GEAR? PUT YOUR KNOWLEDGE TO THE TEST AS **GUITAR WORLD** PRESENTS 666 QUESTIONS DESIGNED TO TICKLE, TEASE AND TORTURE YOUR GUITAR-LOVIN' BRAIN.

SO, DEAR *GUITAR WORLD* READER, you've been reading our magazine all these years, absorbing every little detail you can about guitars, gear, theory and more. Undoubtedly you've remembered some things better than others and had some measure of success with the lessons in our monthly instructional columns.

But maybe you've been wondering just how much you really know about the artists and music represented in our pages. Well, here's your chance to find out.

Over the next many pages are gathered 666 questions that will test your knowledge of guitarists and bands, in every genre, as well as your expertise in the world of guitars, amps and pedals. Our greatest minds have devised questions to assess your grasp of beginning, intermediate and advanced music theory. Plus, we've gathered up hundreds of brain teasers about music lyrics, guitarists' real names, guitar models and shapes—and so much more.

But what would an IQ test be without a scoring system? To discover where you fit in the evolutionary scale of guitarists, simply add up your correct answers and check the graph below. So grab a pencil, and get to work! By the time you're finished, you'll be a little wiser about music—and yourself!

GUITARIST EVOLUTIONARY SCALE
How Do You Score?

| 0-100 CHIMP | 101-200 NEANDERTHAL | 201-300 DUDE | 301-400 "THE MAN" | 401-500 ROCK STAR | 501-666 ROCK GOD |

46
MUSIC TRIVIA:
Style Makers
Guitarists in classic rock, metal, extreme/underground metal, shred, the blues, punk, alternative and Eighties rock. **Plus:** Zakk Wylde, Jimi Hendrix

72
GEAR:
Sound Check
Guitars, amps, guitar shapes, parts of the guitar, pedals and effects, signature and standard guitar models. **Plus:** Stevie Ray Vaughan, Van Halen, Led Zeppelin

96
THEORY:
Class Ax

LEVEL 1:
Scales & Modes

LEVEL 2:
Guitar Theory

LEVEL 3:
Chord Theory

98
HITS & MISCELLANY:
All Faced Up
Song lyrics, guitarists' real names, anagrams and *Guitar World* magazine trivia. **Plus:** Randy Rhoads and Dimebag Darrell

PHOTOGRAPH BY PAMELA LITTKY / ILLUSTRATION BY DAVE CURD

NOV. 2007

VOL. 28 / NO. 11

Ultimate Guitar I.Q. Challenge

A sampling of the 666 brain-bending music and gear trivia questions from *Guitar World's*

1. Poison's original band name was
a) London
b) Waco
c) Paris

2. What name did Rivers Cuomo play under in his pre-Weezer prog project Avant Garde?

3. What D.C. hardcore band did Foo Fighters frontman Dave Grohl play drums for before he joined Nirvana?

4. This amp introduced in 1990 had controls that went to 20 and was endorsed by Spinal Tap's Nigel Tufnel. What model is it?

5. Crate amplifiers got their name because:
a) They used to be shipped in wooden crates.
b) Their first models were housed in unfinished pine boxes that looked like crates.
c) They were sold to stores for a C-rate discount.
d) The original models were battery powered, and a battery's charge is measured in C-rate.
e) Their first choice, PV, was too similar to Peavey.

6. Solve this anagram:
A Bit Uncork

7. Solve this anagram:
Bag of Mold

8. Solve this anagram:
Landward Heaven

9. Where is the House of the Rising Sun?

10. Huddie Ledbetter was the self-styled King of the 12-string guitarists. What was his nickname?

11. He played a Telecaster with a 100-foot lead and his nickname was "The Iceman." Who is he?

12. Lemmy Kilmister was a member of which band before he formed Motörhead?
a) Hogwarts
b) Hawkwind
c) Lord Muttonchop

13. What David Bowie album features guest appearances by Pete Townshend and Robert Fripp?

14. Who replaced Joe Perry in Aerosmith from 1979 until 1984?
a) Jimmy Crespo
b) Jim Beam
c) Steve Stevens

15. Which of his guitar heroes did Dimebag Darrell have tattooed on his chest?
a) Randy Rhoads
b) Eddie Van Halen
c) Ace Frehley

16. Flanging is named after:
a) Electronics whiz Augustus Flanger
b) The flange or rim of a tape reel
c) What it sounds like when you flang a cat across the room

17. When Les Paul ended his endorsement with Gibson, the Les Paul models were renamed SG. What do the initials "SG" stand for?
a) Spanish Guitar
b) Solid Guitar
c) Shecky Greene, Les Paul's main rival at the time
d) Super Gibson

18. These two radical-shaped Gibson models were unsuccessful when introduced in 1958 and discontinued in 1963 after less than a hundred of each model was produced. Now they're extremely popular with rock and metal musicians. What models are they?

19. Which guitar solo did our readers in August 2002 declare the greatest?
a) "Eruption" by Edward Van Halen
b) "Stairway to Heaven" by Jimmy Page
c) "One" by Kirk Hammett
d) "Crazy Train" by Randy Rhoads

20. Which song did we misspell on our cover?
a) "Smoke on the Water"
b) "Stairway to Heaven"
c) "Layla"

21. These lyrics are from which song? "Well, my name is a number / A piece of plastic film / And I'm growin' funny flowers / In my little window sill."

22. What Judas Priest song was cited in the 1990 subliminal-message lawsuit against the group?

23. In 1989, Metallica lost to what band in the Grammy Awards category of Best Hard Rock/Metal Performance?

24. If you have two notes that are a major third apart and you lower the higher note by a half step, what interval is produced?

25. King Diamond was forced to alter his makeup after what famous rocker threatened to sue him? ✱

TWO THOUSAND '08

300 issues and counting. *Guitar World* reaches a major milestone; Jimmy Page, Kirk Hammett, Tony Iommi, Slipknot and others join in the celebration.

Dear *Guitar World*,

I think the best part of the 300th [May 2008]
issue was looking back through past covers and
remembering where I was in life when each cover
graced the shelves. I can remember exactly where
I was when I bought so many different issues and
where I was musically and in life. From my first
September '94 "Pink Floyd Returns" issue, which
I convinced my mom to buy me, to the latest
300th issue and a closetful in between, life
has never been quite the same. Congrats on 300
issues. Keep 'em coming!

—Dustin Smith

JANUARY Jimmy Page offers his most candid discussion of the upcoming Led Zeppelin reunion and his dancing days in the Seventies.
COVER STORY BY BRAD TOLINSKI; PHOTOS BY ROSS HALFIN

FEBRUARY Metallica's Kirk Hammett makes the key tones from his career available to players everywhere with his brand-new signature model Randall amplifier.
COVER STORY BY ALAN DI PERNA; PHOTO BY ROSS HALFIN

MARCH Three years after Dimebag Darrell's untimely death, Dime's longtime girlfriend Rita Haney gives *GW* a revealing look inside the heart and soul of metal's lost cowboy from hell.
COVER STORY BY CHRIS GILL; PHOTO BY NEIL ZLOZOWER

APRIL Edward and Wolfgang Van Halen talk about working and performing together as father and son in Van Halen.
COVER STORY BY CHRIS GILL; PHOTO BY JILL GREENBERG

MAY *Guitar World* celebrates its 300th issue with a detailed retrospective of the magazine's past 28 years.
WRITTEN AND EDITED BY CHRISTOPHER SCAPELLITI; COVER COMPOSITE AND PHOTOGRAPHIC ILLUSTRATION BY DALE MAY

JUNE Slash and Joe Perry, the faces of *Guitar Hero III* and *Guitar Hero: Aerosmith*, talk about what it takes to be a real guitar hero.
COVER STORIES BY RICHARD BIENSTOCK
PHOTOS BY ROSS HALFIN (PERRY) AND
TRAVIS SHINN (SLASH)

JULY Looking back at his 25-year career, Yngwie Malmsteen talks about technique and tone and the new album that will be his magnum opus to end all tour de forces.
COVER STORY BY CHRIS GILL
PHOTO BY DALE MAY

2008 TOTAL ISSUES: 13

AUGUST Dan Donegan explains the meaning behind Disturbed's newest pro-military/anti-war effort, *Indestructible*. "Nobody wants to send their sons and daughters off to war, especially one that we can't all agree on."

COVER STORY BY JOE BOSSO; PHOTO BY DALE MAY

SEPTEMBER *Guitar World* celebrates the 40th anniversary of *Electric Ladyland*, Jimi Hendrix's greatest triumph and one of rock and roll's most vital albums.

COVER STORY BY ALAN DI PERNA; PHOTO BY KARL FERRIS

OCTOBER As the midwest rivers rise and civilizations fall, Slipknot guitarists Mick Thomson and Jim Root find a patch of dry land and talk about their group's apocalyptic new release, *All Hope Is Gone*. "There's some great, beautiful shit in the world," says Thomson, "but the ugliness overtakes the beauty."

COVER STORY BY CHRIS GILL PHOTO BY DALE MAY

NOVEMBER *Guitar World* heads to England to learn how Herman Li and Sam Totman play the insanely precise and blazingly fast solos, harmonies and rhythms that have made DragonForce the biggest name in heavy metal shred. "The better you get," says Li, "the harder it gets because you don't want to repeat yourself."

COVER STORY BY CHRIS GILL PHOTO BY ROSS HALFIN

DECEMBER Metallica's James Hetfield and Kirk Hammett talk about why the band burned its bridges with *St. Anger* and explain how it rose from the ashes to create *Death Magnetic*. "I wasn't a big fan of not having any solos on the last album," says Hetfield.

COVER STORIES BY BRAD TOLINSKI; PHOTOS BY ROSS HALFIN

HOLIDAY Forty years after Black Sabbath's birth, Tony Iommi reflects on his riff-tastic career and his legacy as the electric wizard who defined metal for the ages. "When I look at MySpace, I can't believe all of the bands that are inspired by us. I'm really proud to have had such a positive influence on so many people."

COVER STORY BY CHRIS GILL PHOTO BY ROSS HALFIN

LORDS
OF THE
STING

By
RICHARD BIENSTOCK
Photographs by
ROSS HALFIN

THIRTY-FIVE YEARS AFTER THEIR DEBUT, THE SCORPIONS STILL PACK A LETHAL DOSE OF HEAVY METAL VENOM. GUITARISTS RUDOLF SCHENKER AND MATTHIAS JABS DISCUSS THE HISTORY AND HITS OF GERMANY'S MOST DANGEROUS METALHEADS.

JAN. 2008

VOL. 29 / NO. 1

Rudolf Schenker & Matthias Jabs

he Scorpions guitarists look back at some of the hits that catapulted their band to worldwide

GUITAR WORLD It's been 35 years since the release of *Lonesome Crow*. Listening to the record today, it hardly sounds like the work of the band we've come to know as the Scorpions. The music is very psychedelic and jammy.

RUDOLF SCHENKER We were just trying to find our own way. We liked Black Sabbath, Led Zeppelin, Jeff Beck...all that hard rock stuff. No question about it. But we didn't want to sound like any of them. Also, Germany back then was very much into experimental music—what the international press labeled "Krautrock." All the bands were very progressive, and many used German lyrics. We didn't want to do that either. At the same time, we didn't want to be too commercial. So we made up our own sound. On that first album we had stuff like "Action," which was kind of jazzy, and "I'm Going Mad," which was a little more rock.

GW The Scorpions' big commercial breakthrough in America came with 1982's *Blackout*. The album featured "No One Like You," which was a huge MTV hit. How did that song come together?

SCHENKER "No One Like You" was something I had composed a few years earlier, but I kept it in my pocket because Klaus [*Meine, singer*] didn't like it so much. I don't think he heard the quality. But while we were recording the basic tracks for *Blackout*, Klaus' voice began to give out. It got so bad that after three weeks we had to stop production while he underwent two operations on his vocal cords. During this period I had a lot of free time to compose, and I came up with a few songs to add to the album, like "China White" and "Dynamite." I also pulled out "No One Like You" again. I brought it to the other guys and they said, "Yes, that's a great song. Let's do it." And now Klaus loves it, but he still complains. He says, "I know why I didn't want to do this song. It's a very hard one for me to sing in concert because it's very high!"

GW While Klaus was laid up, you had Don Dokken come in and sing on demos for some of the songs on *Blackout*. How did that come about?

MATTHIAS JABS Dieter [*producer Dieter Dierks*] was working with Dokken at the time and brought Don to his studio [*Dierks Studios*] in Cologne, where we were recording. We got to know each other, and he came in and sang a few pilot vocals while Klaus was in the hospital. You can hear his voice on the backing vocals on "You Give Me All I Need," but otherwise Klaus redid everything once he was better.

GW There was a rumor at the time that Don had replaced Klaus in the Scorpions.

JABS No, that was never going to happen. Don must have spread that rumor himself!

GW Matthias, how did you come up with the harmony guitar melody that opens "No One Like You"?

JABS The first time I heard "No One Like You" it was just the simple three or four chords that run through the verse and chorus, and it had a different name. I think it was called something like "Talk About You." I was sitting with my little four-track listening to the vocal melody, and pretty quickly I had the inspiration to come up with that intro part. Then I came up with the harmony that goes over it. That type of melody was typical of my style, and it's something I brought to the Scorpions. I always did those harmony-lead intros.

GW You play a similar one on "Rock You Like a Hurricane," from 1984's *Love at First Sting*.

JABS Exactly. It's the same principle. It's just what I used to do at the time. It's like, okay, there's a 16-bar intro, and if the song inspired me, that's what I would do. But I've done it now so many times that at some point I stopped, because I didn't want to be too repetitious.

GW You recently released your 16th studio album, *Humanity—Hour 1*. Are you surprised that the Scorpions have lasted this long?

SCHENKER My dream was always for this band to stick together for a long time, but I wasn't sure if it would work out or not. Especially when you have success like we did in the Eighties: the egos get bigger, and there's so much partying and people lose perspective. Then it's really hard to hold a band together because it's getting too crazy. But we went through the hard times of grunge and alternative and have also had the opportunity to try different things, like playing with an orchestra, doing an acoustic record and now, with *Humanity—Hour 1*, releasing a concept album. Plus, we've had some great musicians and managers working with us over the years. And, of course, we've had great fans. We're very thankful for everything we've been able to achieve. ✱

TONY IOMMI & BULLET FOR MY VALENTINE

Bullet for My Valentine's Matt Tuck and Michael Paget seize a rare opportunity to quiz their hero, Black Sabbath's Tony Iommi.

Bullet for My Valentine's Matt Tuck and Michael Paget are granted an audience with metal's sepulchral patriarch, Black Sabbath's own Tony Iommi

The Punks Meet The Godfather

MATT TUCK You're considered by millions to be the godfather of heavy metal. How does that title make you feel?

TONY IOMMI Old! Seriously, though, it's a great honor for people to look to me in that way, probably because it's taken a long time for me to get to this point in my life. Thirty-five, 40 years ago, it was quite difficult and I was struggling like everyone else.

MICHAEL PADGET Did you ever think when you were starting out that you'd be looking back on a career that has spanned numerous albums and so much success?

IOMMI No, you can never think like that. I remember back in 1970 or 1972 when we were doing an interview with some music magazine like *Sounds* or *Melody Maker*, and they were asking us, "Don't you think it's about time you gave up? When are you gonna stop all this?" Those questions were surrounding us even then. But you can never answer them.

TUCK You've had so many great moments on guitar. What has been your proudest achievement as a guitarist?

IOMMI I wouldn't know where to start with this question. I guess, after all the Ozzy years of Sabbath, the biggest jump for me was when we did *Heaven and Hell* with Ronnie [*James Dio, in 1980*], because it was another challenge. There we were, having done all those albums with our first singer, Ozzy, which were really successful, and suddenly we had to change to another singer. It was very hard to go out there and record another album, tour it and make it a hit. But we did it, and we had great success with that lineup, so that was a major achievement for me, personally.

TUCK You've written some enormous riffs over the years. What would you consider to be your best?

IOMMI I like "Into the Void," that's one of my favorites. But the popular ones are "Iron Man" and, for some reason, "Paranoid." I mean, that's the simplest bloody riff in the universe! That song was originally written as a joke, just some filler for the album. That song makes me wanna scream, because that riff is so bloody simple, but it's all people ask about.

Edward & Wolfgang Van Halen

The father and son duo talk about being in the unique position of performing together.

Like Father, Like

APR. '08

GUITAR WORLD Wolfgang, you play several instruments—guitar, drums, keyboards. What drove you toward the bass?

WOLFGANG Well, it was the only open spot. [*laughs*] And the people filling the other spots—drums and guitar—are the two greatest players of those instruments in the frickin' world. I find the bass safe. You don't have to go out on the line.

ED I remember another thing you said at the very beginning: "Can I just groove?"

WOLFGANG I just like to be there to groove and keep the song going.

GW Ed, What's it like to be onstage with your son as a band member, not just a special guest like he was on the previous tour?

ED I have pictures of me sitting in the racquetball court in my pajamas with an acoustic guitar and Wolfgang is probably just two-and-a-half-feet tall. I'll never forget the day I saw his foot tapping along in beat! I knew then, I couldn't wait for the day I'd be able to make music with my son. I don't know what more I could ask for.

JUNE / VOL. 29 / NO. 6

PAUL GILBERT & ROBIN TROWER

After years of worshipping from afar, speed demon Paul Gilbert finally meets and interviews the British blues legend.

PAUL GILBERT Do you remember your first steps on the guitar? Did you learn a pentatonic scale? What were the earliest things?

ROBIN TROWER Chords from a chord book. I just tried to learn chords. It seemed that that's how music works. It didn't take me very long.

GILBERT So the guitar came naturally to you. But what took effort?

TROWER I was never a great practicer. I think it all comes naturally. But that's because I've been playing so long, I think. By the time I became a solo artist, I'd already been playing for 14 years. So even though I didn't practice, I had a lot of experience.

GILBERT Maybe you didn't practice alone in your bedroom, but you were doing a lot of rehearsing for shows.

TROWER Yeah, I had a huge amount of experience then. And when I started to write my own music, the lead work naturally blossomed out of the music I was writing. All the soloing and lead guitar parts come out of the music. The actual lead solo and stuff—it grows out of each song. It's an entity unto itself. Why somebody like Albert King is the greatest is because, compositionally, his solos are beautiful melodies. You want soloing to be free. You want it to be something that you've just invented in that moment. But at the same time, you want it to be compositionally right.

GILBERT So that you're not just babbling, you're telling a story right off the top of your head.

TROWER Absolutely. It's got to be compositionally right for the song, not just some licks you've learned and are overlaying.

GILBERT As you're improvising, are there certain things you focus on to help your improvising? Are you listening to the drummer?

TROWER No. When I'm improvising long, moody solos, I tend to not hear what I'm playing to. I'm sure it's there subconsciously. But I'm so wrapped up in what I'm doing that I'm not consciously hearing what I'm playing to.

The 50 Fastest Guitarists of All Time

Guitar World compiles a controversial list of the ultimate speed demons.

JUL. '08

Trey Azagthoth (Morbid Angel)
Mick Barr
Michael Angelo Batio
Jason Becker
Buckethead
Dimebag Darrell
Paco de Lucia
Marty Friedman
Synyster Gates (Avenged Sevenfold)
Danny Gatton
Paul Gilbert
John 5
The Great Kat
Richie Kotzen
Alexi Laiho (Children of Bodom)
Shawn Lane
Albert Lee
Alvin Lee
Jeff Loomis (Nevermore)
Yngwie Malmsteen
John McLaughlin (Mahavishnu Orchestra)
Steve Morse
John Petrucci (Dream Theater)
Les Paul
Django Reinhardt
Randy Rhoads
Joe Satriani
Chuck Schuldiner (Death)
Alex Skolnick (Testament)
Timo Tolkki (Stratovarius)
Herman Li & Sam Totman (DragonForce)
Steve Vai
Eddie Van Halen
Ben Weinman (Dillinger Escape Plan)
Johnny Winter
Allan Holdsworth
Al Di Meola
Frank Gambale
Chris Impellitteri
Guy Mann-Dude
Maestro Alex Gregory
Vinnie Moore
Uli Jon Roth
Jimmy Bryant
Cliff Gallup
Larry Collins and Joe Maphis "Flying Fingers"
Johnny Hiland
Cary and Larry Parks
Jimmy Olander

And, according to our readers, those we forgot: Kerry King, George Lynch, Michael Romeo, Chris Broderick, Vernon Reid, Joe Stump, David T. Chastain, Marc Rizzo, Joe Pass, Hughie Thomasson, Kirk Hammett, Jeff Waters, Ritchie Blackmore, Danny Gatton...

V Will Rock U

James Hetfield returns to his roots, picks up his original Flying V and vows once again to kill 'em all.
By Brad Tolinski † Photographs by Ross Halfin † Illustration by John Dyer Baizley

Guitar World 40

DEC.2008

VOL. 29 / NO. 12

James Hetfield

**Metallica's main man talks about how the band's new *Death Magnetic* rights some
of *St. Anger*'s wrongs, and also looks at his own progression as a rhythm guitar**

GUITAR WORLD How would you describe *Death Magnetic*?

JAMES HETFIELD I guess I would say that it's a look backward—taking the essence of our earlier style and playing it with our current skills. It's impossible to completely regain your innocence or virginity. When we recorded our first albums, we had no regard for authority or for the way things were supposed to be. We'd walk into a studio and we'd play what we knew and that was that. Some of the engineers would complain and say things like, "You can't hear the vocal, or "You can't hear the guitar...what's that sound?" And we'd say, "That's us! Record it, please." [*laughs*] We tried to capture that attitude again. It's one of the reasons we chose Rick Rubin to produce the album. He's good at capturing the essence of the artists he works with.

GW The new album references the past, but it has its own character.

HETFIELD I'd like to think every one of the albums has its own unique and distinct sound. Some might be harder to listen to. Listening to *St. Anger* is somewhat of a chore for me. [*laughs*] It's cool because it's raw and in your face, but it has just one dimension. You know, "This is anger, and here it is."

GW How important is the guitar sound to achieving that character?

HETFIELD Very important. I'm on this eternal quest to get the best guitar sound in the world, but my vision of what is "the best" changes every time I go into the studio. Sometimes my goal is to make my guitar jump out, and sometimes I want it to lay back. It all depends on what we're trying to achieve with the album. But getting the right sound is essential. I want to feel what I'm playing. When I finally arrive at that sound, the songs get written and played.

GW Each song on *Death Magnetic* features multiple riffs and as many as three solo sections. Did you ever worry about going over the top?

HETFIELD Well, we usually fall victim to ourselves in that respect. We always think there's not enough or there's got to be more, and most of the songs on this album are pretty long. However, we're not too concerned. We're pretty sure radio, be it satellite or whatever, will play them.

The one thing I struggle with these days is quality control. In the early days we only had to write between eight and 10 songs per record, so if a riff wasn't good we just threw it away. But that started to change when we were writing *Load* and *ReLoad*. If a riff wasn't working, instead of throwing it out we'd explore it and try to take it as far as we could to see if there was anything there. We'd end up recording 20-something songs, which was especially challenging because I had to write lyrics for all of them.

On *St. Anger*, the process was even longer; we went through two writing cycles. On this one, there were 16 *full* CDs of ideas with 30 to 40 ID markers on them.

GW Your rhythm guitar playing has had a huge impact on a couple of generations of guitar players. How do you think your guitar playing has changed since, say, ...*And Justice for All*?

HETFIELD I haven't really thought about it. I would say I'm probably a little more precise. It's a little more important to me that the riff is clear. Back then I would just layer parts four times and make it wide. Now I'm more concerned about how sounds work. I'm a little more willing to put up with a sound that's not completely great on its own but fits well within a song.

GW You're considered to be one of fastest and most precise rhythm players in rock history.

HETFIELD [*laughs*] It's not hard for me to play fast. It's just not. And I love that. It might take a little while to warm up to certain songs, but the fast down picking—the really fast double picking in the riffs, especially when I pick up the beat—is just fun.

GW What would you say you've learned since releasing the Black Album in 1991?

HETFIELD On the Black Album we learned how to add muscle to our sound. On *Load* and *ReLoad*, I learned that when you write too many songs, your focus gets watery; it gets diluted. I hate that part of us. We know how to take an okay song and make it good. But the question lately has been, Do we have the discipline to dismiss an average song and say it's not on the record? Do we know when something is not good enough?

We used to have that discipline early on. And I attribute that to having blinders on—that fuckin' attitude that says, "Fuck that, it's not heavy enough to put on the album." In the Nineties we tried to embrace everything, and [*producer*] Bob Rock was good at helping us do that. Each time we did, we opened our eyes a little more, but the discipline kind of went away. We became craftsmen instead of destructors. So from *Load* and *ReLoad*, what I learned is that I can't spread it out over 40 songs. I just can't. I'd rather have eight powerful songs than 14 so-so songs. ✳

TWO THOUSAND '09

Guitar World welcomes the return of AC/DC, Green Day, Slayer and Alice in Chains as Page, White and The Edge go to the movies and Chickenfoot stomps its way to rock and roll superstardom.

Dear *Guitar World*,

At the age of 33, I was given a life sentence—my first time in trouble and I pick a doozy. I am a musician and started playing guitar at 14. When I was sentenced, I figured I would never play the guitar or bass again, and I didn't for the first four years I was in here. But then one day I decided to go to the church and see what was up with the music program. I tried out, and now I play in the church services three to four times a week. I even convinced the chaplain that metal has its place in church: sometimes I take Metallica songs and change the lyrics to make them about God, and people love it. Each month I look forward to the new issue of *Guitar World* so I can practice the lessons and play the songs. The magazine has helped me to become a better player than I was in the free world. And if you think your life is hard or that things couldn't get any worse, trust me, they can. I took for granted what I had, and look where I ended up.

—James Cavazos

JANUARY Angus Young and the boys from Down Under are back with *Black Ice*, their cool new return to the raunch and roll that made them famous. "If you know what you do well and stick to that, I think you can appeal to the different generations. I've got the brain of a teenager anyway."

COVER STORY BY ALAN DI PERNA; PHOTO BY GAVIN BOND

FEBRUARY *Guitar World* gets a sneak preview of Eddie Van Halen's new EVH Wolfgang guitar, the ultimate refinement of his signature ax. "I destroyed a lot of guitars trying to get them to do what I wanted, but I learned something from every guitar I tore apart."

COVER STORY BY CHRIS GILL; PHOTO BY CLAY PATRICK MCBRIDE

MARCH *Guitar World* presents the story behind Led Zeppelin's launch and ascent, and delves into the making of the ethereal and controversial *Led Zeppelin III*.
COVER STORIES BY ALAN DI PERNA AND CHARLES R. CROSS
PHOTO BY JIM MARSHALL

APRIL Surfing buddies Kirk Hammett and Adam Jones compare notes on how they transformed their heavy metal into a worldwide religion.
COVER STORY BY BRAD ANGLE
PHOTO BY ROSS HALFIN

MAY On the 25th anniversary of his *Flex-Able* album, Steve Vai delivers the most in-depth look ever into the making of his shred-tastic debut.
COVER STORY BY ALAN DI PERNA
PHOTO BY DALE MAY

JUNE Birds of a feather Joe Satriani, Sammy Hagar, Michael Anthony and Chad Smith join forces for Chickenfoot, rock and roll's most talked about supergroup.
COVER STORY BY JOE BOSSO
PHOTO BY ROSS HALFIN

JULY In an oral history spanning the Allman Brothers Band's 40-year career, Greg Allman, Dickey Betts and others tell the story behind rock and roll's enlightened rogues.
COVER STORY BY ALAN PAUL; PHOTOS BY RAYON RICHARDS
(CURRENT GROUP) AND JIM MARSHALL (CLASSIC)

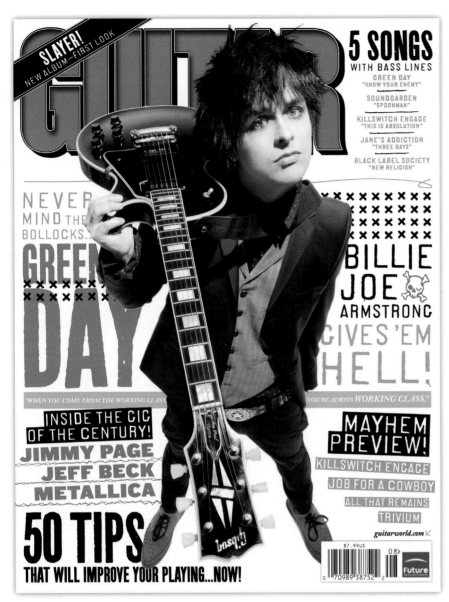

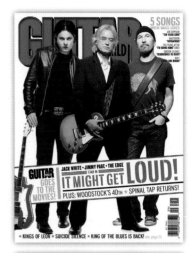

SEPTEMBER *Guitar World* sits down with larger-than-life guitarists Jimmy Page, Jack White and The Edge for a high-level discussion about the making of *It Might Get Loud*.
COVER STORY BY JOE BOSSO; PHOTO BY ROSS HALFIN

OCTOBER Neil Young tells the complete story behind the making of his *Archives Volume 1, 1963 – 1972*, the most ambitious anthology ever created.
COVER STORY BY RICHARD BIENSTOCK
PHOTO BY HENRY DILTZ

AUGUST *Guitar World* talks with Billie Joe Armstrong about the making of Green Day's latest rock opus, *21st Century Breakdown*. "It's about wanting to learn something new and not getting distracted by television addiction and trying to read between the lines of the lies that come at you."
COVER STORY BY ALAN DI PERNA; PHOTO BY ROSS HALFIN

NOVEMBER Slayer's Jeff Hanneman and Kerry King talk about working hard, playing fast and living life on the dark side.
COVER STORY BY BRAD ANGLE; PHOTO BY TRAVIS SHINN

DECEMBER With *Black Gives Way to Blue*, Alice in Chains have a new lease on life. Guitarist Jerry Cantrell talks about the making of the new album and reflects on his band's past glories.
COVER STORY BY CHARLES R. CROSS; PHOTO BY CLAY PATRICK MCBRIDE

HOLIDAY On *God & Guns*, a newly resurrected Lynyrd Skynyrd reclaim their right to bear arms—and to rock and roll.
COVER STORY BY ALAN PAUL; PHOTO BY TRAVIS SHINN

2009 TOTAL ISSUES: 13

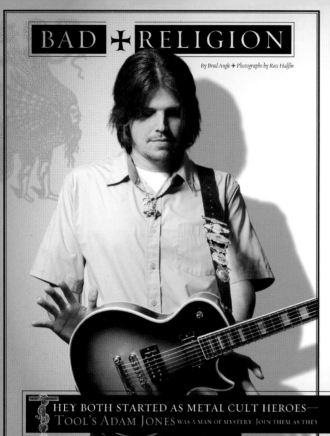

BAD ✝ RELIGION

By Brad Angle ✝ Photographs by Ross Halfin

THEY BOTH STARTED AS METAL CULT HEROES—
TOOL'S ADAM JONES WAS A MAN OF MYSTERY. JOIN THEM AS THEY

METALLICA'S KIRK HAMMETT WAS A MAN OF THE PEOPLE, AND
COMPARE NOTES ON HOW THEY TURNED THEIR MUSIC INTO A WORLDWIDE RELIGION

APRIL 2009

VOL. 30 / NO. 4

Kirk Hammett
& Adam Jones

Metallica's lead guitarist and Tool's six-string visionary talk about their friendship and mutual

GUITAR WORLD Let's start with a little history. How did you guys become friends?

KIRK HAMMETT I've always admired Adam from a distance.

ADAM JONES A far distance.

HAMMETT As far a distance as possible. [*laughs*] We played some shows together in 2006, in Korea, and that's when we started getting to know each other. After those Korean shows, Tool went right to Hawaii. I was also going to Hawaii, because I spend a lot of time there. They were playing a show, and Adam asked me to come onstage and play "Sober" with him. To which I said, "Hell yes!"

JONES Yeah, it was really great. We extended the breakdown in "Sober" where [*Tool vocalist*] Maynard [*James Keenan*] comes in by himself, and we built the song back up into the chorus again. We softly started playing the main riff and let Kirk swim over it. For a guy who didn't prepare at all, he blew my mind! It just kept getting better—more complex and cooler.

HAMMETT It was one of my best onstage jamming experiences, ever. It was totally improvised and really mind-blowing.

GW Adam, in the days before Tool did you ever listen to Metallica?

JONES Absolutely. You always hear about the prog and math stuff that influenced me, but there's also Aerosmith, AC/DC and Metallica. All that stuff has affected me. It's really funny to think back to when I bought ...*And Justice for All*, that one day I would be hanging out or surfing with Kirk.

GW You guys surf together?

JONES Yeah. The first time was in Hawaii, the day after we met. He lent me a long board and took me out to this spot where all the old-timers surf. I'm from California, so I've never had to paddle 30 minutes *anywhere*. [*laughs*] And you have to go out real far in Waikiki to catch the good waves. My arms were getting so tired, and I was so worried I was gonna look like a pussy! [*laughs*]

GW What initially attracted you to Metallica's music?

JONES I definitely have this prog side of me, so I listen for counter rhythms and polyrhythms, and ...*And Justice for All* had stuff in seven and nine. There's even one riff that's in 11, which I really like. But I'm sure you guys don't count it like that, or maybe you do?

HAMMETT I can only count to four, bro. [*laughs*]

JONES Exactly. [*laughs*] We actually do that too. We write weird riffs and sometimes we count them and other times we just feel them. I always felt that the stuff on ...*And Justice for All* was written from Metallica's heart and not their head.

GW Kirk, what do you like about Adam's playing?

HAMMETT I really appreciate that Adam is the prog master. I love the fact that he strives to create progressive music that really stands on its own. I come from a real old-school prog background myself. I love bands like King Crimson, Yes and Genesis. I love Robert Fripp, and I know Adam loves Robert Fripp, as well. I think it's cool that he's carrying that torch.

GW Adam, what attracts you to these artists? Is it strictly their music, or are you also drawn to their ideologies or creative processes?

JONES If I have the chance to find out what David Bowie was thinking when he came up with this or that, I'm absolutely interested. But it's also nice to be immersed in just the song without worrying what it's about. That curiosity can backfire. The funniest time for me was when I found out what the Melvins' song "Boris" was really about. It's from *Bullhead*, which is a very innovative and phenomenal record. I remember listening to the lyrics and being like, This is the purest, most meaningful and heaviest shit I've heard in a long time. Later on, after I befriended [*Melvins guitarist/singer*] Buzz [*Osborne*], I said, "That song 'Boris' really means a lot to me." And he says, "Oh, that song's about my cat." [*laughs*] So it's good to not get too analytical about this stuff.

GW Kirk, how much does musical analysis play a role in Metallica?

HAMMETT Adam really nailed it when he said some people count it and some people feel it. We *totally* feel it. You won't hear anyone in our band saying, "Oh that's in five and this is in seven." We'll say something like, "It's on the upbeat," "It's on the downbeat," "Switch here after you count to five"... It's really simple for us: it comes from the gut and heart rather than the head. Sometimes it does come from the head, and I have to sit down and do the math. But after I've done the math, I just start feeling it again.

JONES Thinking too much will always become distracting. When you think too much, especially when you start to get successful, you can go down paths like, Oh, what will the fans like? What will radio like? But when you keep it in your chest or stomach, it stays about What do *I* like? When you nail that, only then will your excitement be reflected by other people who listen to your music.

GW In the early days Metallica gained its rep and momentum through its cult status, with the tape traders and underground metalheads. Similarly, a cult of fans has always surrounded Tool. I'm wondering what, in your opinions, are the upsides and downsides to becoming a cult phenomenon?

JONES The upside is that you can play onstage and you can fart, and no one knows it. [*laughs*]

HAMMETT [*laughs*] I just totally lost my thought, because that statement was just so profound. ✴

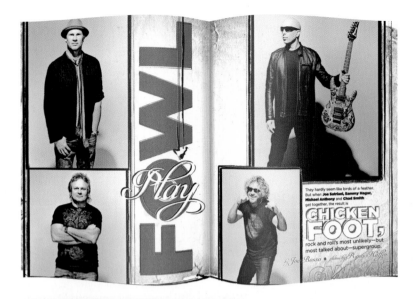

JUNE / VOL. 30 / NO. 6

CHICKENFOOT

Joe Satriani, Sammy Hagar, Michael Anthony and Chad Smith join forces for the supergroup event of the year.

GUITAR WORLD Since you were announced, you guys have been branded a "supergroup." What are your thoughts on this? Do you feel as though there's too much expectation put on you?

SAMMY HAGAR "Supergroup"? Hey, I don't know. We were just trying to make a kick-ass record and be a great band. I love being a part of *this*. [*points to Satriani*]

CHAD SMITH When I think of the word "supergroup," I think of those bands that were kind of artificially put together, where guys auditioned and record company guys got involved and all that. We came together very naturally. Everything was fun, it felt good, there was nothing preconceived about it.

GW Before you guys officially said, "Okay, we're a band," were there any discussions about what you wanted to avoid—problems you had faced in other bands that you didn't want to repeat?

JOE SATRIANI We had no time. We were too busy writing and making the record.

MICHAEL ANTHONY The thing is, we've all played together in various ways: Chad came down to Cabo and jammed with me and Sammy; Sammy and I had a thing going for a while with Neal Schon and [*Journey drummer*] Deen Castronovo; then Joe came down and was possibly going to be a part of that...

HAGAR But we never sat down and said, "Hey, we're gonna be like this, or we're not gonna be like that." Joe came with his riffs, Mikey started playing over them, Chad went loose and laid down the groove, and I started scatting—and that's how it all went down. Song by song, we did it just like that.

GW So there were no discussions beforehand, like, "Well, let's make sure this guy isn't crazy, like so-and-so from my last band"? [*laughs all around*]

SMITH I don't think so. Of course, now that I think of it, you'd have to be crazy to be in this band. Nothing about it makes any sense.

HAGAR Joe won't hang around with me on tour, I guarantee you that. I'm *waaaay* too crazy for him. When I start bringing naked pigs into my hotel room, brother, he'll be long gone! [*laughs*]

APR. '09

Randolf Sanders Wins *GW* Reader Art Contest

Congratulations to Randolf Sanders from Oshkosh, Wisconsin, the winner of the first-ever *Guitar World* Reader Art Contest. For his painting of Pantera guitarist Dimebag Darrell—done in acrylic paint on a 16x20-inch canvas panel—Sanders referenced the Dime photo that appeared on the March 2008 cover of *Guitar World*, then added his own unique touches, including the cemetery gates, tombstones and grim reaper. "I chose Dime because he's not only a guitar god but also because he reminds me so much of my brother, Chad, who died in 1998," says Sanders. "I understand what [*Dimebag's brother*] Vinnie Paul has had to go through."

With nearly 300 submissions—which ran the gamut from sketches on loose-leaf paper to abstract works by professional artists—the contest was packed with entries, making it extremely difficult to pick one winner. We ultimately chose Sanders' piece for its powerful combination of creativity, talent and heart—attributes possessed by Dimebag himself.

SCOTT GORHAM

Thin Lizzy's longtime guitarist reveals the secrets behind the great Irish rock group's signature sound.

GUITAR WORLD If anyone ever fit the description "Rock Star," it was Phil Lynott. What was Phil really like?

SCOTT GORHAM He was the gunslinger, but he was absolutely the most generous guy at the same time. No matter who was working with us at any given time, Phil always wanted to push all of us as equal partners, which was really great. He was a real star, and he knew it, but he didn't dwell on it all that much. He wanted everyone around him to take part in this whole thing. He actively pushed you up to the front of the stage. Back in the very beginning, he actually grabbed me one night by the collar, pulled me up to the front and said, "Don't fookin' move!" [*laughs*], because I was cowering in the back, thinking, What the hell is going on? He wanted you to take part in the whole thing. He wanted you to have your own time in the spotlight.

GW One of the greatest things about the Thin Lizzy sound is the amount of swing in the grooves of even your hardest rocking tunes.

GORHAM A lot of that had to do with [*drummer*] Brian Downey and the way he approached his drum grooves. Brian wasn't a real "slammer" of the snare drum. There was a lot of "ghosting" [*light syncopated accents*] in the parts that he played. He had a real "wristy" thing going with his hi-hat, too.

Then you've got Phil's bass playing, too. He used to joke around and call himself the worst bass player in the business, but he knew that wasn't true. I've played with several Class A bass players and each one was amazed at the things Phil could do, in terms of the notes he picked out, the strength with which he hit the strings and how he kept the groove going, while singing all of the time.

GW The harmonized twin guitars, essential to so many Thin Lizzy classics, exemplify the signature sound of the band. How did you guys work out the harmonized guitar lines?

GORHAM I think a lot of that came from the influence of Irish music, which probably occurred on a subliminal level for us. We weren't intentionally thinking of bringing that sound into our music, but being a guitar player you're like a sponge soaking up all kinds of peripheral musical elements. Because of the way Phil wrote his songs, with lyrics that were very explicit and the strong storyteller aspect, it rubbed off on the guitar players, and we wanted to contribute to the melodic side of the Thin Lizzy sound. We went for the idea of creating signature guitar parts that would work inside the songs. On a lead guitar bit, rather than thinking, Here's my 15 seconds to rip, we thought about where we were in the song, and how to fit harmonized melodies into the songs in just the right way.

The Premiere of *Guitar Aficionado*

In the summer of 2009, the *Guitar World* editorial staff launched its most ambitious spin-off magazine ever: *Guitar Aficionado*, a high-end publication designed for players who are passionate about the finer things associated with the rock and roll lifestyle, including vintage and collectible axes, designer watches and fashion, exotic motorcycles, fine foods and spirits and more. Renowned chef and player Tom Colicchio graced the cover of the first issue, and since then such famous faces as Jimmy Page, Lenny Kravitz and even Academy Award–winning actor Jeff Bridges have appeared on the magazine's cover.

mines a treasure trove of his early songs, demos, videos and memorabilia for his new multimedia project, *ARCHIVES VOLUME 1, 1963-1972*. In this world-exclusive interview, the iconic guitarist tells the complete story behind the making of the most ambitious music anthology ever created. *by RICHARD BIENSTOCK*

GW ★ 55

OCT.2009

VOL. 30 / NO. 10

Neil Young

As his ambitious multimedia project *Archives Volume 1, 1963–1972* **sees daylight, legendary guitarist Neil Young talks to** *Guitar World***'s Richard Bienstock about the evolution of Crazy Horse's metallic edge.**

GUITAR WORLD Let's talk about your process as a guitar player. In particular, around the time of 1969's *Everybody Knows This Is Nowhere*, were there other guitarists who influenced you as far as your pursuit of the louder, noisier side of the music? Jimi Hendrix would be an obvious point of reference, but anyone else?

NEIL YOUNG Not really. I mean, Jimi certainly. I liked him. He was on my radar. But not too many others. [*Producer and occasional Young collaborator*] Jack Nitzsche and I used to listen to the early Jimi Hendrix Experience 45s that came out of London before we did my first solo album. He was the latest, greatest thing from over there, and we were checking it out. Wanted to see what was going on.

GW What about any of the metal players? For example, you were getting pretty thick, detuned tones on songs like "Cinnamon Girl" and "When You Dance, I Can Really Love." Were you aware of, say, Tony Iommi from Black Sabbath, another guy who tuned down his guitar?

YOUNG Not so much. But I love that music. It's like classical rock and roll. The Scorpions, Iron Maiden... That whole thing is quite strong. It's an art form in itself. That's the thing about metal: some people think one band is great and another is just shit, while a normal person standing there couldn't tell the difference between the two. So I was never a metal*head*, but I'll listen to a guy like Zakk Wylde play the guitar. He's good. And I know a lot of metal guys. They come to our shows because there's something we do that I guess they connect with.

GW But there was nothing directly influencing you at the time you were first getting loud with Crazy Horse?

YOUNG Well, you know...when you really listen to it, Crazy Horse didn't get very loud. Not until *Rust Never Sleeps* [*1979*]. The early Crazy Horse, with Danny [*Whitten, guitar*], is not a big, whomp-'em, arena-rock sound. That happened with the second version of the band, when Poncho [*Frank Sampedro*] joined. "Cowgirl in the Sand" and "Down By the River"—when you listen to 'em, they're not that loud. Though they *can* be, especially when we do them now.

GW Much of the "bigness" that's associated with Crazy Horse, I suppose, is a result of the grit in the guitar tones, and also the space between the instruments.

YOUNG Yeah, there's *a lot* of room in those records. Those songs were written to be explored forever. There's no finished version.

GW How would you characterize your lead playing?

YOUNG It sucks! It's just a fucking racket. I get totally lost when I'm playing guitar. I'll just play a melody over and over again and change the tone, bend a string, do all that. I'm totally engrossed in what I'm doing. At one with it. But I suck. I've *heard* myself.

GW Some people would beg to differ.

YOUNG Well, I have *moments* where I really express myself on the guitar. But I can't play acoustic like Bert Jansch, and I can't play electric like Hendrix or J.J. Cale, who are probably the two best electric guitar players I've ever heard. And Jimmy Page, he's a great one. I really love the way he plays. He's so slippery. He's very, very dangerous. Those are three classic guitar players to me. I'm not that.

GW What would you say are your strengths?

YOUNG I have melodies, and I have a sense of rhythm and drive. But it's not about me, anyway—it's about the whole band. It's about *everybody* being there at once. When I play I'm listening for everything, trying to drive it all with my guitar. My guitar is the *whole fucking band*.

GW Perhaps an example of what you're describing would be the famous "one-note" solo in "Cinnamon Girl," which encompasses everything you're talking about: lead, rhythm, melody, drive. Though my contention has always been that it's not really one note...

YOUNG It's not! Everyone says that, but there's about a hundred notes in there. And every one of them is different. Every single one. They just happen to have the same name. [*laughs*]

GW Does it amuse you that people spend so much time evaluating the things you do?

YOUNG You know, I just thought I was playing the right solo. I mean, can you imagine anything else in there? Like, some fucking fast-note thing. Who needs that? It's *rhythm*.

GW That said, is there any particular song or moment on *Archives* that really captures the essence of Neil Young as a musician?

YOUNG No one thing. No one thing. It's too big. There's too much information. And you can zero in as close as you like, but then you wind up going too far, and you gotta pull back out. It's big-picture stuff. But it's all there. You know, one day I'm gonna put out a download update, and when you open it up, there'll just be several photographs of kitchen sinks. [*laughs*] That's it. ✳

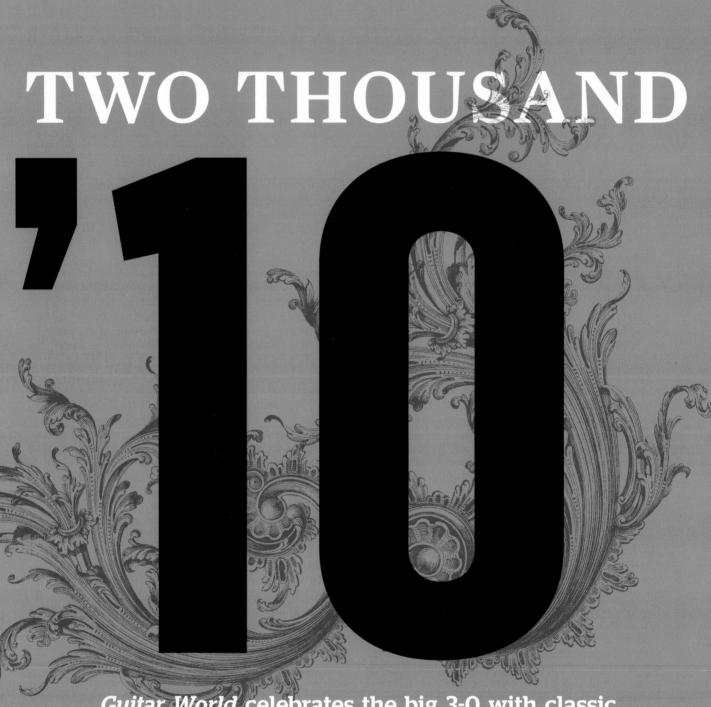

TWO THOUSAND '10

Guitar World celebrates the big 3-0 with classic album retrospectives, tributes to Dimebag and Stevie Ray and a historic joint interview between Eddie Van Halen and Tony Iommi.

Dear *Guitar World*,

I'll be 55 on my next birthday. Just had heart
bypass surgery, got diabetes, rheumatoid
arthritis, and I'm blind in one eye. But I can
see fine out of my other eye, and that's all
I need to read *Guitar World* every month. Even
at this stage of the game, it's hard to accept
limitations on what I can or can't play on my
guitar. I love all kinds of music, and I'm never
disappointed with whatever your next issue
brings. I've learned so much from the magazine
and only wish I had started reading it sooner.
So I just wanted to say thanks. Your devoted
efforts always give a player like me something
to look forward to.

—Marty Becton

ANNIVERSARY Tony Iommi and Eddie Van Halen mark *Guitar World*'s 30th anniversary with a colossal conversation about their careers, friendship and the past three decades of our favorite instrument. "When we toured with Black Sabbath in 1978," says Van Halen, "they scared the shit out of us."

COVER STORY BY CHRIS GILL; PHOTO BY CLAY PATRICK MCBRIDE

JANUARY On the fifth anniversary of his passing, *Guitar World* remembers Dimebag Darrell with tributes from the people who knew him best.
COVER STORIES BY NICK BOWCOTT, CHRIS GILL AND RICHARD BIENSTOCK
PHOTO BY ROSS HALFIN

FEBRUARY Who says you can't have a Number One pop album, play the blues and Twitter at the same time? Meet musical multitasker John Mayer, the world's most famous guitar hero.
COVER STORY BY BRAD TOLINSKI
PHOTO BY F. SCOTT SCHAFER

MARCH The story of Them Crooked Vultures, rock's latest supergroup, featuring John Paul Jones, Dave Grohl and Josh Homme.
COVER STORY BY ALAN DI PERNA
PHOTO BY JUSTIN BORUCKI

APRIL Newly restored tapes from 1969 shed light on the turbulent final months of Jimi Hendrix's life, the recordings he created, and the music that might have been.
COVER STORY BY ALAN DI PERNA
ILLUSTRATION BY GABZ

MAY With a new solo album featuring guest vocals from M. Shadows, Ozzy Osbourne, Andrew Stockdale and others, Slash has been busier than ever following the demise of Velvet Revolver.
COVER STORY BY RICHARD BIENSTOCK
PHOTO BY ROSS HALFIN

JUNE Keith Richards recalls the making of the Rolling Stones' *Exile on Main St.* and how the album's new reissue project became a walk down memory lane.
COVER STORY BY ALAN DI PERNA
PHOTO BY NORMAN SEEFF

JULY On the 20th anniversary of his death, *Guitar World* celebrates blues legend Stevie Ray Vaughan with a detailed look at the making of *Couldn't Stand the Weather* and SRV's early years.
COVER STORIES BY MAC RANDALL AND CHRIS GILL
PHOTO BY JONATHAN POSTAL

SEPTEMBER *Guitar World* presents the players—from Keef to Muddy, from Hetfield to Buddy—whose talents, attitude and style made the guitar the greatest instrument ever.
COVER STORY BY RICHARD BIENSTOCK, ALAN DI PERNA AND CHRIS GILL
PHOTO BY ROSS HALFIN

OCTOBER Zakk Wylde and Alexi Laiho team up for the Berzerkus tour, the freakiest rock show on earth. "Alexi was my first choice for the Berzerkus, because he's part of the new breed of kick-ass guitar players, along with Gus G," says Wylde.
COVER STORIES BY BRAD TOLINSKI AND CHRIS GILL; PHOTO BY DALE MAY

TO BE PUBLISHED:

NOVEMBER ISSUE
on sale September 12

DECEMBER ISSUE
on sale October 19

HOLIDAY ISSUE
on sale November 16

AUGUST Ozzy Osbourne, the godfather of heavy metal, opens up about going sober, firing Zakk Wylde and hiring Gus G. for his latest album, *Scream*. "I was addicted to prescription drugs for 25 years."

COVER STORY BY PETE MAKOWSKI; PHOTO BY ROSS HALFIN

CAST A GIANT SHADOW

By CHRIS GILL *Photos by* CLAY PATRICK McBRIDE

One forged the template for heavy metal. The other advanced it with virtuoso shredding. Together, they shaped the guitar universe as we know it today. TONY IOMMI and EDDIE VAN HALEN mark *GUITAR WORLD'S* 30TH ANNIVERSARY with a colossal conversation about their careers, friendship and the past three decades of our favorite instrument.

GW
46

ANNIVERSARY

VOL. 27 / NO. 6

Eddie Van Halen & Tony Iommi

In this historic roundtable interview, the two titans of hard rock guitar help *Guitar World* celebrate our 30th anniversary by recalling their early years.

GUITAR WORLD You both started out as aspiring drummers.

EDDIE VAN HALEN [*to Iommi*] You did too?

TONY IOMMI That's what I wanted to become originally. My parents wouldn't let me get a set of drums because they were too loud.

VAN HALEN And then you got an electric guitar and became even louder.

GW You both have really well-developed rhythm styles. Do you think your interest in drums had anything to do with that?

VAN HALEN I think it's just inherently built in. When I was growing up and listening to bands like the Dave Clark Five, the groove was what initially got me going. I really like that funky, heavy groove. Obviously you have to have rhythm. If you have rhythm, then you can play anything you need. If you have rhythm and you love music, then play and play and play until you get to where you want to get. If you can pay the rent, great. If you can't, then you'd better be having fun. Playing guitar is the only thing I ever knew how to do.

IOMMI I first played accordion. That was my first actual instrument.

VAN HALEN I think accordion is great. It's hard to play.

IOMMI My father played accordion, and so did many of my relatives. Nobody played guitar back then. People in my family either played drums or accordion, and I went from accordion to guitar.

VAN HALEN I had to learn to play piano because that was the respectable instrument to play.

GW You both have mentioned Eric Clapton as an early influence.

IOMMI Probably because of the whole blues thing. I really liked his playing with John Mayall, which influenced a lot of players back then.

VAN HALEN With me it was all about the live Cream stuff. I don't mean to downplay anything Clapton did, but for me it was also about Cream's rhythm section. Listen to "I'm So Glad" on *Goodbye* and adjust the balance to the right—Jack Bruce and Ginger Baker were playing jazz through Marshalls. To me that is where Clapton's style came from. Clapton was the only guy doing that kind of extended soloing back then.

IOMMI That's right. Later on it was Hendrix and everybody else, but Clapton in those days appealed to a lot of people from his work with John Mayall through Cream.

GW Ed, I understand that in the very early days of Van Halen you originally wanted to call the band Rat Salad, which is the name of a Black Sabbath instrumental.

VAN HALEN We played just about every Black Sabbath song. I used to sing lead on every Black Sabbath song we did—things like "Into the Void," "Paranoid," and "Lord of This World." When we toured with Black Sabbath in 1978, they scared the shit out of us. I'll tell you a funny story that I'll never forget. I walked up to Tony and began to ask him, "Second song on side two of *Master of Reality*..." Tony looked at me and went, "What the fuck, mate?" By that time Black Sabbath had several records out, but we had only one album out so I knew where every track on our first record was. A few years later somebody asked me a question in the same way, and I was going, Oh, you've got to be kidding me. The first thing that popped in my head was that incident with Tony! At first I thought it was odd that he couldn't remember what was on his records, and then it happened to me.

GW Black Sabbath and Van Halen toured together for eight months in 1978. What effect did you have on each other?

VAN HALEN To me, Tony is the master of riffs. That's what I loved. I'm not knocking Ozzy or his singing, but listen to "Into the Void." That riff is some badass shit. It was beyond surf music and jazz. It was beyond anything else I had ever heard. It was so fuckin' heavy. I put it right up there with [*sings the four-note intro to Beethoven's Fifth Symphony*]. What are you going to sing over that? Listen to the main riff, where he chugs on the low E string. It hits you like a brick wall. Every band on the planet still does that. That is a staple of rock and roll.

GW Tony, what did you think of Van Halen?

IOMMI From the very first minute I heard them I knew straight away that they were something special. The way that Ed plays is very different. He came up with a style that's been imitated a million times. And they had great songs. Often after the shows we would get together in my room and chat about guitars. We'd ramble on for about 10 hours before we'd go to bed.

VAN HALEN Or not. [*laughs*] What time is show time? The bus has left without me! That was awesome.

IOMMI That's right! [*laughs*] I really enjoyed that tour. Brian May is the only other guitar player I've ever associated with, and we've never been on tour together.

VAN HALEN I was just telling someone this morning that out of all the people I've ever met—all the celebrities and rock and roll stars—I fuckin' love this guy. He's the sweetest, most humble, down to earth, normal guy. He has no attitude, and look at what this guy has done! I could name a handful of people who I still respect but no longer look up to. After I met them I was like, Fuck you! You're no better than I am as a person. So many people are a bunch of pompous fuckin' pricks. What makes them think their shit doesn't stink? Tony is still like a brother even after all these years. ✶

30 ESSENTIAL BLUES DISCS

Joe Bonamassa and Black Crowes guitarists
Rich Robinson and Luther Dickinson each pick
their 10 essential blues rock albums.

Joe Bonamassa

Jeff Beck—*Truth*
"A road atlas that mapped out the future for English blues and rock."

John Mayall and the Bluesbreakers—*Blues Breakers with Eric Clapton*
"This one inspired an entire generation of blues guitarists. A classic."

Jethro Tull—*Stand Up*
"Titanic in its delivery and its ingenuity."

Muddy Waters—*Electric Mud*
"Anything the blues purists pan immediately generally suits me just fine. This album is no exception."

Free—*Tons of Sobs*
"The record that changed my life. It solidified my commitment to English blues."

Led Zeppelin—*Led Zeppelin*
" 'How Many More Times,' 'You Shook Me,' 'I Can't Quit You.' Enough said."

Rich Robinson

Patto—*Patto*
"They twisted the genre into something different, and I really admire that."

Johnny Winter—*The Progressive Blues Experiment*
"Just filled with incredible guitar playing that really moves me."

Ry Cooder—*Boomers Story*
"One of my favorite albums in any genre."

Taj Mahal—*Happy Just to Be Like I Am*
"I fell in love with Taj's voice and sound the first time I heard him."

The Grease Band—*The Grease Band*
"Everything about them—the singer's voice, the tones, the looseness—just works for me."

The Allman Brothers Band—*The Allman Brothers Band*
"It didn't strike me how heavy and amazing they were until I started writing my own songs."

Luther Dickinson

Jimi Hendrix—*Live at Berkeley*
"You really can't compare Hendrix to anything. He stands alone."

Allman Brothers Band—*At Fillmore East*
"As far as blues rock, this about sums it up."

Free—*Free*
"Paul Kossoff was an amazing guitarist, and his vibrato was crazy. No one else sounds like that."

Led Zeppelin—*Led Zeppelin*
"The vocals and the lyrics and the way they reworked old blues lyrics was brilliant, and that is the traditional blues oral history."

ZZ Top—*Tres Hombres*
"The riffs are disgustingly good. Billy Gibbons is the king of sleazy riffs."

Fleetwood Mac—*Peter Green's Fleetwood Mac*
"Peter Green is the whole package: singing, songwriting, amazing guitar playing."

30 ON 30

As *Guitar World*'s 30th anniversary celebration continues, 30 of the greatest living guitarists go on record about their heroes.

Eddie Van Halen on Eric Clapton

"I never had a guitar lesson in my life, except from listening to Eric Clapton records."

James Hetfield on Tony Iommi
"He inspired me to want to play heavy."

Tom Morello on Steve Vai
"Some instrumental guitar players are lost in a muso fog. Steve Vai is not one of them."

Angus Young on Chuck Berry
"Even on a bad night, Chuck Berry is a lot better than Clapton will ever be."

Joe Perry on Angus Young
"Instead of using all the traditional tricks, he found a way to get inside those licks and be inventive."

Alex Skolnick on Jimmy Herring
"He has the bluesiness of Warren Haynes or Johnny Winter and the vocabulary of John Scofield, with an element of Steve Morse thrown in."

Phil Collen on Ritchie Blackmore
"Ritchie Blackmore was a huge influence because he was flashy. I love really flashy lead guitar playing, and Blackmore's technique is great."

Zakk Wylde on Glenn Tipton and K.K. Downing
"They are the ultimate twin guitarists in metal—they go together."

David Gilmour on Jeff Beck
"I'm horribly, pathetically fannish about Jeff. Ever since I was 20-odd years old, I've revered him and his playing."

Ted Nugent on Jim McCarty
"That's why I immediately went on a gee-hah to get a Byrdland and a Fender Twin amp—because of the crispness, the thickness, the style of McCarty's playing."

Steven Van Zandt on Keith Richards
"I grew up on Keith Richards, and his lead on the Stones' versions of Chuck Berry songs helped reinvent the guitar for Beck, Clapton and Jimmy Page."

Joe Satriani on Jimi Hendrix

"I was a drummer, and I started from watching the Rolling Stones and the Beatles on *The Ed Sullivan Show*. But as soon as I heard Hendrix, that was it."

Slash on Mick Taylor

"People always mention Jimmy Page, Jeff Beck, Angus Young...all the obvious ones. But there are guys like Mick Taylor and Joe Walsh that were as important."

Martin Barre on Leslie West
"I loved Leslie's larger-than-life style, they had great songs, and they were so incredibly tight. In that last respect, they taught Jethro Tull a lot about being a band."

Jason Becker on Marty Friedman
"I feel like every day that I jammed or wrote with Marty was like taking lessons for a year. He taught by example, and with his influence I learned how to be my own unique creative artist."

Steve Vai on Brian May
"I can listen to any player and pantomime their sound, but I can't do Brian May. He's just walking on higher ground."

Richie Kotzen on Eddie Van Halen
"Everyone talks about Van Halen's sound, but it really has to do with his timing, his rhythm style and his phrasing."

George Lynch on Yngwie Malmsteen
"On a pure playing level, players that create music that touches people are always viable. And that's why he's still around and a lot of the other guys aren't."

Billy Gibson on B.B. King

"B.B.'s distinctive one-note style, his sustain and attack, that kind of call-and-response thing between the vocals and the solos... He's taken for granted now, which means he's underrated."

Frank Hannon on Randy Rhoads
"I was infatuated from the first time I heard *Blizzard of Ozz*. Randy was doing everything that Van Halen did, and more."

Scott Ian on Malcolm Young
"Malcolm Young has got to be the most unsung, underrated guitar hero of all time. He's the backbone of AC/DC."

PLUS: Ron Thal on Zakk Wylde • Kim Thayil on Ron Asheton • Rich Robinson on Peter Green
Kirk Hammett on Uli Jon Roth • Nancy Wilson on Neil Young • Elliot Easton on George Harrison
Ace Frehley on Pete Townshend • Mick Mars on Alvin Lee • Dweezil Zappa on Frank Zappa

GUITAR WORLD PRESENTS THE 30 COOLEST GUITARISTS OF ALL TIME

REAL REBELLION IS NOT GIVING UP.

JAMES HETFIELD

BORN August 3, 1963
BAND Metallica
ICONIC GUITAR 1984 Gibson Explorer
COOLEST RIFF "Leper Messiah"–*Master of Puppets*

MOST METAL GUITARISTS would kill to have half of the power and precision of James Hetfield's right hand, not to mention his ability to write the most devastating riffs known to mankind, from "Seek and Destroy" and "Creeping Death" to "Enter Sandman." Of course, most musicians with skills comparable to Hetfield's have such big egos that they become the targets of our murderous intentions.

That's not the case with Hetfield. Years of hard-earned success and fame have not changed his down-to-earth attitude. Even though he has become one of the world's richest rock stars, he hasn't married a supermodel or become a pompous art collector. Instead, he's remained true to his working-class roots, spending his spare time building incredibly cool kustom cars and cruising the streets with his car club buddies, the Beatniks of Koolsville. His kustom masterpieces like "Slow Burn" (a 1936 Auburn boat-tail speedster), "Skyscraper" (a 1953 Buick Skylark) and his daily driver known as "The Grinch" (a 1952 Oldsmobile) are drivable works of art that defy the bland Toyota Priuses, Lexuses and Land Rover SUVs of his Northern California environs like a stiff middle-finger salute wearing a skull ring.

JOE STRUMMER

BORN August 21, 1952 (died December 22, 2002)
BANDS The Clash, Joe Strummer and the Mescaleros
ICONIC GUITAR 1966 Fender Telecaster
COOLEST RIFF "Train in Vain"–*London Calling*

JOE STRUMMER WAS far from the most proficient rhythm guitarist in punk rock, and his tone was often downright wimpy. Yet you'd never find a punk rocker who didn't want to be just like him. Whereas most punk guitarists found inspiration from the same hard rock and proto-metal players that they pretended to despise, Strummer was influenced by reggae, rockabilly, soul, ska and even early New York rap music when most of the world still hadn't heard of the Sugarhill Gang. Those influences helped him develop a truly unique rhythm guitar style that no one has been able to duplicate since.

Perhaps the coolest thing about Joe Strummer is no one could ever predict what he would do next. In 1981, the Clash played 17 consecutive nights at the 3,500-capacity Bond's International Casino nightclub in Manhattan, but when they returned to New York the next year they played two sold-out shows at Shea Stadium as an opening act for the Who. Julien Temple's documentary, *Joe Strummer: The Future Is Unwritten,* reveals what many would perceive as Strummer's flaws: from his hippie squatter roots to the way he dissed former bandmates during the Clash's last gasps. But ultimately, Strummer was a man who simply did wanted he wanted to do without giving a shit what anybody else thought.

THE 30 COOLEST GUITARISTS

49

SEPT. 2010

VOL. 27 / NO. 6

The 30 Coolest Guitarists of All Time

A celebration of the players whose talents, attitude and style have made the guitar the greatest instrument ever.